MONUMENT TO HOOD'S TEXAS BRIGADE

Now being erected on the Capitol Grounds at Austin, Texas, by The McNeel Marble Company, of Marietta, Georgia. The monument will be dedicated May 7, 1910, with State-wide ceremonies

FACING HALF-TITLE

HOOD'S TEXAS BRIGADE

FRONTISPIECE

Hood's Texas Brigade

*Its Marches Its Battles
Its Achievements*

BY

J. B. POLLEY

AUTHOR OF "A SOLDIER'S LETTERS TO CHARMING NELLIE"

ILLUSTRATED

NEW YORK AND WASHINGTON
THE NEALE PUBLISHING COMPANY
1910

Notice

In many older books, foxing (or discoloration) occurs and, in some instances, print lightens with wear and age. Reprinted books, such as this, often duplicate these flaws, notwithstanding efforts to reduce or eliminate them. The pages of this reprint have been digitally enhanced and, where possible, the flaws eliminated in order to provide clarity of content and a pleasant reading experience.

Originally published

New York and Washington:
1910

Reprinted by:

Janaway Publishing, Inc.
732 Kelsey Ct.
Santa Maria, California 93454
(805) 925-1038
www.janawaygenealogy.com

2012

ISBN: 978-1-59641-291-0

Made in the United States of America

CONTENTS

CHAPTER	PAGE
Preface	9
I. Introductory	13
II. Fredericksburg—Yorktown—Eltham's Landing	20
III. Richmond—Seven Pines—Gaines' Mill	29
IV. Gaines' Mill	40
V. Savage Station, Frayser's Farm, Malvern Hill, Kelly's Ford, Freeman's Ford, Thoroughfare Gap, Second Manassas	71
VI. Second Manassas, *Continued*	87
VII. Sharpsburg, or Antietam	112
VIII. Fredericksburg and Suffolk	136
IX. Gettysburg	149
X. Gettysburg, *Continued*	166
XI. Gettysburg to Chickamauga	190
XII. Chattanooga and Knoxville	213
XIII. The Wilderness — Spottsylvania — Cold Harbor — Petersburg	228
XIV. Charles City Road, Darbytown Road, Chaffin's Farm, Williamsburg Road	249
XV. Appomattox	269
XVI. Addenda	283

ILLUSTRATIONS

Monument to Hood's Texas Brigade . *Facing half title page*
General Hood . . . . *Frontispiece*

	FACING PAGE
John H. Kirby	12
Albert Sneed	20
John M. Pinckney	32
Billy Pearce	38
E. K. Goree	48
George S. Qualls	60
John Coleman Roberts	84
Ben M. Baker	90
Dick Pinckney	114
L. P. Hughes	116
William R. Hamby	130
B. Eldridge	132
W. W. Henderson	144
R. M. Powell	164
John D. Murray	200
J. T. Hunter	204
W. H. Burges	220
J. B. Polley	258
W. T. Hill	274
Sam R. Burroughs	288
F. B. Chilton	292
George W. Littlefield	294
F. B. Chilton	328

PREFACE

BIDDEN to write "a fair and impartial history of Hood's Texas Brigade," the author submits the following pages as the result of his labors. While painfully conscious of many imperfections in his work, he yet congratulates himself on having made both an honest and an earnest effort to tell a true story. That the thread of it is spun almost entirely out of material furnished by the memories and diaries of himself and his comrades, and is not strengthened by many references to or quotations from official records, is due to the lack of such records. Little documentary evidence as to the services of the command was saved out of the wreck and upheaval following upon the retreat of Lee's army from Petersburg and its surrender at Appomattox. The loss, however, is not likely to be regretted —the majority of readers being more interested in what is done than in the how and the wherefore of it.

Events are related in the order of their occurrence; and since "deeds speak louder than words," the privilege of characterizing the conduct and performances of individuals, singly and collectively, is left to the reader. Fortitude and courage, trial, endurance, hardship and privation, speak for themselves and need no aid from adjectives and adverbs. Much has been omitted that, forty years ago, would have been of interest, but now would burden the story, and only such movements and operations of the Confederate armies are mentioned as are necessary to show the relation of Hood's Texas Brigade to other commands. The righteousness of the cause for which it fought and suffered is taken as granted and confessed by every fair-minded native-born American.

In brief, the effort of the author has been to relate the acts and achievements of the Southern soldiers whose place was at the front, on the firing line—his own feelings being in perfect accord with those of the writer of the following verses:

THE PRIVATES THAT TRAMPED IT WITH LEE

" While over the Southland the voices
Of speakers and poets let fall
The accents of praise for the chieftain,
So richly deserving it all,
I think it would please the great captain
If he could look down here and see
That some one remembers his heroes,
The privates that tramped it with Lee.

" How oft in his tent at the midnight
He plotted the brilliant campaign,
How oft, ere the daylight was dawning,
They followed in sleet and in rain—
How often they rushed into battle,
Their hearts in a tumult of glee,
The steady, the ready old fellows—
The privates that tramped it with Lee.

" Tho' mighty the brain in its schemes,
The feet at its bidding must run;
The victories on paper are proven
By privates that level the gun.
So, great as the captain we honor
(And great may his fame ever be!)
'Tis shared by the shaggy old heroes—
The privates that tramped it with Lee.

" 'Tis easy in shock of the battle
To pass out of life with a smile,
A hero secure of his laurels;
But to sweat with the rank and the file,
And afterwards live and be patient,
Still struggling, appeareth to me
Yet nobler; and such be the fellows,
The privates that tramped it with Lee.

" They followed their dauntless commander,
Him who to the warrior's art
United the lore of the scholar
And the patriot's temperate heart;

And yet in their zealous devotion
These men were as great as he,
These grizzled, grim, veteran soldiers,
These privates that tramped it with Lee.

" The frosts of the winter are whitening
The locks that the bullets once kissed;
And soon they will meet with a foeman
The stoutest can never resist.
To us they'll bequeath inspiration
When at length, mustered out, they are free
To cross over the River of Silence
And tramp it again there with Lee.

" And so, if the General is conscious
Of things that are done here below,
He'd be glad if the speakers and poets
Some sprigs of their laurels bestow
On such as did win him the glory,
And back him from mountain to sea,
On them, both the dead and the living,
The privates that tramped it with Lee."

Hon. John H. Kirby
A member of the Monument Committee, who subscribed $5,000 to the Monument Fund

HOOD'S TEXAS BRIGADE

CHAPTER I

INTRODUCTORY

AMONG the Texas troops who bore a conspicuous part in the war between the States were the First, Fourth, and Fifth regiments of infantry. They fought in Virginia, Maryland, Pennsylvania, Georgia, and Tennessee, and were the only representatives of their State in the Army of Northern Virginia. Brigaded at first with the Eighteenth Georgia and Hampton's Legion of South Carolinians, and, after the transfer of these commands, with the Third Arkansas, they adopted and yet claim as a distinctive title the name of Hood's Texas Brigade.

Of the details of their organization but brief mention will be made. The twelve companies that composed the First Texas may be said to have straggled to Virginia, where, in the early months of 1861, it was believed the one decisive battle of the war would be fought. They went singly, in couples, and in triplets; but although all arrived in Richmond by June 1, 1861, they were not ordered to the front until July 21, the day the first battle on the fields of Manassas was fought, and so did not reach the Southern army in time to take part in that engagement. Thence, with L. T. Wigfall as colonel, Hugh McLeod as lieutenant-colonel, and A. T. Rainey as major, the First Texas was ordered to the extreme right of the Confederate line, taking position near Dumfries, Va., as support to masked batteries at Cockpit Point.

Wigfall was a politician without military training; McLeod was a valiant soldier in the Texas revolution of 1836, commanded the Santa Fé expedition of 1841, and had languished as a captive in the prison of Perote; Rainey was a lawyer, eminent in his profession. Wigfall, having been elected a senator in the Confederate Congress, resigned his commission in January, 1861. McLeod died about the same date. May 12, 1862, the regiment reinlisted and reorganized, electing Rainey as its colonel, Captain P. A. Work as its lieutenant-colonel, and Captain Matt. Dale as its major. That, as will be seen, was five days after the battle of Eltham's Landing.

The companies that composed the Fourth and Fifth Texas were organized as early as those in the First Texas, and would have proceeded to Virginia as soon but for the refusal of the Confederate authorities to accept their services in that field. After the First Texas arrived in Richmond, though, Mr. Davis decided to accept two more regiments from Texas, and the Fourth and Fifth were at once mustered in—Mr. Davis reserving, however, the right to appoint the field officers of each. They arrived in Richmond in September, 1861, and immediately there was a rush of gentlemen more or less prominent in political affairs to the seat of government, each applying and hoping for appointments to such positions. But all were disappointed. Not one of their number had taken any interest in either regiment prior to its departure from Texas, and as they failed to secure any indorsement of their claims from the rank and file of the two commands, President Davis acted on his own judgment, and appointed John B. Hood colonel of the Fourth Texas, John Marshall its lieutenant-colonel, and Bradfute Warwick its major; Jas. J. Archer colonel of the Fifth Texas, Jerome B. Robertson its lieutenant-colonel, and Q. T. Quattlebaum its major.

Hood and Archer had resigned from the United States regular army and offered their services to the Confederacy. Both were young, gallant, and capable, and each was liked by his regiment. John Marshall was a newspaper man, and, save courage, had no qualifications for military command. Jerome B. Robertson was by profession a physician, but had gone to Texas early enough to join in the pursuit, with a company of Kentuckians commanded by him, of the Mexicans after their retreat from San Jacinto. Later, in 1839 and 1840, he assisted, as commander of a regiment, in repelling the frequent invasions of Mexicans and Indians, and was one of the first to raise a company for Confederate service. Bradfute Warwick was a Virginian, wealthy and adventurous. Educated as a physician, he traveled extensively through Europe, and finally joined the Italian patriot, Garibaldi, and was given a commission in his army, first as a surgeon, and next as a captain. Quattlebaum was a graduate of West Point, but of his record little is known, as, at his own request, he was transferred to another field of service within a week after his assignment to the Fifth Texas.

Thenceforward, promotions among the commissioned officers of the three Texas regiments were in the order of seniority. The only promotions for merit were in cases where company elections were held to determine who should fill places made vacant by death, disablement, transfer, or resignation. To these might be added an occasional promotion from the ranks to an adjutancy, and when, in 1864, color-bearers were entitled to commissions as lieutenants, of privates to the rank of color-bearers and lieutenants. Under the rule of seniority it happened that toward the close of the war the junior captain of a regiment often became a field officer of his regiment. No instance can be cited in Hood's Texas Brigade, and few in any other command, where higher rank was gained by regimental and company officers on account of their merit. As long as an officer remained with his command he took rank only by seniority. This statement applies, of course, only to the Texans. At the beginning of the war there was little law to govern such matters, and commissions were frequently granted by President Davis to men for whom places only could be found in this, that, or the other of the many regiments admittedly lacking competent officers.

Colonels Hood and Archer took command, respectively, of the Fourth and Fifth Texas regiments in October, 1861, holding them in camp near Richmond, and drilling and disciplining them, until about the last of November. Then they marched them over to Dumfries, Va., where they were brigaded with the First Texas and the Eighteenth Georgia regiment, under command of Brigadier-General L. T. Wigfall. Of their stay there in winter-quarters during the winter of 1861-2 much might be told that would be interesting as reminiscences of a far-distant past to the few hundred survivors of the command, but would hardly prove entertaining to the general reader. Their experiences differed little from those of other Confederate commands at that early stage of the war. What difference there was may be attributed to the fact that General Wigfall's imagination was too often quickened by deep potations to be reliable. The colder the night and the more metallic the rustling of the pine tops above his quarters, the more plainly he could hear the rattling of oars in the oar-locks of boats transporting Federal troops across the Potomac who were bent on capturing Cockpit Point, and but for the restraining influence of Colonels Hood and Archer he would have had the brigade on the double-quick twice a week while he remained in command.

As it was, he sent the Fifth Texas on a tramp in the dark through mud more than ankle-deep, one bitter cold night, down to the Point. Colonel Hood, however, surmised that the order was based either on false intelligence or imagination, and therefore did not move the Fourth Texas. To a certain extent, however, Wigfall was excusable. The First Texas had run him half-crazy with its unwillingness to submit to the rigorous discipline he would have enforced, and, in addition, but previous to the arrival of the Fourth and Fifth, had manufactured more than one false alarm just to see what he would do. One night indeed, grown tired of inaction and longing for excitement, the boys of the First took French leave of their officers, and went in a body across the Potomac, and there waked up not only General Sickles and the Union troops then under his command, but spread consternation on the streets of Washington city by the report circulated by themselves that they were the advance guard of the Confederate army. General Sickles assembled his troops in battle array and called lustily for reinforcements, and these were on the way when daylight came and revealed the absence of a single Confederate on his side of the river. In brief, the Texans went over "on a lark," and, having enjoyed it, returned to their quarters before daylight, and for many months the question with Wigfall and the equally ignorant officers of the First Texas was, Who was it that kicked up such a row among our friends, the enemy?

Among the Federal troops then wintering in Maryland opposite Cockpit Point was Duryea's Fifth New York Zouaves. Several times during the winter ice formed on the Potomac thick enough to bear the weight of a man, and far enough out from the shore on either side to let members of the Fifth Texas and the Zouaves get within easy hearing distance of each other. While always in good humor, the conversations were, as a rule, made up of boasts of what one regiment would do to the other should they ever meet in battle, as it was earnestly hoped they would. "We'll wipe your regiment off the face of the earth," threatened the Zouaves. "We'll cover the ground with your ring-streaked and striped bodies," counter-threatened the Texans. Which regiment made good, and how, will be told in its proper place.

Much sickness prevailed among the Texans—more, perhaps, than in commands from the Southern Atlantic States and from Tennessee, where the winters were so nearly equal in severity to those of Virginia. Measles and pneumonia caused the death of many brave young men. Diarrhea led the way to the more fatal complaints. At one time there were not exceeding twenty-five men fit for duty in the Fifth Texas, although it had in camp fully eight hundred men. Nevertheless, much scouting was done, and the enemy was kept in constant apprehension. On one occasion, a party of nine Texans were surrounded by Federal cavalry, and driven for refuge into a house. But they had no thought of surrender. All day long they held the Federal regiment at bay. Night was coming on, though, and to make sure of escape, one of their number climbed to the top of the building. Standing there, he called to his comrades in a tone loud enough to be heard by the enemy: "Keep on shooting, boys—a whole brigade of Confederate cavalry is just beyond the creek, and it'll be here in a few minutes." Hearing the announcement, and not doubting its truth, the Federal commander called his men into line of battle, and taking advantage of the movement, the Texans made a run for it to the timbered valley of a little creek, where, protected by the trees, they could bid defiance to their mounted assailants.

At winter-quarters time hung heavily on the hands of some, lightly on those of others. After a house for each mess in each company was built, there was to be done the fatigue duty needed to keep the camp in good sanitary condition, guard duty night and day around the camp, and picketing at Cockpit Point, each regiment of the brigade in its turn. In addition, when the weather was favorable and the ground dry enough, there was company and regimental drill. Both to give the men employment and to train them in soldierly ways,

Colonels Hood and Archer insisted on daily guard mountings and dress parades. In the way of indoor amusements there were cards, checkers, backgammon, and chess, and, with the cards, more or less gambling for small stakes. The Richmond press was enterprising, and daily papers supplied the news, and in discussing these, announcing and listening to plans of campaigns and comments and criticisms on this, that, and the other subject, there was little time given to such solitary communings with one's self as so often encourages discontent and gloom. The one monotony was the staying in one place—the grievous lack was feminine society.

In preparations for active operations in the field, there was a general shifting about of commands. Among the orders issued was one placing together, as a division to be commanded by the senior brigadier-general, of the Texas Brigade and that of General W. H. C. Whiting. Whiting's brigade—the Third Brigade it is often called in reports—was then composed of the Fourth Alabama, the Sixth North Carolina, and the Second and Eleventh Mississippi regiments. While each of these regiments had taken a prominent and gallant part in the battle of First Manassas, one of them, the Fourth Alabama, was the command in appealing to which at that engagement General Bernard E. Bee fixed upon Jackson the sobriquet of "Stonewall." Whiting, as ranking officer, assumed command of the division, Colonel E. M. Law, of the Fourth Alabama, commanding the Whiting brigade. Thenceforward until after the seven days of battle around Richmond, the division was known and spoken of as "Whiting's division." After those battles Whiting was not with the division, and Hood commanding it, it came to be known as "Hood's division," and Whiting's brigade came to be known as "Law's brigade." In October, 1862, Hood was made major-general of a division composed of Law's, the Texas, Benning's, and Anderson's brigades. At the same time Law was made a brigadier-general and assigned to the command of the old Whiting brigade, and Colonel Jerome B. Robertson, of the Fifth Texas, was also made a brigadier-general and given command of the Texas Brigade.

The Eighteenth Georgia regiment was composed of companies hailing from middle Georgia. Its field officers were

Colonel William T. Wofford, Lieutenant-Colonel S. Z. Ruff, and Major Jefferson Johnson. It was transferred from the Texas Brigade, after the battle of Sharpsburg, to one composed entirely of Georgia troops, and of which Colonel Wofford was made brigadier-general. A brave and gallant command while in the Texas Brigade, it continued the same throughout the war.

Hampton's Legion, as originally organized, consisted of seven companies of infantry, four of cavalry, and one of artillery. During the spring of 1862, this organization was dissolved. The infantry companies, retaining the name of "Hampton's Legion," were formed into a battalion, and assigned to the Texas Brigade before the seven days' battles around Richmond. To it was added another company of infantry, Company H. Its field officers were Lieutenant-Colonel Martin W. Gary, and Major Harvey Dingle. About the close of Longstreet's Knoxville campaign, the Legion was mounted, and ordered to report for duty at Richmond, Va., under Brigadier-General Martin W. Gary. As infantry the Legion had a grit, a staying quality, and a dash that was admirable, and as cavalry it maintained its reputation as a hard fighter.

CHAPTER II

FREDERICKSBURG—YORKTOWN—ELTHAM'S LANDING

The winter of 1861-2, in the latitude of Virginia, was one of great length and severity. The Texans, however, soon grew fairly well inured to the cold, and after the Christmas holidays there was a speedy return of health and appetite—the latter finding pleasant regalement and ample satisfaction in the abundance, variety and excellent quality of the rations then issued and obtainable. In brief, they were beginning to feel in a measure "to the manner born," and very much "at home," when, about the first days of March, 1862, a rumor spread that some general movement of the Southern army was in immediate contemplation. That rumor was based on fact. General George B. McClellan, the so-called "Young Napoleon of the West," was now in command of the Federal army. Abandoning all thought of another "on to Richmond" by the Manassas route, he planned to concentrate his forces on the peninsula below Yorktown, and thence move on the Confederate capital by a route lying between the York and James Rivers. To place his army in position to meet this movement General Jos. E. Johnston, the Confederate commander, made preparations to withdraw from the Manassas line to the south side of the Rappahannock, and in his injudicious haste sacrificed immense stores of military supplies.

The Texas Brigade bade farewell to its winter-quarters on the morning of March 8, 1862, and after a march of two days. over snow-covered ground encamped four miles northwest of Fredericksburg. In the meantime, Wigfall 'had resigned his commission as brigadier-general, and to fill the vacancy thus created, President Davis promoted Hood to the rank of brigadier and assigned him to the command of the brigade. A few days after he assumed command, our Texas scouts reported that Federal General Sickles, with one or more brigades of infantry, had crossed the Potomac at or near Cockpit Point,

ALBERT SNEED
Company F, Fourth Texas Regiment

and was moving toward Fredericksburg. Too ambitious to neglect so favorable an opportunity to display his generalship, and at the same time test the fighting qualities of his command, General Hood at once sought and obtained permission from his superiors to lead the Texas Brigade across the Rappahannock and teach the enemy a lesson. Our march was rapid, but not a man lagged by the wayside. It was a "wild-goose" chase, though; General Sickles not only heard of our approach in his direction in time to evade an attack, but must also have heard the threatening boasts of his presumedly blood-thirsty antagonists; at any rate, when the brigade came to the place where he was said to be encamped, he was not there, having beat a hasty retreat to the shelter of gunboats on the Potomac. The Texas Brigade, therefore, had no recourse but to return to its camp and await another chance to show its mettle.

General Magruder, who with about ten thousand Confederates. was holding McClellan at bay on the Peninsula, now began to call for assistance. Magruder's line extended from the York River at Yorktown, the scene of Cornwallis' surrender to General George Washington during the Revolutionary War, to the James River on the south, a distance of twelve or fifteen miles. Because the abandonment of that line would expose Norfolk to capture, Mr. Davis insisted on holding it. General Johnston deemed such an attempt inadvisable; flanked as the narrow peninsula was by the York and James Rivers, the one navigable as high up as West Point, and the other all the way up to Richmond, it would be a trap, he argued, for the Confederate army. Heavily fortified as was Yorktown at the mouth of York River, its guns could not be relied on to block the way of gunboats into that stream. That way once opened, Federal troops might be landed at points along the stream whence by a march of a few miles they could cut the Confederates off from Richmond. But Mr. Davis was not only commander-in-chief, but insistent, and obeying his orders, Johnston moved his army to Yorktown.

The Texas Brigade moved from Fredericksburg on the 8th day of April, going by railroad to a point near Richmond, and thence marching to Yorktown. It was the first long tramp it had been called on to undertake, and as the roads were too sandy to afford firm footholds, it arrived at its destination on the 15th, footsore and tired. Fortunately for its comfort, it was assigned to no specific duty. Troops which had preceded it had relieved Magruder's weary soldiers. Its adventurous spirits, however, were not content to spend their time in idleness, and so sought sport and excitement in sharpshooting and scouting. Armed as most of the Texans were with Minnie and Enfield rifles, and accustomed as they were to the use of fire-arms from their earliest boyhood, their marksmanship proved so superior to that of the Federals that it was not long before their appearance on the firing line was hailed with delight by their comrade Confederates, and viewed with apprehension by the Federals.

About the first of May General Johnston received information that his opponent, General McClellan, had ordered a general advance of his army. Delaying only long enough to make sure of McClellan's intentions, General Johnston on the 3rd of May ordered the retreat of the Confederate army. But since to the Texas Brigade was assigned the honor of being the rear guard on the road leading from Yorktown to Williamsburg, twelve miles above, it did not move until daylight of the 4th. Formed into line then, it made good use of its legs, and by 10 A. M. overtook the troops under General Longstreet which had halted four miles short of Williamsburg—their object to check the advance of the enemy and give time for the wagon trains to get beyond the danger line. But the Texas Brigade came to no halt; instead, it went steadily on, and taking a right hand road, left Williamsburg to its left—its objective point, the York River at or near Eltham's Landing, where, it was believed by General Johnston, McClellan would make a prompt effort to land a sufficient force to intercept the Confederate retreat and probably capture its wagon and artillery trains. The event proved the truth of the surmise, for on the morning of May 7 a large part of Franklin's Federal division landed there.

On the morning of the 6th the Texas Brigade encamped in the forest, within two miles of the landing. During that day and the following night General Hood located the point at which the landing would be attempted, and early the next morning led the brigade, in advance of all other troops, toward it. His own account of the battle that ensued is to be found in his book, "Advance and Retreat":

"While in bivouac opposite West Point, General Whiting informed me that a large body of the enemy had disembarked at Eltham's Landing; that our cavalry was on picket upon the high ground overlooking the valley of the York River, and instructed me to move my brigade in that direction, and drive the enemy back if he attempted to advance from under cover of his gunboats. Pursuant to imperative orders, the men had not been allowed to march with loaded guns during the retreat. On the 7th, at the head of my command, I proceeded in the direction of Eltham's, with the intention to halt and load the muskets upon our arrival at the cavalry outpost. I soon reached the rear of a small cabin upon the crest of the hill, where I found one of our cavalrymen half asleep. The head of the column, marching by the right flank, with the Fourth Texas in the front, was not more than twenty or thirty paces in my rear, when, simultaneously with my arrival at the station of this cavalry picket, a skirmish line, supported by a large body of the enemy, met me face to face. The slope from the cabin toward the York River was abrupt, and consequently, I did not discover the Federals till we were almost close enough to shake hands. I leaped from my horse, ran to the head of my column, then about fifteen paces in rear, gave the command, 'Forward into line,' and ordered the men to load. The Federals immediately opened fire, but halted as they perceived our long line in rear. Meanwhile, a corporal of the enemy drew down his musket upon me as I stood in front of my line. John Deal, a private in Company A, Fourth Texas, had fortunately, in this instance, but contrary to orders, charged his rifle before leaving camp; he instantly killed the corporal, who fell within a few feet of me. At the time I ordered the leading regiment to change front forward on the first company, I also sent directions to the troops in rear to follow up the movement and load their arms, which was promptly executed. The brigade then gallantly advanced, and drove the Federals, within the space of about two hours, a distance of one mile and a half to the cover of their gunboats. When we struck their main line quite a spirited engagement took place, which, however, proved to be only a temporary stand before attaining the immediate shelter of their vessels of war. Hampton's Brigade, near the close of the action, came to our support, and performed efficient service on the right."

In closing his account, General Hood says: "This affair, which brought the brigade so suddenly and unexpectedly under fire for the first time, served as a happy introduction to the enemy." To that statement he might have added that it was also the first time that he himself commanded in battle a larger force than a single regiment, and had an opportunity to display his generalship. To do justice both to himself and the Texas Brigade, he should have gone more into detail. A private of the Fourth Texas gives the following particulars:

"We marched out of camp that morning, at daylight, each of us wondering where we were going, and not a soul of us suspecting that an enemy was near. We went about a mile and a half, and the Fourth Texas in advance, were passing through a field dotted with pine stumps, and approaching a house situated on the crest of the hill overlooking York River valley. Hood and some member of his staff, and perhaps a courier or two, rode about fifty yards ahead of Company A, the leading company. To the left of the road, and about forty yards from the house, sat a cavalryman, apparently fast asleep on the back of his steed. Hood rode on by him, but had not gone ten steps when a party of Federals, fifteen or twenty in number, sprang from behind the house, and fired a volley at us. For a second, consternation prevailed. Not a man of us had his gun loaded, and there was a pell-mell scattering to take shelter behind the many stumps. Hood wheeled his horse, and shouting, 'Fall into line, men—fall into line,' came dashing back at full speed toward us. Half way to us, he noticed that nobody was paying any attention to him, and he shouted, 'Get into line, men—get into line, Fourth Texas! Is my old regiment going to play hell right here?' Just then a Yankee stepped out from behind the house, and seeing him, John Deal—the one and only one of us that had a loaded gun—dropped to his knees, took careful aim and laid the daring fellow low. In another second every gun in the command was loaded, and the men began moving into line, and having formed a semblance of one, rushed forward to the crest of the hill and commenced firing at the Yankees now in swift retreat across an open field in the valley between us and heavily timbered land. The other regiments of our brigade moved quickly up on the right of the Fourth, and within five minutes such of the Federal skirmishers as were not killed or wounded had fallen back to the protection of the timber.

"Hood then ordered forward a skirmish line, and following it, we crossed the open field in the valley and gained the timber beyond. Then, the Fourth Texas, the only regiment whose movements I know anything about, began hunting for the enemy. But although there was an abundance of Yankees near us, as was evident from the firing on our right and left, not one of them appeared in front of the Fourth. Its only loss was from the volley fired at us on top of the hill. By that, one man was seriously wounded. The same volley, I have always understood, killed Captain Denny, the commissary of the Fifth Texas. As to that, I cannot speak positively; I was having my first experience in being shot at, and was therefore observant of only what occurred in my own regiment, and near at hand. In saying that the other regiments of the brigade moved quickly up on the right of the Fourth Texas, I may be in error, for one or the other of them might have formed on its left."

As adjutant of the Fifth Texas, Lieutenant Campbell Wood should be good authority concerning the movements of his regiment. Writing of the events of the day, he says:

"I am positively certain that the Fifth Texas was assigned to the duty of opening the battle. I am equally certain that no other regiment went in with us, or was at any time during the battle aligned with us. The Fifth was drawn up in line in an old field or meadow back of a little village, when, riding out in front of it, Colonel Archer said: 'Fifth Texas, I have sought and obtained permission for you to open the ball this morning.' Then he gave the orders, 'Right face, file left— Forward! March!' We moved across the opening, and soon struck the timber, taking a road on each side of which was a dense thicket of undergrowth in full leaf. No skirmishers or scouts advanced in front of us, and judging from that fact, I could not believe a battle was imminent. I forgot to say that before giving the command, 'Forward,' Colonel Archer ordered the men to load their guns, but not to cap them.

"We marched down the road toward West Point in column of four ranks, Colonel Archer and Captain Denny rode at the head of the regiment, and I trudged along on foot, immediately behind Archer. Archer and Denny rode slowly, and the men kept close up, talking a little as was usual on a march. Just as we approached quite near to an old shack of a house, a Federal sergeant and eight men jumped from behind it and fired a volley at us. All their bullets excepting one went wild, but that one struck and killed Captain Denny, and he fell from his horse. Archer immediately ordered the men to cap their guns. Many of them, however, had capped theirs when they loaded them, and these men sprang from the ranks and fired at our assailants, killing and mortally wounding every one of them.

"Breaking into a double-quick, and following close on the heels of two or three men Archer had ordered to keep well in advance of us, we went forward several hundred yards and halted. Here we caught a glimpse of some troops in line to the left of our front, and some of our men began to fire at them. Colonel Archer put an instant stop to the firing, being uncertain whether the parties aimed at were friends or foes, and ordered me to take the first platoon of Company D and deploy it in skirmish line to the right of the road. He also, I think, ordered Lieutenant W. T. Hill, or Captain Powell, to deploy the second platoon of the same company on the left of the road. Just at this juncture a couple of young fellows came running to us from our left, to tell us that it was Hampton's Legion that was out there. Archer told me that he thought the First Texas was somewhere on our right, and cautioned me not to fire on it.

"But the First Texas was not on our right, as I soon ascertained and reported; it was the Ninety-fifth Pennsylvania Bucktails. Archer ordered me to give them h—ll and the boys of my platoon did it, for when formed in line of battle the Fifth was struggling through the undergrowth, it passed and counted forty dead bucktails, killed by my platoon in its first volley. The undergrowth was so thick that we could see but a little way ahead. While the regiment was thus advancing, I located the whereabouts of the First Texas by the sound of Colonel Rainey's voice, but whether it came from the right or left, I am not sure. I did not see him, or the First Texas, but I heard him call out to his men, in the shrill, penetrating voice that was so peculiar to him: 'G—d d—n it, boys! Swing around there on the right! The Je-e-e-sus! Did you hear that bullet?'

"The Fifth continued its advance to the river, where the men now pretty well exhausted by their long run over and through the undergrowth, laid down in a cedar thicket, so near the gunboats that we could see the smoke from their smokestacks, and hear the puffing of the steam from their boilers. The fire of their guns, of course, passed over us.

"While lying in the cedar thicket, some troops came up within thirty yards of our right flank, and formed in line facing the river. Thinking they were one of the regiments of our brigade, I walked up pretty close to them and asked what regiment it was. 'Eighteenth Ohio,' came the reply, clear-cut and distinct. I immediately reported the fact to Colonel Archer, and when he had taken a near enough look at them to see they wore blue, he ordered the regiment to move as quietly as possible to the rear, which they did, and an hour later the Fifth got in line with the other regiments of the brigade."

Lieutenant Wood's account is not so widely at variance with that of General Hood as to require any effort to reconcile them. At best, Hood's is but a partial account, many things having happened that day which are unmentioned. General Hood owed Colonel Archer a good turn. At the time he was promoted to a generalcy, Archer ranked him by seniority, and was thus entitled to the promotion in preference to Hood. But as Hood gracefully says in his "Advance and Retreat," when Archer learned of Hood's advancement, he went immediately to that officer's tent, and warmly congratulating him, expressing his entire willingness to serve under him. It was in appreciation of this self-abnegation on the part of Colonel Archer, that Hood gave him, at Eltham's Landing, the privilege of "opening the ball" with the Fifth Texas.

However, "Man proposes and God disposes." Even if the Fifth Texas was first to advance, and went further than other regiments, it was the First Texas that bore the brunt of the battle of the day; for it was the only regiment that came squarely up against a battle line of the Federals, and face to face with it, struggled for and won the victory. Its greater loss than any other regiment attests the greater risk it encountered, and the courage it exhibited. While the Fourth Texas lost but one killed and one wounded, and the Fifth Texas two killed, five wounded and two missing, the First Texas lost fifteen killed, nineteen wounded—more than three times as many as both the other Texas regiments. Among its killed was Lieutenant-Colonel H. H. Black.

What part in the affair the Eighteenth Georgia took, and whether it suffered any loss, cannot be stated. It is probable that it was held in reserve.

CHAPTER III

RICHMOND—SEVEN PINES—GAINES' MILL

Two hours before dawn of the 8th of May, the Texas Brigade was quietly awakened by its officers, and ordered to form in line as quickly and silently as possible, in readiness for rapid marching. No noise was to be made, for during the night the Federals had landed in large force and pushed forward to the hill-tops, and only by the stealthiest of movements could we hope to escape without a fight against overwhelming numbers. In checking the landing and the advance of the enemy on the previous day, we had accomplished all that was desired. Our wagon and artillery trains were far on their way to Richmond, and the troops under Longstreet, whom we had passed beyond Williamsburg, had held McClellan's main army at bay long enough to secure their own safe retreat. The Texas Brigade only was still in danger.

It moved at a lively gait, and by noon overtook the main army, and passing within the picket lines came to its first halt during the day in a thicket of laurels, about three miles from Long Bridge, across the Chickahominy. Here it rested until about 10 P. M. of the 9th, when under a torrential downpour of rain, in a darkness that was almost impenetrable, and over a road knee-deep in mud, and in places waist-deep in water, it straggled to and across the bridge named—each man, as he reached the high ground beyond the Chickahominy, dropping to the ground, and without effort to find his company or regiment, going to sleep. But by 9 A. M. of the next day, order was restored, each soldier with his command, and late afternoon found the Texas Brigade in camp about five miles from Richmond.

The war was now on in good earnest. The over-sanguine, fire-eating secessionists who at the outset predicted that but one battle would be needed to conquer a peace and independence, had withdrawn from the public gaze, and were now busy in search of such governmental employment in their respective States, or under the Confederacy, as would exempt them from military service. Every port in the South was blockaded, and its communication with Europe cut off. Federal troops were stationed or in active movement in every State of the Confederacy except Texas and Louisiana. Union successes marked the beginning months of 1862, both in the East and in the West. Roanoke Island and Fort Macon, in North Carolina, and Fort Pulaski, near Savannah, Ga., had been captured; Fort Henry on the Tennessee River and Fort Donelson on the Cumberland had both fallen, and with them Nashville had been lost. The battle of Shiloh had been fought, but although claimed as a victory by the Confederates, accomplished but little for the Southern cause. As said by a Southern historian, "to the Confederates, Shiloh did not seem to be a defeat, but rather, the disappointment of a hope almost realized."

As offsets to these reverses to, or failures to win on the part of the Confederates, Stonewall Jackson in the Shenandoah valley of Virginia had been keeping the Federal forces there, under Banks, Milroy, Fremont and Siegel, constantly on the go—winning battle after battle from them, and capturing large stores of military supplies much needed by the Southern armies. Jackson's victories, though, were not on a sufficiently large scale to inspire the thoughtful mind of that day with any great confidence. Indeed, much of the confidence inspired by them was lost when it was known that General Johnston was retreating from the peninsula. This retrograde movement insured the loss to the Confederacy of Newport and the navy yard there, and thus put an end to any sanguine hope of building a Confederate navy, for by it the nucleus of that navy would be hemmed up in James River.

There was no corresponding loss of confidence, though, among the Confederates actually in the field in Virginia. They were "built of sterner stuff" than were the many who sought either exemption from any military service or such service only as could be performed in places where the missiles of war were not likely to reach them. Having enlisted as soldiers in a cause they believed just, and having implicit faith in the generals then in command of them, they let no reverses discourage them and remained not only firm and unshaken in determination, but optimistic. As for the Texas Brigade, it had come altogether too far in search of a fight to allow itself to be discouraged. It had tested its mettle at Eltham's Landing, had smelled the smoke of battle, and heard the screech of shells and the hissing of bullets, and had shrunk from none of the dangers, and with Hood in command of it, and Joe Johnston, of the army, why should it fear disaster?

General Johnston placed his army in position south of the Chickahominy to guard all the approaches to Richmond on the north side of James River. McClellan advanced with cautious and seemingly timid deliberation to the north bank of the Chickahominy, and in a few days set his pioneer corps to work repairing the partially destroyed bridges across that stream—in the meantime calling insistently for reinforcements. He then had a force of over 100,000, but Johnston, he claimed, had still more men. He particularly insisted that the large force of Federals at Fredericksburg, under command of McDowell, should be ordered to move over and take position on his right flank. But Mr. Lincoln and his advisers at Washington, although promising much, did little. Least of all would they, for quite a while, consent that McDowell should go farther from Washington than he then was. To let him do so would be to expose the Federal capital to capture by Stonewall Jackson.

Over one of the bridges across the Chickahominy, at last in tolerable repair, McClellan threw two corps of his army which immediately took position at Seven Pines and Fair Oaks station, points east and about eight miles from Richmond. About the same time he extended his right to Mechanicsville, a hamlet about northeast from Richmond, placing it under command of Fitz-John Porter, and protecting it by earth and timber works, abatis and fallen timber. This was about the 24th of May. Learning of it, and also of Jackson's retirement toward Staunton in the Shenandoah valley, Mr. Lincoln consented that McDowell should march to the assistance of McClellan. Informed of the state of affairs, General Johnston decided to attack McClellan before McDowell could arrive, and therefore planned an attack on the Federal right at Mechanicsville by a flank movement. The troops were marching to their positions when intelligence came that Stonewall Jackson had won a great victory at Winchester, and that McDowell was already marching north and away from Richmond, and Johnston abandoned the flanking movement.

Then Johnston planned the battle of Seven Pines—an attack on the two Federal corps then on the Richmond side of the Chickahominy. His orders obeyed in letter and spirit and with proper concert of action, the success promised would undoubtedly have been achieved. But they were not so obeyed. The scene of operations was a wilderness of swampy, heavily-timbered pine land, made almost impenetrable by tangled undergrowth, and traversed by dim roads of which there were no maps accessible; the guides secured were incompetent; jealousy was rife among commanding officers of brigades and divisions, and there was no concert of action; and the upshot was a victory fruitful only in the loss of life. General Johnston needlessly exposed himself, and was wounded just when his presence on the field might have accomplished most good. The command devolved upon General G. W. Smith as next in rank, but before he could thoroughly acquaint himself with the position of his troops, was conferred by Mr. Davis, the President, on General Robert E. Lee, and by his command the assaulting forces withdrew from the field.

Since crossing the Chickahominy, the Texas Brigade had not, as a command, been called into active service. Its men, however, did not remain entirely idle. Occasionally, scouting was ordered; frequently it was volunteered by individuals, by couples and by parties large and small. When the Federals first got foothold on the Richmond side of the Chickahominy, General Johnston himself called for a detail of one hundred and fifty men from the brigade, and sent them forward into the swamps to feel of the enemy and ascertain his position. Going farther and taking greater risks than similar parties from other commands, the Texas scouts not only engaged in several heavy skirmishes and inflicted considerable loss on the Federals, but also secured the only accurate information obtained.

It was intended that the brigade should bear a prominent part at Seven Pines; but although on the ground in proper

JOHN M. PINCKNEY
Company G, Fourth Texas Regiment

place and time, and for the better part of two days exposed to artillery fire and several times to that of musketry aimed at compatriot commands in its front, the most diligent efforts of General Hood failed to secure it an opportunity to meet the foe, face to face. Nevertheless, eighteen of its men were wounded more or less seriously.

General Lee was no sooner in command of the army than he commenced scheming to raise the threatened siege of Richmond before it was fairly under weigh. The plan fixed upon was to reinforce Stonewall Jackson, who was still in the Shenandoah valley, and thus impressing the Federal authorities with the belief that an attack was contemplated on Washington city, cause them to withhold reinforcements from McClellan. That accomplished, Jackson was to make a sudden descent, with his whole force, upon McClellan's right flank and rear in the vicinity of Mechanicsville—his attack to be joined in by the Confederate troops around Richmond.

The plan was brilliant in conception, but was audacious in the extreme. At the date its execution began, Lee had but 57,000 men. With these he must hold at bay McClellan's 115,000, near 80,000 of whom were then strongly intrenched on the south side of the Chickahominy, with outposts within five miles of the Confederate capital, and not only in sight of the city, but in hearing of its church-bells. But Lee did not hesitate; aware that McClellan's bump of caution was of abnormal development, and knowing how insistently and persistently he was appealing for reinforcements, Lee felt confident he would make no immediate advance. On the 11th of June, Whiting's division, composed of his own and the Texas Brigade—the latter strengthened since Eltham's Landing by the transfer to it of Hampton's South Carolina Legion— marched into and through the streets of Richmond with banners flying and drums beating, and boarding trains, set out by way of Lynchburg for the Shenandoah valley, there, as was proclaimed publicly by officers high in rank, to join Jackson in an "on to Washington." Federal spies communicated the tidings to the Federal authorities at once; McClellan knew them two days in advance, and Jackson, never happier than when deceiving an enemy, aided the deception by arranging that Federal surgeons within his lines, but on the eve of departure, should overhear a conversation between certain of his officers in which they spoke of the reinforcements coming and of Jackson's design to essay the capture of Washington.

Arriving at Lynchburg, Whiting's division remained there two days. Then boarding the cars again, it went on to Charlottesville, where it rested another day, and thence proceeded by train to Staunton, at the head of the Shenandoah valley. General Whiting, a brave and capable officer, but with, perhaps, a rather exaggerated sense of his own importance, went in person to General Jackson to report the arrival of his division, receive orders, and incidentally, secure information as to plans and purposes. "Hold yourself and command, sir, in readiness to march at six o'clock Monday morning," was the only order given him, and it was given in the curt tone habitually employed by "Stonewall" when issuing his commands. For two seconds, General Whiting sat silent, waiting for the information that he thought would surely be vouchsafed him. Then with an assurance born of the consciousness that in the old regular army of the United States he ranked the man in whose presence he was, he asked, "In what direction will we march, General?" "That will be made known to you, sir, at the proper time," answered Jackson, and with that, Whiting had, perforce, to be content.

Monday morning came, and to the surprise and mystification of officers and men alike, instead of moving down the Shenandoah valley, the division marched eastward along the road leading across the Blue Ridge from Staunton to Charlottesville.

"Where are we going, Captain?" asked a Texas private, sidling up to the commander of his company. "Damfiknow," was the reply; "but I'll mosey along up to the head of the regiment, and ask the colonel." "Where in the mischief and Tom Walker are we going, Colonel?" queried the captain of the colonel, as after considerable fast walking he overtook that mounted officer. "I'll be durned if I know," answered the colonel; "General Hood hasn't told me yet, but I'll let you know as soon as he does." But when the colonel applied to Hood for the desired information, Hood said, "I don't know," as promptly as did General Whiting when Hood propounded the now burning question to him. Meanwhile the division marched on until, high up on the mountain side, a halt was called. What was said to the regiments of Whiting's Brigade is not known, but to each of those of the Texas Brigade General Hood made a short speech in which he said that the division was now subject to the orders of General Jackson, to whom alone its destination was known, and that to all questions asked, it was Jackson's order that the men should answer, "I do not know." "But, fellow-soldiers," said Hood in conclusion, "while I myself do not know where we are going, I can assure you that such of you as keep up with your command, will witness and take part in stirring and glorious events."

That Hood's words but added to the mystification and increased the curiosity already prevailing, needs not the telling. All that day, and indeed until the morning of June 26th, an "I do' know" preceded the answer given to any question asked, the boys falling into the humor of the thing and making a joke of it. As it was the invariable answer they gave to each other, so it was often that which they gave to officers, and occasionally it served as a means of evading punishment; as, for instance, when General Jackson himself discovered one of them in a tree by the roadside, busily engaged in stuffing alternate handfuls "of the fruit thereof" into his mouth and haversack, and apparently reckless that such depredations were forbidden. It is an old and oft-told story of the war, and readers will remember that growing angry at the "I do' knows," flippantly uttered in response to each of his questions, Jackson finally asked why it was he was so answered, and the impudent fellow replied: "Because them's ole Stonewall Jackson's orders, an' I'm goin' to obey 'em, or bust."

Previous to the halt of the Texas Brigade and his speech to each of its regiments, General Hood had an experience that was amusing enough to be told by himself. There were many stills in the secluded nooks of the Blue Ridge, and by 9 A. M. many of the boys were in a good humor, more than a few were staggering, and apple-jack brandy could be had out of dozens of canteens. To prevent any straggling for the purpose of replenishing empty canteens, Hood authorized the statement, which was industriously circulated and really believed, that small-pox was raging among the citizens living along our route. Riding by himself, half a mile in rear of the brigade, he discovered, lying in the middle of the road and obviously very drunk, a member of the Fourth Texas.

Checking his horse, the general asked: "What is the matter with you, sir? Why are you not with your company?" The stern and peremptory voice brought the culprit to a sitting posture, and looking at the general with drunken gravity, he said: "Nussin much, I reckon, General—I jus' feel sorter weak an' no account." "So I see, sir," said Hood; "get up at once and rejoin your company." The fellow made several ineffectual attempts to obey, but each time fell back on the ground, and a few sober stragglers coming along just then, Hood ordered them to take him in charge and conduct him to his company. But as they approached to carry out the order, the fellow found voice to say between hiccoughs: "Don't you fellers that ain't been vaccinated come near me—I've got the small-pox—tha's wha's the masser with me."

The stragglers shrank back in alarm, and the general, laughing at the way his own chickens had come home to roost, said, "Let him alone, then—some of the teamsters will pick him up," and rode on.

That day—it was the 16th of June—Whiting's division marched twenty long miles, halting, shortly after dark, in the vicinity of a station on the railroad leading from Staunton, via Charlottesville, to Gordonville, known as Meechuam's. Thence, on trains and on foot—riding ten miles and footing it twenty, in alternation with other troops—we proceeded by way of Gordonsville to the neighborhood of Frederick's Hall, distant about ninety miles from Richmond—arriving there in the afternoon of June 21, and camping in a dense woodland. By dark every regiment and brigade under Jackson's command was on hand, and lest information of their presence be carried to the enemy, were surrounded by a line of cavalry and infantry pickets whose orders were to allow the passage of neither soldier nor citizen beyond their line, unless he had a pass signed by Jackson himself. In addition, and in aid of the outside picket line, around each separate command a guard was stationed whose duty it was to prevent all straying from camp. Such restrictions upon freedom of movement were not resented, however; the troops had been constantly on the move for ten days or more, and rest was not only needed but gratefully enjoyed.

At midnight of the 22nd—he would not start sooner lest he violate the injunction, "Keep the Sabbath day holy"—Jackson mounted his horse, and accompanied by a single courier, rode at a gallop toward Richmond, to report the whereabouts of his command to General Lee, and to plan for concert of movement between his own and the troops then near Richmond. He reached the city at 2 P. M. of the 23rd, and an hour later had made his report to General Lee and was in conference with him, Longstreet, A. P. Hill and D. H. Hill. The plan agreed upon was, briefly, this: Jackson was to march from Ashland at 3 A. M. of June 26th—the date and hour set by himself—and following the dividing ridges between the Pamunkey and Chickahominy Rivers, place his command in rear and flank of the right wing of the Federal army, and turn and dislodge it; A. P. Hill, upon notification that Jackson had crossed the Virginia Central Railroad, to move his command across the upper Chickahominy, and approaching Mechanicsville, attack the enemy there at sound of Jackson's signal guns; Longstreet and D. H. Hill, when A. P. Hill had driven the enemy from Mechanicsville, to find passage across the bridge at that place to the north side of the Chickahominy —Longstreet's troops taking position on the right of A. P. Hill's command, between it and the river, and assisting it to drive the Federals down the river—D. H. Hill's forces to march eastward and find position on Jackson's left. Jackson was enjoined to bear well to the left, " press forward toward the York River Railroad, close upon the enemy's rear, and force him down the Chickahominy, and if possible, cut him off from his base of supplies at the White House on the Pamunkey River."

General Lee was taking risks that a commander less courageous and less confident of the courage of his army would not have taken. The passage to the north side of the Chickahominy of A. P. Hill's 11,000 men, D. H. Hill's 10,000, and Longstreet's 9,000, left on the south side of that stream but 30,000 Confederates, under command of Generals Holmes, Magruder and Huger, to hold in check the nearly 80,000 soldiers of the four Federal corps then in line on the Richmond side of the stream, with their intrenched advance at Fair Oaks and Seven Pines. However, Lee knew the hesitating disposition of his opponent, McClellan, and events justified the risks taken.

The mystery with which General Jackson surrounded his movements was so well-preserved that it was not until June 24 that McClellan suspected he was approaching Richmond. Greatly perturbed by the suspicion, he wired Stanton, the Federal Secretary of War, for positive information. On the 25th Stanton replied that Jackson was either somewhere between Gordonsville and Luray, or in the mountains of West Virginia. On the same day, Banks and Fremont, then in the lower Shenandoah valley, were apprehensive that Jackson would descend on them. McClellan placed no faith in Stanton's information, for replying to him, he wired: "I am inclined to think that Jackson will attack my right and rear. The rebel force is stated at 200,000, including Jackson and Beauregard."

Jackson's command marched from Frederick's Hall on Monday, the 23rd, but owing to the excessive heat, the lack of water along the route traveled, and the necessity of repairing bridges destroyed by the Federals in a movement against Hanover Court House ordered by McClellan, did not make the rapid headway expected. It did not reach Ashland until the night of the 25th. Resuming its tramp at early dawn of the 26th, it crossed the Virginia Central Railroad about 9 A. M. Thence, the Texas Brigade, preceded by a strong line of skirmishers, deployed on each side of the road, began a march which, if undelayed, would have brought it by the middle of the afternoon in contact with the main body of the enemy. The Federal commander, though, had not been idle, for not only had he obstructed the roads by felling large trees across them and destroying bridges, but had posted cavalry north of the Totopotomoy Creek to give notice of the approach of Confederates and to delay it. This cavalry fled in such haste before our skirmish line as to abandon large quantities of supplies, and even the food that was cooking. But they set fire to the bridge over the boggy little Totopotomoy Creek, and the repair of that occupied so much time that it was after dark before the head of Jackson's column reached Hundley's Corner, about six miles east of Mechanicsville.

BILLY PEARCE
Company D, Fifth Texas Regiment

Jackson's failure to arrive sooner at Hundley's Corner produced its embarrassments. On receiving notice that he was crossing the Virginia Central Railroad, A. P. Hill led his command to the north side of the Chickahominy, and placed them in position to make an assault on the enemy at Mechanicsville as soon as Jackson's signal guns should be heard. These not sounding by 3 p. m., the hour when it was calculated Jackson would begin the attack, and fearing that longer delay might " hazard the failure of the whole plan," Hill ordered an assault by his troops. This attack uncovered the Mechanicsville bridge, and across it D. H. Hill and Longstreet led their respective commands, and joined in the fray with such spirit and determination as to force the Federals back on Beaverdam Creek behind almost impregnable intrenchments. These they held against repeated furious assaults by the Confederates until night brought cessation of battle. But during the night McClellan received positive information that Jackson was coming down on the rear of his army, and at early dawn of the 27th he abandoned his position at Beaver Dam, to concentrate all his forces along the previously intrenched crest and side of the ridge lying between the Chickahominy on its south, and Powhite Creek on its north or northeast.

Powhite Creek empties into the Chickahominy, and is a narrow, deep-channeled and brisk-flowing little stream fed by the swamps and morasses hidden in dense, thickly undergrown forests which begin about two miles from its mouth, and extend far to the east. Emerging from these tangled woods, it runs for half a mile between undulating meadows, its course marked by a narrow skirt of trees and passing the meadows, hides itself again in the recesses of a forest that continues to its outlet. On the highest point of the ridge south of it, and almost exactly opposite the upper end of the meadow land north of it, the Federals, on the morning of the 27th, massed twenty pieces of heavy field artillery.

CHAPTER IV

Gaines' Mill

The troops at Hundley's Corner were early astir on the fateful morning of June 27th, 1862, and were no sooner astir than they commenced inquiring as to the result of the battle at Mechanicsville and Beaver Dam, away off on their right. But little positive information was to be had, yet that little was encouraging and inspiring; although at great sacrifice of life, the Federals had been driven from their strongholds, but were still standing defiant behind intrenchments lower down the Chickahominy to which they had fallen back and from which it needed only the appearance of Jackson's command in their rear to compel them to retreat. But eager as were both commanding officers and their men to move forward and test conclusions, A. P. Hill's unauthorized and premature attack on the 26th caused many delays.

Moving at an early hour, D. H. Hill led his forces over from Mechanicsville toward Hundley's Corner—his orders and object, to lead the advance down the Chickahominy toward the York River Railroad. By 9 A. M. his column had passed the corner, and following close on its trail, went Ewell's command. By this time it was past midday. About 1 P. M. Whiting's division moved from the corner, and bearing to the right, late in the afternoon formed in line confronting that of the enemy —the position taken, opposite the high point of the ridge south of the little creek upon which the Federals had massed their twenty pieces of heavy field artillery—the center of the Texas Brigade exactly opposite these guns—the First Texas, Fifth Texas, Hampton's Legion and all but two companies of the Eighteenth Georgia, in the forest where lay the swamps and morasses, and the Fourth Texas in reserve, on the right of the Eighteenth Georgia. On the right of the Texas stood Whiting's Brigade, under command of Colonel E. M. Law. Next on the right was Pickett's Brigade.

McClellan's withdrawal from Beaver Dam in the early morning necessitated a readjustment of the lines of Longstreet and A. P. Hill, and it was 11 A. M. before the troops of either were in position to begin another assault. But though they fought well and gallantly, and made charge after charge, each was repulsed with terrible loss to the assailants, the twenty pieces of massed artillery doing most effective service for the Federals against every attack upon them over the high plateau of open meadow land, and the swamps and undergrowth elsewhere in the Federal front, making rapid advance through them possible. Brigade after brigade of the Confederates that essayed to move forward across the meadow was halted by the murderous fire of the artillery, and, save Trimble's Brigade, driven to retreat. But although that command did not fall back, it went no further than a depression on the near side of the ridge immediately north of Powhite Creek. There taking shelter from both bullets and shells, it kept up, for two long hours, an ineffective fire from smooth-bore muskets loaded with buck and ball.

"Long before we moved forward that morning," writes a member of the Fourth Texas, "we began to hear the noises of the fierce battle that was raging far away on our right front. We were but three miles on our way to it when evidences of its severity presented themselves in the persons of wounded men, these increasing in numbers as we went nearer and nearer to the firing line. When close in rear of A. P. Hill's command, we not only saw individual stragglers by the score, but regiments of them that were seemingly beyond the control of their officers. Still further on, the signs of battle, and of failure and perhaps defeat, became more numerous, and more than one of the boys expressed the opinion that we had come too late to do any good. But Whiting and Hood urged us on with what speed could be made over roads obstructed by artillery and wagon trains, a constantly increasing press from the front of the skulking and the wounded, and large and small squads of prisoners."

In his report of the battle of Gaines' Mill, which is dated July 19, 1862, and is to be found in Vol. XI, Part II, page 568, of War of the Rebellion records, published by the United States government, General Hood says:

"Arriving on the field between 4 and 5 P. M., I was informed by Colonel J. M. Jones, of General Ewell's staff, that his troops were hard pressed and required assistance. Line of battle was formed at once with the Hampton Legion, Lieutenant-Colonel M. W. Gary commanding, on the left, with orders to gain the crest of the hill in the woods and hold it, which they did, the Fifth Texas, Colonel J. B. Robertson commanding, engaging the enemy on the right of the Legion, and the First Texas, Colonel A. T. Rainey commanding, on the right of the Fifth Texas. The brigade moved gallantly forward, soon becoming engaged from left to right. The battle raged with great fury all along the line as these noble troops pressed steadily on, forcing the enemy to gradually give way.

"Directing in person the Fourth Texas regiment, Colonel John Marshall commanding, on the right of my line, they were the first troops to pierce the strong line of breastworks occupied by the enemy, which caused great confusion in their ranks. Here the Eighteenth Georgia, Lieutenant-Colonel S. Z. Ruff commanding, came to the support of the Fourth Texas, and these regiments pressed on over a hotly contested field, inclining from right to left, with the Fifth Texas on their left, taking a large number of prisoners and capturing fourteen pieces of artillery, when night came on and farther pursuit of the enemy ceased. The guns were captured by the Fourth Texas and Eighteenth Georgia, and a regiment was taken prisoners by the Fifth Texas regiment."

In his book, "Advance and Retreat," General Hood gives a more detailed account of the battle. In that he says:

I moved on with all possible speed, through field and forest, in the direction of the firing, and arrived, about 4.30 P. M., at a point on the telegraph road, I should think not far distant from the center of our attacking force. Here I found Gen. Lee, seated upon his horse. He rode forward to meet me, and extending his usual greeting, announced to me that our troops had been fighting gallantly, but had not succeeded in dislodging the enemy: he added, "This must be done. Can you break his line?" I replied that I would try. I immediately formed my brigade in line of battle with Hampton's Legion on the left.

In front was a dense woods and ugly marsh, which totally concealed the enemy from us, but the terrible roar of artillery and musketry plainly revealed, however, that thousands and thousands of living souls were struggling in most deadly conflict for the mastery of that field, and I might say, almost under the shadow of the Capitol of the infant Confederacy. My line was established, and moved forward, regiment by regiment, when I discovered, as the disposition of the Eighteenth Georgia was completed, an open field a little to its right. Holding in reserve the Fourth Texas, I ordered the advance, and galloped into the open field or pasture, from which point I could see at a distance of about eight hundred yards, the position of the Federals. They were heavily entrenched on the side of an elevated ridge running a little west and south, and extending to the vicinity of the Chickahominy. At the foot of the slope ran Powhite creek, which stream, together with the abatis in front of their works, constituted a formidable obstruction to our approach, whilst batteries, supported by masses of infantry, covered the crest of the hill in rear, and long range guns were posted on the south side of the Chickahominy, in readiness to enfilade our advancing columns. The ground from which I made these observations was, however, open the entire distance to their entrenchments.

In a moment I determined to advance from that point, to make a strenuous effort to pierce the enemy's fortifications, and, if possible, put him to flight. I therefore marched the Fourth Texas by the right flank into this open field, halted and dressed the line whilst under fire of the long range guns, and gave positive instructions that no man should fire until I gave the order; for I knew full well that if the men were allowed to fire, they would halt to load, break the alignment, and, very likely, never reach the breastworks. I moreover ordered them not only to keep together, but also in line, and announced to them that I would lead them in the charge. Forward march was sounded, and we moved at a rapid but not at a double-quick pace. Meantime, my regiments on the left had advanced some distance to the front through the wood and swamp.

Onward we marched under a constantly increasing shower of shot and shell, whilst to our right could be seen some of our troops making their way to the rear, and others lying down beneath a galling fire. Our ranks were thinned at almost every step forward, and proportionally to the growing fury of the storm of projectiles. Soon we attained the crest of the bald ridge within about one hundred and fifty yards of the breastworks. Here was concentrated upon us, from batteries in front and flank, a fire of shell and canister, which ploughed through our ranks with deadly effect. Already the gallant Col. Marshall, together with many other brave men, had fallen victims to this bloody onset. At a quickened pace we continued to advance, without firing a shot, down the slope, over a body of our soldiers lying on the ground, to and across Powhite creek, when, amidst the fearful roar of musketry and artillery, I gave the order to fix bayonets and charge. With a ringing shout we dashed up the steep hill through the abatis, and over the breastworks, upon the very heads of the enemy.

The Federals, panic-stricken, rushed precipitately to the rear upon the infantry in support of the artillery: suddenly the whole joined in the flight toward the valley beyond. At this juncture some twenty guns, stationed in rear of the Federal line on a hill to my left, opened fire upon the Fourth Texas, which changed front, and charged in their direction. I halted in an orchard beyond the works, and dispatched every officer of my staff to the main portion of the brigade in the wood on the left, instructing them to bear the glad tidings that the Fourth Texas had pierced the enemy's line, and were moving in his rear, and to deliver orders to push forward with the utmost haste. At the same moment I discovered a Federal brigade marching up the slope from the valley beyond, evidently with the purpose to re-establish the line. I ran back to the entrenchments, appealed to some of our troops, who, by this time, had advanced to the breastworks, to come forward and drive off the small body of Federals. They remained, however, motionless. Jenkins' command, if I mistake not, which was further to our right, boldly advanced and put the brigade to rout. Meantime, the long line of blue and steel to right and left wavered, and, finally, gave way, as the Eighteenth Georgia, the First and Fifth Texas, and Hampton's Legion gallantly moved forward from right to left, thus completing a grand left wheel of the brigade into the very heart of the enemy. Simultaneously with this movement burst forth a tremendous shout of victory, which was taken up along the whole Confederate line.

I mounted my horse, rode forward, and found the Fourth Texas and Eighteenth Georgia had captured fourteen pieces of artillery, whilst the Fifth Texas had charge of a Federal regiment which had surrendered to it. Many were the deeds of valor upon that memorable field.

The general and the private under his command view a battle from quite different standpoints. The one observes the movements of corps, divisions, brigades and regiments, and takes little note of the units composing these organizations—the other, himself one of the units, observes the conduct of individuals. The one takes note of general details, the other, of minute. We will now let the privates tell what they witnessed and heard, what they did and what they suffered. The evidence they give may be conflicting, but it must be kept in mind that few persons see, hear and remember alike. A member of the Fourth Texas says:

"The forenoon of June 27th, 1862, was well-advanced before the Texas Brigade left its bivouac. D. H. Hill's division marched over to Hundley's Corner, that morning, from Mechanicsville, and as it was to take position on the left of Jackson's line, it and Jackson's troops moved before Whiting's division did. Once in motion though, to the southwest, Whiting's division made few halts. We had gone but a few miles when sounds of the battle made by A. P. Hill's division, away off to our right, came to our ears and quickened our steps. Whiting's orders were to take position on Jackson's right. Law's brigade led the advance which was made to the music of a constantly increasing roar of artillery and musketry.

Along about 4 P. M. we came under the fire of the enemy's heavy artillery, passing, as we moved rapidly forward, the ordnance trains and the batteries of Confederate commands then at the front—the batteries awaiting the call to action, but delayed in receiving it by the difficulty of finding places in the woods and swamps, from which to do execution. Further on, squads of prisoners, a few wounded men and many stragglers commenced passing through our lines. About this time General Hood placed the Fourth Texas in reserve, and led the other regiments of the brigade toward the front to the assistance of troops already there. They were not long in finding work to do, and did it nobly.

The Fourth Texas had a long wait before it went into action. According to my recollection, it was well on to 6.30 P. M. before Hood had his line established and ready for the general advance that was to be ordered. Law's brigade, it is likely, had by this time found its place, advanced against the enemy and met with repulse. Colonel Columbus Upson, then a volunteer aide on General Whiting's staff, after the war a member of Congress from West Texas, but now in the Great Beyond, is authority for this assertion. Generals Hood and Whiting, said Colonel Upson, met in the open field.

Pointing to the battery, fourteen guns of which were captured by the Fourth Texas that very day, Whiting said: "That battery ought to be taken, Hood." "Then, why has it not been taken?" asked Hood. "Because," replied Whiting, "the position is too strong. My brigade is composed of veteran troops, but they can do nothing with it." "I have a regiment that can take it," declared Hood, and scarcely waiting for Whiting's assent to his undertaking the task, galloped in the direction of the Fourth Texas.

Because it left them to the leadership of a colonel whose rank had been secured through political pull, and who, though admitted to be brave to a fault, was not deemed competent to direct the regiment in battle, both officers and men of the Fourth Texas deeply regretted the promotion of Hood to the rank of brigadier-general. Learning of this, Hood promised that he himself would lead them into their first battle. He had not done this at Eltham's Landing, no opportunity having offered. Now the situation was entirely different. For hours the brave Federals in our front had successfully resisted the many efforts of the Confederates to dislodge them. Unless this was done, the battle was lost to the Confederates, and thousands of lives had been sacrificed in vain. Promotion for himself was to be won, distinction for the regiment he had so carefully trained was to be gained. The tide "which, taken at its flood, leads on to fortune," was in full sweep, and seizing the golden moment, Hood made good his promise.

Taking command of the Fourth Texas, he moved it forward in column to a dry ravine running parallel with the course of Powhite Creek, on the south bank of which stretched the long lines of intrenchments occupied by the Federals. Here the regiment formed in line of battle, and was admonished by Hood not to fire a gun until he gave the command to do so. Thence, it went at a quick step toward the front, ascended the north slope of a ridge—passing, just before reaching the crest, over a long line of Confederates lying flat on the ground, and thus sheltering themselves from the enemy's fire. Arrived at the crest, the Fourth came in sight and range of the Federal infantry and artillery. These immediately opened fire on us, and comrades began to halt or sink to the ground, wounded or dead. Though now within one hundred and fifty yards of the enemy's first line, it was hid from our view by the tops of the tall trees bordering Powhite Creek. Our pace accelerated by the incline down which we went, and the murderous fire to which we were exposed, we moved rapidly on until, looking between the trunks of the trees, we had a view of the first line of intrenchments. Without halting us, General Hood shouted an order to take aim and fire, and this obeyed, gave the commands, "Fix bayonets. Charge!" In an instant, almost, bayonets were fixed, and with a yell that sounded high above the noise of battle, we sprang forward, into and across the little creek, into and through the cunningly constructed abatis, and at the enemy holding the first line of breastworks. The onset was so furious and determined, that seized with panic, the first line of Federals, taking time only to fire a few scattering shots, took to precipitate flight. Their panic communicated itself to the troops in the two lines behind them, and they, too, fled, pell-mell, and probably with a prayer that the devil might save the hindmost, up and over the ridge in their rear.

At this point, if nowhere else along Powhite Creek, the Federals were protected by three lines of breastworks. The first hugged the south edge of the narrow skirt of timber, probably fifty yards wide, which grew in the valley of the stream; the second lay fifty steps back of the first, and the third the same distance back of the second—the last two stretching along the side of the ridge south of the creek, each of them so elevated that troops in either could, without endangering comrades in their front, join in resisting attack. The extra care manifested in providing defenses here, was probably due to the circumstance that it was the only point on the Federal line where a rush on it was not prevented by undergrowth or marshes.

The panic into which the coming of the Texans threw the Federals was not simply complimentary and encouraging; it was also inspiring and persuasive, and loading and firing as they ran, the Texans followed in fast pursuit of their swiftly retreating antagonists. Arrived at a road that ran along the summit of the ridge, and there pausing an instant for breath, we saw on our left thousands of the Federals fleeing from the intrenchments which had been assaulted by the First and Fifth Texas, the Hampton Legion and the left wing of the Eighteenth Georgia. Casting our glances next to our right, the same comforting spectacle of wild and confused flight appeared. A moment later a wild, joyful yell from our right informed us that the Confederates there, who since noon had been fighting at long range, or if they attempted any, had not made a successful charge, were in rapid pursuit of the now demoralized foe.

It is due the other regiments of the Texas Brigade to say, that but for the advantage of open ground which the Fourth Texas had, they would have kept well in line with it, and have shared the glory it won. As it was, advancing to the assault over swampland and through densely matted undergrowth, it was impossible for either regiment as a whole to arrive within striking distance of the breastworks as soon as the Fourth Texas did. The right wing of the Eighteenth Georgia, however, had the advantage of open ground, and it joined with the Fourth Texas both in the rush upon the breastworks and in the subsequent capture of artillery. In General Hood's official report, he places the Eighteenth Georgia as a command, with the Fourth Texas in the capture of the artillery. That he is mistaken, and that only a few companies of the regiment are entitled to share in the glory of that achievement, is evident from the fact that in the volume of Confederate Military History which recounts the deeds of Georgia troops, no hint of such claim is given.

While regaining breath at the road mentioned, an incident occurred which, trifling as it was, will bear telling. Beyond the road was an acre of land inclosed by a high and strong fence, and in its center stood an unoccupied log stable. Behind the stable, a Union soldier of a more combative spirit than was possessed by his tribe, had sought a lurking-place from which to resist any further advance of the Confederate army. Desiring, apparently, to take a pot shot at the Fourth Texas, this soldier very carelessly exposed himself to the view of his enemies. Seen by slow-talking but fast-moving Stringfield, that worthy sprang forward, and climbing over the fence, ran, gun in hand, toward the stable. Presuming that a mite of encouragement would not be wasted, Lieutenant L. P. Hughes, a mild-mannered gentleman who never takes the

E. K. GOREE
Company H, Fifth Texas Regiment

name of the Lord in vain, but falls short of it only by a hair's-breadth, sang out, "Go it, Stringfield—go it! Kill him, dod damn him, kill him!"

Combined with Stringfield's ardor and the reckless impetuosity of his onset, this adjuration came near inviting disaster to him. For when he came within twenty feet of the stable, the Federal behind it decided it was time for him to exercise the right of self-defense, and accordingly, stepped out from behind the stable, and pointed a capped, cocked and loaded gun at the bold Confederate. But time was not vouchsafed him to pull trigger. Wolff, a German, who stood near Lieutenant Hughes, realized the peril in which his compatriot stood, and raising his rifle from the hollow of the arm in which its barrel rested, shot the rash Federal through the heart.

The pause at the road lasted hardly one minute. The artillery at whose capture we aimed, had withheld its fire while the timber on the creek and the ridge south of it hid us from view. But as the Fourth Texas came into sight on the road, it reopened, hurling shot, shell and canister at us with a rapidity and in a volume that warned us we had yet much to accomplish ere we laid just claim to victory. Heeding the hint, the Texans and such Georgians as had joined them, formed into line of battle in a peach or pear orchard, about three hundred yards beyond the road, called to that point by General Hood, who, it should be mentioned, had left his horse in the ravine where we had first formed into line, and was still afoot. It should also be stated that the artillery we were after stood on a high hill slightly to the left of our line of advance from the ravine, and that we now faced almost at a right angle to that line, the batteries, about three hundred yards distant, with a deep hollow down the middle of which ran a steep-banked, tortuous gully, almost impassable except at a few places, between us and them.

In the rush down and up the slopes, across the creek and through abatis, companies had scattered and lost their places, and probably five minutes elapsed ere the regiment was in battle array, and during these the batteries got its range and poured upon it a withering and deadly fire under which many brave men fell. Cool and sylvan as the orchard might have felt and appeared under other circumstances, it was not now a spot on which to linger, and therefore, no sooner was the line reformed than Hood gave the command to charge. As in stentorian voice he called, "Attention!" Major Warwick, who at daylight that morning, against the protest of his physician, had left a sick bed and galloped out to join his command, and who like Hood was on foot, cried, "Wait a second, General—let me lead the charge!" and sprang in front of the regiment. As the command "Charge!" fell from Hood's lips, the line surged forward for the race down the slope. But the gallant Warwick took scarcely a dozen strides before a fragment of a shell struck and mortally wounded him, and he fell to the ground.

Never did a regiment make better time than the Fourth Texas did, down to and into and across the gully in the middle of the hollow; there was need for speed, for only when there could the men hope to escape, for a second or two, the storm of lead and iron that fast depleted their ranks—it being impossible, they knew, for the guns to be sufficiently depressed to bear on them. Falling again into a semblance of a line as they scrambled out of the gully, and moving at their best speed up the hill on the crest of which the guns were posted, they gained half-way ground before again coming under fire, and then only under that of two pieces. These, however, were denied the time to fire a third shot, for before the second left their muzzles, the Texans won the crest, the artillerists fled and the guns were ours.

Halting on this crest a minute to regain formation, the Fourth Texas pushed rapidly on toward the Chickahominy. A couple of hundred yards from the artillery, it encountered a squadron or more of cavalry, United States dragoons, they called themselves. These charged gallantly, but unavailingly. Met with bullet and bayonet, many steeds soon galloped riderless, many brave cavalrymen lay on the ground, wounded or dead. That scrimmage over, Major Townsend, then in command—General Hood had come no further than the battery— decided that the regiments had gone far enough, and so called a halt. It was then in the timber bordering the Chickahominy. It was fast growing dark, and he did not care to assume the responsibility of going further. While he waited for orders and instructions the First Texas approached within near range of the Fourth, and in the darkness mistaking it for a Federal command, commenced firing at it. "Lie down—lie down," was shouted along our line by both men and officers, while others sought to inform the First Texas who they were. Before it could be made to understand, though, Lieutenant L. P. Lyons, of Company F of the Fourth Texas, in his anxiety to see that all of his company obeyed the order to lie down, stood for a moment on his feet, and was mortally wounded. . . .

From what State hailed the troops over whom the Fourth Texas passed on the crest of the ridge where it first came under direct fire, was a question as much discussed during the war as since. When asked, as we came to them, who they were, the majority who spoke at all, answered, "Alabamians." Not knowing then on what part of the field Law's brigade was, many of us jumped at once to the conclusion that we had caught the Fourth Alabama regiment "showing the white feather." The Fourth Alabama, however, denied the harsh impeachment, and their negative being proven beyond dispute, the matter remained one of doubt and speculation. The first light on the subject came in 1905, forty years after the close of the war. Governor William C. Oates, of Alabama, in his book entitled, "The War between the Union and the Confederacy, and its Lost Opportunities," admits that the Fifteenth Alabama regiment was the sinner. As he was then a lieutenant in one of the companies, his acknowledgment "of the corn" must be held as conclusive, and none the less so because he relegated to a comrade the task of relating the incident. That comrade, after telling that the Fifteenth took position on the crest of the hill where we found it, at about 2 P. M., and while there the men lay flat on the ground, and that finally, details sent back for ammunition returned and the men began to fill their cartridge-boxes, says: "About the time we got through, we looked down the hill in our rear, and there came the Fourth Texas, half-bent, as if looking for a turkey." Being against himself, that statement will not be disputed. Other assertions made by the comrade, however, are not only challenged, but positively denied. The Fourth Texas made no halt at the line of the Fifteenth Alabama to rectify their own line, to fire a volley, and to reload and fix bayonets. Nor did the Fifteenth Alabama, as an organized body, advance with the Fourth Texas. As to these matters, the comrade has mistaken a lively imagination for a poor memory.

Justly proud of the achievements of the Fourth Texas at Gaines' Mill, survivors of Hood's Texas Brigade were astounded when, in 1898, their title to the laurels won by that regiment in that battle was questioned. That Hood and Whiting, Jackson and Lee, and Jefferson Davis, the president of the Confederacy, had erred in crediting the Fourth Texas with being the first to penetrate the lines of the enemy, and to capture, unassisted save by the Eighteenth Georgia, the fourteen pieces of artillery, was too incredible for belief. A lively tilt, with the pen, at once began in the columns of the *Confederate Veteran* in the October number, 1898, in which had appeared an article over the signature of Adjutant Cooper, formerly of Pickett's Brigade, in which the claim of the Texans was assailed, and the laurels awarded them credited, exclusively, to Pickett's Brigade.

Fortunately for the Texans, the evidence on which they relied was of record in official reports and in history; unfortunately for the Virginians, Adjutant Cooper, at the very outset, blundered into details concerning the movements of Pickett's Brigade that shatter his contention beyond repair, physical facts as well as oral and written testimony of unimpeachable character, showing that, if he tells the truth, his claim in behalf of Pickett's Brigade is absolutely baseless. In that October number of the *Veteran* he says:

" The sun shone brightly and the atmosphere was clear, and every move that Lee's troops made could be plainly seen by the enemy. Pryor's line advanced to the attack, and in a short time were almost annihilated. Pickett with his five regiments went in on a double-quick, and being hid by the smoke of battle, approached to within thirty or forty yards of the first line of intrenchment, where in the intense heat and the dense smoke, *they involuntarily threw themselves flat upon the ground and commenced firing*. The roar of musketry was so terrific that it was impossible to hear anything else. The men knew, however, that heavy work was intended, as each man had his eighty rounds of ammunition. This continuous firing was kept up, neither side knowing the proximity of the other, on account of the smoke. *Finally, the firing of the enemy somewhat slackened and the sun set, as it were, in blood, with neither side having gained any advantage. At the slight lull in the enemy's fire, General Pickett ordered a charge, to which his brigade responded promptly."*

Following this paragraph, Adjutant Cooper tells how the Union troops melted away as the Virginians rushed forward and at them, and how, without another halt, and without again involuntarily throwing themselves flat upon the ground, the sons of the Old Dominion swept on and captured the fourteen guns in advance of any other command. In view of his admission that his brigade did not charge the enemy until the sun had set, his claim is an absurdity.

In none of the official reports of Confederate generals commanding that day is the time at which the general advance began given as later than 7 P. M. The sun set on June 27, 1862, in the latitude of Virginia, not earlier than 7.30. This gave half an hour for the Fourth Texas to pass over the 1320 yards of ground that lay between the ravine in which Hood first formed it into line and the batteries. Moving leisurely, at the rate, say, of two miles an hour, one can walk that distance in $22\frac{1}{2}$ minutes. Pickett's Brigade at 7 P. M. was fully half a mile to the right of the Fourth Texas, and fully that distance further than the Fourth from the batteries in question, which were, at least, two hundred yards to the left of the direct line of advance of the Texas regiment. For Pickett's Brigade to have reached the guns first, even had not its men " involuntarily thrown themselves flat upon the ground " within " thirty or forty yards of the first line of intrenchments," it must have moved entirely across the front of Whiting's Brigade, and, for two hundred yards, across that of the Fourth Texas. It was not possible, though, for it to move across the front of either of those commands, for, after beginning their advance at 7 A. M., half an hour before sunset, neither of them halted until the Federals had taken refuge in the lowlands of the Chickahominy, and the batteries had been captured by the Fourth Texas and part of the Eighteenth Georgia.

It should be remembered that the Fourth Texas did not move leisurely, when making the charge that day. Any soldier ever in action knows that such a withering, destructive fire as was poured upon the Confederates that afternoon, puts speed in the legs of the slowest, the weariest and the bravest. Save for probably two minutes at the road, and five, at the farthest, in the peach and pear orchard, the Fourth Texas made no halt between starting point and the batteries. Pride and patriotism, esprit de corps, and the dangers threatening, each enjoined and assisted in securing rapidity of movement.

Hood was as ambitious as he was brave and daring. The stars and wreath of a major-generalship hung in the near perspective. Like Henry of the Wynd, in the combat between the clans, Chattan and Quhile, he "fought for his own hand." Not a Texan there, whether by birth or adoption, but shared his spirit, and resolved to maintain the reputation for desperate courage won for the "Lone Star State" by the heroes who at the Alamo fought and died that their compatriots might at San Jacinto fight and win. Therefore, Hood urged speed, and the Fourth Texas made speed—such speed, indeed, that before sunset they seized and silenced the batteries which all day long had played such havoc in the Confederate lines.

Of the half a hundred or more old comrades of the Fourth Texas whose testimony has been sought, not one of them but remembers distinctly and declares unhesitatingly that the sun was yet shining above the tree-tops in the west when his regiment drove the enemy from these guns. I was wounded in a narrow lane that led from the road running up and down the ridge south of Powhite Creek, toward the peach and pear orchard in which Hood formed the remnants of the regiment for its direct charge upon the guns. I saw the regiment in line there, and just behind it, General Hood—his left hand raised above his head and grasping the bough of the apple tree under which he stood—his right hand holding an uplifted sword—the fact that he held the sword made evident to me by the circumstance that its bright blade reflected the rays of the still shining sun. As the regiment moved down the hill in its direct charge upon the batteries, Austin Jones, who was also wounded, and I, went slowly to the rear, and until we got three-fourths of the way to Powhite Creek, the sun shone in our eyes. In confirmation of my own recollection on this question, I have a letter written to me by General Stephen D. Lee, May 27, 1899, in which he says that just before sundown on the 27th of June, 1862, he was on top of the Garnett house, across the Chickahominy from the battlefield, with field-glasses in his hands, through which he was watching the progress of the fight; that President Davis was in the yard below him, and that he (Lee) was reporting his observations to Mr. Davis; that he saw the lines carried by the Confederates, but did not know by what command they were first broken until messengers brought the information to Mr. Davis that 'Hood's Texans had swept everything before them, piercing the lines and driving the enemy before them in the greatest disorder.'

I have said this much about the claim of Pickett's Brigade, simply because not to deny the justice of that claim would be to acquiesce in it. Especially, should it be denied in a history whose sole aim is to record the achievements of the Texas Brigade. That command has never sought to wear laurels won by other commands, but it insists on keeping those fairly won by itself, bright and untarnished even by the idle suspicion cast upon them by the members of Pickett's Brigade.

It was when we first came in view of the Federals that we suffered our heaviest loss. Whatever their panic later, they exhibited no lack of steadiness then, and under the accurately aimed volleys of shot and shell they poured into us, more than a hundred of our bravest and best fell wounded or dead. But thinned as the line was by the fearful discharges, the Texans closed to right or left, as need was, to fill the gaps made in the line, and pushed swiftly and resolutely on. Of the courage displayed by both men and officers, I can say no more than that it was splendid. It is useless to say more, for it is only brave men that unflinchingly face "the grim monster, Death"; the coward shrinks appalled and trembling from him. When thunder of cannon and roar of musketry, whistling of bullets and shrieking of larger missiles combine in one grand volume of sound; when grape and canister, round shot and fragments of burst shells sweep the bosom of the earth like a tidal wave from the wide ocean, to say that men who breast the storm shoulder to shoulder, and seeking no shelter, press on without halt until victory is won, or death or wounds lay them low, as did the Texans at Gaines' Mill, are brave and heroic, is to attribute to them virtues inseparable from their deeds."

No one soldier sees all that occurs in the battle in which he participates; it is impossible he should. Officers and privates do not see alike even when observing the same occurrence, for they look from different angles and standpoints. That being the case, as between officers and privates on the firing line and taking active part in the engagement, how can a general in command of a body of men in action, be expected to know all the many important and unimportant incidents that transpire while his men are advancing under fire, or are in battle?

Generals Lee, Jackson, Whiting and Hood give in their official reports but surface accounts of this or that movement —it is to the private, and the officer whose duty places him almost in line with the private, we must go for particulars, for the minutiae—all the many incidents that make the story of a battle interesting. That the accounts they give are often in conflict with each other, and seldom agree precisely with those that appear in official reports, should not discredit them. No two persons, ordinarily, exactly agree in their relation of incidents in daily, peaceful life, and why should not soldiers differ in their accounts of happenings on fields of fierce and sanguinary conflict?

Comrade William R. Hamby, a member of Company B, Fourth Texas, tells the following story of his experiences and observations:

"On the morning of the 26th of June, we left our camp near Ashland, Va., about fifteen miles north of Richmond, as the advance guard of Stonewall Jackson's corps, marching toward Cold Harbor, then in the rear of the Federal army. Nearly all of the afternoon and far into the night we could hear heavy firing on our right in the direction of Mechanicsville. About three o'clock in the afternoon we passed an old Virginia farmer sitting on his fence by the roadside. His negroes were in the field cutting wheat. He was delighted to see us and waving his hat, said: 'Hurry on, boys: the Yankees have just gone flying over the creek.' While he was cheering us, Reilley's battery, of our brigade, pulled down the fence and ran into the field just in the rear of where the old man was sitting and opened fire upon the enemy, who had burned the bridge and had taken position on the hill beyond the creek in front of us. The first shot from Reilley's guns was a surprise to the old man. He fell backward from the fence and exclaimed: 'My God! a battle here on my plantation!' and then, turning to his negroes, shouted to them to get to the woods as fast as their legs could carry them, and he led the procession. Company B were thrown forward as skirmishers. The enemy were soon dislodged from their position, and we continued to drive them back until we went into bivouac for the night.

"Early in the morning on Friday, June 27, we were again on the march through fields, crossing creeks, climbing hills, and finally wading a swamp about one hundred yards wide and waist-deep in mud and water. After crossing the swamp, we climbed another hill and passed through a pine forest into the edge of an old field, where a conference was held between Generals Lee, Whiting and Hood, which ended by Lee and Whiting riding rapidly away. In a short while General Lee returned, and addressing Lieutenant Walsh of Company B, inquired for General Hood, who was only a short distance from us and who heard the inquiry. He at once saluted General Lee, who said that the efforts to break the enemy's lines in front of us had been unsuccessful and that it was of the utmost importance to do so. General Hood replied: 'We will do it.' As General Lee turned his horse to ride away, he lifted his hat and said: 'May God be with you!'

"Just before we were ordered into battle, and while heavy firing could be heard in our front and on each flank, Captain Owens, of our regiment, was talking to some comrades of the battle in which we expected soon to be engaged, and, drawing his sword and waving it over his head, repeated the following lines from Scott's 'Marmion:'

> "'The war that for a space did fail
> Now, trebly thundering, swelled the gale,
> "On Stanley!" was the cry:

> A light on Marmion's visage spread
> And fired his glazing eye;
> With dying hand above his head,
> He shook the fragment of his blade
> And shouted "Victory!"
> "Charge, Chester, charge! On, Stanley, on!"
> Were the last words of Marmion.'

"While they were the last words of Marmion, they were almost the last words of gallant Tom Owens, who fell mortally wounded in less than half an hour from the time he quoted them with such prophetic inspiration.

"The other regiments of our brigade—Hampton's Legion of South Carolinians, the First Texas, the Fifth Texas and the Eighteenth Georgia—were at once ordered forward on our left. Our regiment, the Fourth Texas, moved by the right flank farther into the field, fronting the Federal lines, which appeared to be about half a mile in front of us. From our position we could form some idea of what was required of us. At the farther side of the field the enemy occupied a steep hill covered with timber; at the foot of the hill was a creek whose banks afforded protection by abatis and log breastworks; at the top of the hill was another line of infantry behind intrenchments and supported by artillery.

"The troops in front of us who had failed to break the enemy's line were retreating in disorder, and to use the language of General Whiting, our division commander, 'some were skulking from the front in a shameful manner.' The conditions confronting us vividly recalled the remark Hood had made when he was colonel of our regiment, that he 'could double-quick the Fourth Texas to the gates of Hell and never break their line.'

"About six o'clock in the evening our line was formed under fire from the enemy in front of us and from artillery that enfiladed us on our right and left. General Hood had assumed personal command of the regiment and ordered us to dress to the center upon our colors and not to fire until he ordered us to do so. We started at quick-time march with our guns at 'right shoulder shift.' The fire from the enemy was falling upon us like drops of rain from a passing cloud, and as we advanced their messengers of death grew thicker until they came in teeming showers, 'while cannon to the right and cannon to the left volleyed and thundered.' At every step forward our comrades were falling around us. When we were within about one hundred and fifty yards of the enemy we passed over a line of our own troops lying upon the ground. They had gone that far, but would not go farther. A young lieutenant of that regiment was pleading with his men to go forward; and when they would not do so, he said they had disgraced their flag, and, throwing away his sword, he seized a musket and joined our ranks; but the brave boy had gone only a short distance when he was killed. As we passed this regiment, Lieutenant-Colonel Warwick snatched up their colors, and, like the standard bearer of the Tenth Legion of Ancient Rome, told them to follow their flag, but they did not do so. With that flag in one hand and his sword in the other, the gallant Warwick fell after he had crossed the second line of fortifications.

"General Hood was in our front until we were within about one hundred yards of the creek, when he wheeled his horse to the right and ordered us to fix bayonets and charge at double-quick. Here the fire of the enemy was poured into us with increasing fury, cutting down our ranks like wheat in the harvest.

"More than half of our regiment had fallen upon the field, although we had not fired a gun. Raising the Rebel yell, we dashed across the creek (which we found to have steep banks, in some places twenty feet high, with sides cut to form a ditch, and climbed over the breastworks, when the enemy gave way in confusion. The Federal colonel in command of the line broken by the Fourth Texas says: 'All along the line our fire was opened on the enemy and maintained in a most vigorous manner. Nothing could have been better done. The effect upon his ranks were perceptible, and the slope of the hill bore testimony to the steadiness and accuracy of our fire, yet he moved steadily along until up and onto us. When unable to resist, our line broke.'

"We fired into their retreating ranks as they ran up the hill, and reloading as fast as we could, we followed them over their second fortifications, when their entire line gave way in disorder, but continued to fire as they retreated. A Federal officer who was on their second line says: 'The enemy made a final and desperate effort to break through our lines, and were successful, but not until our weary men were trampled upon. The attack was desperate, and so was the defense. The noise of the musketry was not rattling as ordinarily, but was one intense metallic din.' This position of the Federals was strong and well-selected, and their double line of defenses ought to have been held against almost any force that could have been thrown against them.

"After we crossed their second line of defenses, eighteen pieces of artillery massed on an elevation in the rear of their lines on our left opened a heavy fire of grape and canister upon us. Without halting to re-form our lines, we charged the batteries, capturing fourteen cannon; but one battery, with four guns, succeeded in escaping before we reached them, which we had the satisfaction of capturing a couple of months later in the second battle of Manassas. We then turned upon the retreating infantry and drove them through an old orchard.

"In a short while we felt the ground begin to tremble like an earthquake and heard a noise like the rumbling of distant thunder. It was a regiment of United States cavalry charging us. This regiment was one of the most famous in the United States army. Albert Sidney Johnston had been the colonel, Robert E. Lee had been the lieutenant-colonel, and J. B. Hood had been a lieutenant before resigning to enter the Confederate service. The captain of Hood's old company commanded the regiment in the charge, and was captured by us.

"To hear the trumpets sounding the charge, to see the squadrons coming toward us at full speed, and to see their sabers glistening in the sunlight of the dying day like a flame of fire from heaven was a spectacle grand beyond description, and imparted a feeling of awe in the bravest of hearts. When they were within about forty yards of us, we poured a volley into them and prepared to receive them on our bayonets; but our one volley had done dreadful execution. Horses and riders fell in heaps upon the ground, and the groans of the wounded and the shrieks of the dying could be heard above the roar of the battle as the setting sun shed a fading light over

GEORGE S. QUALLS
Company G, Fourth Texas Regiment

the battlefield. Captain McArthur, who succeeded to the command of the regiment after the battle, in his official report says: 'The regiment charged under a most galling fire until all the officers but one had been struck down, and, being without officers, wheeled to the right and came off in as good order as could be expected.'

"After the charge of the cavalry had been repulsed, we pushed on to the brow of the hill overlooking the valley of the Chickahominy. Desultory firing continued until it was so dark we could not distinguish friend from foe a few yards from us; in fact we were fired upon by our own troops, resulting in the killing of Lieutenant Lyons, of Company F, of our regiment.

"The gentle breezes of that night in June were whispering requiems for the brave spirits who had fought their last battle when our regiment was re-formed in line about nine o'clock by General Hood, who counted only seventy-two present; but others reported during the night who had been separated from us in the darkness in the latter part of the battle.

"The charge of the Fourth Texas at Gaines' Mill was a dearly bought victory; but it broke the Federal lines around Richmond, and for a time, at least, the capital of the Confederacy was saved. Out of less than five hundred who went into the battle, we lost two hundred and fifty-two men and twenty-three officers, killed and wounded, including Colonel Marshall, Lieutenant-Colonel Warwick, and Major Key.

"With a detail of one man from each company in the regiment, I stood picket that night at the corner of the garden fence of a farmhouse which we were informed had been the headquarters of General Fitz-John Porter, whose corps we had fought that day. As the rations issued to us at Ashland on the 25th had been exhausted, and as our commissary trains were far in the rear, we went on duty with empty haversacks. We had been at our post some hours, and could hear the Federal troops, pushing their retreat across the bridges of the Chickahominy as fast as possible, while the loneliness of the night was increased by the wail of the whip-poor-wills that came to us from the swamps below us. We were recounting the incidents of the day and of the baptism of fire through which we had passed, when we heard the tramping of horses and the clanking of sabers coming toward us from the direction of our own lines. When they were within a short distance of us, we halted them and demanded who they were, supposing them to be a scouting party of our own cavalry. Although it has been nearly fifty years since then, the answer we received will never be forgotten. A pompous voice rang out clear and distinct, 'Major-General McCall, of the Grand Army of the Potomac,' which evidently came from one who had straightened himself up in his stirrups so as to get the answer out strong and forcible. Our surprise can scarcely be imagined, as we had heard that General McCall was in command of the Federal forces the previous day at the battle of Mechanicsville. We at once demanded their surrender, but instead of doing so they put spurs to their horses and dashed by us down the hill towards their own line, followed by a volley from us.

"General Morell, whose division formed the left wing of Porter's corps in the battle of Gaines' Mill, in his final report says: 'The Confederates made their first attack about twelve o'clock upon the right, which was handsomely repulsed. The second attack was made about 2.30 and the third about 5.30 o'clock, each extending along my entire front, and both, like the first, were gallantly repulsed. The fourth and last came (about 6.30 P. M.) in irresistible force, and swept us from the ground.'

"General Seymour, whose division went to the support of General Morell's division, in reporting the actions of his artillery, after we had broken the Federal lines, says: 'The batteries which had already played an important part now endeavored to drive back the Confederates and opened with rapidity and precision, but could not contend successfully against the bullets of the infantry at short range. Captain Easton, nobly encouraging and cheering his men, fell, and his battery (six guns) was lost with him. Captain Kerns was wounded early in the battle, but in spite of his wound kept the field; and when the enemy came upon his battery, he loaded and fired the last shots himself and brought four of his guns off the field. Captain De Hart's battery did its best service, keeping its ground and delivering its fire against the advancing enemy. Captain De Hart was here wounded. All displayed the greatest gallantry; but no efforts could repel the rush of a now successful foe, under whose fire rider and horse went down and guns lay immovable on the field.'

"General R. E. Lee, in his official report of the battle, in speaking of the breaking of the enemy's lines, says: 'The dead and wounded marked the way of the intrepid advance, the brave Texans leading, closely followed by their no less daring comrade, driving the enemy from the ravines to their first line of breast-works, over which the impetuous column dashed up to the intrenchments on the crest of the hill, which were quickly stormed and fourteen pieces of artillery captured.'

"The day following the battle of Gaines' Mill, General Jackson, in riding over the ground where the Fourth Texas had charged, exclaimed, 'The men who carried this position were soldiers indeed,' and in his official report of the battle said: 'In this charge, in which more than a thousand men fell, killed and wounded, before the fire of the enemy and in which fourteen pieces of artillery were captured, the Fourth Texas, under the lead of General Hood, was the first to pierce these strongholds and seize the guns. Although swept from their defenses by this rapid and almost matchless display of daring and desperate valor, the well-disciplined Federals continued to fight with stubborn resistance as they retreated.'

"General Whiting, our division commander, in his official report of the battle, said: 'The battle was severe, hotly contested, and gallantly won. I take pleasure in calling special attention to the Fourth Texas, which was the first to break the enemy's line and enter his works. Of the other regiments in the division, it would be invidious and unjust to mention one above another.'"

Writing of the part taken by the Fifth Texas in the battle of Gaines' Mill, Captain W. T. Hill, who was then first lieutenant of Company D of that regiment, says:

"On the night of June 26, 1862, the Fifth Texas bivouacked with its comrade regiments of the Texas Brigade at Hundley's Corner, several miles from the battlefield of next day. The sleep we got might have been more restful but for the excitement caused by the carelessness of advance cavalry scouts. They let a bunch of their horses stampede, and as the animals came directly toward us, and from the front, they were thought to be a body of the enemy's cavalry charging down upon our camp, and the regiment was hurriedly called to arms. On the morning of the 27th the Texas Brigade resumed the march, the Fifth Texas in the advance.

"Shortly before noon, General Jackson rode by us, on his way to the front. At the head of the regiment he found General Hood, who, tired of motonous marching and impatient to get to fighting, said to him: 'General Jackson, the enemy keeps well out of my way—what shall I do?' 'Press on, sir—press on,' replied Jackson. But although we did press on, it was not until about 4.30 P. M. that the brigade reached a point on the telegraph road near the firing line, then occupied by troops under command of General Longstreet. They and the troops under General A. P. Hill had begun their terrible fighting on the 26th and were still at it. Here, the brigade was formed into line of battle such that from right to left the regiments, excepting the Fourth Texas, stood, the Eighteenth Georgia, First Texas, Fifth Texas and Hampton's Legion. The Fourth Texas was being held in reserve, and later, led by General Hood himself, went into action on the right of the Eighteenth Georgia. Between the four regiments then in line of battle was quite a wide space, the Fifth Texas taking position at least a third of a mile from the ground over which the Fourth made its grand charge.

"Line of battle was formed in comparatively open ground, but in front of us was a forest of heavy timber. Just before we entered that timber many members of a Georgia regiment came running in great disorder from the front, and right into us, calling out as they came near, 'Don't go any further, men—you'll all be killed if you do.' Our men denounced them as cowards, thinking thus to shame them, and this failing, sought to hold them back by a show of bayonets. But no effort availed to halt their mad flight, and rushing between the bayonets they fled to the rear. Continuing our advance under a heavy artillery fire, we entered the boggy marshes in which Powhite Creek had its source, and beyond it came to a ridge occupied by the braver comrades of the cowards we had met. Halting here to give time to the slow-movers of the regiment to catch up with their companies, we fired about three rounds in the direction of the enemy in our front, who were concealed from view by the timber.

"While thus halted, we saw, some distance in front of us, a lone Georgian whom a shot in the head crazed, and who, standing upright, was making the wildest and oddest gesticulations imaginable, with his arms. Two of our men ran out to him, and brought him back to a place of safety. Just after crossing the marsh a cannon ball came rolling slowly down the hill. Nobody feared it—it was moving, apparently, with too little momentum to be at all dangerous. But we knew better when it struck a member of Comapny I in the stomach and drew from him a scream of pain that was fearful to hear. Its movement arrested by impact with the poor fellow's body, it stopped within ten feet of him. The soldier received from it a mortal wound; one of his comrades told me next day that he died from the effect of the blow, his body having swollen to near the size of a flour barrel.

"It is but fair to the men whose retreat we endeavored to stop to say that they were armed only with old-style, smoothbore and short-range muskets carrying 'buck and ball,' or one ball and three buckshot. Such weapons were only dangerous at closer quarters than their bearers had gotten to the enemy. The Federals, though, carried Springfield rifles of long range and large caliber, and so had much the advantage of their poorly armed antagonists. But when the Fifth Texas, which was armed with Enfield rifles, moved up to the ridge, the advantage shifted to the side of the best marksmen, and that, it soon appeared, the Texans were. Many of the Georgians, notably those whom we met in retreat, had soon decided it was time for them either to get further from, or move closer to the enemy, and had chosen the getting further as the safer alternative. That no such choice was forced upon the Texans, is evident from the circumstance that after three carefully aimed volleys from them the Union troops immediately in their front got out of range so rapidly and numerously as to leave but few in the line to receive the charge of the Fifth that was immediately ordered.

"Again with a loud yell, our line sprang forward. At the very outset, Sergeant Onderdonk, of Company A, our flag-bearer, was shot down. R. A. Brantley, of Company D, sprang forward and, seizing the flag, bore it bravely through the battle then on, and continued to bear it gallantly until, just before the battle of Second Manassas, it was resigned to another member of the regiment. The effort by the Federals still remaining in line to stay our advance was fruitless; many of them were killed outright, the others chased through their encampment. This was a sea of white tents. Planned for the occupation of a large force, it had been carefully laid off and kept remarkably clean. After passing into the open ground beyond the camp located, the Fifth Texas continued its advance to the crest of a hill in a large field and there halted to readjust its alignment. As formed, our line overlapped, on the right, several of the cannon previously captured by the Fourth Texas. Approaching these guns at the same time we did, came some scattering men belonging to the Fourth Texas, who for some cause had failed to keep up with their comrades, then in front of us on our right and out of sight.

"Having restored its line, the Fifth Texas marched southeast through the field, in the direction of Grapevine Bridge, about two hundred yards. Neither friend nor foe coming within its view, it countermarched and took position again near the cannon. For about ten minutes nothing happened. Then bullets commenced flying over our heads from the rear, and facing about, we saw a line of troops bearing the Federal flag coming toward us through the encampment. As they emerged from the protection of the tents, we began to fire on them. But there was no fight in them—that was taken out the moment they saw a Rebel regiment in their front. Without firing another shot, they lowered their flag and commenced waving hats and handkerchiefs in token of surrender. So anxious, indeed, were they to surrender, that they came running toward us as though they recognized us as dearly beloved but long lost brothers, and our men had actually to push many of them back to prevent them from getting right in among us. Unfortunately, too, although offering every other evidence of surrender, they forgot, or at least, many of them did, to throw down their guns. As a consequence of this failure on their part, many were fired on at close range by individual members of the Fifth Texas. I was lucky enough to save the life of one of them. As one of my company was in the act of firing on him—the two were hardly ten feet apart—and the Federal still had his rifle—I knocked up the Confederate's weapon.

"The regiment surrendering was the Sixth New Jersey. Judging from the fact that it came from the direction we supposed the First Texas to be, we argued that it was driven back and into our arms by that regiment. Previous to its capture by us, a lone cannon fired many times at us from a hill half a mile east of the Fifth, but did no damage. Between this gun and Grapevine Bridge, stood a division of the enemy, massed in column, which had evidently come that far to the front with a view of reinforcing their assaulted lines. They came too late though; there were no longer any lines at the front to reinforce.

"On our march to the battle ground that morning, when four miles or more from it, the Fifth, and I suppose, all the other regiments of the Texas Brigade, was ordered to deposit blankets, knapsacks and other impediments to rapid motion, by companies, in piles. Over these, guards were placed, the men being told that wagons would come along to transport and return them to the owners. But to this day no wagons, with our all, have overtaken us. Our loss was total and serious. We never secured an outfit of clothes and blankets to compare with those abandoned. The Fifth Texas supplied itself liberally from the stores left in the Federal camps, but along with what they took they got army lice enough for a large division of troops.

"As already said, the Fourth and the Fifth Texas entered the battle about one-third of a mile apart. The Fourth moved, I think, southeast, while the Fifth moved south or a little southeast, their lines of advance converging at such angles as, had not the Fourth had much the shorter line, and the easier to make speed over, would have brought the two commands together at the batteries. General Hood remained with, and directed the movements of the Fourth, until it began the charge from the orchard where it halted to re-form, on the batteries. When the Fourth got under headway, he sent for his horse, and when the animal came, rode to the front to find that the Fourth Texas and the Eighteenth Georgia had captured the batteries, and the Fifth Texas, a whole regiment of the enemy. This would indicate, that long and difficult as was the route forward pursued by the Fifth, it had not tarried by the way, but had moved promptly and vigorously. As from the beginning of the advance till night came, no regiment of the brigade came within view of the Fifth, it played the part of a lone knight on the field, anxious to meet and defeat the enemy, but unable to do so because of his rapid disappearance and continued absence. It carried with the battle 800 men. Its losses in killed and wounded were few.

"On the morning of the 28th, in company with other officers, I looked at the fortified position of the enemy which the Fourth Texas had assaulted so successfully, and wondered how any of the assailants escaped with their lives. Not again during the four years of war was another such charge made. General Jackson did right in mentioning the Fourth Texas in his official report as having been the first Confederates 'to pierce these strongholds and seize the guns.' Nor was it fulsome and undeserved praise he bestowed when the day after the engagement, while surveying the ground over which the Fourth Texas charged, he said to General Hood, 'The men who carried this position were soldiers indeed.'"

As a supplement to the foregoing account of the part taken by the Fifth Texas in the engagement of Gaines' Mill, the following anecdote will not come amiss. Its truth is vouched for by more than one of the survivors of the Fifth Texas. As introduction to it, it must be told that Lieutenant-Colonel J. C. Upton was in command of the Fifth Texas when the New Jerseyans surrendered, Colonel J. B. Robertson having been wounded before the Fifth came so far. Upton was one of that adventurous, self-reliant and plain-mannered class of people to whom military uniform and a long unwieldy sword were nuisances. That day, a woolen overshirt constituted his uniform, and while his sword trailed at his side, he carried in his right hand, as was his habit, the long-handled frying pan in which was fried the bacon for himself and mess. But for the look of command in his eyes and the deference paid him by his command, one would never have suspected his rank.

Having made up their minds to surrender, both the men

and the officers of the Sixth New Jersey were in haste to relieve themselves of the unwelcome job; apparently, each of them thought, "if it were done when 'tis done, then 'twere well it were done quickly." The privates and non-commissioned officers had naught to do save drop their guns. The commissioned officers, though, must, to play the game of war with dignity, surrender their swords to equals or superiors in rank. Therefore, their first inquiry of their captors was, "Where is your commanding officer?" "There he stands," said a Texan, pointing to Colonel Upton. But there was so little of the commanding officer in Upton's make-up and pose, that for half a minute the Federal officers stood in doubt. Reassured of his rank, however, they rushed toward him from all parts of their line, each man endeavoring to be the first to reach him. When the foremost officer unsheathed his sword and holding it by the blade, proffered it to Upton, he said, "Just drop it on the ground, will you." "Indeed, I will not," said the Federal indignantly. "As major of the Sixth New Jersey regiment of infantry, I tender the weapon to you as token that I am your prisoner, and I insist, sir, on your instant acceptance of it." "Well," said Upton, "hand the thing to me," which was immediately done, Upton taking the sword in his left hand, as he also did the next one tendered. Then noticing that twenty or more of the same weapons were on their way to him, and unwilling to lay aside the frying pan that was yet in his right hand, he crooked his right arm and as each sword was presented, laid it in the crook of that soon heavily loaded limb. At first, the swords taken behaved with commendable decorum, but ere the last was laid on the pile of them, they began to get crosswise, and to slip and slide about in a way that soon put each of them pointing in a different direction.

At this juncture, Colonel Upton became aware of a commotion at the far end from him of the almost surrendered regiment. Springing to the top of a nearby log, the armful of sabers dangling in every direction, he shouted to a Texan who seemed to be having trouble, "Say, Big John Ferris, what the mischief and Tom Walker are you trying to do now?" "I'm trying to keep a lot of these d—d Yankees from escaping," came back the response in a stentorian voice. "Let them go, you infernal fool," returned Upton, " let them go; we'd a d——d sight rather fight 'em than feed 'em."

It is matter for regret that no accounts of the parts taken in the battle by the First Texas, the Eighteenth Georgia and Hampton's Legion are forthcoming. The two or three companies forming the right wing of the Eighteenth Georgia, being in open, unobstructed ground, moved forward in line with the Fourth Texas, and assisted in the capture of the batteries, but the other companies of the regiment could not make the same headway over the ground in their front. That over which the First Texas and Hampton's Legion had to pass was probably the most difficult, and their movement forward was so retarded by swamp and morass, fallen timber and the profusion of vines and undergrowth, that it was practically impossible for them to gain the enemy's lines as soon as the regiments on their right.

In his official report, General Hood gives the losses of the brigade, as follows:

Hampton's Legion—Two killed, 18 wounded, none missing.
Eighteenth Georgia—Sixteen killed, 126 wounded, 3 missing.
First Texas—Fourteen killed, 64 wounded, none missing.
Fourth Texas—Forty-four killed, 207 wounded, 1 missing.
Fifth Texas—Thirteen killed, 62 wounded, none missing.

But he does not correctly state the number of killed and wounded in the three Texas regiments. In these, the First Texas had 20 killed and 56 wounded; the Fourth Texas, 75 killed and 176 wounded, and the Fifth Texas, 15 killed and 52 wounded.

CHAPTER V

SAVAGE STATION, FRAYSER'S FARM, MALVERN HILL, KELLY'S
FORD, FREEMAN'S FORD, THOROUGHFARE GAP,
SECOND MANASSAS

ON the day following that of Gaines' Mill, the Texas Brigade counted up its losses and buried its dead. Many had fallen dead on the field of honor; others lived long enough to send last messages to their loved ones, and still others lingered and died in hospitals amid utter strangers. Wrapped in a blanket, the soldier's shroud, the bodies of such comrades as died on the field were laid side by side in shallow trenches, each regiment's dead to itself. At the head of each body was placed a rough, rudely lettered board to tell whose it was, and then the earth was heaped in a high mound over the common grave. A few, whose bodies, it was thought, their friends would likely desire to remove, were buried in separate graves.

On the morning of the 29th, the enemy in the meantime having made good his escape to the south side of the Chickahominy, and being now so little desirous of capturing Richmond as to be making his best speed down the James River and away from it, Whiting's division followed Jackson's troops in pursuit—a body of Texas scouts leading the advance of Jackson's command. Inasmuch as, although under fire of both artillery and musketry at Savage Station on the afternoon of the 29th, at Frayser's Farm on the 30th—where, by the explosion of a shell from a Federal battery, nearly all of Company M of the First Texas was killed or wounded—and at Malvern Hill, on the 1st of July, where it lay exposed for long hours to the merciless fire of Federal artillery, the Texas Brigade took active part in neither attack nor repulse, the description of these battles is left to the general historian. Suffice it here to say, that owing to blunders and misunderstandings, absence of reliable maps of the country, the incompetency of the guides secured, and various other causes, the defeat of the Federal army was not as complete and overwhelming as it should have been, and as General Lee sanguinely hoped it would be.

McClellan having accomplished the "change of base" to which he was driven by the Confederate commander, and betaken himself, with his army, to the protection of the gunboats in James River, at Harrison's Landing, General Lee ordered Longstreet to remain in the vicinity of the Landing, and observe his movements, and recalling Jackson's command from the front, ordered it to Culpeper Court House, north of the Rapidan. General Pope—the puissant Federal general who, from headquarters "in the saddle" bombastically proclaimed that he was accustomed in the West, where up to that date he had served, to see only the backs of the enemy, and that with the army under him there would be no retreats, and who was then commanding "the Army of Virginia," composed of the corps of Banks, Fremont and McDowell, was making demonstrations indicating an intention to move down on Richmond, and Jackson was sent to administer a check to his puissancy.

Whiting's division, though, not belonging properly to Jackson's command, was returned to that of Longstreet, and about the 10th of July was ordered into camp on the Mechanicsville road, three miles from Richmond. Here the Texas Brigade remained idle and at rest until the 8th of August. Since June 11th it had been almost constantly on the move—its days of rest few, its marches long and wearisome, its hardships many, its dangers great, its losses in battle heavy, and it was grateful indeed for the lengthy exemption from hard service. To the Texans at this place came long-delayed letters, and our captures from the Federal army large, a great deal of much-needed clothing, and with the latter, that pest of the soldier, the body louse. Up to this time we had no acquaintance with the animal—thenceforward to the close of the war, he remained with us.

On the 8th of August the brigade folded its tents, and shouldering its guns began the marching that, with but few rests, was to continue until December of that year. It marched light, each man having by this time learned what weight he could comfortably carry, and therefore, dispensing with all superfluities. Still, we could not reduce the weight to be carried to less than about thirty-six pounds. A gun weighed about ten pounds, the cartridge box, cap-box, bayonet and the belts and straps to which these hung, another ten, and the roll of blanket and tent, or oil-cloth, still another ten. Add to these the weight of the haversack, in which not only provisions but under-clothing and many other necessities were carried, and the total, on a fair estimate, was never less than thirty-six pounds, and often went a little beyond forty. A canteen full of water weighed at least three pounds.

For three days the march was leisurely. On the 11th, haste was enjoined. Jackson had engaged in battle with Pope at Cedar Run, near the mountain of the same name, on the 9th, and had not only defeated the Federals but inflicted upon them a heavy loss. He held the field until the night of the 11th, and then learning that his antagonist had received reinforcements and would move against him with an overwhelming force, he retired to the south side of the Rapidan. Thither Longstreet hastened, and on the 15th took position along the Rapidan, on the right of Jackson—the Texas Brigade, at Raccoon ford. On the 20th, there was a simultaneous advance by both Confederate commanders across the Rapidan and toward the Rappahannock—Whiting's division, now under command of General Hood and hereinafter to be spoken of as Hood's division, leading Longstreet's advance. General Lee himself was now up and directing the Confederate army.

Learning of the advance, and fearing to join battle, General Pope hastily retreated to the north side of the Rappahannock, taking position there to command all fords in his front. The Texas Brigade followed rapidly, and at Kelly's ford came under a heavy artillery fire and had a light skirmish with the rear-guard of the enemy. Here it was that Captain Reilly, commanding one of the batteries attached to the brigade, let his imperfection of sight lead him into trouble with his superiors. While yet the cannonading on both sides was in progress, a lone horseman rode into the river at the ford, bearing a white flag. Swearing that although he could see man and horse distinctly, he could see no flag, Reilly trained and fired a gun at the fellow, the round shot plunging into the water three feet to his right. That not calling him to a halt, Captain Reilly, still insisting that he could see no white flag, fired two more shots, one of which struck the water a few feet to the left of the horseman, and the other, five feet in front of him. Hardly, though, was the last shot on its way, when an aide-de-camp dispatched by General Hood came at full speed, and halting near Captain Reilly, shouted: "General Hood says stop your d—d foolishness—that man is bearing a flag of truce." "An' so, be Jasus, he is," confessed Reilly with a grin, "but in the name of St. Pathrick an' all the ither hoully saints, whoy didn't the spalpeen hould the domned white rag high enough for an Irishman to persaive it?"

At Freeman's ford, on the following day, occurred the funniest incident that ever precipitated a conflict between bodies of armed men. Having crossed Hazel River, the Texas Brigade formed in line just inside of a field of corn in good roasting ear. On the other side of the field and on the south side of the Rappahannock, yet lingered a Federal brigade. The Confederates were hungry, the Federals in the same fix, and roasting ears in sight, each wanted a share of them. Each in position to watch the other from its main line, neither of the opposing brigades had out a skirmish or picket line. Two soldiers, the one a Dutchman belonging to the Union army, the other a Prussian serving in the Confederate, happened to be in the field at the same time, gathering corn, and each fastidious as to quality, each wandered toward the center of it, and just when each had an armful of roasting ears, they came face to face.

Neither uttered a word, but dropping the corn, each rushed at the other and began to pound him with his fists. That proving slow work, they clinched, and finally falling, began a mighty wrestle for supremacy that was punctuated by vigorous kicks and thrusts at each other. Which was first worsted, which first raised the cry for help from his compatriots that was immediately joined in by the other, will never be known, the two cries arising so nearly simultaneously. The Federals were first to move to the rescue, but the Texans were not far behind them in starting—the lines of battle meeting about the center of the field—and for a few minutes there was a hot fight, the First and Fifth Texas bearing the brunt of it and each losing men. The Fifth, however, might have escaped any loss, had it not carried the Lone Star flag on an unusually long staff. Floating high above the corn, this flag caught the eye of an expert Federal artillerist, and the shell he fired at it exploding just in front of it, Major Whaley and another man were killed outright, and four men were wounded. Although under fire, the Fourth Texas, Eighteenth Georgia and Hampton's Legion suffered no loss.

On the 22nd, General Lee's effort was to force a passage across the Rappahannock and bring on an engagement. That night, Confederate cavalry raided Catlett's station, and captured, among other things, General Pope's dispatch book. Forwarded to Lee, this revealed the exact location of each command of Pope's army, of its pressing need of reinforcements, and of the dates on which these were expected to arrive. Lee immediately changed his plan of operations. Obeying his instructions, Jackson made a flank movement, and passing well around the Federal right flank, arrived on the afternoon of the 26th, at Bristoe's station, seven miles from Manassas Junction, the main depot of supplies for Pope's army. Having destroyed these, he marched on the morning of the 27th to the plains of Manassas, the scene of the battle of that name, and by his seemingly erratic movements in that section, set the Federal commanders far and near to guessing where he might be found.

Nevertheless, Jackson's command was in grave peril. Only by the speedy arrival of Longstreet's columns could disaster to it be averted. Longstreet, however, was held on the south side of the Rappahannock by the main Federal army until the 26th, when, learning that Jackson was in his rear and imagining there was a chance to capture him and his whole command, Pope opened the way for Longstreet's advance by a rapid retreat in the direction of Washington. At 2 P. M. of the same day, the 26th, the Texas Brigade began its longest and most exhausting march. On a bee-line, it was about thirty miles to Groveton, the little town near which Jackson was practically hemmed in—by way of Thoroughfare Gap, it was nearly, if not quite, forty. All that night and until after sunset of the next, the men tramped steadily but wearily and sleepily on—their only rest, that taken in the five minutes of every hour allowed them. All knew that Jackson's men were in peril and that only by their timely arrival could he hope to escape defeat and capture, and all willing to do their best, there was no grumbling, no voluntary straggling, and but little lagging.

The sky was cloudless, the sun hot, the dust thick, and places where we might fill our canteens with water, few and far between; but still, although feet blistered, legs grew wearier and wearier, flesh sweltered and bones ached, and after each brief rest we rose to our feet stiff and sore, we moved on and on—toward the last, too near the point of exhaustion to bestow a glance of admiration on the beautiful scenery through which we were passing, and almost too tired even to respond, with a cheer, to the grateful salutations of the bevies of ladies fair who at the little towns on our route stood on the streets to encourage us by their approving smiles. Indeed, so fatiguing became the march of the 27th, so sleepily and unobservantly did we plod along, that few saw the gruesome spectacle of the corpse in gray uniform that hung by the neck from the limb of an oak, scarcely two hundred yards from the road we followed. It was that of a self-confessed spy, who, lured by the promise of an immense sum of gold, had undertaken to delay the march of Longstreet's troop long enough to afford time for Pope and his lieutenants to capture or destroy Jackson and his men.

The night of August 27th was one of sound slumber and imperatively needed rest. Awaking next morning, refreshed and vigorous, the men lighted their fires and clustering around them were cooking and eating their slender rations when the announcement was made that at 8 A. M. the march would be resumed. Thoroughfare Gap, although yet half a day's journey distant, was in plain view, and through it we must pass, and beyond it reach, in order to relieve Jackson and his brave men. It was occupied by the enemy when in the afternoon we approached it, and Law's brigade and skirmishers from the Texas took an active part in the fighting that followed, and which resulted in the retreat of the enemy. The way clear, the

Texas Brigade marched through the gap, following the railroad track, and shortly after sunset went into bivouac on a hill-side just beyond.

An hour later, everybody except Bill Calhoun, of Company B, Fourth Texas, was resting comfortably. He was an oddity of whom the Texas Brigade was proud, for although usually sad of countenance and melancholy of mien, in his bosom dwelt a spirit of drollery that was constantly effervescing and running over. His mess-mate and bed-fellow was Davidge. Carrying out a well-conceived plan for an equitable distribution of baggage, Davidge, on the morning of the 28th, was intrusted with the transportation of the blankets and tent-cloths of the mess—Bill Calhoun with that of the provisions and the frying-pan. Davidge straggled, and when camping time came, was not on hand. Confident that he would soon put in his appearance, Bill prepared supper for the mess, and Davidge still remaining absent, ate it all himself. Then lighting his pipe, between puffs he chatted with such of his company as would listen and respond. The responses, after a while, growing few and sleepy, he declined an invitation of a friend to share the friend's blankets, and remarking that Davidge would surely be along soon, stretched himself out on the bare ground, and was soon asleep. But the night was cool enough to make some covering necessary, and though Bill endured the hardness of his couch and the chilliness of the air without a murmur until midnight, he could endure it no longer. Standing erect in the midst of the 2500 recumbent forms that darkened the moonlit hill-side, he broke into magniloquent apostrophe:

"Oh, Davidge, Davidge!" he cried, "friend of my bosom and possessor of my blanket, where art thou, Davidge, this cold and comfortless night? Art thou, indeed, false to thy many professions, false to the sacred obligations of the true and loyal friendship thou hast so often and fervently declared, and oblivious of duty, forgetful of the friend who has confided to thee even the well-worn blanket on which he dependeth for protection from the chilling blasts of winter? Art thou now peacefully and blissfully, but alas, ungratefully, reclining on some hospitable feather bed and dreaming of the joys that will be thine 'when this cruel war is over,' or art thou, beguiled and betrayed by the demon of intemperance that hath bestowed upon thee such a damnable thirst for apple-jack, wallowing like a filthy and disreputable hog in the dirt before the door of some far-away mountain still-house, while I—thy friend and mess-mate, thy boon companion in happiness and adversity—stand here alone, a homeless, houseless, blanketless orphan, his wandering and faltering footsteps guided only by the pale light of yonder refulgent orb of night, his shivering body covered only by the blue canopy of the sky, his restless slumber watched over only by the myriads of twinkling stars that shine in the heavens above him? Alas, Davidge, thou hitherto trusted friend and companion and confidant of my youth and my manhood! Thou hast been weighed in the balance and found wanting. The surrounding and circumambient circumstances and facts furnish proof strong as holy writ, that I have been duped, deceived and outwitted, and ungratefully left to encounter the slings and arrows of misfortune alone and unsustained by any human aid." And dropping suddenly from the sublime to the ridiculous, Bill nudged the nearest man with his foot, and in a voice of entreaty that would have melted the hardest of hearts, said: " Say, Bill Hamby, roll over just a little bit, and let me get under the shadow of your blanket. If you don't, ere the morning's dawn illumines the eastern horizon, I'll be a standing monument to man's inhumanity to man."

The morning of the 29th dawned unclouded, but full of portentous sound. From the direction of Groveton came the deep bellows of artillery and the dull indistinct roar of musketry. General Pope was obviously early at work in his effort to bag Jackson's little army before that of Longstreet could reach and relieve it. Shortly after sunrise, the Texas Brigade —the only command that had passed through the gap—was in motion toward the sound of the firing. In advance of it went Lieutenant-Colonel John C. Upton, of the Fifth Texas, in command of one hundred and fifty skirmishers and with. orders to keep the way clear for the brigade. He obeyed these orders both in letter and spirit, for although opposed by infantry, cavalry and artillery, he put them to retreat and advanced so rapidly, and the brigade followed so close on his heels, that General Longstreet more than once sent orders forward to halt the Texas Brigade until the troops in its rear could overtake it.

By 11 A. M. Upton drove the Federals beyond the cut in an unfinished railroad, in which Jackson's men, although sorely beset, were yet holding their ground, and coming up, Law's Brigade fell into line of battle to the right of Jackson, and the Texas Brigade on the right of Law's—the other troops as they arrived extending Longstreet's line a mile or more to the right of the Texas Brigade. Approximately Longstreet's line faced to the northeast, Jackson's to the southeast, thus forming an obtuse angle, the Federal lines running parallel with those of the Confederates, but northeast and southeast of them.

The Texas Brigade formed along the southwestern edge of a strip of timber extending far to its right, but only a short distance to its left. In front of this strip of timber, lay an open, slightly undulating wheatfield, or meadow into which, in front of the Fifth Texas, Eighteenth Georgia and Hampton's Legion, the woods jutted. Across the wheatfield, which in front of the First and Fourth Texas was about three hundred yards wide, stood a rather dense forest, covering, perhaps, four hundred acres of land, which immediately in front of those regiments was about three hundred and fifty yards wide—its northeast edge approaching within thirty yards of the crest of the slope on whose southwest side it lay. From that crest, the ground sloped rapidly for a couple of hundred yards to one of the prongs of Young's branch, and beyond the prong, rose as rapidly until its highest altitude reached, it stretched off toward Bull Run Creek in a fairly level plateau, dotted sparsely with clumps of young pine and cedar.

Having secured position on his right, Longstreet seemed disposed to let Jackson maintain the contest unaided save by the artillery under his command, which he posted on the high hills just to the left of Law's Brigade. Assisted by that, Jackson's men repulsed every one of the five successive, well-planned, bravely-led and gallant assaults made upon them during the afternoon. Then at the point of exhaustion, they made their first urgent appeal for help. Longstreet still loth to extend it, General Lee, at sunset, ordered Hood's division forward. In five minutes from the time Lee gave the order, it was advancing, a strong line of skirmishers in its front. Much to its surprise, the Texas Brigade was not fired upon by even Federal skirmishers until, having crossed the wheatfield and passed through the timber beyond that, it came to open ground. There, the enemy's skirmishers opened a brisk fire upon our own, but continued it only a few minutes and then fled. The twilight is short in Virginia, and troops moving in line of battle through a woodland obstructed by undergrowth, make slow headway, and by the time the main line of the brigade reached the open ground, and descending the slope, crossed the branch at its foot, it was too dark to distinguish friends from foes at ordinary musket range.

Somehow, too, it happened that Law's and the Texas Brigades moved forward on converging lines. Owing to this circumstance, one of Law's regiments passed across the front of the First Texas, and when halted at the branch to perfect its alignment, stood exactly in front of the Fourth Texas. This failure to move straightforward, on parallel lines, combined with the darkness to intermingle the two brigades and create confusion. While a semblance of order was being restored, from the hill-side in our rear came the flashes and reports of many small arms, fired, obviously, by opposing bodies of troops. Staff officers immediately galloped in that direction, but before they had gone half-way the firing ceased, and as if by magic, a line of camp-fires appeared all along the crest of the ridge in our rear. Five minutes later, the Texas Brigade was ordered to move by the left flank, which placed the First Texas in the lead. We had gone scarcely a hundred yards, though, when a loud peremptory "Halt!" broke the silence that had fallen on the field, and the next moment a shot rang out, and was followed by several others.

At the word, the brigade came to a sudden stop, the men standing motionless with wonder. A minute later the strange caution came whispered from man to man, all along the line, "Silence! We are surrounded by the enemy." It was the truth, and for a minute or more, a sadly humiliating truth, since to be surrounded presaged speedy capture and resulting shame and mortification. But our humiliation lasted but a second or two; with arms still in our hands, we could fight our way out, or die; and thus resolving, we asked each other in whispers how in the mischief we had got ourselves into such a trap. It had been easy to do so; moving forward on converging lines, the two brigades of the division had simply driven themselves, wedge-like, into the unoccupied space between two Federal brigades—the darkness of the night and the suddenness of the movement having prevented them from discovering our passage. When, however, they did discover it, they moved closer to each other and thus closed the gap through which we had entered. But in doing that, they made the gap between themselves and the brigade on their left wider than was safe, and through this, after midnight, we stole, with bated breaths and noiseless steps, back to the line from which we had started.

The loss of the Texas Brigade on the 29th was light. As now recalled, but two of its men were wounded, and one captured. Colonel Work, of the First Texas, was one of the wounded. While advancing with his regiment in the darkness and over strange ground, he ordered his men to shoot at everybody that appeared in the front. The men, however, were unwilling to do this, lest they fire into their friends, and coming at last within sixty yards of a line of troops standing silent and motionless, refused to fire at them. Work insisted they were Yankees, and to prove it, unwisely pushed forward alone to decide the question. But when within twenty yards of the suspected line, he ran up against a vidette whom he took to be a lone Confederate, and asked if the troops just beyond him were not Yankees. "You are a rebel, d—— you," instantly exclaimed the vidette, making a movement to bring his gun to his shoulder. But before he could level it, Colonel Work sprang at him, wrested the gun out of his hands, and aiming at him, pulled the trigger.

His gun in an enemy's hands, the vidette fled, but he need not have done so, for only a snap of the cap rewarded the efforts of Work to shoot him. Work pursued, but had gone hardly five steps when he ran against the muzzle of a gun in the hands of another Federal. Dropping the gun he held, Work knocked the weapon of his new assailant to one side, and its shot went wild. Then remembering he wore a pistol, Work reached for it, but before he could draw it, the Federal clubbed his gun and struck the colonel over the head with it. The blow did not fell the plucky Confederate, but it sent him reeling backwards, and one of his spurs caught in the undergrowth and tripped him up. The Federal rushed on him to administer the coup-de-grace, but just then Captain W. H. Gaston of the First Texas heard the racket, and surmising that his doughty colonel was in pressing need of reinforcements, came up in a run. Not caring to fight two Confederates with an unloaded gun, the Federal took to his legs.

It was Bill Calhoun that was captured. Davidge, whose untimely absence the night before had been so eloquently lamented and denounced by him, having that morning put in an appearance, Bill went forward with his comrades of the skirmish line in high good humor with himself and everybody else. Unluckily, however, his desire to get in close range of a Yankee, in order, as he said, " to show the blue-bellied cuss what a feller from ole Brushy can do in the way of quick shootin'," led him too far to the front. As with cocked gun held in his hands across his breast, he passed a little clump of cedars, one of the " cusses " he was in search of stepped out, and leveling a gun at him, cried, " Surrender, you d—d rebel! Surrender, or I'll blow your brains out."

Noting at a glance that the Federal " had the drop on him," and that in the shadow of the cedars stood other soldiers in blue, Bill released the clutch of his fingers on his gun, and letting it drop with a clang to the rocky ground, exclaimed, "Surrender? Why, of course I surrender—who in h—ll's talkin' 'bout not surrenderin'?" Such an odd way of submitting to capture so amused the Federal that he forgot to lower his gun, but held it aimed in the general direction of his captive—its barrel moving up, down and sidewise in time to the laughter that shook his form. " See here, Mister," called Bill, " please quit pintin' yer gun at me—hit mout go off unbeknownst to yer, an' eff hit do, hit's jest as apt ter hit a feller as ter miss him."

With the morning of the 30th, came another unclouded sky. At sunrise, General Pope wired to Washington that he had won a great victory, that the Confederates were in full retreat and that he was making preparations for a vigorous pursuit. An hour later, he discovered that Lee's army was yet in his front, ready to test conclusions with his own. It was 1 P. M., however, before the Federal commander renewed the contest by an attack along the whole length of Jackson's line—his most desperate and determined assault being on the Louisiana and Virginia Confederates occupying the railroad cut. It was a gallant affair on both sides, the courage and steadfastness of the assailed being fairly matched by the daring and determined bravery of the assailants.

Line after line of the Federals moved forward, their battle-flags waving, their alignments as straight as though they were on the parade ground, and their men stepping boldly, briskly and confidently. When within a hundred and fifty yards of the red-clay embankment behind which crouched the Confederates, a loud resounding huzza would burst from the throats of the men, and they would spring forward in a seemingly reckless charge. But in a minute's time the scene would change. As they came within fifty yards of their waiting opponents, the flash, the smoke and the roar of three thousand well-aimed rifles would burst from the embankment, a wild, blood-curdling Confederate yell rise high above the din of battle, and when the smoke lifted, the survivors of a fire as terrible and destructive as was ever hurled at a foe could be seen fleeing back to the Union lines, up and across a hill-side darkened by the forms of their dead, dying and wounded. It was both a saddening and a magnificent spectacle. While the sympathies and hopes of the Texans on the skirmish line a mile away to the right, went with the troops that so pluckily held the railroad cut, they made no attempt to conceal their admiration of the splendid daring, the American courage of the assailants.

Although they repulsed the enemy at every point on their line, Jackson's men were not made of iron. The strain on them was terrible, the pressure unceasing, and at 4.30 P. M. General Jackson called for assistance. The artillery of Longstreet and Colonel Stephen D. Lee was first to give it—its enfilading fire on the left flank of the still advancing Federals sweeping them down in long rows. At the moment it appeared most effective and demoralizing, Longstreet ordered his command forward, and it went with a will and a vim that carried consternation to the Federals and soon put them to flight.

Springing into line when the order reached them, each man eager for the fray, the Texas Brigade moved rapidly across the wheat-field into the woods beyond—the Eighteenth Georgia in the center; on its right Hampton's Legion and beyond that the Fifth Texas, and on its left, the Fourth Texas, and beyond that the First Texas. Some little skirmishing took place in the woods, but it was only when the open ground beyond the timber was gained that the main forces of the enemy were encountered. The alignment of the five regiments, as a brigade, was lost when they entered the timber, and as each seemed bent on making a record that should be distinctively and peculiarly its own, there was so little concert of action between them that any attempt to describe their movements as a brigade would be confusing both to writer and reader. Instead, each regiment will be given space to tell its own story through the medium of the official report of its immediate commander, and the pen of one or more of its members. But only such parts of the reports will be given as relate to the battle of August 30.

To economize space, official and non-official reports and accounts will appear in the order in which the regiments stood, looking from the left to the right. That will give the report of Lieutenant-Colonel P. A. Work, of the First Texas, first place. The official reports of the battle of Second Manassas are to be found in Part II, Volume XII, of War of the Rebellion Records. Colonel Work says:

The regiment, having been withdrawn from the ground occupied by it on the battleground of the evening previous, was placed in position about daylight of the morning of August 30, with its left resting upon the turnpike road at the point occupied by it the day previous. During the day I received instructions through Capt. W. H. Sellers, assistant adjutant-general, to keep the regiment at attention, and advance to attack the enemy whenever ordered. By Captain Sellers I was informed that General Kemper's Brigade would be advanced simultaneously with the Texas Brigade, moving diagonally across the front of the latter; that mine would be the directing regiment, and would move slowly, with its left flank resting upon the turnpike road, the other regiments of the brigade inclining and gradually wheeling to the left, so that at the proper point the Texas and Kemper's Brigades would present an even, unbroken front.

John Coleman Roberts
Company C, Fourth Texas Regiment

About 4 or 4.30 P. M. I was ordered to advance, when I at once put the regiment in motion. After having advanced about 125 yards, I was informed by the acting adjutant of the regiment, W. Shropshire, that the Fourth Texas Regiment had not moved, when, supposing my movement premature, I halted and dispatched a messenger to ascertain the truth. Before the return of the messenger, Lieut. James Hamilton, aide-de-camp, galloped up and informed me that the Fourth Texas was some 150 yards in advance of me. I at once moved at the double-quick and soon came upon a line with the Fourth (just after moving out of the timber into the large open field where the engagement took place). As the regiment advanced, a battery of the enemy fired into us repeatedly, but before either this or any other regiment of the brigade could charge upon it, it limbered up and moved off at a rapid gait up the turnpike road, until it reached an orchard upon an elevated, commanding position, where it halted and again opened fire upon us. This regiment continued to advance up the turnpike road, with its left resting thereon, until halted in a hollow, by an order delivered by a courier (Barbee, I believe). From this hollow I received an order (through Barbee) to move forward to the second hollow beyond the one I was then in, where I would halt and receive orders, which order I executed, moving forward to the hollow designated and halting, exposed to the fire of the above-mentioned battery while crossing the two intervening ridges. I failed to receive any orders at this place, and it was at this last-mentioned hollow that I discovered that I was alone. I had been watching so intently the battery in my front and the movements of the troops in its immediate vicinity, that I did not know when the other regiments of the brigade left me. Discovering that I was alone, I called to Templeman (acting as courier) and asked as to the whereabouts of the other regiments. He could not then inform me, but said that he would ascertain and let me know, and galloping off, soon returned, stating the Fourth Texas had crossed the creek opposite my right flank, had moved up and taken a battery upon a ridge which he pointed out, and had moved on over the ridge after the infantry support. I at once moved by the right flank across the creek and upon the ridge designated. Having moved the right of the regiment to the top of the ridge, and placed the regiment under cover from an enfilading fire from two batteries, to wit, the one above mentioned at the orchard, and the second on a ridge running parallel to the one upon the top of which my right was then resting, I advanced, myself, to a point from which I hoped to discover the locality of the Fourth Texas. I heard a heavy firing of musketry or rifles down in the hollow in front of where I was standing, but, owing to a swell or second ridge upon the descending slope to the hollow, not a man could I discover.

About this time Barbee galloped up and informed me that all of the brigade were down in the hollow, were hard pressed, and needed assistance. Selecting a place where I could pass the ridge with as little loss as possible, I fronted the regiment and moved forward some 35 yards to a depression crossing the ridge. Once in this depression, I believed I could cross the ridge protected wholly from the fire of the orchard battery, and partially from the battery upon the parallel ridge. Just as the regiment had reached the depression alluded to, and just as I was in the act of giving the order to move by the right flank, Captain Sellers brought me an order to take my regiment under cover, and was so earnest that he gave the order to right-about before I could give it myself. As the regiment moved back over this 35 yards, a heavy fire of grape and canister was opened on us from the two batteries above mentioned, and it was here that several were wounded. Having brought the regiment under cover, I was directed by Captain Sellers to move down into the hollow, where flowed the creek spoken of above, and there rest. About the time I reached the last-mentioned hollow quite a number from the several regiments of the brigade joined me, and, falling into the ranks, remained until their respective regiments successively reached the hollow and formed upon this.

We lost 3 killed and 7 wounded. It is proper to state, that of the killed, one, R. B. Stephens, of Company E, was killed by a rifle ball while skirmishing, and a second, —— Walker, of Company E, was killed while with the scouts, under Lieutenant-Colonel Upton, of the Fifth Texas.

It is a matter of regret that I received no notice and did not discover the movements of the other regiments of the brigade in time to have changed my front and contributed the best efforts of the regiment in aiding in taking the battery captured, and in the attack upon the troops routed by them.

CHAPTER VI

SECOND MANASSAS (*Continued*)

THE Fourth Texas held place in the line of battle, on the right of the First Texas, and between that regiment and Hampton's Legion. Relating the movements of the Fourth on the 30th, one of its survivors writes:

"In front of the Fourth as it emerged from the timber, stood two lines of the enemy's infantry in battle array— the first, a hundred yards or so from the timber—the second, beyond Young's branch. Beyond the second was posted on commanding ground a battery of four guns, which, from the time we came in view of it, poured shot and shell into our ranks with an accuracy of aim that caused much loss. The first line seemed panic-stricken by the mere sight of us, for holding its ground only long enough to fire one volley, and that aimed too high to do much execution, it about-faced in one movement and the quickest time on record, and receiving our fire in its rear, fled at a speed that soon took it out of sight and range. Then, neither consulting Colonel Carter, nor giving him time to utter a command, the men of the Fourth, moved by a common impulse, began a charge upon the battery.

" The Federal infantry in our front, beyond the branch, fired two or three volleys at us as we plunged down the slope, and into and across the little stream, but it no sooner saw us moving up the hill toward it, than it, too, took to precipitate flight. The battery, though, held its ground, and as we neared it, began to hurl at us grape and canister that tore great gaps in our ranks. Behind it lay, in a thicket of cedars, a regiment whose special duty it was to support it, but when that saw the two lines in front break into flight, it also broke and fled, leaving the battery entirely without support. Then, feeling themselves deserted, the men belonging to the battery abandoned it and made for the rear, leaving only their captain to stand by it. And that he did, with a courage and heroism that, although wasted on the impossible, deservedly won the admiration and even the sympathy of the foes he was doing his best to destroy. Even when we had come within forty yards of the guns, he stood at the only loaded one, and was in the act of discharging it when he was shot down. That gun was loaded with grape and canister, and, huddled together as the regiment then was, each man of us seeking to be the first to lay hands on a cannon, had he discharged it, fully one-half of the Fourth Texas would have been wounded and killed.

"The battery captured, the Fourth Texas formed in line facing in the direction of the enemy—forming, according to my recollection, in a low swale not over fifty yards beyond the battery and at no time advancing beyond the swale. Not another Confederate command was in sight, either to right or left, and naturally, our men felt lonely, the colonel, anxious. To move forward, might be to invite disaster—to fall back, was to abandon the trophies we had won at a terrible sacrifice —to stay there and, Micawber-like, wait 'for something to turn up,' was not military conduct. The enemy solved the problem. While Colonel Carter and other officers consulted as to what should be done, it was discovered that a large force of Federals, hidden from view in the valley of Young's branch —which, making a bend to the right below where we had crossed it, was now on our left—was moving on our rear.

"One glance over the brow of the hill convinced Colonel Carter that at such a crisis, 'discretion was the better part of valor,' and he moved the regiment, by the right flank, back to Young's branch, at the point where we had crossed it, and thence up it a couple of hundred yards, where it halted and remained until after sunset. We were not there more than five minutes, when a magnificently arrayed Confederate brigade—it was Kemper's, I think—came marching up to and over us, on its way to take part in the battle. 'What are you fellows skulking here for?' asked one of its men. 'We are not skulking,' replied a red-haired Texan: 'we are just holding this branch for you folks to hide in when the Yankees up yonder on the hill whip you back.' 'They'll never do that,' boasted the man of Kemper's Brigade. But he boasted too soon, for in less than twenty minutes, he and many hundreds of his brigade came running back to the branch for shelter from the bullets that pursued them. 'I told you you'd come back a-runnin', said the red-headed Texan, but there was no rejoinder.

"Of what the other regiments of the Texas Brigade did, I have little personal knowledge. We had evidence of what the Fifth Texas had done in the ghastly, horrifying spectacle that met our eyes as, while lying in the branch, we looked at the hill-side then in our rear, nearly an acre of which that regiment had covered with killed and wounded Zouaves, the variegated colors of whose gaudy uniforms gave the scene, when looked at from a distance, the appearance of a Texas hill-side when carpeted in the spring by wild flowers of many hues and tints.

"Certainly the career of the Fifth New York Zouaves was neither a long nor a brilliant one. While camped in 1861-2 across the Potomac River, from the Fifth Texas, it is said they threatened that if they ever met the Fifth Texas in battle, they would 'wipe it off the face of the earth'—the Fifth Texas in retort, declaring that if it ever met the Zouaves, it would cover the ground 'with their ring-streaked and striped bodies.' At Gaines' Mill, the Fifth New York Zouaves encountered the Fourth Texas, and driven in confusion from the first line of works there, defeated, could only boast of the speed that enabled them to outstrip their comrades of other regiments in a wild, go-as-you-please race to the protecting shelter of the Chickahominy swamplands; at Second Manassas, they met the Fifth Texas, and instead of wiping that command 'off the face of the earth,' as they had boasted they would, were themselves, as a command, practically annihilated. Certainly, the laurels they won on fields of battle were not many, for the survivors of Second Manassas proved too few to maintain a separate organization, and for the remainder of the war, served only on details, as guards and nurses at prisons and hospitals. Blotted from history by the Fifth Texas, the regiment has remained 'unhonored and unsung,' save in so far as that has been done in song and story laudatory of the Fifth Texas, or descriptive of 'Carnage Hill,' as by Union veterans, the hill-side on which so many of its men were killed, has been called.

"In all the annals of warfare, ancient and modern, no greater mortality was ever inflicted in the same space of time by as few men as were engaged in the affair. Actual and careful account made after the battle was over for the day, disclosed that 443 of the Zouaves were killed, and that of these, 294 fell dead in the tracks where they stood when the Texans of the Fifth fired their first volley. Only ten prisoners were taken, and of these but four were wounded. One of the wounded, an officer, said, while being taken to the rear, that not over fifty of the regiment escaped death, wounds, or capture. Against that estimate should be placed the fact, vouched for by many members of the Fifth Texas, that at least twice that number were seen to reach the shelter of timber beyond Young's branch.

"Captain Mark Kerns, the commander of the battery captured by the Fourth Texas, deserves more than a passing notice. A Virginian by birth, no braver soldier than he served in either army. His experience with the Texans was somewhat similar to that of the Zouaves. His battery was one of those that were massed on the high hill south of Powhite Creek, at the battle of Gaines' Mill. There he was lucky enough, when the capture of the position seemed inevitable, to escape with four of his guns. With these same four guns he fought the Fourth Texas again at Second Manassas. That night, members of the Fourth Texas returned to the battery, and finding its gallant commander still alive, offered to carry him to a hospital for surgical attention. But he declined such aid, saying that he knew he was mortally wounded and must soon die, and that all he asked was to be let die by his guns, as he had sworn to do when given command of them. His wish was respected, and the watch, the keep-sakes and the letter he wrote were a few days later sent through the lines to the parties he named."

Another member of the Fourth Texas, General William R. Hamby, writes as follows:

"Resuming our march early in the morning of August 29th, we could hear cannonading in our front, causing our column to press forward in a forced march, as we knew Stonewall Jackson was already engaged. We struck the enemy near

LIEUTENANT BEN M. BAKER
Company B, Fifth Texas Regiment

the village at Groveton about the middle of the forenoon, and at once formed line of battle, the Texas Brigade on the right of the turnpike leading from Warrenton across Bull Run to Centerville, and Law's Brigade of our division on the left of the pike and connecting with the right of Jackson's line. The balance of Longstreet's Corps forming to the right of the Texas Brigade, thus placing us about the center of the Confederate line of battle. Our line was formed in the edge of a narrow strip of timber; in our rear was a small glade or abandoned field; our skirmish line was at the further side of the timber in front of us; in front of our skirmish line was an open field some three hundred yards wide; then came another body of timber in which the enemy had formed their lines. Their sharp shooters and their artillery kept up a regular fire, but did little execution.

"Late in the afternoon we were ordered forward, but had scarcely cleared the outer edge of the woods where our skirmish line had been on duty before we met the enemy advancing to meet us. Raising a shout we charged them at double quick and drove them from the open field back through the woods; while passing through this timber a cavalry charge was made along the pike to our left, but was soon repulsed; we then crossed another field, passing over a small creek and advanced up a hill into another body of timber. Night had overtaken us sometime before we entered this last woods, which was probably three-fourths of a mile from where we started. The conflict here was close and obstinate and continued until it was so dark we could not distinguish friend from foe. The Federal and Confederate lines were badly mixed, resulting in many cases of hand-to-hand conflict. It was here that Lieutenant-Colonel Work, then in command of the First Texas, was struck on the head with a gun by a Federal soldier. The dense woods only added to the darkness and the embarrassment of a battle at night, which is the most undesirable service in which a soldier can engage. While our losses had been comparatively small that day, yet many of those brave Texans were destined to join the innumerable caravan on the shores of the great beyond before the setting of another sun. We were far advanced inside the Federal lines and practically surrounded on three sides. We remained in this position until after midnight, when we quietly withdrew and returned to the same position we held before the fight commenced, bringing with us a few prisoners and several flags as the result of the engagement. The prisoners were New York troops and said they belonged to Hatch's Brigade.

"In consequence of our withdrawal General Pope, the Federal commander, fell under the erroneous impression that General Lee's whole army was in retreat and telegraphed that fact to Washington and issued orders that his troops be thrown 'forward in pursuit of the fleeing rebels,' but he soon became convinced that the rebels were not retreating, but were still in strong force along his entire front, and before the close of the day he realized that the 'fleeing rebels,' as he termed General Lee's army, not only had no intention of retreating, but were actually advancing, and then it was the matter of but a few hours when the pursuers became the pursued.

"During the forenoon of August 30, sharp firing was kept up between the skirmish lines of the opposing armies. In addition to the whistling of the minie balls that would occasionally hit a man in our lines, the Federal Artillery on a hill about half a mile in front of us were shelling the woods in which we were located and while not doing much damage, were very annoying. As the shells came shrieking through the tree tops over our heads, they seemed to say, 'Where are you? Where are you?' and when they burst there is no question but what they plainly said, 'Found you.'

"About three o'clock we witnessed an artillery duel between the Confederate batteries on our left and the Federal artillery in our front. Our guns were under the direction of General Stephen D. Lee, who at that time was a colonel of artillery. The enemy's batteries were silenced and our batteries advanced at a gallop about 200 yards in front of our lines and again opened fire, with shot and shell and doing great execution. It was one of the most brilliant artillery actions it was ever my fortune to witness. The fire of our guns was so rapid and so accurate that the Federal infantry, then seriously threatening Jackson's line to our left, were broken and their artillery forced to change position and seek shelter.

"It was about four o'clock, or possibly some later, in the

afternoon of August 30th, when we were again ordered forward. We advanced through the timber in front of us and were met by the enemy in the open field near where we had met them the previous day. Again raising a yell and charging at double quick we drove them from the field through the timber to another field and across a creek where we made a short halt, re-formed our lines and prepared for another charge. The battery on the crest of the hill in our front and their infantry supports were subjecting us to a heavy fire. While we were re-forming our lines, Albert Nicholls of Company B, Fourth Texas, broke ranks and ran some thirty or forty steps up the hill towards the enemy to pick up a hat which he said had been left there for him by a gentleman from New York. We started at a run, firing and reloading as we advanced, and but for the fact that the enemy over-shot us, we would never have reached the top of the hill, and yet with that in our favor we lost heavily in making that charge of about 200 yards. The Fifth Texas was to our right and came in contact with the Fifth New York Zouaves, as gallant a regiment of soldiers as ever fired a gun. The New York Regiment covered the Fifth Texas, while in front of the Fourth Texas was a battery of artillery. The Zouaves were dressed in blue jackets, red trousers and white leggins, and presented a picturesque appearance, but out of 490 who went into action that day, 297 of them fell where they stood, and I verily believe if any one had been disposed, he could have walked from one end of their line to the other without touching the ground. The officers and men of the battery shared a similar fate, standing to their guns until we were upon them, the most of them being either killed or wounded before they permitted their four guns to fall into our hands, but the troops supporting the battery fled in disorder. When the Fifth Texas fired their last volley into the ranks of the Zouaves, their right could almost cross bayonets with the left of the New Yorkers. The valor of the Zouaves was only exceeded by the gallant charge of the Texans.

"It was a singular coincidence that the Zouaves and the battery which suffered so heavily at the hands of the Texans at Second Manassas should have also fought us at Gaines' Mill the 27th of June previous, when the Zouaves lost about one-third of their number while the battery lost two of their guns, besides many of their men killed and wounded. The battery was composed of Pennsylvania soldiers and was commanded by Captain Mark Kerns, who although wounded early in the day at Gaines' Mill, stayed with his guns until the Federal line was swept from the field, and at Second Manassas, although nearly all his men had fallen, he loaded and fired his guns until he himself was struck down when we were only a few steps from him. When we reached the gun beside which he fell, with his life blood fast ebbing away, he said: 'I promised to drive you back, or die under my guns, and I have kept my word.' After crossing the hill on which Kerns' battery was located we deflected somewhat to the left, while the Fifth Texas, Hampton's Legion, and Eighteenth Georgia had gone to the right, thus widely separating us from these regiments of our brigade. We pushed on after the retreating Federals down the hill across a small hollow and came in contact with the Pennsylvania Reserves, who were in a pine thicket in front of us. We here discovered the enemy in heavy force on the hill to our left and almost in our rear. We were being enfiladed by both infantry and artillery, which forced us to change direction and fall back, as we were then about half a mile in front of the balance of the Confederate line on this part of the field. The friendly sides of a ravine protected us somewhat until we could re-form our line and take a survey of the situation. We then crossed the hill in our rear, keeping up a rapid fire and holding the enemy at a safe distance when the Fourth Texas was joined by the First Texas, who had been engaged on our left and nearer the turnpike. The Federals came up within about 200 yards of our line; the intervening space between the two lines was covered with the dead and wounded, both Union and Confederate. It was on this part of the field where Sergeant Bible, of Company E, and Charley McAnnally and Niles Fawcett, of Company B, and others were killed, besides many wounded, myself among the number.

"A comrade who was wounded and unable to leave the field gives a graphic description of his surroundings. He said he laid on that field as the sun was slowly sinking behind the hills, and as the shadows of night came on, the feelings that came over him were beyond his powers of expression; midway between two lines of battle with shot and shell from friend and foe falling thick, and every few moments some poor unfortunate would cry out in anguish, 'Oh, God, I am hit again.' His mother from his infancy had taught him to pray, but on this day the thought of prayer never entered is mind, and yet, he says, he could embrace every act of his life in a single thought.

"Evans' Brigade soon came up to our support, followed soon thereafter by a general advance of the entire Confederate line which swept the Union forces from the field. The battle continued until darkness put an end to the conflict, the Confederate lines being about two miles in front of where we had started, but if an hour more of daylight had remained, Pope's army would have been captured or destroyed, as many organizations left the field in a rout, and to use the language of a distinguished Federal officer, 'The road was filled with fleeing men, artillery and wagons, all leaving the field in a panic, the shadows of night enabling them to escape in safety across Bull Run.'

"A short time before the battle commenced, James Thomas, of Company B, Fourth Texas, remarked to some of his comrades that if he went into the battle that day he knew he would be killed. Captain McLaurin, then in command of the company, heard the remark and told him if he felt that way for him not to go into action, and that he would send him to the rear on a special detail, but Thomas promptly declined and said he would rather be killed than to be left in camp on any kind of a detail when his regiment was at the front fighting. In less than an hour from that time he was killed in our charge up the hill in front of Kerns' battery.

"In striking contrast to the foregoing, there was another soldier, who had the habit of skulking and who had done so in the engagement the previous day. As soon as we were ordered to advance his captain said to him, calling him by name, 'I noticed your conduct in the fight yesterday, and if you attempt to skulk to-day I will have you court-martialed and shot,' to which the man replied, 'Captain, there is no use talking, I just can't stand it; do with me what you please.'

He was detailed to the litter corps and made one of the most useful soldiers in the army and achieved a reputation for bravery on the field that made him honored and respected by all who knew him.

"I remained at the field hospital some ten or twelve days until all the wounded who were able to be moved were transferred to the hospital at Warrenton, when I took an ambulance and followed the army into Maryland, reaching the brigade at Hagerstown September 13, while the B. & O. bridge was being destroyed. The route I traveled from the field hospital led by the deep cut in the bed of the railroad in front of Jackson's line, where I saw hundreds of dead bodies still unburied, who were piled up like railroad crossties, and were being buried by having the earth from the embankment above thrown upon them. The stench was sickening and the sight appalling.

"The genius and generalship of General Lee never shone with greater splendor than in the second battle of Manassas, which will go down in history as one of the great battles of modern warfare. The Confederate position was strong and well selected against which the Federals frittered away much of their strength in their repeated and unsuccessful assaults upon Jackson's line, and when final orders were given to advance, there was scarcely a halt in the entire Confederate lines until the battle ended. General Lee with 50,000 men was opposed by General Pope, the Federal commander, with an army of 70,000. The Confederate losses were 7244, while the Federal losses were 14,462 men, in addition to thirty pieces of artillery, 20,000 stand of small arms, numerous flags and a large amount of army stores. No troops in General Lee's army bore a more conspicuous part in this great battle or contributed in a greater degree to achieve the victory than Hood's Texas Brigade, but the honors they won were bought at the price of 627 killed and wounded, of which the Fifth Texas alone lost 239."

In his official report, Lieutenant-Colonel B. F. Carter says:
"After our return to the position of the previous day, early on the morning of the 30th, we rested on our arms in line of battle during the day. Soon after four o'clock in the after-

noon we were ordered to advance in the same line of battle as the day previous, the First Texas, on our left, being the directing battalion. Company A (Captain S. H. Darden) was deployed as skirmishers in our front early in the morning; was engaged with the enemy during the day. Passing through the skirt of wood we rested in, we advanced through the first field, thence through the second skirt of timber to the next field. While yet in the wood a heavy firing of musketry commenced on the right of our brigade, but no enemy appeared in front of my regiment. As we emerged from the wood I discovered a battery stationed on the hill beyond the small creek, supported by infantry in strong force, who opened fire on us. The distance to the creek at the bottom of the hill was about 300 yards. We advanced in double-quick down the hill to the creek, where we halted in accordance with your orders, and were pretty well protected by the banks and some trees growing there. Here the regiment, somewhat broken in our rapid advance, was quickly re-formed. We had halted scarcely a minute when I discovered the right of the brigade advancing up the hill, and immediately ordered the regiment to charge the battery. Two or three guns on the right of the battery were directly in front of my regiment, at about 100 yards distance from the creek, on a small eminence sloping gradually to the bottom, the ground being bare and smooth. We were greeted with a terrific fire of grape, canister, and musketry, and my principal loss was sustained here. The regiment responded gallantly to the order to charge, and carried the hill and battery on the run, utterly routing the supports, and killing the gunners, who stood to their guns until we approached to within twenty paces. I hurried the regiment rapidly forward to the next valley beyond the hill, where a dry, shallow ravine afforded some protection from the fire of the enemy, who had taken refuge on the next hill, covered with a growth of short pine, and were keeping up a sharp fire of musketry on us. The Eighteenth Georgia formed in the same ravine on our right, but the First Texas had disappeared from my left, and I did not see it any more until our return to the creek. While advancing through the first field, before meeting the enemy, I had received a caution to look well to my left; that we had no supports there, the Third Brigade being held as a support for the batteries, and not advancing. In crossing the different hills, and especially from the battery hill, I discovered large masses of the enemy on our left moving down at right angles to the course we were going. We remained in the shallow ravine spoken of several minutes, driving the enemy from the short pines in front by our fire, when I discovered the Eighteenth Georgia was moving by the right flank away from me along the ravine, and about the same time the enemy commenced firing on me from a wooded ridge to my left and in rear of my left flank. I sent Adjutant Price to Colonel Wofford, of the Eighteenth Georgia, to ascertain where he was going; to tell him the enemy were moving in large force around our left flank, and ask him for support. The reply received was he could not come, but was going to the right. I found myself exposed with my weakened force to an increasing fire from the enemy in front, on my left, and in rear of my left, with no support on either flank, and not a Confederate soldier but my own regiment in sight. To meet the movement of the enemy around my left, I changed front perpendicularly to the left across the ravine we occupied, and finding myself uncovered by this movement, I fell back about fifty yards to the dry bed of a shallow cross-ravine, where for some time we maintained a steady fire on the enemy. Here several of my men fell from the severe crossfire of the enemy, and some of the wounded, I fear, were taken prisoners here. The ravine we were in extended to the left, up the hill on which the battery was situated that we had taken. In the prolongation of it on the opposite side of the hill, was a thin hedge of small growth, affording a partial protection. Seeing no prospect of supports, and believing my whole command would be sacrificed in the present position against the immense number of the enemy, I ordered the regiment to march by the left flank, keeping it as well as possible under cover of the ravine and hedge spoken of. The movement was executed with remarkably good order, the enemy being kept at a respectful distance by our rapid fire. Reaching the small creek, the regiment was formed under cover of its banks, and soon afterward, by your orders, I moved up the creek by the right flank and connected with the First Texas, now on my right. Throwing out skirmishers to the front on the hill-side, covering the captured guns with their fire, we rested here until dark. We were not again engaged.

"About half an hour after forming in the creek, while resting, General Evans rode up from the woods in our rear and was cheered by our men, to whom he addressed a few words in return.

"I cannot speak too highly of the officers and men of my command. The coolness, good order, and prompt obedience to orders displayed under the most trying circumstances, and the daring courage in the charge, were worthy of the reputation the Fourth had already established. The skulkers, if any, were so few as to escape observation.

"Our loss was severe, including some of the best officers. Major Townsend fell, badly wounded in the leg, while gallantly leading the right of the regiment in its charge on the battery. Previous to and during the action, he had rendered invaluable services to me, and his loss was greatly felt by his regiment.

"Captain (D. U.) Barziza, Company C; Captain (James T.) Hunter, Company H; Lieutenant (M. C.) Holmes, Company H, and Lieutenant (A. D.) Jeffries, Company D, were all wounded in the same charge—the first and last slightly; the other two severely.

"Lieutenant (C. E.) Jones, Company H, and Lieutenant (T. I.) Johnson, Company D, were killed on the field in the same charge, and died as brave men should, in the front of battle, and their loss is irreparable to their companies and the regiment.

"Color-Sergeant Francis, of Company A, fell severely wounded while leading the colors in front of the regiment, and they were gallantly borne the remainder of the action by Color-Corporal Parker, of Company H."

Lieutenant-Colonel M. W. Gary's official report of the movements of Hampton's Legion is next in order and is as follows:

"The fight was opened about three o'clock by an attack of the enemy upon the left wing of our army. About four o'clock the brigade was ordered to advance, the Legion in line of battle, with the Fifth Texas Regiment on the right and the Eighteenth Georgia on the left. I ordered Captain H. J.

Smith's company thrown forward as skirmishers. We had gone about a quarter of a mile when the skirmishers became hotly engaged with the Duryea Zouaves near where we had engaged the enemy the evening before. We received the volley and charged upon them and delivered our fire at short range, killing, wounding, and capturing a large number. They were completely routed, and as they retreated over the ravine and up the hill a large number were killed and wounded by the well-practised aim of the men of the entire brigade. The whole brigade moved forward in hot pursuit under a heavy fire of grape and canister, driving the enemy back to their reserves, capturing a large number of prisoners and a battery. Seeing that in our eager pursuit we were about to be flanked by the enemy on the right and left, I commanded the Legion to halt as it was ascending the hill from the deep ravine. We were then ordered to move by the right flank. We gained the woods under a heavy fire, and immediately advanced upon the enemy. Perceiving that they were now outflanked, they fled in confusion after the first volley, the Eighteenth Georgia, Legion, and Fifth Texas still pursuing. We were then hotly engaged around the Chinn house, where the brigade captured several pieces of artillery. At this place, the brigade of General Evans came up in gallant style and relieved us.

"During the fight, Lieutenant B. E. Nicholson captured a stand of colors. Private Henry Brandies, Company C, also captured a beautiful flag.

"The colors of the Legion were the first that were planted upon a battery of four guns, which was successfully turned upon the enemy by Lieutenant J. H. M. James and Private John Pios, of Company C, assisted by several members of Company H, who were practised artillerists.

"I cannot mention in too flattering terms the splendid courage evinced by the officers and men of the Legion. Major J. H. Dingle had his horse shot under him and again won new laurels by his untiring gallantry, being always in the thickest of the fight. Captain L. C. McCord was shot down at the head of his company, wounded in three places. His first lieutenant, J. D. Palmer, fell at his side dangerously wounded, and his second lieutenant, T. A. G. Clarke, shared the same fate. Lieutenant R. A. Tompkins, acting-adjutant, was wounded while rallying the men. Lieutenant John W. Austin, of Company F, was wounded while leading his company. Lieutenant James McElroy, of Company A, who fought with conspicuous courage, was wounded. Sergeant J. H. Satterfield, the color-bearer, was wounded. Never was a flag borne with more dashing courage than he displayed, as the bullet-rent folds will attest. Captain T. M. Logan, by his brilliant fighting, won the admiration of every one. Captain R. W. Tompkins distinguished himself by his cool and practical courage. Lieutenant W. Edward O'Connor, in command of a scouting party, acted with his usual gallantry and rendered important information as to the movements of the enemy. Lieutenant W. A. B. Davenport, (J. J.) Exum, (J. J.) Cleveland, and (J. H. M.) James, commanding their respective companies, proved themselves gallant guardians of the honor of their commands."

Reporting the movements of the Eighteenth Georgia, its colonel, William T. Wofford, says:

"On the morning of the 30th ultimo I was directed by Captain W. H. Sellers, your adjutant-general, to hold my regiment in line of battle to move against the enemy at three o'clock that evening; that our brigade would move after General Kemper's brigade had entered the woods in our front. The enemy having commenced the attack, I received orders to advance my regiment. On my right were Hampton's Legion and Fifth Texas and on my left the Fourth and First Texas. As we passed the field in front of our line the brigade moved in splendid order, and with a shout, advanced through the second strip of woods on the enemy's lines, which we carried so quickly that no halt was perceivable. The right wing of my regiment encountered the Fifth and Tenth New York Regiments supporting and in front of a battery of the enemy. We pursued these fleeing regiments to the ravine at the foot of the hill in front of the battery, killing and taking prisoners nearly every man, with the assistance and co-operation of Hampton's Legion and Fifth Texas. As we advanced on the battery up the hill from the branch, my regiment captured the colors of the Tenth New York Regiment. As our brigade charged the battery and carried it most gallantly, the left of my regiment passed over four guns, and my color-bearer mounted one of the pieces and waved the colors over the captured trophy. Observing a second battery immediately in front and on a hill, I gave the order to move rapidly to the ravine between the two batteries, where I halted the regiment to take breath. At this moment, Colonels Gary, of Hampton's Legion, and Robertson, of Fifth Texas, came to me and said that we were being flanked on our left by a large body of the enemy, which caused us to move by the right flank up the ravine to the woods. I halted my regiment as soon as my left was covered by the woods, and moved in line to the second battery through the woods and over a slight declivity, to within forty yards of the enemy's guns and their lines of support, composed of two regiments of infantry placed on the right and left of the battery. At this battery I had no support but a fragment of a regiment (supposed to be the Holcombe Legion), which fought with much spirit and gallantry. Sergeant Weems, my color-bearer, who bravely moved in front of the regiment, was shot down in forty yards of this battery; also two others—Sergeants McMurray and Jones. Seeing my men falling rapidly, and having no support and no reinforcements arriving, I withdrew my regiment in the same order that we approached the battery, through the woods to the branch to the right of where we took the first battery, were I found the First and Fourth Texas Regiments, when I halted and formed on their right, and where we remained until you came to us.

"My regiment lost in killed 19, and wounded 133. Among the former were Lieutenant (S. V.) Smith, commanding Company K, and Lieutenant (E. L. Brown), of Company E.

"I cannot find words to express the gallantry of my regiment, both officers and men. Nearly all the men lost were killed where we first encountered the two New York regiments of Zouaves, and at the second battery. It would be invidious to speak especially of any man or officer where all did their part so well, but the great gallantry of my color-bearer, Sergeant Weems, who was shot down almost at the mouth of the guns of the second battery, entitles him to particular notice."

Captain W. T. Hill, of the Fifth Texas, contributes the following account of the movements of that command:

"Until 3 P. M. of the 30th, there was no disturbance of the peace except such as was produced by occasional discharges of small arms and artillery. At three o'clock the enemy advanced in force against Jackson, and for an hour, one of the most terrible battles of the war raged. Jackson was pressed so persistently and heavily, that at 4 P. M. General Longstreet was ordered by General Lee to join in the battle, and if possible, drive the enemy from the field. Longstreet gave the necessary commands to his subordinates, and, in line with the other brigades of the corps, the Texas Brigade moved forward—my company, then on the skirmish line in front of the Fifth Texas, being ordered to form on its right when overtaken by it. The brigade marched across an open field, and through a skirt of timber, and in the open ground beyond the timber, encountered the enemy, as, in line of battle he stood awaiting attack—the Fifth New York Zouaves standing directly in front of the Fifth Texas, but overlapped by the length of my company, when that fell in on the right of the Fifth Texas.

"Thus it happened that when the Fifth Texas, its men yelling their loudest, came out of the timber into the open ground, it came, practically, face to face with the Zouaves, who, in their red, white and blue uniforms, stood in as perfect alignment as if on dress parade. The Zouaves were first to fire, but most of their shots went far astray from the mark: they killed only two of our men, but wounded several others. Lieutenant-Colonel Upton, sad to say, was one of the killed. Following almost on the instant, but with far better aim, was the volley of the Fifth Texas, and seemingly, one-half of the Zouaves fell, cut down in their tracks. Appalled by such a storm of lead as fell among them, and by the sight of so many fallen comrades, the surviving Zouaves, seized with panic, wheeled and took to flight. With a shout, the Fifth Texas followed, continuing the slaughter down to and until two hundred yards beyond Young's branch. There, remembering that his orders were to move no further forward than Young's branch, Colonel Robertson called a halt.

"This halt, however, was not of long duration. Hardly

had the last slow-coach of the regiment come up and found his place in line, when somebody—a private, it was thought to have been, but nobody ever knew who—shouted at the top of his voice, 'Forward!' Then, as General Hood said, 'the Fifth Texas slipped the bridle.' Hearing that 'Forward,' every man of the regiment sprang to his feet, and with a yell, dashed forward at his topmost speed, reckless that at this time we were two or three hundred yards in advance of the foremost regiment of the brigade then in sight, and that, as had been the case when they fell upon the Zouaves, not a single Confederate command was in view on our right.

"What effort, if any, was made by officers to stay this second charge of the Fifth Texas, I do not remember. But we had not gone far, when a line of Federals sprang up from the ground where they had been lying so flat we could not see them, and poured a volley into our ranks that was terribly destructive—many of our men falling dead or wounded. But undismayed, the Fifth returned the fire, and with effect even more deadly than was theirs. Broken and demoralized by it, they fled, and following them, went the Fifth Texas, yelling, loading and firing as they ran. The pursuit carried the regiment into open ground, and there it came in view and range of two batteries—one on its left, and the other on its right, at the Chinn house.

"As out of breath in the chase of infantry whose fleeter-footedness had taken them out of sight, we came finally to a halt, and looking to the right and left, saw what we were 'up against,' we felt ourselves lost and bewildered orphans. It was not comfortable, by a long shot, to be five hundred yards or more in advance of our army, under the enfilading cross-fires of two well-served batteries, and with enemies innumerable presumably waiting, just over the hill, to capture or destroy us. To stay where we were, was suicidal—to go straightforward was to get further from support—and to retreat, not a man of us dared suggest to another. The officer in command of the regiment—our officers were killed or disabled, that day, too rapidly for one to know which one commanded at this or that place—solved our doubts and fears; although around the Chinn house, Federal infantry was heavily massed, we were far beyond the range of their rifles, and might, in order to secure protection from the artillery, safely lessen the distance between us, and therefore, he orderd the regiment to double-quick, by the right flank, down the slope of the hill toward the Chinn house, into a gully, two hundred yards away.

"We obeyed the order with alacrity, each man going at his best speed, and the lame and the slow-coaches getting over the ground as fast as any of their comrades. But we had barely passed the gully, found safety in the pine and cedar thicket beyond it, and gotten into a semblance of alignment, when an unknown voice again shouted the command, 'Forward!' and joining on the left of D. R. Jones' division, which just then came in line with us, we made such a vigorous and determined assault on the Federal lines at the Chinn house, as to force the enemy into retreat down a breach and valley leading in the direction of Sudley ford on Bull Run Creek. It took us until night, though, to get the Federals into the humor for going. They fought gallantly and stubbornly, and inflicted a severe loss on us. Exactly what our losses were in the day's fighting, I cannot say. The Fifth Texas carried into the action about 800 men, but after the fighting was over, only 400 answered to roll-call."

Because of a change of commanders on the field, two official reports were required to tell the part the Fifth Texas took in the battle of the 30th—one from Colonel J. B. Robertson covering what occurred up to the time he was disabled, and one from Captain King Bryan, acting major, who succeeded Robertson in the command. Colonel Robertson reports as follows:

"My regiment was on the right of the brigade. I was ordered to keep well-closed on the left of the First Regiment Texas Volunteers, which was the battalion of direction. I was notified that General Kemper, with his brigade, was on my right, and that I need have no uneasiness about my right flank. As the brigade moved across the first field to the timber held by the enemy's skirmishers, a change of front forward on the left battalion made it necessary to move my men at a run across the field. At the edge of the timber the enemy's skirmishers were encountered by my skirmishers and driven back to a point in the timber about 100 yards from the open field beyond. Here I encountered the regiment of the enemy that had deployed as skirmishers, who had rallied on their right. I ordered the regiment to fire on and charge them. They broke and were closely pressed to the open field, where we encountered a second line of the enemy in the Fifth Regiment New York Zouaves, who, after permitting the fleeing regiment to pass its lines, presented a solid front for a short time.

"Their stand was but momentary. They gave way before the impetuous charge of my men and fled, leaving the field strewn with their dead and wounded. Such was the impetuosity of the charge and the unerring aim of my men, that very few, if any, of that regiment reached the hill beyond. My charge was continued across the branch and up the hill, in the direction of a heavy battery the enemy had playing on us from the hill beyond.

"Seeing nothing of General Kemper's brigade or any other of our forces on my right, and no support visible in my rear, I ordered my regiment to halt under the crest of the hill. Seeing Major (Captain) Sellers, assistant adjutant-general, I went to him for orders. He ordered me to halt. I returned to the center of my regiment, which was but a few steps up the hill, and found that my right wing had failed to receive the order to halt, and had passed over the crest of the hill, and was advancing under a murderous fire from two of the enemy's batteries. As these batteries swept the field over which our reinforcements had to come, I determined to charge the one immediately in my front, in preference to recalling my right. It was here that I first missed my gallant lieutenant-colonel, J. C. Upton. His fall was the cause of my right not getting the order to halt.

"The charge was gallantly made; the battery cleared and passed; the enemy fleeing before us. As I passed down the hill beyond the battery taken, I observed the enemy in still heavier force than any we had encountered on the hill before us. They were drawn up in three lines of battle, the rear line of which was moving by the left flank at a run, for a point of timber on my right, some 400 yards distant. Seeing no support on my right, it was evident that I must gain this point of timber before him to prevent my right from being turned. I sought Colonels Wofford, of the Eighteenth

Georgia regiment, and Gary, of the Hampton Legion, and announced the movement of the enemy and my determination to move by my right flank to the timber. They assented to the move, and I moved by my right flank up the hollow as rapidly as the exhausted condition of my men would permit me. We gained the woods, the head of my column leading the enemy's by some fifty yards, when we fired into them and drove them from the woods. After getting distance sufficient to cover the command, I ordered a halt, intending to collect my men and giving them a few moments' rest (they had made three separate charges and continued the run for one and one-half miles and were very much exhausted) and await our reinforcements.

"Before my lines were well-formed, a regiment of our forces came up through the woods from the rear. As it passed my lines, the command of forward was given. My command, mistaking it for them, moved forward, and thus became considerably scattered by intermixing with that regiment. We rallied and advanced to their right through the orchard and passed the house, driving the enemy from his position there, and gained the hollow beyond. Near the gate beyond the garden, I was struck down, and must refer to the report of Captain Ike N. Turner, who was left in command, Captain K. Bryan, my acting major, being wounded.

"The separation of the regiments of the brigade during the battle probably increased the casualties in my regiment, interfering to some extent with its efficiency, and demonstrated the absolute necessity of having brigade commanders present with brigades at all times during the engagement.

"My flag was borne into action by Color-Sergeant W. V. Royston, of Company I; next by Corpl. J. Miller, Company B; Private C. Moncrief, Company C; Private Shepherd, Company B; Sergeant Simpson, Company A; Private J. Harris, Company D; Sergt. F. C. Hume, Company D, all of whom were shot down while gallantly bearing the flag in front of the regiment. It was borne through the remainder of the fight by Private Farthing, Company D.

"I had three companies left without a commissioned officer, viz., Companies C, H and I, but they pressed forward without faltering.

"Where all behaved so nobly distinctions cannot, with propriety, be made. All, both officers and men, sustained well the reputation of the Lone Star flag, under which they fought through the battle. Among the list of killed I have to lament the death of the brave and chivalrous Lieut. Col. John C. Upton, who fell while gallantly leading the right wing of his regiment to victory. My list of killed is 15, wounded 245, missing 1. The regiment captured three stands of colors and two batteries. Six guns and quite a number of prisoners were sent to the rear."

Following the above report of Colonel Robertson, comes that of Captain King Bryan, who was that day acting as major of his regiment. No report from Captain Turner is to be found. After saying that he (Bryan) was not wounded before Robertson was, and that he succeeded Robertson in the command, Captain Bryan relates what happened after Robertson was wounded; that is, after the Fifth Texas halted in the hollow beyond the house referred to by Colonel Robertson. He says:

"By the time the line was halted and formed, General Evans' brigade had come up on our left, when the command, forward, was given, and the Fifth Texas and Hampton's Legion moved off in good order to the edge of the field. Being then within 80 yards of the enemy, another of our impetuous charges swept that wing of the enemy's line away like chaff before the wind, the right remaining intact, supported by a battery and another strong line of infantry formed perpendicularly to the other line, distant from the Chinn house about 600 yards. Another battery was near the Chinn house on the left and in rear of the line we had assailed and broken. The pursuit was rapid, the rush being mainly directed toward the last mentioned battery; but this was managed with such precaution as to move in time to effect its escape, we capturing two caissons only. In the charge some confusion occurred on our right which caused me to hasten to that flank, and coming in contact with a brigade of fresh troops, I moved rapidly along its line, appealing to it to move faster, not knowing what might be awaiting us beyond the house. The pursuit was conducted to the left of the house and through the orchard and yard. On the east of the house is a wide hollow, and in it a mass of timber running northeast, beginning opposite the house and extending in the direction named about 700 yards, when it turns more to the eastward, leaving a large open field on the north. At the head of the hollow, about 400 yards from where the timber makes the turn to the eastward, was a battery. Opposite this point or turn in the timber, and on the ridge upon which the Chinn house stands, rested the left of that perpendicular line, which consisted of two heavy regiments. Being delayed by going to the right, on arriving east of the house I had the satisfaction of seeing our flag at the timber, it having pursued that far and halted, and was waving briskly, that the men might see and rally to it. I recognized the tall and manly forms of Captains J. S. Cleveland and Turner with it and directing its movements. I found a number of our men who had been forced to take shelter in a deep wash in the side of the ridge from a terrible flank fire poured upon them from the perpendicular line described. It was this fire during this pursuit and subsequent advance upon it which caused our very heavy losses on that day. We were not allowed to remain long in our then secure position. A small brigade came up, moving toward the last mentioned line of the enemy, and the only unbroken one on that part of the field.

"As the brigade reached our thinned ranks, the command forward was given, and all started off in the new direction with the same spirit which had characterized their previous movements on that day, but gradually settled down to conform to the movements of the brigade. Our flag dashed up the slope to the center of the brigade, and then led on in the direction of the enemy. About this time I joined the colors and remained near them. I found Captain Turner and Sergeant Hume, of Company D, and privates Jimmy Harrison and G. W. Farthing, of the same company, with them, Captain Cleveland having just fallen, dangerously wounded in the neck, having discharged his every duty as an officer and soldier, to his company and his country. Harris had the flag when I joined the party. His enthusiasm was such that it could not be restrained. He would from time to time rush to the front a distance of 60 or 70 yards, face to the advancing line, wave the flag and shout, ' Come on '; but we were soon deprived of his gallant and cheering example. He was cut down by a severe wound in the right thigh, falling far in the van of our line. Sergeant Hume took the flag when young Harris fell, and bore it high above all others which were then floating over the field, as a beacon to our men who had been separated from it. Sergeant Hume, after bearing the flag about 200 yards, was also shot down. Being near him, I received the colors from him as he fell, and carrying them a short distance I transferred them to Private Farthing, who carried them through the remainder of the day.

"The brigade had steadily followed our flag, but I now discovered that the line had diminished by the men falling behind, and the nearer we approached the enemy the greater was this evil; but as vacancies occurred in the rank they were promptly closed from the flanks. On arriving within 70 yards of the enemy I found that we had not more than 200 men in line and in supporting distance of the flag; but the hill-side was covered with those who had fallen behind, yet slowly advancing, still loading and firing as they came, the nature of the ground being such that they could shoot over us with effect upon the enemy. I halted the colors and closed the line upon them, intending to await the coming up of those scattered men before advancing the attack further. Here I discovered that the whole command devolved upon me, all evidence of any other organization than that of the Fifth Texas having disappeared from the field. In this I was assisted by Captain Turner; but the enemy would not permit our delay. By the time the line had closed upon the flag, which had halted immediately in front of the colors of his left regiment, the commander of that regiment dashed through his lines to the front and commanded his men to charge, the left of which had gotten in motion, when some well-directed shots from our side brought the officer and his horse both down. This was followed by a yell and a rush from our side, which, together with our well-directed fire, completed the work. They broke by the left flank, and fled behind the batteries at the head of the hollow, the whole line following in the same trace. On discovering this, we halted and poured our fire upon them as they passed. We might have made an advantageous movement and cut off the rear of their line, but their right was obstructed from our view by high ground until they reached a point about opposite to our left, and we deemed victory too secure to hazard the result by a movement the certainty of which could not be clearly foreseen. We pursued, keeping up our fire till the last one had taken shelter behind their guns.

"Our attention was now attracted to the open field north of the timber. Here was to be seen the heaviest line of the day advancing steadily across the field, firing rapidly as they advanced upon our troops (Jenkins' brigade) who had fought upon the right and up through the timber, and at that time occupying a position in the timber fronting this line. Now that we had disposed of our immediate foe, our next impulse was to assist our friends, and accordingly we turned our fire upon the flank of the advancing line, moving forward at the same time, the range being too great for our fire to be fully effective; but we had not gone more than 150 yards when we encountered the line of fire from the enemy's battery, which was playing across our front upon General Jenkins, when it was determined to move down to the timber by the right flank to a point opposite General Jenkins' line, and there file out and form upon his left. In this movement I was wounded and had to quit the field, when the command devolved upon Captain Turner.

"We went into the last attack with the new brigade not expecting to act a very conspicuous part in the new drama, but rather, as auxiliaries to the brigade, and I felt surprised and disappointed when I found that we had the whole work left upon our hands. Yet we shrank not from the responsibility, and with the smiles of fortune upon our side, we succeeded in breaking the line, though it was fully five times our strength. This was the third heavy line the Fifth Texas had encountered that day, in each instance achieving complete success. But for the timely breaking of that line the fortunes of the day might have been changed. Had it remained intact ten or fifteen minutes longer it might have co-operated with the heavy line then advancing upon our front, before which our men had to yield ground for a time, by flanking our position in the timber. Such a movement at that time must have been attended with very disastrous results to us."

CHAPTER VII

SHARPSBURG, OR ANTIETAM

BELIEVING that the only hope of the South for success against the great numbers and resources of the North lay in rapid fighting, General Lee moved his army toward Maryland. Jackson led the advance—marching northward on July 31—Longstreet's command marching in the same direction on the 1st of September. The weather was excessively hot, the roads dusty, the tramp a weary one. But there was no grumbling, and but little straggling, for large accessions to our ranks were promised, and high hopes were entertained that the presence of the victorious Confederate army in Maryland would go far toward securing the independence of the South and peace between it and the North.

Having, on the 31st of August, buried its dead, the Texas Brigade marched northward on the morning of September 1, and on the 5th forded the Potomac River at Point of Rocks—the men keeping step, as best they could on the slippery bottom, to the tune of "Maryland, My Maryland," played by Collins' brass band. But the reception it and other Confederate commands were accorded by the Marylanders was as nearly freezing as the waters they waded—the truth being that they were entering a section of the State the residents of which were, as a rule, pronounced Unionists. Two days later, the brigade camped on the Monocacy, near Frederick City, whence, on the 10th, it marched on to Hagerstown.

At Frederick City, General Lee had his army in a position that created well-founded alarm in Washington and all over the North. The Federal army was practically without a commander, the authorities having lost faith in both McClellan and Pope. For a brief space of time, the game was in General Lee's hands. Not knowing it, though, he divided his army, sending Jackson, with all his command and nearly half of Longstreet's, up the river to capture Harper's Ferry, then held by a force of 11,000 Federals who, he feared, might interrupt his communications with Richmond by way of the Shenandoah valley. The order for the movement was embraced in Special Order No. 191, and in this was disclosed not only Lee's plans but the position and the place it would likely be in the near future, of every command in his army. A copy of that order fell into the hands of a careless staff officer, and was used by him as a wrapper for cigars. The bundle was lost, and picked up on the street by a Unionist; he smoked the cigars and sent the wrapper to General McClellan, who, by that time, was in command of the Federal army.

McClellan got possession of the order on the 13th. Up to that date, his movements had been characterized by even more caution and timidity than he had displayed when approaching Richmond in May; but informed by the order that Jackson was at Harper's Ferry and Longstreet at Hagerstown, he felt that his opportunity had come, and immediately ordered his army forward—his aim, to crush Longstreet before Jackson could rejoin him. Thus it happened that in the late afternoon of the 13th his advanced forces came in contact with the Confederates, under D. H. Hill, left by Lee, who rode with Longstreet to Hagerstown, to hold the gaps in the range of mountains between Hagerstown and Frederick City.

Hearing the sound of Hill's guns, and informed by a scout that the whole Union army was moving against the small force then under his command, General Lee realized the peril in which he had placed his army by dividing it. Up to that moment he had believed Jackson would have ample time to capture Harper's Ferry and return to him before any advance was made by the Federals. But he might yet, he thought, contest the passage of the gaps through which McClellan and his army must come, long enough to reunite his scattered troops, and he therefore, on the morning of the 14th, ordered Longstreet's command to the aid of Hill.

Hood's division left its camp at Hagerstown in a frame of mind that threatened insubordination. At the close of the last day's fighting at Second Manassas, Texas scouts captured quite a number of well-appointed ambulances and their teams. Hood ordered them distributed among the regiments of his division, but Major-General Shank Evans, under whose command the division temporarily fell on the 1st of September, interfered, ordering the captured vehicles and teams turned over to his South Carolina brigade, for its exclusive use. Hood refused to do this, and, placed under arrest by Evans, was ordered by Longstreet, a friend and crony of Evans in the old United States army, back to Culpeper Court House, to await trial on charges to be preferred by Evans. The matter coming to Lee's ears, he countermanded Longstreet's order by directing that Hood should remain with the army, but did not release that officer from arrest. And, therefore, since September 1, Hood, bereft of command, had followed in rear of the Texas Brigade.

Feeling that the commander they most trusted was deeply wronged, the officers and men of the division had given loud expression to their indignation, and now as they marched toward what might be another battle, their wrath grew intense. The Texans, naturally, felt most aggrieved, and were most outspoken. Coming late in the afternoon to where General Lee sat on his horse by the side of the road, almost within the range of the enemy's guns, each man as he passed gave expression to the resolve that if any fighting was done by the Texas Brigade, Hood must command it. General Lee was not inattentive, and understanding the full significance of the demand, he raised his hat courteously and replied, " You shall have him, gentlemen." The men began to cheer, but " when the gallant Hood, his head uncovered and his face proud and joyful, galloped by to his rightful place at the head of the division, the cheers deepened into a roar that drowned the volleys of the hundred cannons that were even then vengefully thundering at the gap. And, as the same order that released Hood from arrest, relieved the division of Evans, and left the ambulances in possession of it, happiness was at once restored.

Having reached the summit of Boonesboro Gap, Hood's division took position on the left of the turnpike, its right resting upon that road. From this point the advance of McClellan's long lines could be seen moving up the slope in their front, evidently intending to dislodge the Confederate forces posted on the sharp ridges overlooking the valley to the east. Half an hour later, Hood moved the command to the right of the turnpike, our troops on that side having been driven back. In the new position taken, the men were ordered to fix

DICK PINCKNEY
Company G, Fourth Texas Regiment

bayonets, and when the enemy came within a hundred yards, to fire and charge. The charge was made to the accompaniment of a Confederate yell, and sent the Federals flying pellmell.

The Confederates on the left of the pike, however, yielded ground to the enemy, who, advancing, took strong position near the western foot of South Mountain. This fact reported to General Lee, he decided to fall back toward Sharpsburg—the movement beginning on the morning of the 15th, and Hood's division, assisted by artillery and cavalry, forming the rear guard, and holding the Federals in check until the other troops of Longstreet's command marched quietly to their destination west of Antietam Creek. This was no easy task. The three days' rations issued to the division on the 13th included no meat, and were therefore the sooner exhausted. No clothing or shoes had been furnished it since it left Richmond, and in a month and a half of hard marching and harder fighting hundreds of the men had become ragged and barefooted, while lack of provisions forced them to subsist on green corn and green apples. Nevertheless, they remained in high spirits, and contended as gallantly with the enemy as ever, on the 15th and during the forenoon of the 16th, when they overtook the main army, then in line west of Antietam Creek, confronting the Federals in position on its east side.

On the afternoon of the 16th Hood's division took position in an open field in front of the Dunker or Saint Mumma church—the Texas Brigade on the left, Law's on the right—and against it, about an hour before sunset, advanced Hooker's Federal corps. With that it contended until a late hour in the night, and, when the firing had in great measure ceased, was so close to the enemy that it could distinctly hear his orders to troops being massed on his front.

From General Hood's official report is taken the following: "I was ordered to take position in line of battle on the right of the road leading to Boonesborough, but soon received orders to move to the extreme left, near Saint Mumma church, on the Hagerstown pike, remaining in this position, under fire of the shells from the enemy, until nearly sunset on the evening of the 16th. The enemy, having crossed higher up the Antietam, made an attack on the left flank of our line of battle, the troops of this division being the only forces on our side engaged. We succeeded in checking and driving back the enemy a short distance, when night came on, and soon the firing ceased. . . . The officers and men of my command having been without food for three days, except a half ration of beef for one day, and green corn, General Lawton, with two brigades, was directed to take my position, to enable my men to cook.

"On the morning of the 17th, about 3 o'clock, the firing commenced along the line occupied by General Lawton. At 6 o'clock, I received notice from him that he would require all the assistance I could give him. . . . Being in readiness, I at once marched out on the field in line of battle, and soon became engaged with an immense force of the enemy, consisting of not less than two corps of their army. It was here that I witnessed the most terrible clash of arms, by far, that has occurred during the war. The two little giant brigades of this division wrestled with this mighty force, losing hundreds of their gallant officers and men, but driving the enemy from his position and forcing him to abandon his guns on our left. The battle raged with the greatest fury until about 9 o'clock, the enemy being driven from 400 to 500 yards. Fighting, as we were, at right angles with the general line of battle, and General Ripley's brigade being the extreme left of General D. H. Hill's forces and continuing to hold their ground, caused the enemy to pour in a heavy fire upon the rear and right flank of Colonel Law's brigade, rendering it necessary to move the division to the left and rear, into the woods near the Saint Mumma church, which we continued to hold until 10 A. M., when General McLaws arrived with his command, which was at once formed in line and moved forward, engaging the enemy. My command was marched to the rear, ammunition replenished and returned at 12 M., taking position, by direction of the general commanding, in rear of the church, with orders to hold it. About 4 P. M., by order, the division moved to the right, near the center, and remained there until the night of the 18th, when orders were received to recross the Potomac."

General Hood is liberal in this report of the praises he be-

CAPTAIN L. P. HUGHES
Company F, Fourth Texas Regiment

stows upon subordinate officers of the division. Among the Texas officers complimented by him is Major W. H. Sellers. Of him he says: "Too much cannot be said of the members of my staff, the chief, Major W. H. Sellers, having his horse shot while ably directing the Texas Brigade at the battle of Manassas during the time of my being sent for by the commanding general to receive additional orders. He has proven himself competent to command a brigade under all circumstances. This distinguished officer, together with my two aides, Major B. H. Blanton and Lieut. James Hamilton, had their horses shot during the battle at Sharpsburg while most gallantly pushing forward the troops and transmitting orders." He also mentions the gallantry and the valuable services rendered to him of his Texas couriers, Privates M. M. Templeman, T. W. C. Lake, J. P. Mahoney, James Malone, W. E. Duncan, J. A. Mann, W. J. Barbee, W. G. Jesse, J. J. Haggerty, and J. H. Drake. But he does not mention the tears that coursed down his cheeks, and the sobs that choked his utterance, when he saw his brave men falling fast before the merciless fire of the outnumbering enemy, and his every appeal for aid to them was met by the statement that there were no troops to send to their relief until McLaws should arrive.

To this report General Hood appends a list of the casualties in the division from the date of its departure from Richmond—the list showing that the Texas Brigade lost at Freeman's Ford, 10 men; at Second Manassas, in the two days' fighting, 628 men; and at Sharpsburg, in the two days' fighting, 548 men.

From the report made by Colonel W. T. Wofford, of the Eighteenth Georgia, as commander of the Texas Brigade, it is necessary to quote but few passages—his report as a whole being covered by those of the regimental commanders. Speaking of the movement to the right and in front of the church mentioned by General Hood, Colonel Wofford says: "While we were moving to this position, the enemy opened a heavy fire upon us from their long-range guns, which was continued after we were in position, and resulted in the wounding of a lieutenant and a private of the Fourth Texas. Late in the evening of the 16th, we were ordered by General Hood to move by the left flank through the open field in front of the church and to its left about 700 yards, to meet the enemy, who, it was then ascertained, had commenced to cross Antietam Creek to our left. We then formed line of battle and moved up to a corn-field in our front, and awaited the advance of the enemy, who had, by this time, opened on us a brisk fire of shot and shell from some pieces of artillery which they had placed in position immediately in our front and to the left of our lines, wounding one officer and some dozen men. . . .

"While our line of battle rested upon the corn-field, Captain Turner, commanding the Fifth Texas, which was our right, had been moved forward into some woods, where he met a party of our skirmishers driven in by the enemy, whom he engaged and finally drove back, with the loss of one man. Our skirmishers, consisting of 100 men, under the command of Captain W. H. Martin, of the Fourth Texas, who had been moved into the woods in front and to the left of the Fifth Texas, were hotly engaged with the enemy, but held their ground until they had expended all their cartridges, and then fell into our line of battle, about 9 o'clock at night, about which time we were relieved by General Lawton's brigade, and were withdrawn from the field to the woods in rear of Mumma church, for the purpose of cooking rations, our men not having received any regular allowance in three days.

"At 3 o'clock in the morning of the 17th, the picket firing was very heavy, and at daylight the battle was opened. Our brigade was moved forward at sunrise, to the support of General Lawton, who had relieved us the night before. Moving forward in line of battle in the regular order of regiments, the brigade proceeded through the woods into the open field toward the corn-field, where the left encountered the first line of the enemy. Seeing Hampton's Legion and Eighteenth Georgia moving slowly forward, but rapidly firing, I rode hastily to them, urging them forward, when I saw two full regiments, one in their front and the other partly to their left. Perceiving at once that they were in danger of being cut off, I ordered the First Texas to move by the left flank to their relief, which they did in a rapid and gallant manner. By this time, the enemy on our left having commenced falling back, the First Texas pressed them rapidly to their guns, which now poured into them a fire on their right flank, center and left flank from three different batteries, before which their well-formed line was cut down and scattered; being 200 yards in front of our line, their position was most critical. Riding back to the left of our line, I found the fragment of the Eighteenth Georgia regiment in front of the extreme right battery of the enemy, located on the pike running by the church, which now opened upon our thinned ranks a most destructive fire. The men and officers were gallantly shooting down the gunners, and for a moment silenced them. At this time the enemy's fire was most terrific, their first line of infantry having been driven back to their guns, which now opened a furious fire, together with their second line of infantry, upon our thinned and almost annihilated ranks. . . .

. . . . .

"During the engagement . . . I was drawn to the left of our line, as it first engaged the enemy, who had succeeded in flanking us on the left, and to escape from being surrounded, changed the direction to left-oblique, thus causing large intervals between the regiments on the left and right of the line. The Fifth Texas, under the command of Captain Turner, moved with spirit across the field and occupied the woods on our right, where it met the enemy and drove and held them back until their ammunition was exhausted, and then fell back to the woods with the balance of the brigade. The Fourth Texas, which in our line of battle was between the Fifth and First Texas, was moved by General Hood to the extreme left of our line on the pike road, covering our flank by holding the enemy in check.

"The brigade went into action numbering 854, and lost, in killed, wounded and missing, 560—over one-half.

. . . . .

"Without specially naming the officers and men who stood firmly to their post during the whole of this terrible conflict, I feel pleased to bear testimony, with few exceptions, to the gallantry of the whole brigade. They fought desperately: their conduct was never surpassed. Fragments of regiments, as they were, they moved boldly upon and drove before them the crowded lines of the enemy up to their cannons' mouths, and, with a heroism unsurpassed, fired upon their gunners, desperately struggling before yielding, which they had never been forced to do before."

Lieutenant-Colonel S. Z. Ruff, commanding the Eighteenth Georgia, says in his official report: "The next morning, 17th instant, just after daylight, the brigade was drawn up in line of battle, and ordered to lie down under cover of the hill from a terrible storm of shell that the enemy's batteries were at that time pouring into the woods. A heavy firing of musketry had been going on in our front for some time. About 7 A. M. the brigade was ordered to move forward in the direction of the firing. Advancing about a quarter of a mile through the timber, we came upon the enemy posted in front of a piece of corn, and immediately opened fire upon them. After one or two rounds they gave way, and fell back to a considerable distance in the corn. Advancing, with the left of the regiment resting on the right of the Legion, which had its left upon the turnpike, we drove the enemy in fine style out of the corn and back upon their supports. At the far edge of the corn, the ranks of the retreating line of the enemy unmasked a battery, which poured a round or two of grape into our ranks with terrible effect; but it was soon silenced by our riflemen, and the gunners ran away. At this moment we discovered a fresh line of the enemy advancing on our left flank in an oblique direction, threatening to cut us off, and our ranks being reduced to less than one-third their original strength, we found it necessary to fall back. At the edge of the woods we met supports and rallied on them a part of our men; but the regiment was too much cut up for further action, and in a short time, in connection with the whole brigade, was taken from the field.

"We carried 176 men into the action, and lost 101 in killed, wounded and missing; most of the missing are either killed or wounded."

Lieutenant-Colonel M. W. Gary, of Hampton's Legion, says: "The battle opened about day-break along the whole line. The Legion was placed to the left of the brigade, the Eighteenth Georgia being to its right. We began to advance from under cover of woods in rear of a church, and engaged the enemy as soon as we emerged from them, the enemy being in line of battle near the edge of the cornfield immediately in our front. We advanced steadily upon them, under a heavy fire, and had not gone far when Herod Wilson, of Company F, the bearer of the colors, was shot down. They were raised by James Estes, of Company E, and he was shot down. They were then taken up by C. P. Poppenheim, of Company A, and he, too, was shot down. Major J. H. Dingle, Jr., then caught them and began to advance with them, exclaiming, ' Legion, follow your colors!' The words had an inspiring effect, and the men rallied bravely under their flag, fighting desperately at every step. He bore the colors to the edge of the corn near the turnpike road, on our left, and, while bravely upholding them within 50 yards of the enemy and three Federal flags, was shot dead. I immediately raised the colors and again unfurled them amid the enemy's deadly fire, when Marion Walton, of Company B, volunteered to bear them. I resigned them into his hands, and he carried them gallantly and safely through the battle. Soon after the death of Major Dingle, I discovered that the men to our right were falling back from being flanked on the right. I went to the fence of the turnpike road, and discovered, about 200 yards distant, a brigade of the enemy in line of battle, covering our entire left flank. I immediately ordered the men to fall back under the crest of the hill. I then rallied them and reformed them, and remained with the brigade the remainder of the day. . . . Strength of battalion in action, officers and men, 77. Killed, 3 officers and 3 privates; wounded, 3 officers and 46 privates."

Lieutenant-Colonel B. F. Carter, commanding the Fourth Texas, says in his official report of the battle of the 17th:

"Soon after daylight the brigade formed line of battle in regular order, the Fifth Texas being on my right and First Texas on my left, and about 7 A. M. were ordered to advance. I received no order as to which was the directing battalion, but, advancing diagonally to the right through the woods, we entered the open field on the right of the turnpike road. Here the fire upon us became severe, and, owing to our troops being in front of us, and the dense smoke pervading, we were unable to return the fire or see the enemy clearly. Still advancing, I came directly behind the Eleventh Mississippi, when I received the order from Captain Sellers for the Texas Brigade to halt. Halting, I ordered the men to lie down. At the same moment, the Eleventh Mississippi was ordered to advance, and a portion of two companies on my right, mistaking the order, advanced with them. After a moment I received an order from General Hood to move to the left until the left of my regiment rested on the crest, in advance, next to the turn-pike road. Moving left-oblique in double-quick, I occupied the position indicated, and was then ordered by General Hood to move directly up the hill on the left of the troops then advancing.

"The enemy then occupied the hill in strong force, which receded before our steady advance. Arriving on the top of the hill, at the intersection of the corn-field with the turnpike, I found the enemy not only in heavy force in the corn-field in front, but occupying a ravine in the field on the left of the turnpike, from which position they poured a destructive fire upon us. I discovered at once that the position was untenable, but if I fell back the troops on my right who had entered the corn-field would be surrounded; so, wheeling my regiment to the left, I posted the men along the fence on either side of the turn-pike, and replied as best we could to the tremendous fire of the enemy. We held this position for some time, until the troops in the corn-field on my right were falling back, when I ordered the regiment to move along the line of fence by the left flank. This movement, however, exposed us so much that we fell back directly under the hill. Here I ordered the regiment to halt and form, but at the same moment received an order from General Hood to move by the left flank into the woods. Forming here, I advanced on the left of the turnpike up to the fence at the edge of the field, and rested in this position until I was ordered by Colonel Wofford to fall back to the point we started from in the morning, where the remnant of the brigade was formed. . . .

"I cannot speak in too high terms of the conduct of both officers and men of my command. Exposed to a tremendous fire from superior numbers, in a position which it was apparent to all we could not hold, they fought on without flinching until the order to fall back was given. These men, too, were half-clad, many of them barefooted, and had been only half-fed for days before. The courage, constancy and patience of our men is beyond all praise."

In the omitted part of his report, Colonel Carter, among other things, states that he carried into action about 200 men. The list of casualties that he appended is not published, but elsewhere it appears that the Fourth Texas lost 10 killed and 97 wounded.

Gallant Captain Ike. N. M. Turner commanded the Fifth Texas during the engagements of the 16th and 17th at Sharpsburg, and is as laconic in his report as he was brave in action. He says: " About 8 o'clock at night (on the 16th) we were relieved, and retired to the woods in rear of the church. Slept until about day, when firing commenced in front. We were called to attention; thrown around the hill in line of battle to protect us from grape and shell. We had not occupied this position more than half an hour before we were ordered out as support for the Third Brigade. We caught up with said brigade where our first line had been fighting. Here the Fifth was ordered to halt, by Major (Captain) Sellers, and allow the regiments on the right of the Third to advance. While lying here, General Hood rode up, ordering me to incline to the right, press forward, and drive the enemy out of the woods, which we did. The enemy twice tried to regain their position in the woods by advancing a force through the lower edge of the corn-field, which we repulsed. From a point of timber about 400 yards to our front and left, I discovered strong reinforcements marching out by the left flank down a hollow, which protected them from our fire. Allowing them to get within 75 yards of us with lines unbroken, I saw we would soon be hard pressed. Sent four times to Major (Captain) Sellers for support, determined to hold my position as long as possible. My men were out of ammunition, the enemy not more than 100 yards in my front, no support, no ammunition; all of our troops had fallen back on my left; I deemed it prudent to fall back also.

" Officers and men, with few exceptions, behaved well.

" The casualties of the regiment were 5 killed and 81 wounded."

The brunt of the battle of the 17th on that part of the line occupied by the Texas Brigade, fell upon the First Texas, and its men bore it like the heroes they were. By their bravery on that field of carnage they proved that, given the same opportunity, either one of the Texas regiments could be depended on to do all that mortals may to punish a foe and wrest from him a victory. The Fourth Texas had its day at Gaines' Mill, where it was the first Confederate command to break the enemy's lines; the Fifth Texas secured its opportunity when at Second Manassas, having exterminated the Zouaves, it "slipped the bridle," as General Hood said, and breaking loose from the brigade, went a mile to the front and never ceased fighting as long as its men could see to aim; it was the turn of the First Texas at Sharpsburg, and, when weighed in the balance, it was not found wanting. As expressed in the nomenclature of camp, at Gaines' Mill it was the "Hell-roaring Fourth" that carried off the honors; at Second Manassas it was the "Bloody Fifth," and at Sharpsburg it was the "Ragged First."

Lieutenant-Colonel P. A. Work commanded the First Texas at Sharpsburg. That part of his official report in which he relates the movements of the regiment is as follows:

"The brigade, having been formed in order of battle upon the ground occupied by it on the night of the 16th, in the following order, to wit, First Texas in the center, Eighteenth Georgia left center, Fourth Texas right center, Fifth Texas on the right flank, and Hampton's Legion on the left flank, was moved forward to engage the enemy about — o'clock, the latter having made an attack upon our forces occupying a position in front of this brigade. Advancing through the woods some 200 yards, under a heavy fire of grape, canister and shell from the enemy's artillery, the brigade emerged into an open clover field some 200 to 250 yards in width, across which the forward movement was continued for some 150 to 200 yards, when, it being discovered that the left flank of the brigade was exposed to attack, I was ordered to move by the left flank, following a corresponding move of the Eighteenth Georgia and Hampton's Legion upon my left, which I did until ordered to move by the right flank, which was also done.

Advancing now by the right flank (my original front), I entered a cornfield and soon became engaged with a force of the enemy, driving them before me to the farther side of the cornfield. As soon as the regiment became engaged with the enemy in the cornfield, it became impossible to restrain the men, and they rushed forward, pressing the enemy close until we had advanced a considerable distance ahead of both the right and left wings of the brigade. Discovering that this would probably be the case when my men first dashed forward, I dispatched you two different messengers, to wit—Capt. John R. Woodward, Company G, and Private A. G. Hanks, Company F—stating that I was driving the enemy and requesting you to hurry up the regiments on my right and left to my support. It was not until we reached the farther side of the cornfield that I could check the regiment. By this time we had broken the first line of battle of the enemy and had advanced to within some thirty steps of his second line, secreted behind a breastwork of fence rails thrown up in heaps upon the ground, when a battery of artillery some 150 or 200 yards in our front was opened upon us. My men continued firing, a portion of them at the enemy's men and others at the artillerists, the result of which was that the enemy's second line broke and fled, and the artillery was limbered up and started to the rear, when the whole fire of my regiment was concentrated upon the artillerists and horses, knocking over men and horses with such effect that the artillery was abandoned. Very soon, however, a force of the enemy was moved up to the support of this artillery, when it again opened fire upon us.

"Just at the farther side of the cornfield was the point where I was in great doubt as to the proper move to be made by me. I was aware that my regiment had advanced 150 or 200 yards farther than the regiment upon my left, so diverging as to leave a wide interval between the right flank of the Eighteenth Georgia and my left, thus exposing both regiments to attack—the Eighteenth upon the right and the First Texas upon the left flank. I was aware at the same time that a heavy force of the enemy was massed upon my left, and felt confident that in case I moved farther to the front I would be attacked upon my left and rear and annihilated. Had I moved forward to carry the enemy's battery I would have exposed the regiment to attack from three different directions, to wit, from the front from infantry and artillery and upon the left and rear from infantry. I am told also by some of the men that had I advanced a little farther to the front my right flank would have become exposed to attack, and am assured that some distance to my front, and obliquely to my right, was a large force of the enemy. This I did not discover myself. At this juncture I dispatched Acting Adjutant W. Shropshire to say to you that unless the regiments upon my left were moved up quickly to my relief and support upon my left, I would be forced to abandon my position and withdraw. Before the return of Shropshire a fire of musketry was opened upon me from my left and rear, which determined me at once to withdraw, as I had but a handful of men left, all of which must have been slain or captured had I remained longer. I at once gave the order to fall back and the few men remaining to me retired, turning to fire upon the enemy as rapidly as their pieces could be loaded and fired.

"I entered the engagement with 226 men, officers (field and staff) included, of which number 170 are known to have been killed and wounded, besides twelve others who are missing, and, doubtless, also killed or wounded.

"During the engagement I saw four bearers of our State colors shot down, to wit: First, John Hanson, Company L; second, James Day, Company M; third, Charles H. Kingsley, Company L, and fourth, James K. Malone, Company A. After the fall of these, still others raised the colors until four more bearers were shot down. Not having seen plainly who these were, I am unable to give their names in this report, but will do so as soon as, upon inquiry, I can ascertain.

"It is a source of mortification to state that upon retiring from the engagement our colors were not brought off. I can but feel that some degree of odium must attach under the most favorable circumstances, and although such are the circumstances surrounding the conduct of this regiment, the loss of our flag will always remain a matter of sore and deep regret. In this connection it is but proper to state, in addition to that detailed in the above and foregoing report, the additional circumstances and causes which led to its loss. When the order to retire was given, the colors began the movement to the rear, when the color-bearer, after roving but a few paces, was shot down. Upon their fall some half dozen hastened to raise them, one of whom did raise them and move off, when he was shot down, which was not discovered by those surviving. While falling back, and when we had nearly reached the cloverfield hereinbefore alluded to (being still in the cornfield), I gave the order to halt, and inquired for the colors, intending to dress upon them, when I was told that the colors had gone out of the cornfield. Then I gave the order to move on out of the corn and form behind the crest of a small ridge just outside of the corn and in the cloverfield. It was when I reached this point that I became satisfied our colors were lost, for I looked in every direction and they were nowhere to be seen. It was then too late to recover them. There was no one who knew the spot where they had last fallen, and, owing to the density of the corn, a view of no object could be had but for a few feet. By this time, also, the enemy had moved up and was within some thirty-five or forty yards of my left (proper) and rear, and another force was following us. No blame, I feel, should attach to the men or officers, all of whom fought heroically and well. There was no such conduct upon their part as abandoning or deserting the colors. They fought bravely, and unflinchingly faced a terrible hail of bullets and artillery until ordered by me to retire. The colors started back with them and when they were lost no man knew save him who had fallen with them. It is perhaps due to myself to state that when I determined to retire I requested Captain (U. S.) Connally to give the order upon the right and stepped to the left to direct Captain Woodward to give the order upon the left, from which point I moved on to the extreme left, to discover, if possible, the locality of the enemy attacking from that quarter, in order to be prepared to govern the movements of my regiment, so as to protect it as far as possible from danger and damage. While I was at the left thus engaged, the regiment commenced the movement to the rear, and, not being near the center, I was unable, owing to the density of the corn, to see where the colors were and when they fell.

"Capt. John R. Woodward of Company G acted in the capacity of major during the engagement, and aided me greatly in directing the movements of the regiment. Major (Matt)

Dale, acting as lieutenant-colonel, had moved from the right and was conferring with me as to the propriety of advancing or at once withdrawing, when he was killed. Feeling that it was madness to advance with the few men left, I remained for several minutes after the fall of Major Dale, awaiting orders and information as to what my movements should be, being unwilling to withdraw as long as I had the ability to hold my then position without orders to do so."

Colonel Work submitted with his report a list of the casualties in the First Texas, but it is not published. It is known, however, that the First Texas carried into action on the morning of the 17th, 226 men, officers and privates, and in the tabular statement of killed and wounded made by Surgeon Lafayette Guild, Medical Director of the Army of Northern Virginia, its losses are given as 45 killed and 141 wounded.

As evidence that the flag of the First Texas was not captured, but was simply found lying on the ground and picked up by a Federal soldier, the following excerpt from a letter, dated December 17, 1908, and written by former Lieutenant W. E. Barry, of Company G, Fourth Texas, to George A. Branard, of Company L, First Texas, will be conclusive. At Eltham's Landing Branard, a member of the color-guard of his regiment, in the absence of the regular color-bearer, bore the flag so daringly and gallantly as to deserve and receive an appointment as color-bearer. Early in the action at Sharpsburg he was disabled, and handed the flag to one of his guard. Since the date of the letter he has passed over into the Great Beyond. Lieutenant Barry says:

I was captured that morning of September 17th, 1862, in a lane that ran in front of the cornfield in which your regiment fought so long and desperately, and was delivered by my immediate captors to some cavalry under command of a major. While standing by the side of a public road, I saw approaching from the Federal front a party of infantry soldiers, one of whom was waving a flag that I immediately identified as that of the First Texas. When the party came up, the major asked what flag it was and where it had been captured. The reply of the man who held it was: "I did not capture it, Major—I found it in the cornfield." The major then asked me if I knew the flag. "Yes," said I as the soldier handed it to me, "I know it well; it is the flag of the First Texas regiment." And kissing it reverently I returned it to the soldier and asked him where he got it. He repeated his statement that he had found it in the cornfield, and then told me that thirteen men lay dead within touch of it, and that the body of one of the dead lay stretched across it. From the description he gave of that body, and from subsequent information, I have not a doubt that it was the corpse of Lieutenant R. H. Gaston, a brother of Captain W. H. Gaston, of the First Texas.

Writing of the battle of Sharpsburg, and of his observations and experiences as a member of the Fourth Texas, Comrade W. R. Hamby says:

"The Librarian of Congress in a recent letter to the Texas State Librarian, asking for information touching Hood's Texas Brigade, says: 'The known statistics of these regiments are so remarkable that if missing figures can be obtained it will establish a record equaled by few, if any, organizations in the Civil War, or indeed in modern warfare.'

"When a soldier has been wounded, he has the scar to show for his wound. When a regiment or brigade claims to have suffered heavily in battle, you ask for the list of killed and wounded. Judged by this standard, no brigade in the Confederate Army has more bloody laurels or stands higher on the roll of honor than Hood's Texas Brigade. This article, however, will only attempt to describe the action of the brigade in the battle fought near Sharpsburg, Md., September 17, 1862.

"After the battle of South Mountain, September 14, we were the rear guard of the army on the march to Sharpsburg. On the morning of September 15, with a detail of one hundred men under Major Sellers, I was with the rear guard of the rear guard; and after the army crossed the Antietam, we were on the skirmish line along the west bank of that stream, until the 16th. In the meantime the brigade had formed a line of battle along the Hagerstown and Sharpsburg Turnpike, near the Dunkard church. This modest and hitherto unknown church was destined soon to become historical, as it was the storm center of the great battle fought September 17, 1862, called Sharpsburg by the Confederates, and Antietam by the Federals. The church was about a mile north of the town of Sharpsburg and about a mile west of the Antietam River. From the church north, along the west side of the pike, the woods extended about a quarter of a mile to an open field, extending still farther north several hundred yards. Across the pike east of the church were open fields, somewhat rocky and hilly, extending about half a mile north, and intersecting with a cornfield. East of the fields were woods extending toward the river.

"About sunset, the evening of the 16th, the Federal skirmish line was seen advancing through the woods east of us, closely followed by lines of battle in echelon with banners waving, drums beating, and bugles blowing. It was a magnificent spectacle, and looked more like they were on a grand review than going to battle. Our thin single line presented a striking contrast. Since leaving Richmond, about one month previous, we had marched over two hundred miles, and had participated in engagements at Freeman's Ford, Thoroughfare Gap, Second Manassas, and South Mountain, and had lost six hundred and thirty-eight men, killed and wounded. For the past several days, we had subsisted chiefly on apples and green corn. Many of us were barefooted and ragged, and all of us were foot-sore, weary, and hungry, but full of patriotic ardor and inspired faith in the justice of our cause.

"The fight was opened by the artillery on our right, between us and Law's Brigade, which was composed of the 4th Alabama, 6th North Carolina, 2d Mississippi, and 11th Mississippi. They were as gallant soldiers, either collectively or individually, as ever fought a battle. Among the first to enter the field, they were on the firing line when the last shot was fired. Both brigades advanced across the field with our skirmish line in front, which fell in with the main line as we entered the woods. The action continued for some time after dark; and when firing ceased, the two lines were so close together that they could hear each other speak. We knew this was only a preliminary skirmish, as we could tell from the sounds in front of us that the Federals were massing their troops for a desperate battle the following day. In this position we remained until far into the night, when we were re-

GENERAL WILLIAM R. HAMBY
Company B, Fourth Texas Regiment

lieved by General Lawton's division, and marched a short distance to the rear. After a long delay, some flour was issued to us, which was the first ration of any kind we had received since leaving Hagerstown; but before the flour could be cooked and eaten, the battle of Sharpsburg had begun.

"It was scarcely daylight Wednesday morning, September 17, when the Texas Brigade was ordered in line of battle, and by sunrise it had crossed the pike in front of the Dunkard church and entered the meadow to take the place of the troops who had relieved us only a few hours before. The 5th Texas was on the right of the brigade, and as it entered the field was ordered into the woods east of the cornfield, where the fighting had occurred the previous evening. The 4th Texas, 1st Texas, 18th Georgia, and Hampton's Legion entered the meadow in the order named, and at once encountered a heavy fire. The troops in front had lost half their numbers, had exhausted their ammunition, and were retiring, and the smoke was so dense that the enemy could scarcely be seen to return his fire. The 4th Texas was ordered by the left flank, to the left of the brigade, up the side of a hill towards the pike. In this formation, the 4th Texas, Hampton's Legion, 18th Georgia, and 1st Texas advanced and drove the Union lines out of the open fields, back upon their reserves across the pike on the west and beyond the cornfield on the north.

"The enemy's reinforcements appearing in strong numbers on the left, the 4th Texas changed from front to left flank and took position along the pike near the south edge of the cornfield. A short distance to the rear were some stone bowlders, behind which some of our wounded were placed to protect them as far as possible from further injury; but even then several were struck the second and some the third time. Hampton's Legion and the 18th Georgia were farther into the cornfield, facing a galling fire from infantry and artillery with a steadiness unsurpassed. The 1st Texas had advanced some distance beyond the remainder of the brigade toward the north side of the cornfield, breaking two lines of the enemy and forcing them to abandon a battery and take shelter in the ravine north of the field. Three times the enemy tried to check the 5th Texas in the woods east of the cornfield, and each time broke and fled before their intrepid advance.

"The Texas Brigade was now only a skirmish line; in fact, all of the Confederates on this portion of the field scarcely covered a fourth of the Federal front. It was yet early in the morning, although the battle had been hot and furious for some hours. In addition to the infantry and artillery on front and flanks, the heights above the Antietam were crowned with long-range batteries that poured a merciless fire; while the fresh troops of the Union forces seemed inexhaustible as they were thrown upon the fragments of the Confederate lines. The earth and sky seemed to be on fire, and it looked like here would be the Thermopylæ of the Texas Brigade. With sublime courage the 1st Texas held their advanced position in the cornfield against overwhelming numbers, and retired only to escape annihilation. Unsupported and with both flanks uncovered, the 4th Texas, Hampton's Legion and the 18th Georgia met the advancing enemy from across the pike and drove them back and held their line. Many of the men had exhausted their ammunition and supplied themselves from the cartridge boxes of the dead and wounded around them. They were holding a position they knew they could not retain; yet men never fought better, and they withdrew only to keep from being surrounded. Falling back slowly below the crest of the hill, the line moved through the field, crossed the pike and took position in the woods near the church. The Fourth Texas was then ordered up through the woods west of the pike near the edge of the field on the north, where they remained about an hour, defiantly waving their flag over empty muskets, when they were ordered to rejoin the other regiments of the brigade. The Fifth Texas, finding their ammunition exhausted and that they were being flanked, retired and also rejoined the brigade. By this time the morning was far gone, and the Federals had advanced down both sides of the pike within a short distance of the line held by the remnants of Hood's division, who stood facing them almost exhausted and practically without ammunition.

"At last the long-looked-for reinforcements arrived, and again the enemy were driven back upon their reserves. The Texas Brigade was then ordered a short distance to the rear for a fresh supply of ammunition, and again returned to the front about noon and found the woods near the church lately

LIEUTENANT B. ELDRIDGE
Company E, Fifth Texas Regiment

occupied by them, in possession of the enemy; but as our line advanced, the Federals fell back across the pike into the field, about three hundred yards beyond the church. We steadily held our line near the pike until about sunset, when we were moved a short distance to the right, where we remained in line of battle until the night of the 18th, when the entire army withdrew and re-crossed the Potomac into Virginia.

"If the reinforcements had reached the firing line before the Texas Brigade and Law's Brigade were forced to abandon their advanced positions, the Federals would have been swept from the field and another triumph would have been added to the list of Confederate victories. Our dead lay in rows upon the ground, where they had fought a fruitless fight; and instead of a Confederate victory, it was an indecisive contest, giving hope and courage to the Federals and depressing in its effect upon the Confederates.

"The battle of Sharpsburg was fought with desperate courage by both the gray and the blue, and the 17th of September, 1863, stands out conspicuously as the bloodiest day in American history . . . More men were killed and wounded that day than on any other one day during the war between the States, and I doubt if the dead and wounded ever lay thicker upon any field than was seen from the old Dunkard church north, for more than half a mile. The action commenced about daybreak, and by sunset the bloody work had ended.

"The First Texas went into battle with 226 men, and lost, in killed and wounded, 186, a loss of eighty-two per cent. As one flag-bearer would fall, another would seize the flag, until nine men had fallen beneath their colors. Official records show that the First Texas lost more men, killed and wounded, in the battle of Sharpsburg, in proportion to numbers engaged, than any other regiment engaged, either Federal or Confederate, in any other battle of the war. The Fourth Texas went into the fight with 200 men, and lost 107; the Fifth Texas went into the fight with 175 men, and lost 86; the Eighteenth Georgia went into the fight with 176 men, and lost 85; Hampton's Legion went into the fight with 77 men, and lost 55, including four flag-bearers. In the aggregate the Texas Brigade went into the fight with 854, rank and file, and lost 519, killed and wounded, including sixteen flag-bearers, a loss of over sixty per cent. This does not include the 'missing,' many of whom were, no doubt, killed or wounded."

Both armies were completely exhausted by the fighting and constant moving to and fro on the 17th, and each welcomed the night that came to call a halt on the terrible slaughter. While his army rested, Lee summoned his corps and division commanders to meet him. General Stephen D. Lee, who was present, says: "As each commander came up, General Lee inquired quietly, 'General, how is it on your part of the line?' To this inquiry, Longstreet, apparently much depressed, replied to the effect that it was as bad as could be—that his division had lost terribly, his lines had been barely held, and there was little better than a good skirmish line along his front, and he volunteered the advice that General Lee should cross the Potomac before daylight. D. H. Hill came next. He said that his division was cut to pieces, that his losses had been terrible, and that he had no troops to hold his line against the great odds against him. He, too, suggested crossing the Potomac before daylight. Next came Jackson. He quietly said that he had to contend against the greatest odds he had ever met. He had lost many generals killed and several division and brigade commanders were wounded, and his losses in the different commands had been great. He, too, suggested crossing the Potomac before daylight. Next came Hood. He displayed great emotion, seemed completely unmanned, and replied that he had no division. General Lee, with more excitement than I ever witnessed him exhibit, exclaimed, 'Great God, General Hood, where is the splendid division you had this morning?' Hood replied, 'They are lying on the field where you sent them, sir; but few have straggled. My division has been almost wiped out.'

"After the opinion of all had been given, there was an appalling stillness over the group. It seemed to last several minutes, when General Lee, apparently rising more erect in his saddle, said: 'Gentlemen, we will not cross the Potomac to-night. You will go to your respective commands, strengthen your lines, send two officers from each brigade toward the ford to collect your stragglers, and get them up. Many others have already come up. I have had the proper steps taken to collect all the men who are in the rear. If McClellan wants to fight in the morning, I will give him battle again!'"

McClellan, though, did not want to fight next morning. All day long of the 18th, Lee's army awaited assault—inviting it, challenging it, tempting it—but none was made. Then apprised of large reinforcements to his antagonist, and knowing he could hope for none, Lee, during the night, placed his army on Virginia soil.

On the 21st, General Lee wrote to Senator Wigfall, of Texas, a letter that furnishes evidence of his high estimate of the services of the Texas Brigade. In it, he said:

"I have not heard from you in regard to the new Texas regiments which you promised to raise for the army. I need them very much. I rely upon those we have in all our tight places, and fear that I have to call upon them too often. They have fought grandly and nobly, and we must have more of them. Please make every possible exertion to get them on for me. You must help us in this matter. With a few more regiments such as Hood now has, as an example of daring and bravery, I could feel more confident of the campaign."

CHAPTER VIII

FREDERICKSBURG AND SUFFOLK

OCTOBER 1st found the Texas Brigade, its numbers reduced below that of an average sized regiment, encamped around a bold and very large spring of clear, cold water, three miles north of Winchester. Within the next two months a reorganization of the army was effected, and there was much shifting about of commands. General Hood was promoted to a major-generalcy, and given command of a division composed of Law's and the Texas Brigades, and Anderson's and Benning's Georgia Brigades. Colonel Jerome B. Robertson, of the Fifth Texas, was made brigadier-general and assigned to command of the Texas Brigade, and the Eighteenth Georgia and Hampton's Legion were transferred to other brigades, the Texas Brigade securing in their stead the Third Arkansas. This regiment consisted of nine companies of Arkansans and one of Kentuckians that, like those of the First Texas, had straggled to Virginia. Meeting at Lynchburg, Va., in July, 1861, these ten companies had organized into a regiment, with Albert Rust as colonel, ———— Barton as lieutenant-colonel, and Van H. Manning as major, and began their active service in West Virginia, and placed then under command of Jackson, became veteran soldiers.

Colonel Law was also made brigadier-general, and assigned to the command of the brigade heretofore mentioned as Whiting's or Law's and sometimes as the Third Brigade. That brigade lost in the all-round shuffle of regiments, the Second and Eleventh Mississippi, getting in their places the Forty-fourth Alabama and the Fifty-fourth North Carolina. Subsequently, it lost the Sixth and Fifty-fourth North Carolina and secured in their places the Fifteenth and Forty-seventh Alabama Regiments.

A law having been enacted by the Confederate Congress creating that rank, Longstreet and Jackson were made lieutenant-generals and assigned to duty under General Lee, who divided his army into two corps—the First, under Longstreet, embracing the divisions of McLaws', R. H. Anderson, Pickett, Ransom and Hood, and the First Corps of Artillery—this artillery consisting of the Washington (Louisiana) Artillery, under Colonel J. B. Walton, and Alexander's Battalion, under Lieutenant-Colonel E. P. Alexander. The Second Corps, under Jackson, was composed of the divisions of D. H. Hill, A. P. Hill, Ewell, Jackson's old division, and numerous batteries of light artillery. The Reserve Artillery was placed under command of Brigadier-General W. N. Pentleton, and the cavalry, under that of Major-General J. E. B. Stuart.

The stay of the Texas Brigade in camp near Winchester was long and restful. Barring the guard and fatigue duty necessary to preserve order and keep the camp cleanly, and occasional short drills, the men had little to do. Access to the most fertile and productive section of Virginia, and uninterrupted communication with Richmond by two routes, enabled the quartermaster and commissary departments to supply large quantities of needed clothing and shoes, and ample, if not abundant, rations. Here, too, came to the army the mails withheld from it since its departure from Richmond.

October 26th, Longstreet's Corps broke camp, and falling into line, marched to the southeast, keeping within striking distance of the Federal army, which about this time came south of the Potomac and moved out toward Richmond. Our movement was unhurried, and although we had the Blue Ridge to ascend and descend, was not fatiguing; the roads were in excellent condition; water, that great need of marching infantry, plentiful, cold and clear; the weather propitious, and the air cool and bracing. Our destination was Culpeper Court House, and Jackson, with his corps, being assigned the duty of guarding the passes of the Blue Ridge, we marched slowly on—Hood's division by way of Manassas Gap, where Benning's Brigade had a brisk skirmish with a large body of Federal cavalry. On the 7th of November Longstreet's Corps was in position behind Robertson River, near Culpeper Court House.

McClellan remained in command of the Federal army but a few days after it came south of the Potomac, General Burnside being assigned to the command on November 5, and relieving McClellan on the 9th. Burnside was far more successful in fixing a fashion in which to wear whiskers than in conducting the operations of a large army. He planned a demonstration with a large force in the direction of Gordonville, calculating that while General Lee guarded against that, the Federal army could reach Fredericksburg in advance of the Confederates, and place itself between the latter army and Richmond. But, though left in doubt for a day or two, Lee penetrated the designs of the Federal commander, with the result that when Burnside's advance reached Fredericksburg, it found the south side of the Rappahannock well-protected. Moving on down from the upper Rappahannock, Burnside soon had his army in line on Stafford Heights, the line of hills at the south foot of which the river runs. Thither marched also Lee's army—Longstreet's Corps taking position along the range of hills on the south side of the stream, its left extending around the city and for a mile or two above it, its right, to within a mile of Hamilton's crossing, a little railroad station five miles below Fredericksburg—Jackson's corps on the right of Longstreet's.

Hood's division held the right of Longstreet's corps—the Texas Brigade, the center of the division, being stretched out in line in the open valley. The main fighting was done by McLaws' division at Marye's Hill, and by Jackson's troops in the vicinity of Hamilton's crossing, and between that and the river. As save through its scouts and skirmishers, the Texas Brigade took no active part in the battle, a description of the engagement will be left to the general historian. The enemy commenced crossing to the south side of the Rappahannock, at daylight of the 11th. It took him all that day and the next to get his army across and in line, and the battle, therefore, did not begin until the morning of the 13th. During the 11th and 12th, however, the 350 pieces of artillery, many of them guns of long range, that General Burnside had stationed on Stafford Heights in positions commanding every part of the wide valley south of the Rappahannock, kept the air hot with flying projectiles, and there was hardly a minute of either day but was marked by the roar of a cannon, the bursting of a shell, or the passage of round shot. Out of range of the cannon, as a rule, the men of the Texas Brigade stood passive but deeply interested spectators of events as they occurred on their right and left. At one trivial incident which transpired, they were stirred to mirth that was long and loud.

The Forty-fourth Alabama and the Fifty-fourth North Carolina regiments of Law's Brigade were made up, as a rule, of conscripts—young men under twenty, and old men—dressed in homespun, and presenting a very unsoldierly appearance. But there were no cowards among them. Ordered to drive back a force of the enemy which was coming too near our lines for safety, they not only sprang forward in a charge of surprising recklessness, but continued the charge until, to save them from certain capture, General Hood peremptorily recalled them. As they passed the Texas Brigade on their return, one old fellow halted, wiped the powder-grime from his weather-beaten and time-furrowed face with the sleeve of his coat, and wrathfully exclaimed: "Durn ole Hood, anyhow! He jess didn't have no bus'ness 't all ter stop us when we'uns was uh whippin' them ar durn blue-bellies ter h—ll an' back, an' eff we'uns hadder bin you Texikins, he'd never o' did it."

How the battle of Fredericksburg would end was a foregone conclusion. Lee and his 80,000 men held a position as impregnable to any assault that could be made on it by Burnside's 116,000, as were Stafford Heights to the 80,000. Repulsed with great slaughter at every point of the line they attacked, the Federals abandoned the contest and recrossed the Rappahannock. Then, having within six months driven McClellan from before Richmond, defeated Pope at Second Manassas, won all the honors from McClellan, when again his antagonist at Sharpsburg, and forced General Burnside to a halt, General Lee ordered his army into winter quarters. These to be constructed by the army, the Texas Brigade was assigned heavily timbered ground. But it was so late in the season, and there was such likelihood, the men thought, of an early spring campaign, that they were content to erect only temporary structures. Accustomed and inured by this time to many discomforts, they deemed it a waste of labor and time to build cabins they might have to vacate in a month or two.

But as in that month or two they would feel the need of

amusement, they contributed liberally in labor and funds toward the erection of a single story, log theater, in which they might listen to concerts and see plays given and performed by the members of Collins' Band, assisted by such other talent as was to be found in the army. The weather was cold and dry, although snow lay on the ground for days at a time; fuel was abundant, guard and fatigue duty light, and drilling not required, and with little else for the men to do, the theater had a large patronage—General Hood being a frequent attendant, and even General Lee being, on one occasion, an auditor. The favorite amusement in the day-time, when snow lay on the ground, was snowballing. This began with battles between individuals, but soon extended to companies, regiments and brigades. On one occasion, there was a battle royal between brigades of Hood's division in which generals, colonels and many other subordinate officers participated—the alignments and movements of the opposing brigades being conducted in regular military style, with regiments carrying their flags, and drums and fifes in full blast. Indeed, such a racket was made that day by the Confederate army—for the sport was not confined to one division alone—that the Federals on the other side of the Rappahannock took alarm, and at least one of their cavalry regiments saddled its horses in readiness to meet an expected attack.

The Texas Brigade was not mistaken in believing that its stay in winter quarters would be short. About the middle of February, 1863, there were indications of a move upon Richmond, or Petersburg, from the direction of Suffolk. President Davis and the members of the Confederate Congress, which was then in session, became quite uneasy, and to allay their apprehensions, General Lee ordered Pickett's and Hood's divisions to the neighborhood of the capital city. The two commands marched on the 15th—Pickett's division halting on the Chickahominy, but Hood's passing through Richmond and camping between that city and Petersburg—the Texas Brigade, on Falling Creek, four miles south of Richmond.

The change was a welcome one. It brought us within easy access of the "Texas depot," a warehouse in the city rented by the officers of the brigade, in which was stored for safe-keeping all such private property of members of the command as could not be carried on the march. In addition, Hood being exceedingly liberal in granting passes, it enabled the men to make frequent visits to the city and indulge in the many recreations it afforded. Its nearness to the main depot of supplies for the army had its advantages. Hood a favorite with both civil and military authorities, his requisitions on the quartermaster department were honored to such an extent that the ragged were clothed and the bare-footed shod. Hats, however, were not to be had until some inventive genius —a member of the First Texas, it was said—hit upon a novel scheme of securing them from the passengers on trains that passed through the brigade camp.

A high bridge across the creek insured the slowing up of the train at the point on the track most suitable for the execution of the scheme. A train due, all men in need of hats, and many that did not need them and only went along to assist their friends, would form in line on one side of the track, each with a brush made of the tops of young pines in his hands. As the train came by, a shout would be raised that, sounding high above the roar and rattle of the train, would excite the alarm or curiosity of the passengers who, springing to the windows, would stick their heads out, and as at that moment the brushes were brought into play, off the hats of the poor innocents would tumble. The first losers being plain, unassuming citizens, were laughed at by the authorities as the victims of a practical joke. But when, as soon happened, a brigadier-general, the numerous members of his staff, and half a dozen members of Congress on their return from some junketing trip, lost their cocked and stove-pipe hats at the same place and in the same high-handed way, complaint was made and heeded, and thereafter there were no linings up along the track, and the Texans and Arkansans that were still hatless were compelled to make other calculations.

The rest of the brigade was not disturbed until the 18th of March. Then it was discovered that some movement was in progress or contemplation by General Hooker, who in January had been given command of the Federal army at Fredericksburg, vice General Burnside, removed, to gobble up Mr. Davis, his cabinet and all the members of Congress. The blow was to come from the direction of the Peninsula, and to guard against it, the Texas Brigade was routed out of its camp and marched in haste through Richmond, down the Brook turnpike toward Ashland. When within five miles of Ashland, an order from General Lee recalled it, he having assured himself that no danger threatened the capital of the Confederacy. Night close at hand, and the order of recall not enjoining haste, General Hood ordered the command into camp until morning.

Until nearly sunset, the day had been clear and comfortably warm. At that hour, though, the sky clouded, and a brisk cold wind blew from the north. By midnight, the wind lay and snow commenced falling, and fell so heavily that by daylight the ground was covered with it to the depth of three or four inches, and it was still falling rapidly. General Robertson, who, on account of his democratic ways and a certain fussiness over trifles, was by this time called "Aunt Pollie," lost no time after sunrise in putting the brigade in motion toward Richmond—the objective point of the day's march being the camp we had vacated the day before. Called into line at 8 A. M. the men set forth in the blinding snow-storm, their speed hastened by a natural longing to partake of the viands, liquid and otherwise, so easily to be procured in Richmond since a learned justice of the peace there had decided that the military authorities had fractured the constitutions of both the State of Virginia and the Southern Confederacy when they prohibited the sale of liquor by the drink.

There was much straggling, but strange to say, it was not in the rear but all to the front. When at last fairly in the city, the brigade disintegrated, so to speak, every soldier not a teetotaller making a flank movement to right or left. So sudden, surprising and inexplicable was the depletion of ranks, that when Aunt Pollie looked back through the obscuring mist of yet fast-falling snow down the short and attenuated line of shadowy figures following in his wake, he could give expression to his feelings only by exclaiming, "Where the blankety blank is the Texas Brigade?" He was about to send details in quest of the absconders, but luckily, General Hood was near by and intervened. West Pointer that Hood was, he not only knew Texas and Arkansas tastes and temperaments, but was not unwilling they should be occasionally indulged.

Calling to Aunt Pollie, he said, " Let 'em go, General—let 'em go; they deserve a little indulgence, and you'll get them back in time for the next battle."

About this time, General Longstreet, then at Petersburg and in temporary command of all Confederate forces in southeastern Virginia and northeastern North Carolina, learned that a great deal of bacon and corn was in the hands of citizens living along the coast south of Norfolk. To collect and transport this to points accessible to the Confederate army, he ordered Hood's division to Suffolk, with instructions to hold the Federal forces there closely within their lines and enable wagon trains to haul from the country north of the Chowan River all the bacon and forage to be found. Hood moved his division about the 1st of April, and passing through Petersburg, proceeded to the neighborhood of Suffolk, by way of Jerusalem and the Blackwater River. But the forts and intrenchments of the Federals at Suffolk were so surrounded and protected from land assault, by water, that to accomplish their capture was out of the question. Hence, while the Texas Brigade did a great deal of picketing, skirmishing and scouting, it engaged in no battles, and its losses were slight—the most notable and the most regretted being that of the daring Captain Ike N. M. Turner, of the Fifth Texas.

General Hood halted at the camp of the Fourth Texas one day to speak to Colonel Key about some unimportant matter. Noticing, however, that Bill Calhoun stood near, and knowing something of his unique character, Hood winked at Key, and in a loud tone, said: " Detail an officer and twenty-five of your best men, Colonel, and have them report to me at my headquarters within an hour. I have set my heart on securing possession of one of those gunboats down on the Nansemond River, and I feel sure that many men can easily capture it."

Bill heard the challenge, and without a moment's hesitation accepted it. Stepping forward, and laying a hand on the neck of the horse Hood rode, he touched his hat in salute, and looking straight into Hood's eyes, said:

"Now look here, General Hood, eff you've jest got to have a gunboat, speak up like a man an' say so, an' the Fourth Texas will buy you one. But hit ain't a goin' ter go foolin' roun' any o' them big boats down on the river, fur they say the durn things are loaded. Besides, hit'll take swimmin' ter gat at 'em, an' there's mighty few of us kin do it."

It was in January, 1863, previous to the departure of Hood's division from Fredericksburg, that General Burnside, seeking to restore the prestige he had lost in his blundering essay against Lee in December of 1862, and thus ward off impending dismissal from high command, ordered his army to undertake the famous "Mud march"—his aim, to cross the Rappahannock above Fredericksburg and fall upon Lee's left flank. He had hardly made a start, though, when a tremendous storm of wind, rain and snow began, and compelled the abandonment of the project. The only opposition to the movement offered was by the Confederate cavalry, the infantry of Lee's army making no move whatever. One of the grimmest jokes ever perpetrated on the commander of an army, was that of the Southern troopers who placed on trees near the roads on which the Federals were advancing, large and plainly lettered signs bearing the legend, "This is the way to Richmond."

Following immediately on this grand faux pas, came an order relieving Burnside from command, and appointing "Fighting Joe" Hooker as his successor. General Hooker had his hands full at once. The Federal army had deeply resented the removal of McClellan from its command after the battles around Richmond. It had no time to voice its protest until he was restored to command, just before the battle of Sharpsburg. As it was thought he would be allowed to continue in command, the disaffection ceased. When, however, he was again removed, and Burnside appointed to succeed him, the disaffection revived, and growing greater as events proved the incapacity of the new commander, reached its height when he was removed and Hooker appointed. Another cause for disaffection was the Emancipation Proclamation issued by President Lincoln when assured by his advisers that the battle of Sharpsburg, or Antietam, as they called it, was a decisive victory for the Union arms. Many of the officers in high command, and especially those who had served in the regular army, were far from hostile to slavery. A large

LIEUTENANT W. W. HENDERSON
Company B, Fifth Texas Regiment

proportion of the private soldiers, especially in regiments raised in the large cities of the North, looked with bitter aversion upon the negro.

For quite a while after General Hooker took command, his army appeared to be undergoing a process of disintegration. Not only were there as many as 200 desertions a day, but the soldiers at the front were encouraged and advised to desert by their friends and relatives at home, and every aid given them. Practically the entire army yet resented the removal of McClellan, and the appointments first of Burnside and then of Hooker, and believed that the Federal government would be forced to restore McClellan to command and abandon its policy of emancipation. What with deserters and those absent by leave, 85,000 men, of whom 4000 were commissioned officers, left the army and scattered all over the North.

But the disaffection in the Union army neither became revolt nor lasted long. By the middle of April most of its men and officers had returned to it, and it had been reorganized and in various ways improved. When its numbers approached 100,000, General Hooker commenced looking for a route by which he could fall upon Lee's army, and defeating it, march his army on to Richmond. Hitting upon that least expected by his wary opponent, he set his army in motion. Instead of seeking to force a passage of the Rappahannock, he marched to fords above the mouth of the Rapidan, and there crossing, threw the bulk of his troops into the Wilderness country and concentrated them at Chancellorsville.

This movement was so well-planned and executed that not until the morning of May 1st did General Lee learn that, practically, the whole of the Federal army had crossed the Rappahannock and was advancing upon him. In fact, Hooker then had fully 70,000 men at Chancellorsville, Lee, a scant 20,000, and General Sedgewick was advancing from Fredericksburg on the right flank of these. But Hooker made a grave blunder. Instead of gaining position, as he might easily have done on his arrival at Chancellorsvile, in the open country a mile and a half southwest of Chancellorsvile, where he could have kept vigilant watch on the movements of the Confederates, he halted his troops so far back in the dense forest as to allow Lee to form his line also in the timber, and thus conceal his small force. Having this advantage, Lee held the overwhelming forces arrayed against him in check until Jackson made a long detour through the thick woods, and late in the afternoon of the 3rd, fell upon the Federal rank flank, and putting it to rout, compelled the retreat of the Federal host to the north side of the Rappahannock.

May 1st, General Lee wrote to Longstreet, directing him to recall Hood's division from Suffolk, and march it and Pickett's division forthwith toward Chancellorsville. The letter did not reach Longstreet until May 2nd. At that date, the wagon trains of Hood's division were far down on Chowan River, thirty miles south of Suffolk, engaged in hauling army supplies from that section. To withdraw from Suffolk before the trains were recalled would have been to subject them to capture. Therefore, the investment of Suffolk was continued until the 3rd of May, when, the wagons being on the east and safe side of Blackwater River, Hood's division withdrew to and crossed that stream, and on the 4th set out on its two days' march to Petersburg. Early on that day, though, it learned that the battle of Chancellorsville had been fought and won, and that General Jackson had been mortally wounded. Its assistance no longer needed, the speed of its march abated. Marching leisurely through Petersburg and Richmond, it moved on to Fredericksburg, and after a fortnight's stay in that neighborhood, to Verdiersville, in the Wilderness, and thence to the Rapidan River, at Raccoon ford.

The date of the departure of the Texas Brigade from the Rapidan is not recalled. On the afternoon of June 18th, it camped in timber near the little town of Millwood, on the western slope of the Blue Ridge. On the 19th it was ordered to Snicker's Gap and took position on the summit of a mountain where for three days it remained invisible in the clouds that enshrouded its camp. On the 23rd it returned to Millwood, and next day, the 24th, began the march that carried it across the Potomac at Williamsport, Md., through Greencastle, Pa., and on to Chambersburg, Pa. At Williamsport, it halted long enough to swallow rations of whisky. Non-imbibing members of the command gave their doles to comrades that liked the stuff, and as a result, it was of the breadth, more than of the length of the road, that many soldiers that afternoon found cause of complaint. "A fellow-feeling makes us wondrous kind," it is said, and it was that fellow-feeling, perhaps, that made the Texas regimental commanders look with indulgent eyes on the disorder which marked the first few miles of the march from Williamsport. The commander of the Third Arkansas, though, did not appear to be possessed of any fellow-feeling, for he found summary cures for the tortuous locomotion of his men in the cold waters of the various little streams crossing the route.

The Texas Brigade, on the afternoon of the 27th, camped in a grove of magnificent timber about a mile north of Chambersburg. Commissary trains were belated, and when long after dark they arrived, brought only slender rations of rancid bacon and musty flour. In the country roundabout there was a superabundance of all kinds of eatables. The Federal soldiers that had marched through Virginia had taken, with the strong hand, whatever they wanted from the people down there, not even offering to pay in greenbacks. General Lee's order strictly prohibited depredations on private property, but would there be any violation of that order if Confederate soldiers persuaded the good citizens of Pennsylvania to sell them provisions and accept in payment therefor Confederate money? Surely not.

There was no violence used, no threats of any kind made by any Confederate soldier, and none of the citizens complained of having been intimidated and robbed. The greater part of the supplies that found their way into camp were paid for in Confederate money, the rest were voluntary offerings. Soldiers as hungry as were the Confederates could not be expected to refuse proffers of food, even when they suspected such proffers were made through unwarranted fear of ill-treatment. The demanding and the giving were both good-humored; not a house was entered save upon invitation, or consent obtained; not a woman or child was frightened or insulted, not a building was burned, or ransacked for hidden silver and other valuables; all that was wanted, all that was asked for, all that was accepted, was food. And thus it happened that a member of the Fourth Texas who came into the camp of the Texas Brigade after dark on the 30th of June was able to write as follows:

"Rejoining the brigade late that night, at its camp near Chambersburg, and being very tired, I lay down near the wagons and went to sleep. Awakened next morning by Collins' bugle, and walking over to the camp, I witnessed not only an unexpected but a wonderful and marvelous sight. Every square foot of an acre of ground not occupied by a sleeping or standing soldier, was covered with choice food for the hungry. Chickens, turkeys, ducks and geese squawked, gobbled, quacked, cackled and hissed in harmonious unison as deft and energetic hands seized them for slaughter, and scarcely waiting for them to die, sent their feathers flying in all directions; and scattered around in bewildering confusion and gratifying profusion appeared immense loaves of bread and chunks of corned beef, hams, and sides of bacon, cheeses, crocks of apple-butter, jelly, jam, pickles, and preserves, bowls of yellow butter, demijohns of buttermilk, and other eatables too numerous to mention.

"The sleepers were the foragers of the night, resting from their arduous labors—the standing men, their mess-mates who remained as camp-guards and were now up to their eyes in noise, feathers and grub. Jack Sutherland's head pillowed itself on a loaf of bread, and one arm was wound caressingly half-around a juicy-looking ham. Bob Murray, fearful that his captives would take to their wings or be purloined, had wound the string, which bound half a dozen frying chickens around his right big toe; one of Brahan's widespread legs was embraced by two overlapping crocks of apple-butter and jam, while a tough old gander, gray with age, squawked complainingly at his head without in the last disturbing his slumber; Dick Skinner lay flat on his back—with his right hand holding to the legs of three fat chickens and a duck, and his left, to those of a large turkey—fast asleep and snoring in a rasping bass voice that chimed in well with the music of the fowls. . . .

"The scene is utterly indescribable, and I shall make no further attempt to picture it. The hours were devoted exclusively to gormandizing until, at 3 P. M., marching orders came, and leaving more provisions than they carried, the Texans moved lazily and plethorically into line—their destination, Gettysburg."

CHAPTER IX

Gettysburg

COINCIDENTALLY with the northward march of Longstreet's corps from the vicinity of Millwood, Va., General Jeb. Stuart, at the head of all the cavalry belonging to the Army of Northern Virginia, save the brigades of Robertson and Imboden, began a ride that, whatever its aim and hope, served only to detach his command from the army and deny to General Lee early and accurate information of the movements of the Federal army. Not until June 29th did General Lee learn, and then only through a scout traveling on foot, that General Hooker had led the Union army to the north side of the Potomac, and was marching it toward Gettysburg. This news called for an immediate change of plan. Ewell's corps, then far to the north on the march to Harrisburg, the capital of Pennsylvania, was recalled, and A. P. Hill's corps was sent across South Mountain to Cashtown, a little town on the turnpike leading from Chambersburg to Gettysburg, eight miles east of the latter.

The topographic features of the country around Cashtown were peculiarly favorable for a defensive battle, and for drawing supplies from the fertile Cumberland valley west of South Mountain. The presence there of the Confederate army threatened not only Washington and Baltimore, but as well, Philadelphia, and so seriously, that General Lee could safely count on drawing the enemy to his front and thus relieving his rear from danger. Therefore, he proposed to concentrate his army there, and that he might have ample time for that, his express orders both to Hill and Ewell were, that they should not bring on a general engagement until the concentration was effected. Whether it was Hill that was at fault, or General Pettigrew, the commander of a brigade in Heth's division, need not be argued, the fact remaining that instead of halting at Cashtown, Pettigrew, whose brigade led Hill's advance on the 30th of June, moved his command beyond, toward Gettysburg, in search of shoes for his men. In the vicinity of Gettysburg the brigade encountered Buford's Federal cavalry, and after a hot skirmish with those troopers, hastened back to Cashtown, somewhat the worse for wear.

Pettigrew's report of the mishap that had befallen his command, excited General Hill's curiosity " to discover what was in his front," and setting at naught the positive instructions of the commander-in-chief, he ordered the divisions of Heth and Pender forward, next morning, to Gettysburg. Near the town they were confronted not alone by cavalry, but by two largely outnumbering corps of Federal infantry. In the engagement that ensued, the Confederates soon got the worst of it, and knowing that Ewell was approaching Cashtown, Hill appealed to him for aid. Changing the course of his march, Ewell took position north of Gettysburg, nearly at right angles to the line occupied by Heth and Pender, and falling upon the right flank and rear of the Federals, soon had them in rapid and confused retreat.

Meantime, having ordered Ewell and Hill to Cashtown, General Lee remained at Chambersburg. There was no need of hurry, he thought, and hence, he delayed putting Longstreet's corps in motion toward the rendezvous, until the morning of July 1st. Even then he ordered only the divisions of Hood and McLaws' forward—Pickett's division being left at Chambersburg, and Law's brigade, of Hood's division, at New Guilford, to perform services cavalry should have been there to undertake. Lee himself rode across the mountain with Longstreet. He had gone but a few miles when he overtook the head of Longstreet's column, and ordered it to halt and await the passage of Ewell's fourteen-mile long wagon train and the division of infantry, Johnson's, that guarded it. Then he and Longstreet rode on up the mountain side, and having gained the summit, General Lee, writes a Virginian historian, " heard with amazement the noise of the battle which Hill had begun that day at Gettysburg, at sunrise; for his express orders had been, both to Hill and to Ewell, that they should not bring on a general engagement until after the concentration of his army at Cashtown, and now Hill was engaged, at the very beginning of the day, in hot contention eight miles away from Lee's selected defensive position where 'the strength of the hills' would have been his, in the open country about Gettysburg, where mere numbers would have greatly the advantage in an engagement."

It was not amazement alone that Lee must have felt—it was also indignation and apprehension. It was a grave and unique situation for the commander of an army, to be in an enemy's territory without cavalry at hand—his positive orders disobeyed, two corps of his army, Hill's and Ewell's, out of place, and the other, Longstreet's, neither in place nor near enough to be available either as an attacking or reserve force, a fierce battle in progress miles distant from where he had planned it, and himself without more information as to the whereabouts and movements of the enemy than had been secured, two days ago, from a scout who traveled on foot. It is but natural that, taking it for granted, the battle had been forced on Hill and Ewell, resolved to make the best of it, knowing his imperative and immediate need of correct information concerning the enemy, and remembering that he had enjoined upon his cavalry chief to keep constantly in touch with his right wing, his first expression should be of wonder where Stuart was, of fear that he had met with disaster.

General Lee reached Cashtown shortly before noon, and there awaited reports from the battle-field. A call for assistance came from Hill, and Lee rode rapidly on to Gettysburg, arriving there in time to witness Ewell's advance, the driving of the Federals through the streets of the town, and the capture of about 5000 prisoners—the beginning of a struggle which, continued with spirit and determination that day, would have secured for the Confederate army the identical position south of the town that was that night and early next day occupied by the Union army. Observing the confusion of the enemy as they broke into retreat from this and that point, and aware of the importance of seizing upon Cemetery Ridge and Culp's Hill before General Meade, then in command of the Federals, could arrive with his main army, Lee ordered Ewell to " press these people, and secure the hill if possible."

But neither the ridge nor the hill was secured. Early and Ewell each called on Hill for support, and Hill would assist neither. All that General Lee could do was to urge Longstreet to hurry forward the divisions of Hood and McLaws, neither of which was at that hour—5 P. M.—within ten miles of the scene of contention, and again say to Ewell that he would support his advance as soon as he could, and that he wished Ewell to use whatever opportunity he had to advance and hold the ground in his front. Early pushed his men forward; Ewell delayed to re-form his lines on the left of Early; Early's command, Gordon's brigade leading, had the enemy again on the run. At that moment, when Confederate victory needed but a last rush forward to clinch it, Early halted Gordon's brigade, and although, as he confesses in his official report, he had no faith in a report that a large force of the enemy was advancing on the York Road, ordered it to march to the relief of General Smith, then far back in the rear. The pursuit by other troops at once halted—Ewell desiring to have Gordon's brigade on the firing line, and to have Johnson's division, then guarding Ewell's wagon train, on the ground to extend his line to the eastward, scale Culp's Hill and turn the Federal right. It was after sundown when Johnson's division came on the field, and too late for another advance. But for the untimely and absolutely unnecessary withdrawal of Gordon's brigade, success must have crowned the efforts of the day, and Lee must have won the heights of Gettysburg. As it was, at nightfall of July 1st, the Federal army held Cemetery Ridge and Culp's Hill, and these advantages more than counterbalanced its losses during the day.

After nightfall of July 1 General Lee conferred with Generals Ewell, Early and Rodes. To his proposal that Ewell attack the enemy at daylight next morning, that officer demurred, saying it would be better to make a gradual approach on the Federal position for the westward. After a moment's thought, Lee said: "Perhaps I had better draw you around to my right, as the line will be very long and thin if you remain here, and the enemy may come down and break through it." But while advising the approach from the westward, Ewell was not willing to make it, and when he declared that he could not only hold the ground then in his possession but could also, next morning, capture Culp's Hill, Lee began to consider the advisability of making an attack on the enemy's left from the westward, simultaneous with that of Ewell on his right, and finally observed: "Well, if I attack the enemy's left, Longstreet will have to make the attack." Then he added, musingly: "Longstreet is a very good fighter when he gets in position and gets everything ready, but he is so slow."

Following this conference, Lee had another with Hill and Longstreet. The latter urged the withdrawal of the army from before Gettysburg and the placing of it between Meade's army and Washington, thus forcing the Federal commander to offer battle or expose the capital city of the Union to speedy capture. This was an enlargement of Lee's suggestion that Ewell should move around to the right. Relying, however, on Ewell's promise and assurance that on the morrow he would capture Culp's Hill, and arguing it unsafe, in the absence of Stuart and his cavalry, to march eastward, General Lee decided against Longstreet's contention, and resolving to make a contemporaneous attack on both flanks of the enemy, ordered Longstreet to bring up his two divisions then on the way as quickly as possible, and next day, at as early an hour as practicable, assault the Federal left.

The truth is, that while he was a great general, a profound and wily strategist, a consummate master of the art of war, Robert E. Lee, the commander of the Army of Northern Virginia, was in temperament a game cock. The mere presence of an enemy aroused his pugnacity, and was a challenge he found it hard to decline, and at Gettysburg, impossible. In his official report of the battle of Gettysburg, he says: "It had not been intended to deliver a general battle so far from our base unless attacked. But coming unexpectedly upon the whole Federal army, to withdraw through the mountains with our extensive trains would have been difficult and dangerous." Acting in direct disobedience to the orders he had received, Hill and Ewell had brought on a general engagement; it was fairly in progress; the pugnacity inherited from a long line of fighting ancestors thrilled the nerves of the Confederate commander and dominated an ordinarily cool judgment; the enemy invited and challenged a contest, and contest he should have.

Hood's division, Law's Brigade excepted, said a regretful good-by to its camp near Chambersburg, at 2 P. M. of July 1, and, falling behind McLaws' already moving division, began the march across South Mountain to Gettysburg—the Texas Brigade, too heavily burdened, inside and out, with the extra rations supplied by the citizenship of the country to make active exercise a pleasure, but still able to keep going. But a short distance was covered, when from an intersecting road Ewell's long wagon-train, under protection of Johnson's division, came into the Chambersburg and Gettysburg turnpike, ahead of McLaws' leading regiment. Just then General Lee and General Longstreet rode up, and, aware of the confusion and delay sure to result should the train and two columns of infantry attempt to move, side by side, along the turnpike, General Lee, himself, ordered McLaws to halt his column and await the passage of the train and its guard.

Four hours, at least, were consumed by this delay. The length of the train, guess-work, neither division, brigade, nor regimental commanders could say when the way would be clear, and we could only wait, sitting and standing by the roadside. And when, finally, we began to move on in the wake of the last wagon, it was to go a hundred yards or so, and then stop and stand still, not daring to sit down, for five, ten or twenty minutes at a time. Nothing is so wearing on infantry as such halting progress, and when, at 2 A. M. of July 2, near Cashtown, the Texas Brigade was allowed to rest secure from interruption, the boys lost no time in divesting themselves of their accouterments, stretching themselves out on the bare ground and falling asleep.

At 4 P. M the men of the Texas Brigade were awakened from their deep slumber, and within ten minutes were on their way to Gettysburg. Falling into a swinging route step, they made the distance without a halt, arriving near the headquarters of General Lee, on Seminary Ridge, not later than an hour after sunrise. Held here for perhaps an hour and a half, they then moved a mile or more to the south and east, into a little valley where water and fuel were easily accessible. Here they were notified that rations would be issued as soon as the commissary wagons could be brought up, and as about that time the skillet wagon drove up and unloaded each regiment's share of cooking utensils, fires were built and skillet lids put on to heat, preparatory to cooking the flour that was to be issued. While his comrades attended to culinary affairs, Ferdinand Hahn, of the Fourth Texas, strolled to the top of a nearby elevation, and edged up as near as he dared to a group of general officers and their staffs. Among the generals were Longstreet, Hood, and Lee, with each of whom he had a personal acquaintance acquired prior to the war, while he was a clerk at the Menger Hotel in San Antonio, and they its guests. He remained in hearing distance of the group, probably, half an hour. Returning then to his company, he said:

"You might as well quit bothering with those skillet lids, boys—it'll not be twenty minutes before we are on the move again."

"What have you heard, Hahn—what have you heard?" a dozen voices eagerly inquired.

"Only this," he replied. "I got up pretty close to General Lee, and old Longstreet and Hood, a while ago, and while I stood there, an officer rode up, and adressing General Lee, reported that the Yankees were moving troops on to Round Top. General Lee at once turned his glasses in that direction, and after looking through them a minute or two, said: 'Ah, well, that was to be expected. But General Meade might as well have saved himself the trouble, for we'll have it in our possession before night.' That means, of course, that we'll have to take it, and to do it, we'll have to move from here as soon as Hood can send orders."

Sure enough, not ten minutes elapsed before the brigade was called to attention and marched toward the position from which, later, it advanced against Round Top—not six hours had passed before it was fighting, its men bleeding and dying, in the rocky fastnesses of Devil's Den and under the lofty, precipitous cliffs that guarded the approach from the west to the crest of Cemetery Ridge and the Round Tops.

The movement now made was but preparatory. While still adhering to his resolve to deliver battle, General Lee had not yet decided from what line Longstreet's troops should advance. If at this hour he betrayed anger and disappointment, it was not at the failure of Longstreet's command to be up sooner—it was because of Ewell's failure to seize Culp's Hill, or even to attack the Federals there with promising vigor: if he manifested anxiety and impatience, it was not due to the slowness and deliberation with which Longstreet moved his troops, for this he had expected—it was due to the delay of the officers he had sent out, at daylight, to reconnoiter the ground. Not until they reported to him, which was close on to mid-day, did he announce his plan to Longstreet. Previous to that time, though, he himself rode to his left wing and instructed Hill and Ewell to lead their commands forward as soon as they heard Longstreet's guns open.

In this connection the testimony of Longstreet is relevant. In his book, "From Manassas to Appomattox," he says:

"It was some little time after General Lee's return from his ride to the left before he received the reports of the reconnoissance ordered from his center to his right. His mind, previously settled to the purpose to fight where the enemy stood, now accepted the explicit plan of making the opening on his right, and to have the engagement general."

The following excerpt from "Confederate Military History" is also relevant. The incident related occurred at the time General Lee was instructing Longstreet and his division commanders concerning their movements:

"Lee pointed out to McLaws, on the map, the position on the Emmitsburg road, at right angles to that near the peach orchard, that he desired him to occupy, telling him to gain that, if possible, without being seen by the enemy. Longstreet interposed, directing McLaws to place his line parallel to the turnpike. Lee promptly made reply: 'No, General, no: I want his position perpendicular to the Emmitsburg road,' thus clearly indicating his design to move squarely upon the Federal left."

To enable the reader to understand the relative positions of the two contending armies on July 2, 1863, an attempt at description is necessary. Cemetery Ridge, occupied that day by the Federal army, runs first northward, then, with a sharp curve, eastward, and then, again bending, southward for a short distance. In shape, it is not unlike a fish-hook—Round

Top Mountain at the southern end of the stem—Little Round Top half a mile further north—Cemetery Hill in the bend—the town of Gettysburg in a valley, a mile north of Cemetery Hill—Culp's Hill at the barb of the hook. From Little Round Top to Cemetery Hill is barely three miles, while from Culp's Hill—at the barb of the hook—measuring straight across the curve is scarcely a half mile. Owing to the curvature at the end of the hook of the Federal line, that line was scant three miles long, and no part of it was over an hour's march from another. In half an hour, the Federals could concentrate two-thirds of their entire force at any given point on it.

About a mile west of Cemetery Ridge, running parallel with it but extending further northward, lies Seminary Ridge. On July 2 the Confederate line stretched along the crest of Seminary Ridge, from a point opposite Round Top to another opposite the town of Gettysburg: here turning eastward, it followed around the curve of Cemetery Ridge, and, bending with that curve to the southward, terminated at a point opposite and east of Culp's Hill—its shape being also much like that of a fish-hook. Because of its length—seven miles, at the least—and because, also, there could be no cutting across bends, it would have required hours for the Confederates to concentrate a heavy force at any given point.

Culp's Hill dominated Cemetery Hill and the ridge to the south as completely as did either of the Round Tops. That in the possession of the Confederates, the Federal position would have been untenable. Aware of this, of how easily the Federals could concentrate, and of how difficult concentration would be to the Confederates, General Lee planned for a simultaneous assault by all of his troops. If at all points of their line the Union troops were kept busy repelling attack, success would depend on pluck and endurance, and not simply on position and numbers. Assailed at all points with the vigor and determination characteristic of the Army of Northern Virginia, the elect of which was then at hand "to do or die," the facilities of the enemy for rapid shifting of forces would be of small avail.

The Federal commander intended, and so ordered, that his lines should be formed along the crest of Cemetery Ridge, north of Round Top. But mistaking a wooded hill, west of the crest a short distance, for the main ridge, the Federal General Sickles took position on that, slightly in rear of the peach orchard, the position McLaws was enjoined by General Lee to gain. To connect with Hancock on his right, and to rest his left on Round Top, Sickles faced Birney's division southwestward, Humphrey's northwestward. The Emmitsburg road ran southwest from the town of Gettysburg, diagonally across the valley between Cemetery and Seminary ridges. It skirted the base of Cemetery Hill and passed just west of the peach orchard. This orchard is northwest and nearly a mile from Little Round Top. Between it and the mountain, and beyond a skirt of timber, was a wheat field. South of the wheat field, and in the space between the two little branches that form what is known as Plum Run, and which come together at a point about opposite the center of the depression between the Round Tops, is Devil's Den. Beneath its tall timber, and between the abundance of large, irregularly-shaped boulders that covered fully half its surface, grew an almost impenetrable thicket of shrubs, vines, and small timber. East of it rose the frowning, precipitous cliffs which marked the western boundary of Cemetery Ridge, and which extended along the west bases of the two Round Tops. The slope of Round Top to the south, although rough, was not precipitous, and the ground south of that mountain was comparatively open and level.

In preparation for the battle of the 2d, Hill was ordered to extend his line further to the right, Anderson's division being chosen for the purpose. This division met such opposition from the Federals that it was not until 1 P. M. that it got into position. In the meantime Law's brigade joined its division, Hood's. Anderson's division in line of battle, General Pendleton was ordered by General Lee to conduct Longstreet's command to its position by a route concealed from the enemy. McLaws' division was to form on the right of Anderson's— Hood's on the right of McLaws'. In the effort to conceal the movement much time was occupied, and it was 3 P. M. before the troops were in position.

General Hood made no official report of the operations of his division at Gettysburg. June 28, 1875, though, he forwarded an account of them to General Longstreet—the account embracing all that was done up to the time he (Hood) was wounded. The letter containing the account was published by Hood in his book, "Advance and Retreat," beginning on page 55. He says:

"Whilst lying in camp, not far distant from Chambersburg, information was received that Ewell and Hill were about to come in contact with the enemy near Gettysburg. My troops, together with McLaws' division, were put in motion upon the most direct road to that point, which, after a hard march, we reached before, or at sunrise on the 2nd of July. So imperative had been the orders to hasten forward with all possible speed, that on the march my troops were allowed to halt and rest only about two hours, during the night from the 1st to the 2nd of July.

"I arrived with my staff in front of the heights of Gettysburg shortly after daybreak, as I have already stated, on the morning of the 2nd of July. My division soon commenced filing into an open field near me, where the troops were allowed to stack arms and rest until further orders. A short distance in advance of this point, and during the early part of the same morning, we were both engaged, in company with Generals Lee and A. P. Hill, in observing the position of the Federals. General Lee—with coat buttoned to the throat, saber-belt buckled around the waist, and field-glasses pending at his side—walked up and down in the shade of the large trees near us, halting now and then to observe the enemy. He seemed full of hope, yet, at times, buried in deep thought. Colonel Freemantle, of England, was ensconced in the forks of a tree, not far off, with glass in constant use, examining the lofty position of the Federal army.

"General Lee was, seemingly, anxious you should attack that morning. He remarked to me: 'The enemy is here, and if we do not whip him, he will whip us.' You thought it better to await the arrival of Pickett's division—at that time still in the rear—in order to make the attack; and you said to me, subsequently, whilst we were seated together near the trunk of a tree: 'The General is a little nervous, this morning; he wishes me to attack: I do not wish to do so without Pickett. I never like to go into battle with one boot off.'

"Thus passed the forenoon of that eventful day, when in the afternoon—about 3 o'clock—it was decided to no longer await Pickett's division, but to proceed to our extreme right and attack up the Emmitsburg road. McLaws moved off, and I followed with my division. In a short time I was ordered to quicken the march of my troops, and to pass to the front of McLaws.

"This movement was accomplished by throwing out an advanced force to tear down fences and clear the way. The instructions I received were to place my division across the Emmitsburg road, form line of battle, and attack. Before reaching this road, however, I had sent forward some of my picked Texas scouts to ascertain the position of the enemy's extreme left flank. They soon reported to me that it rested upon Round Top Mountain: that the country was open, and that I could march through an open woodland pasture around Round Top, and assault the enemy in flank and rear: that their wagon trains were parked in rear of their line, and were badly exposed to our attack in that direction. As soon as I arrived upon the Emmitsburg road, I placed one or two batteries in position and opened fire. A reply from the enemy's guns soon developed his lines. His left rested on or near Round Top, with line bending back and again forward, forming, as it were, a concave line, as approached by the Emmitsburg road. A considerable body of troops was posted in front of their main line, between the Emmitsburg road and Round Top Mountain. This force was in line of battle upon an eminence near a peach orchard.

"I found that in making the attack according to orders, viz., up the Emmitsburg road, I should have first to encounter and drive off this advanced line of battle; secondly, at the base and along the slope of the mountain, to confront immense boulders of stone, so massed together as to form narrow openings, which would break our ranks and cause the men to scatter whilst climbing up the rocky precipice. I found, moreover, that my division would be exposed to a heavy fire from the main line of the enemy in position on the crest of the high range, of which Round Top was the extreme left, and, by reason of the concavity of the enemy's main line, that we would be subject to a destructive fire in flank and rear, as well as in front: and deemed it almost an impossibility to clamber along the boulders up this steep and rugged mountain, and, under this number of cross fires, put the enemy to flight. I knew that if the feat was accomplished, it must be at a most fearful sacrifice of as brave and gallant soldiers as ever engaged in battle.

"The reconnoissance of my Texas scouts and the development of the Federal lines were effected in a very short space of time; in truth, shorter than I have taken to recall and jot down these facts, although the scenes and events of that day are as clear to my mind as if the great battle had been fought yesterday. I was in possession of these important facts so shortly after reaching the Emmitsburg road, that I considered it my duty to report to you, at once, my opinion that it was unwise to attack up the Emmitsburg road, as ordered, and to urge that you allow me to turn Round Top, and attack the enemy in flank and rear. Accordingly, I dispatched a staff officer, bearing to you my request to be allowed to make the proposed movement on account of the above stated reasons. Your reply was quickly received: 'General Lee's orders are to attack up the Emmitsburg road.' I sent another officer to say that I feared nothing could be accomplished by such an attack, and renewed my request to turn Round Top. Again your answer was, 'General Lee's orders are to attack up the Emmitsburg road.' During this interim I had continued to use the batteries upon the enemy, and had become more and more convinced that the Federal line extended to Round Top, and that I could not reasonably hope to accomplish much by the attack as ordered. In fact, it seemed to me that the enemy occupied a position by nature so strong—I may say impregnable—that, independently of their flank fire, they could easily repel our attack by merely throwing and rolling stones down the mountain side as we approached.

"A third time I dispatched one of my staff to explain fully in regard to the situation, and suggest that you had better come and look for yourself. I selected, in this instance, my adjutant-general, Colonel Harry Sellers, whom you know to be not only an officer of great courage, but also of marked ability. Colonel Sellers returned with the same message, 'General Lee's orders are to attack up the Emmitsburg road.'

Almost simultaneously, Colonel Fairfax, of your staff, rode up and repeated the above orders.

"After this urgent protest against entering the battle of Gettysburg according to instructions—which protest is the first and only one I ever made during my entire military career—I ordered my line to advance and make the assault.

"As my troops were moving forward, you rode up in person; a brief conversation passed between us, during which I again expressed the fears above mentioned, and regret at not being allowed to attack in flank around Round Top. You answered to this effect: 'We must obey the orders of General Lee.' I then rode forward with my line, under a heavy fire. In about twenty minutes, after reaching the peach orchard, I was severely wounded in the arm, and borne from the field.

"With this wound terminated my participation in this great battle. As I was borne off on a litter to the rear, I could but experience deep distress of mind and heart at the thought of the inevitable fate of my brave fellow-soldiers, who formed one of the grandest divisions of that world-renowned army; and I shall ever believe that had I been permitted to turn Round Top Mountain, we would not only have gained that position, but have been able finally to rout the enemy."

General J. B. Robertson, commanding the Texas Brigade, says in his official report:

The division arrived on the ground in front of the position of the enemy that we were to attack but a few minutes before we were ordered to advance. I therefore got but a glance at the field on which we had to operate before we entered it. I was ordered to keep my right well closed on Brigadier-General Law's left, and to let my left rest on the Emmitsburg pike. I had advanced but a short distance when I discovered that my brigade would not fill the space between General Law's left and the pike named, and that I must leave the pike, or disconnect myself from General Law on my right. Understanding before the action commenced that the attack on our part was to be general, and that the force of General McLaws was to advance simultaneously with us on my immediate left, seeing at once that a mountain held by the enemy in heavy force with artillery to the right of General

Law's center was the key to the enemy's left, I abandoned the pike, and closed on General Law's left. This caused a separation of my regiments, which was remedied as promptly as the numerous stone and rail fences would allow.

As we advanced through this field, for half a mile we were exposed to a heavy and destructive fire of canister, grape, and shell from six pieces of their artillery on the mountain alluded to, and the same number on a commanding hill but a short distance to the left of the mountain, and from the enemy's sharpshooters from behind the numerous rocks, fences and houses in the field.

As we approached the base of the mountain, General Law moved to the right, and I was moving obliquely to the right to close on him, when my whole line encountered the fire of the enemy's main line, posted behind rocks and a stone fence. The Fourth and Fifth Texas Regiments, under the direction of their gallant commanders (Colonels Powell and Key), while returning the fire and driving the enemy before them, continued to close on General Law to their right. At the same time, the First Texas and Third Arkansas, under their gallant commanders (Lieutenant-Colonel (P. A.) Work and Colonel Manning), were hotly engaged with a greatly superior force, while at the same time a heavy force appeared and opened fire on Colonel Manning's left, seriously threatening his left flank, to meet which he threw two or three companies with their front to his left flank, and protected his left.

On discovering this heavy force on my left flank, and seeing that no attack was being made by any of our forces on my left, I at once sent a courier to Major-General Hood, stating that I was hard pressed on my left; that General McLaws' forces were not engaging the enemy to my left (which enabled him to move fresh troops from that part of his line down on me), and that I must have reinforcements.

Lieutenant-Colonel Work, with the First Texas Regiment, having pressed forward to the crest of the hill and driven the enemy from his battery, I ordered him to the left, to the relief and support of Colonel Manning, directing Major (F. S.) Bass, with two companies, to hold the hill, while Colonel Work with the rest of the regiment went to Colonel Manning's relief. With his assistance, Colonel Manning drove the enemy back, and entered the woods after him, when the enemy reoccupied the hill and his batteries in Colonel Work's front, from which Colonel Work again drove him.

For an hour and upward these two regiments maintained one of the hottest contests, against five or six times their number, that I have witnessed. The moving of Colonel Work to the left, to relieve Colonel Manning while the Fourth and Fifth Texas were closing to the right on General Law's brigade, separated these two regiments from the others. They were steadily moving to the front and right, driving the enemy before them, when they passed the woods or ravine to my right. After finding that I could not move the First and Third to the right to join them, I sent to recall them, ordering them to move to the left until the left of the Fourth should rest on the right of the First; but my messenger found two of General Law's regiments on the left of my two (the Fourth and Fifth Texas), and did not find these regiments at all.

About this time my aide, Lieutenant Scott, reported my two regiments (the Fourth and Fifth Texas) in the center of General Law's brigade, and that they could not be moved without greatly injuring the line. I sent a request to General Law to look to them.

At this point, my assistant and inspector-general reported from the Fourth and Fifth that they were hotly engaged, and wanted reinforcements. My courier, sent to General Hood, returned, and reported him wounded and carried from the field. I sent a messenger to Lieutenant-General Longstreet for reinforcements, and at the same time sent to Generals (George T.) Anderson and Benning, urging them to hurry up to my support. They came up, joined us, and fought gallantly; but as fast as we would break one line of the enemy, another fresh one would present itself, the enemy reinforcing his lines in our front from his reserves at the base of the mountain to our right and front, and from his lines to our right and front, and from his lines to our left. Having no attack from us in his front, he threw his forces from there on us.

Before the arrivals of Generals Benning and Anderson, Col. J. C. Key, who gallantly led the Fourth Texas, up to the time of receiving a severe wound, passed me, being led to the rear. About the same time, I learned of the fall and dangerous wounding of Col. R. M. Powell, of the Fifth, who fell while gallantly leading his regiment in one of the impetuous charges of the Fourth and Fifth Texas on the strongly fortified mountain.

Just after the arrival of General Anderson on my left, I learned that the gallant Col. Van H. Manning, of the Third Arkansas, had been wounded and carried from the field, and about the same time, I received intelligence of the wounding and being carried from the field of those two able and efficient officers, Lieut. Cols. K. Bryan, of the Fifth, and B. F. Carter, of the Fourth, both of whom were wounded while bravely discharging their duty.

Colonel R. M. Powell
Fifth Texas Regiment

Captain (J. R.) Woodward, acting major of the First Texas, was wounded near me while gallantly discharging his duty.

The Fourth and Fifth Texas, under the command of Majors (J. P.) Bane and (J. C.) Rogers, continued to hold the ground of their original line, leaving the space over which they had made their successive charges strewn with their dead and wounded comrades, many of whom could not be removed, and were left on the field. The First Texas, under Lieutenant-Colonel Work, with a portion of Benning's brigade, held the field and batteries taken by the First Texas. Three of the guns were brought off the field and secured, the other three, from the nature of the ground and their proximity to the enemy, were left. The Third Arkansas, under the command of Lieutenant-Colonel (R. S.) Taylor, ably assisted by Major (J. W.) Reedy, after Colonel Manning was borne from the field, sustained well the high character it made in the earlier part of the action.

When night closed the conflict, late in the evening, I was struck above the knee, which deprived me of the use of my leg, and prevented me from getting about the field. I retired some 200 yards to the rear, leaving the immediate command with Lieutenant-Colonel Work, the senior officer present, under whose supervision our wounded were brought out, our guns secured, and our dead on that part of the field buried.

About 2 o'clock that night, the First Texas and Third Arkansas were moved by the right to the position occupied by the Fourth and Fifth, and formed on their left, where the brigade remained during the day of the 3rd, keeping up a continuous skirmishing with the enemy's sharpshooters, in which we had a number of our men severely wounded. I sent my assistant adjutant-general, Capt. F. L. Price, at daybreak to examine the position of the brigade, and report to me as soon as he could, and, while in the discharge of that duty, he was either killed or fell into the hands of the enemy, as he has not been seen or heard of since.

About dark on the evening of the 3rd, the brigade, with the division, fell back to the hill, and formed in line, where it remained during the 4th. . . .

In this, the hardest fought battle of the war, in which I have been engaged, all, both men and officers, as far as my observation extended, fully sustained the high character they have heretofore made. Where all behaved so nobly, individual distinction cannot with propriety be made.

CHAPTER X

Gettysburg—(*Continued*)

To know what a battle is, one must be in the thick of it—must one's self feel the consciousness of danger, the stern resolve to brave that danger, and the delight of giving play to that instinct of the human being to kill and destroy whoever and whatever bars his way. It is not like coming face to face with "the grim monster, Death," by accident, or under the impulse which bids one to do all he may to save the life of another, for in neither of these cases is the risk taken deliberately as the soldier takes that assumed when he moves forward to the firing line.

Hitherto, the Texans had fought on ground over which they could move rapidly in line, and where the enemy was accessible—where the terror caused by their daring rush and swift on-coming counted large. Here at Gettysburg the foe lay concealed behind stone fences at the base of the ridge and mountains, or flat on the ground on the crest of ridge or mountain. If, when the line of Federals under General Sickles was routed, the Texans obeyed orders and held their left on the Emmitsburg road, thus moving up the valley between the road and Cemetery Ridge, the enemy's fire came down their line from right to left, from one flank to the other; if, obeying the natural impulse to face the Federals opposing them, they disobeyed orders and moved toward and against these, they went into a bend of the Federal line, and subjected themselves to a fire from both artillery and musketry, from the front and on both flanks.

Either movement was a forlorn hope, and desperate; neither offered immunity from annihilation—neither promised success. But while such volunteer soldiers as the Texans and Arkansans, while in camp or on the march, willingly obeyed such orders as were given, when they came in contact with the enemy, and the fight was on and their blood grew warm, each man of them fought "for his own hand," and in his own way.

General Robertson's orders were to keep the left flank of the brigade on the Emmitsburg road, and its right flank in touch with the left of Law's brigade. The distance from the road to Law's left made this impracticable. Law's brigade soon found that by moving north, up the Emmitsburg road, it would have the enemy on its right flank; therefore, it abandoned the effort, and, facing to the east, began an attack on the enemy posted at the base and on the crests of Cemetery Ridge and the Round Top, thus leaving the right flank of the Fifth Texas, if it continued its advance northward, exposed to a flank fire. Noting this, and also fearing that if it continued northward, the enemy would drop down on its rear, between it and Law's brigade, the Fifth Texas also faced east, and the Fourth Texas followed its lead.

The Third Arkansas, however, as will be seen from Colonel Manning's report, hereafter given, clung to the Emmitsburg road, and the First Texas stayed with it. Of the movements of the First Texas, we will let a private, James O. Bradfield, of Company E of that regiment, speak in advance of its commander. The incidents that make a battle memorable and are most thrilling are seldom mentioned and never narrated in detail by field officers of a regiment.

"Hood's division held the right flank of our army. . . . We began forming our line of battle on a wide plateau leading back to the rear, while in front about 200 yards distant was a skirt of timber on the brow of a hill which led down to the valley below. In this timber, our batteries were posted, and as the Texas Brigade was forming immediately in their rear, we were in direct range of the enemy's guns on the mountain beyond. As our artillery began feeling for their batteries, the answering shells struck our lines with cruel effect. The Fourth Texas suffered most severely. As they were passing this zone of fire, one shell killed and wounded fifteen men. It certainly tries a man's nerve to have to stand still and receive such a fire without being able to return it.

"Just here occurred one of the little incidents that, happening at times like this, are never forgotten. In our company was a tall, robust young fellow named Dick Childers, who was noted for the energy and talent he displayed in procuring rations. On this occasion Dick's haversack was well stocked with nice biscuits which a kind Dutch lady had given him. As we were marching by the right flank, our left sides were turned towards the enemy. A shell from the mountain in front struck the ground near our batteries, and came bouncing along across the field, and as Dick happened to be just in the line of fire, it struck him, or rather, his haversack, fairly, and scattered biscuits all over that end of Pennsylvania. But the strange part of it is, that it did not knock the man down, but so paralyzed him that he fell, after it had passed, and lay there unable to move a muscle. The litter bearers picked him up and laid him on a stretcher, as if he had been a log. The boys all contended, however, that it was the destruction of Dick's rations, and not any shock the shell gave, that paralyzed him.

"We marched onward by the right flank, about a quarter of a mile, moving parallel with the enemy's lines, and halting, left-faced and formed for work. We were on the brow of a hill which here sloped quite abruptly down into the narrow valley. We could see the enemy's lines of battle—the first on the level space below us, behind a heavy rock fence; the second, at the top of a ridge a hundred or two yards further on, while still further, and entirely out of our reach, at the summit of the higher range, their batteries were posted so as to sweep the whole space over which we were to advance. Their battle flags floated proudly in the breeze, above the almost perfect natural breastworks formed by the fence and the large rocks that crowned the low ridge upon which they stood. There were but two small cannon on the lower ridge, and these were captured and pulled off the hill by the First Texas regiment.

"About 2 o'clock in the afternoon, the order was given to advance all along the line. We moved quietly forward down the steep decline, gaining impetus as we reached the more level ground below. The enemy had already opened fire on us, but we did not stop to return it. 'Forward—double quick,' rang out, and then Texas turned loose. Across the valley and over the little stream that ran through it, they swept, every man for himself. The first man down was my right file man, William Langley, a noble, brave boy, with a minie-ball straight through the brain. I caught him as he fell against me, and laid him down, dead. As I straightened up to move on, that same familiar 'spat' which always means something, sounded near, and looking around, I saw Bose Perry double over and catch on his gun. He did not fall, however, but came on, dragging his wounded leg, and firing as he advanced. But it was getting too hot, now, to pay attention to details.

"The enemy stood their ground bravely, until we were close on them, but did not await the bayonet. They broke away from the rock fence as we closed in with a rush and a wild rebel yell, and fell back to the top of the ridge, where they halted and formed on their second line. Having passed the rock fence, and as we were moving on up the hill, an order came to halt. No one seemed to know whence it came, nor from whom. It cost us dearly, for as we lay in close range of their now double lines, the enemy poured a hail of bullets on us, and in a few minutes a number of our men were killed or wounded. We saw that this would never do, and so, without awaiting orders, every man became his own commander and sprang forward toward the top of the hill at full speed.

"By this time, Benning's brigade, which had been held in reserve, joined us and together we swept on to where the Blue Coats stood behind the sheltering rocks to receive us. Just here, and to our right, in a little cove called the 'Devil's Den,' which was covered by the Fourth and Fifth Texas, Law's Alabama and Anderson's Georgia brigades, occurred one of the wildest, fiercest struggles of the war—a struggle such as it is given to few men to pass through and live.

"The opposing lines stood with only the sheltering rocks between them—breast to breast, and so close that the clothing of many of the enemy was set on fire by the blaze from the Confederate rifles. This continued for some time, but finally, our fire grew so hot that brave as they were, the Federals could no longer endure it, but gave way and fled down the slope, leaving us in possession of the field. The Lone Star flag crowned the hill, and Texas was there to stay. Not alone, however, for just to our right stood Benning—'Old Rock'—that peerless old hero than whom no braver man ever lived. Striding back and forth in front of his line, he was calling to his gallant Georgians: 'Give them h—ll, boys—

give them h—ll,' and the 'boys' were giving it to them according to instructions.

"On the right of Benning stood Anderson and Law, and the Fourth and Fifth Texas, as firm as the rocks which sheltered them. I cannot hope to describe the deeds of daring and heroism that were enacted. Beyond the valley in our front, on the summit of the practically impregnable ridge that stretched north toward Gettysburg, stood the enemy's batteries, 200 guns. Of these, about forty were playing in close range upon the position we occupied. Their fire and that of our own batteries, and the constant roar and rattle of thousands of muskets, made the earth tremble beneath our feet, while the fierce, angry shriek of shells, the strident swirl of grape and canister as they tore hurtling through the air and broke like a wave from the ocean of death upon that devoted spot, the hissing bullets, and their 'spat' as they struck rock, tree or human flesh—all this, with the shouts and imprecations, the leaping to and fro and from boulder to boulder of powder-begrimed men, seemingly gone wild with rage and excitement, created a scene of such indescribable, awe-inspiring confusion that an on-looker might well believe that a storm from the Infernal regions was spending its fury in and around a spot so fitly named, 'The Devil's Den.' Had it not been for the protection afforded us by the large rocks and boulders which lay scattered over the hill-top, no living thing could have remained on its summit.

"The fearful artillery fire of the enemy was intended to cover the massing of their infantry, who were now to make one more grand effort to regain the ground they had lost. Our boys prepared for this by gathering up all abandoned muskets within reach, and loading them. Some of us had as many as five or six lying by us, as we awaited the attack.

"We had not long to wait, for soon the long blue line came in view, moving in gallant style up the valley. The Federals were led by splendid officers, and made a noble charge: but when they met the murderous fire from behind the rocks where we crouched, they faltered. Only for a moment, though, and on they came right up to the rocks. Again they faltered, for now, most of their officers were down. Again it was but for a second, and cheered on by some of the bravest men I have ever seen, they rallied in the very face of death, and charged right up to the muzzles of our guns.

"There was one officer, a major, who won our admiration by his courage and gallantry. He was a very handsome man, and rode a beautiful, high-spirited gray horse. The animal seemed to partake of the spirit of the rider, and as he came on with a free, graceful stride into that hell of death and carnage, head erect and ears pointed, horse and man offered a picture such as is seldom seen. The two seemed the very impersonation of heroic courage. As the withering, scathing volleys from behind the rocks cut into the ranks of the regiment the major led, and his gallant men went down like grain before a scythe, he followed close at their heels, and when, time and again, they stopped and would have fled the merciless fire, each time he rallied them as if his puissant arm alone could stay the storm. But his efforts were, in the end, unavailing; the pluck of himself and his men only made the carnage the more dreadful, for the Lone Star banner and the flag of Georgia continued floating from the hill, showing who stood, defiant and unyielding, beneath their folds.

"In the last and most determined charge they made on us, the gallant officer made his supreme effort. Riding into our very midst, seeming to bear a charmed life, he sat proudly on the noble gray, and still cheered on his men. 'Don't shoot at him—don't kill him,' our boys shouted to each other; 'he is too brave a man to die—shoot his horse and capture the man.' But it could not be. In a second or two, horse and rider went down together, pierced by a dozen balls. Thus died a hero— one of the most gallant men that ever gave up his life on the red field of carnage. Though it was that of an enemy, we honored the dead body as if it had been that of one of our own men. Such courage belongs not to any one army or country, but to mankind.

"It was about this time that a spectacular display of reckless courage was made by a young Texan, Will Barbee, of the First Texas. Under twenty years old, he was ordinarily a jolly, whole-souled lad, not at all given to extraordinary performances. But when a fight was going on, he went wild, seemed to have no sense of fear whatever, and was a reckless dare-devil. Although a courier for General Hood, he never failed to join his regiment, if possible, and go into battle with it. On the present occasion, when General Hood was wounded, Barbee hunted us up. In the hottest of the fight, I heard some one say, 'Here comes Barbee,' and looking down from the rock on which I was lying I saw him coming as fast as his little sorrel horse could run, and waving his hat as he came. Just before reaching us, the sorrel fell, but Barbee did not stop to see what had happened to the brute. He hit the ground running, and snatching up a gun as he came, was soon in line.

"About five paces to my left was a large, high rock behind which several of our wounded were sheltering themselves. To the top of that, where the very air was alive with missiles of death, Barbee sprang, and standing there, erect and fearless, began firing—the wounded men below him passing up loaded guns as fast as he emptied them. But no living being could stay unhurt long in such a fire. In a few minutes, Barbee was knocked off the rock by a ball that struck him in the right leg. Climbing instantly back, he again commenced shooting. In less than two minutes, he was tumbled off the rock by a ball in the other leg. Still unsatisfied, he crawled back a second time, but was not there more than a minute before, being wounded in the body, he again fell, this time dropping on his back between the rock that had been his perch, and that which was my shelter. Too seriously wounded this time to extricate himself from the narrow passageway, he called for help, and the last time I saw him that day, he was lying there, crying and cursing because the boys would not come to his relief and help him back on to the rock.

"There were many in the regiment as brave as Barbee, but none so reckless. The best blood of Texas was there, and in the Fourth and Fifth Texas, and General Lee could safely place the confidence he did in Hood's Texas Brigade. But God must have ordained our defeat. As was said by one of the speakers at a reunion of 'the Mountain Remnant Brigade': 'At the first roll of the war drum, Texas sent forth her noblest and best. She gave the Army of Northern Virginia Hood's matchless brigade—a band of heroes who bore their country's flag to victory on every field, until God stopped them at Little Round Top.'"

HOOD'S TEXAS BRIGADE

Another private, Val C. Giles, of Company B, Fourth Texas, has placed his observations and experiences as a participant in the fighting at Gettysburg on record. His view of it is from a humorous standpoint, and any lightening of the shadows of war is always acceptable. He writes:

"It was near 5 o'clock when we began the assault against an enemy strongly fortified behind logs and stones on the crest of a mountain, in many places perpendicular. It was more than half a mile from our starting point to the edge of the timber at the base of the ridge, comparatively open ground all the way. We started off at quick time, the officers keeping the column in pretty good line until we passed through the peach orchard and reached the level ground beyond. We were now about four hundred yards from the timber and the fire from the enemy, both artillery and musketry, was fearful.

"In making that long charge our brigade got 'jammed.' Regiments overlapped each other and when we reached the woods and climbed the mountains as far as we could go, we were a badly mixed crowd.

"Confusion reigned supreme everywhere. Nearly all our field officers were gone. Hood, our major general, had been shot from his horse. Robertson, our brigadier, had been carried from the field. Colonel Powell of the Fifth Texas was riddled with bullets. Colonel Van Manning of the Third Arkansas was disabled and Colonel Carter of my regiment lay dying at the foot of the mountain.

"The sides of the mountain were heavily timbered and covered with great boulders, that had tumbled from the cliffs above years before, which afforded great protection to the men.

"Every tree, rock and stump that gave any protection from the rain of minie-balls, that was poured down upon us, from the crest above us, were soon appropriated. John Griffith and myself pre-empted behind a moss-covered old boulder about the size of a 500-pound cotton bale.

"By this time order and discipline were gone. Every fellow was his own general. Private soldiers gave commands as loud as the officers—nobody paying any attention to either. To add to this confusion, our artillery on the hill in our rear was cutting its fuse too short. The shells were bursting behind us, in the treetops, over our heads, and all around us.

"Nothing demoralizes troops quicker than to be fired into by their friends. I saw it occur twice during the war. The first time we ran, but at Gettysburg we couldn't.

"This mistake was soon corrected and the shells burst high on a mountain or went over it.

"Major Rogers, then in command of the Fifth Texas regiment, mounted an old log near my boulder and began a Fourth of July speech. He was a little ahead of time, for that was about 6.30 o'clock on the evening of the 2d. Of course, nobody was paying any attention to the oration as he appealed to the men to 'stand fast.' He and Captain Cussons of the Fourth Alabama were the only two men I saw standing. The balance of us had settled down behind rocks, logs and trees. While the speech was going on, John Haggerty, one of Hood's couriers, then acting for General Law, dashed up the side of the mountains, saluted the major and said: 'General Law presents his compliments and says hold the place at all hazards.' The major checked up, glared down at Haggerty from his perch and shouted: 'Compliments, hell! Who wants compliments in such a damned place as this? Go back and ask General Law if he expects me to hold the world in check with the Fifth Texas regiment.'

"The major evidently thought he had his regiment with him, while, in fact, these men were from every regiment in the Texas Brigade all around him.

"But I must back to my boulder at Gettysburg. It was a ragged line of battle, strung out along the side of Cemetery Ridge and in front of Little Round Top. Night began settling around us, but the carnage went on. It is of that night that I started out to speak.

"There seemed to be a viciousness in the very air we breathed. Things had gone wrong all the day and now pandemonium came with the darkness.

"Alexander Dumas says the devil gets in a man seven times a day, and if the average is not over seven times he is almost a saint.

"At Gettysburg that night it was about seven devils to

each man. Officers were cross to the men, and the men were equally cross to the officers. It was the same way with the enemy. We could hear the Yankee officer on the crest of the ridge in front of us cursing the men by platoons, and the men telling them to go to a country not very far from them just at that time. If that old satanic dragon has ever been on earth since he offered our Saviour the world if He would serve him, he was at Gettysburg that night.

"Every characteristic of the human race was presented there, the cruelty of the Turk, the courage of the Greek (old style), the endurance of the Arab, the dash of the Cossack, the fearlessness of the Bashibazouk, the ignorance of the Zulu, the cunning of the Comanche, the recklessness of the American volunteers and the wickedness of the devil thrown in to make the thing complete.

"The advance lines of the two armies in many places were not more than fifty yards apart. Everything was on the shoot; no favors asked, and none offered.

"My gun was so dirty that the ramrod hung in the barrel, and I could neither get it down nor out. I slammed the rod against a rock a few times and drove home ramrod, cartridge and all, laid the gun on a boulder, elevated the muzzle, ducked my head, halloed 'Look out!' and pulled the trigger. She roared like a young cannon and flew over my shoulder, the barrel striking John Griffith a smart whack on the left ear. John roared, too, and abused me like a pickpocket for my carelessness. It was no trouble to get another gun there. The mountain side was covered with them.

"Just to our left was a little fellow from the Third Arkansas regiment. He was comfortably located behind a big stump, loading and firing as fast as he could, and between biting cartridges and taking aim, he was singing at the top of his voice:

> "'Now, let the wide world wag as it will,
> I'll be gay and happy still.'"

"The world was wagging all right—no mistake about that, but I failed to see where the 'gay and happy' part came in.

"That was a fearful night. There was no sweet music to soothe the savage beast. The 'tooters' had left the shooters to fight it out, and taken 'Home, Sweet Home' and 'The Girl I Left Behind Me' off with them.

"Our spiritual advisers, chaplains of regiments, were in the rear, caring for the wounded and dying soldiers. With seven devils to each man, it was no place for a preacher, anyhow.

"A little red paint and a few eagle feathers were all that was necessary to make that crowd on both sides the most veritable savages on earth. 'White-winged Peace' didn't roost at Little Round Top that night. There was not a man there who cared a snap for the Golden Rule or that could have remembered one line of the Lord's Prayer. Both sides were whipped and all were mad about it."

Another member of the Texas Brigade, John C. West, of Company E, Fourth Texas, relates an interesting story of his experiences and observations at Gettysburg, saying:

"This was my first experience in a general engagement, and though we had marched all night of July 1, reaching the battlefield about 10 o'clock A. M. on the 2d, the interest and excitement and novelty of the occasion kept me up with my eyes and ears wide open. Our brigade was on the extreme right of the Confederate line, with perhaps one other brigade on our right. We marched and counter-marched and rested until about three o'clock in the afternoon, when we came into line in the edge of timber opposite Little Round Top and Devil's Den. I could see the Federal batteries, or rather the location of them, by the smoke of discharge. They were about half a mile or more from us. This was the first actual contact and full view of our enemy. We stood in column of fours, with our faces towards our right, for some time, during which the batteries commenced to play on us, and the first shot—which I recognized—seemed to be a solid shot, which struck the ground about 50 or 60 feet from the line and passed by on a bound over us, scattering dust and dirt over our company. The next shot passed about an equal distance beyond us, tearing up the earth. The third shot hit our line about eight feet in front of me, knocking off one soldier's head and cutting another in two, bespattering us with blood.

"Just then we fronted to the left, facing the battery. There was a short pause. I saw General Hood on horseback about 300 or 400 yards obliquely to my left, just out of direct range of the battery fire, in the edge of the timber. He took his hat, held it above him in his right hand, rose to his full height in his stirrups, and shouted in a stentorian voice, 'Forward! steady; forward!' We started across the open field. As we moved on I heard the word passing down the line, 'Quick, but not double quick!' We went in pretty fair order across the field. As we entered the timber and brush our line was more broken. We soon struck a stone fence; then came a branch. Lieutenant Joe Smith, Company E, wet his handkerchief, wrung it out and tied it around his head as he moved up the slope, which we had now reached. Bullets and grapeshot were coming thick and fast. A bullet passed through his head; examination afterwards showed 11 holes through the folded handkerchief. I think it made a white mark for a sharpshooter. As we advanced up the steep side of the mountain we encountered boulders from the size of a hogshead to the size of a small house. Our line at times could hardly be called a line at all. The battery was taken. The First Texas suffered the brunt of the battle. After we were up on the first ridge the ground was so rough and broken that it was impossible to form a straight line, but it was quite evident to me from the sounds on our left that we were in advance of our center. From this position we made sallies to our front, over rocks and boulders and timber. It was impossible to make a united charge. The enemy were pretty thick and well concealed. It was more like Indian fighting than anything that I experienced during the war. They had sharpshooters in trees and on high places that made it exceedingly dangerous to appear in any open place. One bullet passed through my beard and grazed my left ear. Another missed the top of my head about an inch. Both struck the rock against which I was sitting. I abandoned the position instanter. Just in front of us, perhaps 50 yards, was a comparatively open space on rising ground, very small in extent. It seemed almost certain death to attempt to pass it. Singly and in squads we made several experiments to test the presence of the enemy beyond, and every time, night or day, a shower of bullets greeted us. About 10 o'clock on the night of the 2d Goldsticker of Company A ventured out. He was mortally wounded, and lay there many hours calling for help. I can hear his plaintive cry, 'Water! water! Great God, bring me water!' but there was no truce. Death released him before the dawn. Poor Goldsticker! He was a gambler, a German and a Jew, but he died at the front!

"We held our position among the rocks all night and until about 5 o'clock in the afternoon of the 3d. Colonel Carter of the Fourth was severely wounded, afterwards captured, and died in the Federal hospital. Major Winkler was also wounded. Private Champ Fitzhugh of my company was also captured, and I saw him no more, until by a strange coincidence I met him in May, 1864, at 12 o'clock at night in the swamp on the bank of the Mississippi River, each of us attempting to cross the river. We crossed together in a canoe with Yankee gunboats above and below us. (This by way of parenthesis.)

"From 3 to 5 o'clock on the afternoon of the 3d the battle raged in the center on the left of our brigade. We had received the notice that the artillery on the whole line would open about 2 o'clock, and upon cessation of artillery fire the entire line would move forward. This order was carried out, and when our artillery opened the enemy answered as promptly as if a telephone message had said, 'Shoot now.'

"This cannonade was the grandest and most sublime circumstance I ever saw or heard. I can conceive of nothing grander, more portentous, or awful. An earthquake, a cyclone, a thunderstorm, a hurricane, all in one, could not be more terrific. It sounded veritably as if hell had broken loose and the unchained demons and furies were shrieking in the air. It was grand, sublime and glorious. The anticipation of the assault which was impending at the close of this fearful storm inspired the hearts of men with the joy of battle, which so filled us that there was no room for fear. While the earth quivered the storm ceased and the forward movement began. Our end of the line, crooked and curved by the broken condition of the ground, made no progress. We were already in advance of the troops on our left. When the contest seemed hot on our left and towards the center we moved to the front, hoping to find a weak place or an opening for flank movement, but the enemy evidently recognized the importance of that position, and we could gain no advantage there, but the fight grew fast and furious on our left. We could see nothing, but the Confederate yell and the Yankee huzzah alternated back and forth with such regularity for nearly an hour as to satisfy us that a critical moment was approaching at that point and that we were in danger of being flanked. Soon the 'huzzah' advanced so far as to create uneasiness in our part of the line, and directly notice came from our left to 'get out of here as quickly as you can.' We did not consider the order of our going, but rushed down the slope with better speed than we had been able to make coming in. As we had obliqued to the right coming up the mountain, and now obliqued to the left coming out, we struck the open field several hundred yards to the right of the stone fence and branch which we had crossed, and looking to our right, saw the Yanks in full line in the open field. We went across the field under fire without regard to tactics. Bullets were pretty thick and hit about us with that peculiar searching 'zip-zip' which suggests rapid locomotion.

"Mr. H. Van Dusen of Company C, Fourth Texas, was just in front of me about 10 feet. I heard a bullet hit him and saw him tumble over. I thought he was dead, and I so reported when our regiment got together after dark. Some man said, 'No; he is over there by a tree.' I went to the place and found Van Dusen with head bound with a white cloth. The bullet had struck him in the head, but failed to penetrate. He went to the field hospital, was afterwards captured and got among Dutch kinsfolk in Pennsylvania. It was said that they offered him every inducement to abandon the Confederacy, which he declined, went to prison, and was afterwards exchanged. He survived the war and returned to Texas."

Of what the Third Arkansas did on that 2nd day of July is officially told by Colonel Van H. Manning, as follows:

"About four o'clock on the evening of July 2, I was ordered to move against the enemy, keeping my right well connected with the left of the First Texas Regiment, and hold my left on the Emmitsburg Road, then some 200 yards in my front and out of view.

"Upon reaching this road, I discovered, from the direction the directing regiment was taking, that I could not with the length of my line carry out the latter order; hence I decided to keep my line on a prolongation of the line formed by the troops on my right. After marching in line of battle at a brisk gait (part of the way at a double-quick) for about 100 yards, all the time exposed to a destructive fire from artillery, we engaged the enemy at short range, strongly posted behind a rock fence at the edge of the woods. We drove him back with but a little loss, for a distance of 150 yards, when I ascertained that I was suffering from a fire to my left and rear. Thereupon, I ordered a change of front to the rear on first company, but the noise consequent upon the heavy firing then going on swallowed up my command, and I contented myself with the irregular drawing back of the left wing, giving it an excellent fire, which pressed the enemy back in a very short while, whereupon the whole line advanced, the enemy fighting stubbornly, but retiring.

"Soon I was again admonished that my left was seriously threatened, when I ordered the command back fifty to seventy-five yards, to meet this contingency. He was again driven back, and I stretched out my front to twice its legitimate length, guarding well my left, and advanced to the ledge of rocks from which we had previously been dislodged by the enemy's movement on my flank. I experienced some annoyance from the exposure of this flank up to this moment, when the Eleventh Georgia Regiment joined to my left. The Fifty-ninth Georgia Regiment, coming also at this time, occupied the line with my command. Some little time after this I was disabled by concussion and wound on my nose and forehead. The command then devolved on Lieutenant Colonel Taylor, who will report his operations subsequent to this time.

"It would be invidious to make special mention of gallantry in either officers or men when all did so well, fighting greatly superior numbers and at great disadvantage. I might safely assume that the bearing of the entire command was of the highest creditable character.

"No guns or colors were captured, and but few (some

twenty-five) prisoners, a number of whom were sent to the rear with wounded men."

No report by Colonel Taylor is to be found.

Of the First Texas, Lieutenant-Colonel P. A. Work says:
"The regiment, together with the brigade having been ordered forward to the attack about 4 P. M., continued to advance by the front for a distance exceeding half a mile, the Fourth Texas upon the right and the Third Arkansas upon the left, when Company I, commanded by Lieutenant J. H. Wooters, and thrown out as skirmishers, engaged the skirmishers of the enemy, driving them back upon a regiment supporting the enemy's battery, and then, aided by volunteers from this (First Texas) regiment, engaging the regiment and artillery, succeeded in driving back the regiment and silencing the enemy's guns, taking and holding possession of the latter.

"While this regiment was closely following our skirmishers, and had reached to within 125 yards of the enemy's artillery, the Third Arkansas Regiment on my left, became hotly engaged with a strong force of the enemy upon its front and left, thus leaving my left flank uncovered and exposed, to protect which I halted, and threw out upon my left and rear Company G, commanded by Lieutenant B. A. Campbell (some forty men), which soon engaged the enemy and drove them from their threatening position to the left and the front of the Third Arkansas. It was while in the execution of this order that Lieutenant Campbell, a brave and gallant officer, fell, pierced through the heart.

"Owing to the failure (as informed by Brigadier-General Robertson) of the troops that were assigned to the position on the left of this (Robertson's) brigade to arrive promptly, neither this nor the Third Arkansas was able to advance, without advancing against a vastly superior force, and with the left flank of the Third Arkansas (protecting my left) exposed to attack.

"After the lapse of several minutes, Benning's brigade made its appearance, but instead of occupying the ground to the left of Robertson's brigade, so as to enable the latter to move forward with its left flank secure from attack, it occupied the ground still occupied, by a portion at least, of this brigade, the

Fifteenth Georgia Regiment falling in and remaining with the First Texas Regiment. After several ineffectual efforts upon the part of both the commanders of the Fifteenth Georgia and myself to separate the men of the two regiments, we gave the order to move forward when both regiments, thus commingled, moved forward and occupied the crest of the hill, some 100 yards or more to the front, and where the enemy's artillery was stationed, where we remained until the close of the day and until two o'clock on Friday morning.

"During the evening of the 2nd an incessant fire was kept up by this regiment, and the enemy was several times repulsed in their efforts to retake the hill. My position was such that I was enabled to pour a deadly enfilading fire into the enemy as they advanced through a wheat field to attack the troops in position on my left, and I have no doubt that this fire contributed greatly to the repulse of the enemy attacking our forces some 300 or 400 yards on my left.

"Once during the evening the troops on my left were driven back, and my left was exposed, when, directing Captain H. E. Moss, Company D, to take charge of the colors, and retaining them there with a few men to hold the hill until the regiment could safely retire, I ordered the regiment to fall back to a stone fence about 100 yards in my rear. The major part of the regiment and the Fifteenth Georgia fell back as ordered, but quite a large number, having noticed that the colors were not moving to the rear, refused to withdraw, and remaining upon the crest of the hill, succeeded in holding the enemy in check in their immediate front, and obliquely upon their front and left, until the troops upon my left had been re-formed and were again advancing, when I directed Major F. S. Bass to return to the crest of the hill with the body of the regiment, and, with Captain D. K. Rice, of Company C, proceeded myself to collect together all fugitives, slightly wounded, and exhausted men, and placed them so as to protect my right and rear from an attack in that quarter, one of my advanced scouts in that direction having reported to me that a column of the enemy was moving down a ravine or hollow and threatening me in that quarter.

"Having made every disposition to guard my right and rear, I placed Captain D. K. Rice in charge of such defense, and proceeded to the Third Arkansas Regiment, of which General Robertson had ordered me to take charge. After the loss of some half hour in searching for the Third Arkansas, I found Lieutenant-Colonel Taylor and Major Reedy, of that regiment, both alive and uninjured, and in charge of the regiment, which was doing its duty nobly and well.

"Late in the evening a terrific fire of artillery was concentrated against the hill occupied by this (the First) regiment, many were killed and wounded, some losing their heads, and others so horribly mutilated and mangled that their identity could hardly be established, but notwithstanding this, all the men continued heroically and unflinchingly to maintain their position.

"Immediately after dark, having detailed Companies E and I for the purpose, I sent three pieces of the artillery captured to the rear. There were three other pieces—two at one point and one at another—that I was unable to remove, for the reason that they were located between the lines of the enemy and our own, and were so much exposed that they could not be approached except under a murderous fire. While they could not be removed by us, neither could they be approached by the enemy, for the same fire that drove the artillerists from their guns and the infantry from their support, was ever in readiness to keep them in check and drive them back. . . ."

"Every man of the regiment proved himself a hero. Hundreds might be mentioned, each of whom with reason and propriety might point to his gallant acts and daring deeds, and the lieutenant-colonel commanding feels that he cannot call attention to the bearing of a few only of those, without doing some share of injustice to those not mentioned; and though he is urged to mention the names of Privates W. Y. Salter, Company I; J. N. Kirksey and G. Barfield, of Company B, and W. J. Barbee, of Company L, for great and striking gallantry, and does mention them, he feels that he is neglecting others of equal merit. Private Barbee, though a mounted courier, acting for Major-General Hood, entered the ranks of his company, L, and fought through the engagement. At one time he mounted a rock on the highest pinnacle of the hill, and there, exposed to a raking, deadly fire of artillery and musketry, stood until he had fired twenty-five shots, when he received a minie-ball wound in the right thigh, and fell.

"Having exhausted their original supply of ammunition, the men supplied themselves from the cartridge boxes of their dead and disabled comrades, and from the dead and the wounded of the enemy, frequently going in front of the hill to secure a cartridge box. Many of the officers threw aside their swords, seized a rifle, and going into the ranks, fought bravely and nobly.

"The regiment lost in killed 25, in wounded 48, and missing 20, a list of the names of whom, giving the company and character of wound of those wounded, is hereto annexed as part of this report."

In the report of Major John P. Bane, of the Fourth Texas, is told what that regiment did. He says:

"About 4.30 p. m., the 2nd instant, we were ordered to advance on the enemy, who occupied the heights about one and one-fourth miles distant, the Fifth Texas, the directing battalion, on my right, and the First Texas on my left. Advancing at double-quick, we soon met the enemy's skirmishers, who occupied a skirt of thick undergrowth about one-quarter of a mile from the base of the cliffs, upon which the enemy had a battery playing upon us with the most deadly effect.

"After a short pause, while repelling the skirmishers, I was ordered by General Robertson to move by the right flank, so as to cover all the ground between us and the directing battalion. Moving about 200 yards, I met the enemy in full force in a heavy wooded ground, sheltering themselves behind rocks, from which, after a sharp contest, he was driven to the heights beyond in our front and in close proximity to the mountain, and there I was pained to learn that the gallant Lieutenant-Colonel B. F. Carter was severely wounded while crossing a stone wall near the base of the mountain. I was also informed that Colonel John C. G. Key, while gallantly urging the men to the front, was severely wounded. The command then devolved upon me. Many of the officers and men had been killed and wounded by this time.

"Finding it impossible to carry the heights by assault with my thinned ranks, I ordered my command to fall back to the skirt of timber, the position then occupied being enfiladed by the batteries on the left, and exposed to heavy fire by musketry in my immediate front. Being joined by the Fifth Texas on my right, I again attempted to drive the enemy from the heights by assault, but with like results. · Again, being reinforced by the Forty-eighth Alabama, commanded by the gallant Colonel James L. Sheffield, and the Forty-fourth Alabama, whose commander I did not learn, we again charged their works, but were repulsed, and then, under the order of General Law, I ordered my command to fall back under cover of the timber on a slight elevation within short range of the enemy. I formed my regiment in line of battle, leaving the battle-field contested ground.

"At the dawn of day, I had a stone wall about two feet high thrown up, which afforded some protection to the men occupying the position from which we had driven the enemy, until sunset of the 3rd instant, at which time I was ordered to move my command, in conjunction with the remainder of the brigade, by the right flank, to occupy the ground from which we first advanced upon the enemy.

"I accord to each and all of my officers and men my warmest congratulations for their continued and unceasing gallantry during the entire engagement."

Lieutenant-Colonel King Bryan, of the Fifth Texas, writes:
"Colonel R. M. Powell having fallen into the hands of the enemy, it devolves upon me as lieutenant-colonel of the regiment, to report the part taken by it as far as came under my observation in the action of July 2 and 3, near Gettysburg, Pa.

"About 4 P. M. on the 2nd instant, General Hood's division was drawn up in line of battle, fronting the heights occupied by the enemy. The Fifth Texas Regiment occupied the right of the brigade, resting on General Law's left, whose brigade was the one of direction. At the word, 'Forward,' the regiment moved forward in good order. The enemy had a line of sharpshooters at the foot of the first height, behind a stone fence about three-fourths of a mile from our starting point, which distance was passed over by our line at a double-quick and a run.

"At our approach, the enemy retired to the top of the first height, protected by a ledge of rocks. A short halt was made at the stone fence, to enable those who had fallen behind to regain their places. When the command 'forward' again fell from the lips of our gallant colonel, every man leaped the fence and advanced rapidly up the hill-side. The enemy again fled at our approach, sheltering himself behind his fortified position on the top of the second height, about 200 yards distant from the first.

"From this position we failed to drive them. Our failure was owing to the rocky nature of the ground over which we had to pass, the huge rocks forming defiles through which not more than three or four men could pass abreast, thus breaking up our alignment and rendering its re-formation impossible. Notwithstanding the difficulties to overcome, the men pressed on to the pass of the precipitous stronghold, forcing and securing the enemy's second position, many of our officers and men falling in passing the open space between the heights. Here we halted, there being small clusters of rocks far below the elevated position of the enemy, which gave us partial protection. From this position we were enabled to deliver our fire for the first time with accuracy.

"Seeing that the men were in the best obtainable position, and deeming a further advance without reinforcements impracticable (a great many of the regiment having been already disabled) I looked for Colonel Powell, to know his next order. Failing to see him I concluded at once that he, like many of his gallant officers and men, had fallen a victim to the deadly missiles of the enemy, which were being showered like hail upon us. I moved toward the center, passing many officers and men who had fallen, having discharged their whole duty as true soldiers. I had not proceeded far when I discovered the prostrate form of our noble colonel, who had fallen at his post, his face to the foe. I hastened toward him, when I received a wound in my left arm. On reaching the colonel, I found that he was not dead: but seeing the rent in his coat where the ball had passed out, my fears were excited that his wound would prove mortal. The hemorrhage from my own wound forced me from the field, leaving the command upon Major Rogers.

"The officers and men of my wing of the regiment continued to discharge their duties in a manner worthy of our cause so long as I remained upon the field, and from their conduct heretofore I would not hesitate to vouch for them during the remainder of the battle."

Following Colonel Bryan's report is that of Major J. C. Rogers, who says:

"I have the honor to forward a continuation of the report of the part taken by the Fifth Texas Regiment in the action of the 2nd and 3rd instant after the wounding of Colonels Powell and Bryan, when the command devolved upon me, the regiment still holding the position as left by Colonel Bryan, firing with accuracy and deadly effect.

"The order to fall back came from some unknown source, and, finding that the regiments on our right and left had retired, it became necessary to follow. I therefore gave the order for the regiment to about face and retire to the rear, which they did in good order until they reached the position mentioned in Colonel Bryan's report as the second position of the enemy, and here they were halted and re-formed, in connection with the other regiments. From the exhausted condition of the men, it was deemed necessary to remain here for a few moments.

"The regiments were again ordered forward, and obeyed in the most gallant manner, and regained their first position, which they held as long as it was tenable; and a further advance being impracticable, owing to the nature of the ground as expressed in Colonel Bryan's report, they again retired in good order to an open space about fifty yards in rear, when here it was discovered for the first time that nearly two-thirds of our officers and men had been killed and wounded.

"Only a few moments were here consumed to allow the men to recover their breath, when, in obedience to orders, I again moved the regiment forward to attack the enemy in their impregnable position. The coolness and determination of the men and officers were equal to the occasion. They advanced boldly over the ground strewn with the bodies of their dead and dying comrades to the base of what they knew to be an impregnable fortification. We held this position until it was discovered that we had no supports either on the right or left and were about to be flanked, and therefore were again compelled to retire, which the regiment did in good order, to the point mentioned in Colonel Bryan's report as the second position of the enemy, which place we were ordered to hold at all hazards, which we did.

"Just before day on the morning of the 3rd, orders reached me that breastworks must be thrown up, and the position held. The order was obeyed. During the day, constant skirmishing was kept up with the enemy, which resulted in the loss to us of many of our best scouts. Late in the evening, in obedience to orders, I about-faced my regiment, and marched three-quarters of a mile to the crest of the ridge from which the charge of the day previous commenced. Here we threw up breastworks, behind which we remained during the night.

"I would respectfully beg leave to call attention to the valuable assistance I received from Colonel John S. Cleveland in the management of the right wing of my regiment, and Captain T. T. Clay on the left; also, to the heroic conduct of T. W. Fitzgerald, of Company A, who was color-bearer. He pressed gallantly forward, and was badly wounded far in front. J. A. Howard, of Company B, color-corporal, then took the flag, and remained firmly at his post. He was almost instantly killed. The colors were then taken by Sergeant W. S. Evans, of Company F, who flaunted them defiantly in the face of the foe during the remainder of the fight, always advancing promptly to the front when the order was given.

"The general conduct of officers and men was beyond all praise."

In the report of Surgeon Lafayette Guild, medical director of the Army of Northern Virginia, the losses at Gettysburg of the regiments composing the Texas Brigade are given as follows:

Third Arkansas—Killed, 26; wounded, 116.
First Texas—Killed, 24; wounded, 54.
Fourth Texas—Killed, 14; wounded, 73.
Fifth Texas—Killed, 23; wounded, 86.

Making a total of 87 killed and 329 wounded. Any differences between this and a summation of regimental reports of losses may be accounted for by the fact that in losses reported by regimental commanders, missing men who afterwards rejoin their regiments are included.

Judged by its losses, which are usually held true criterions of the gallantry of a regiment and the dangers it faced, the Third Arkansas bore the brunt of the battle at Gettysburg.

CHAPTER XI

Gettysburg to Chickamauga

THAT General Lee's plan of battle for July 2nd contemplated a united and practically simultaneous assault upon the whole length of the Federal lines at Gettysburg, may be held as established beyond controversy by the facts when viewed in the light of a discriminating, dispassionate judgment. Longstreet's opening guns were to be the signal for Hill, holding the center of the Confederate line, and Ewell, holding its left, to move their veterans forward and engage the Federals in their respective immediate fronts. The object in view was two-fold; such a general attack would engage the attention of the enemy at all points and prevent the withdrawal by him of forces from unthreatened positions for the purpose of reinforcing those seriously menaced; and, with every Confederate command on the firing line, instant advantage could be taken of any confusion created in the enemy's ranks by such successes as might be won by Longstreet's men.

Why Ewell and Hill failed to act in concert with Longstreet, as unquestionably they were instructed, has never been satisfactorily explained. It is doubtful if it can be. Hill, two hours and a half after Longstreet began his assault, did send forward a few of his brigades, and three of these advanced to the very foot of Cemetery Ridge and captured eight pieces of artillery, while another, Wright's, reached the summit of the ridge and seized and, for a while, held twenty Federal cannon. This cut in two the Federal line, and had the success thus gained been promptly utilized, the Federal army would have been compelled to retreat. Hill, though, did not rise to the occasion, but held his other troops in line, but inactive, a mile to the rear, when they should have been well to the front.

At the time Wright's gallant brigade seized the twenty

cannon on the crest of Cemetery Ridge, two regiments of
Law's brigade, fighting on the extreme right of the Confederate army, were crossing the valley lying between the two
Round Tops, and advancing rapidly toward Little Round
Top; the Texas and Benning's brigades had fought their way
to the base of the precipitous cliffs forming the west wall of
the same mountain, driving the enemy before them; and Mc-
Laws' division had advanced beyond the Peach Orchard, the
enemy fleeing in confusion and dismay before it. If then
Ewell had but moved his men forward in a determined assault,
and thus given employment to the Union forces in his front,
Federal General Warren could not so easily have found a brigade and a battery to lead at full speed to the crest of Little
Round Top, and, with them, drive the Alabamians to the shelter of Devil's Den. But Ewell made no movement of any
kind until just before sunset—after Longstreet's battle had
ended through exhaustion, and the Federal line was re-estab-
lished and Little Round Top heavily manned and gunned.

Then Johnson's division assaulted and captured the first
line of Federal intrenchments on Culp's Hill, and Early's
division forced its way to the crest of Cemetery Ridge, and
for a while held the works there. But not only were both
Johnson's and Early's forces left wholly unsupported, but
Federal General Hancock, noting that Longstreet's command
had ceased to advance and that danger no longer menaced the
Union center and left flank, withdrew troops from these points,
and drove both Johnson and Early back. The success which
attended the movements of Johnson and Early proves, beyond
controversy, that the enemy's position in their front was far
from impregnable. Had they made their assaults as soon as
Longstreet's signal guns were fired, or at any time while Hood
and McLaws' divisions were driving the Federals before them,
and before these divisions had spent their strength and, hopeless of aid from either Hill or Ewell, were retiring from their
hard-won vantage ground, the chances of victory would have
been overwhelmingly in favor of the Southern army.

Of whatever needless delay, slow and deliberate movement,
and unwillingness to give battle, General Longstreet may be
accused and may have been guilty, there was yet abundance
of time after the divisions of Hood and McLaws went into

action, in which, by united effort, to drive the Union army from its stronghold and put it to rout. In Volume III of Confederate Military History, the author of the volume says:

Longstreet's bold fight had, undoubtedly, won the day, if Hill's corps had, in its entirety, performed its assigned duty. The writer witnessed, from Seminary Ridge, the hurried movement of troops from Meade's right on Culp's Hill and the Cemetery, toward his broken center and left.

Whatever the omissions and shortcomings of Longstreet, Hill and Ewell; out of time with each other as were the assaults made by the Confederates on right, left and center of the Union position, General Meade was not only disheartened by the day's contest, but so alarmed for the safety of his army, as to be ready to retreat. That night he held conference with his subordinate commanders, and with them discussed its advisability. General Hancock's chief of staff has put on record the statement that for the Union army "it was indeed a gloomy hour." While they deliberated, though, and when an agreement was almost reached to fall back to the line of Pipe Creek, and there halting in defensive position, cover the approaches to Baltimore and Washington, one of their scouts appeared, bringing with him dispatches he had captured from a courier sent by President Davis to General Lee, in which Mr. Davis refused to comply with Lee's urgent request that a Confederate force, under General Beauregard, be concentrated at Culpeper Court House to threaten Washington. This information relieved Meade of apprehensions for the safety of the Federal capital, and he decided to hold on another day at Gettysburg.

General Lee was not disheartened by the failures of July 2nd. Knowing the temper and spirit of the rank and file of his army and having unbounded confidence in its ability and willingness to accomplish any task he might assign it, and the lust for battle still inspiring him, he determined to renew on the morning of July 3rd the attack as first planned. Accordingly, Longstreet, reinforced by Pickett's division, which had come up late in the afternoon of the 2nd, was ordered to again attack the Federal left—Ewell, at the same time, to assault the Federal right, and Hill to move simultaneously and with his whole force against its center. But when the morning of July 3rd dawned, it was discovered that two Federal corps had taken possession of and fortified the Round Tops, and as these dominated the Confederate right and protected the Federal center, General Lee abandoned the plan, and resolved to make a vigorous and well-supported assault on Cemetery Ridge, hoping thereby to break through the Union center and take its right in reverse.

It is not within the province of this volume to give an account of a battle in which the Texas Brigade took no direct and active part, and of which its members caught but fleeting glimpses, and heard only the noises. Beginning about 1 A. M. for an hour or more, 140 Confederate and 70 Federal cannon belched forth their thunders and dealt destruction to everything living within their range. Flame and smoke rose from the long lines of the opposing ridges; the roar of the guns was deafening to the ears of all within miles of the conflict, and a dense dark cloud of smoke settled down between the opposing armies and concealed them from each other. General Francis A. Walker, Hancock's chief of staff, says of the effect of the Confederate artillery:

The whole space behind Cemetery Ridge was in a moment rendered uninhabitable. General headquarters were broken up; the supply and reserve ammunition trains were driven out; motley hordes of camp-followers poured down the Baltimore pike, or spread over the fields to the rear. Upon every side caissons exploded; horses were struck down by the hundreds; the air was filled with flying missiles; shells tore up the ground and then bounded for another and, perhaps, more deadly flight, or burst above the crouching troops and sent their ragged fragments down in deadly showers. Never had a storm so dreadful burst upon mortal man.

Then began the brave and heroic, the superbly magnificent, the awe-inspiring charge of Pickett's and Pettigrew's divisions. Language beggared, it would yet remain undescribed and indescribable. Even those whose fortune it was to witness it can grasp but a small part of its splendid pluck and daring. Still, it failed. Resolute, fearless and indomitable as were the assailants, the assailed were equally so; American valor was matched against American valor, and having the advantage in position, the Federals, standing manfully to their guns, shattered the Confederate columns and drove them back. The courage manifested that day by the Union soldiers proves that it was not to their lack of pluck that their failures and defeats were due—it was to the timidity of their commanders. It has never been confessed, but in effect and deed, McClellan, Pope, Burnside, Hooker, Meade, and even Grant, each in his turn acknowledged Robert E. Lee as his superior in generalship. Not one of them ever attacked or dared attack him with equal forces. Each insisted on having as nearly two men to his one as was possible, and this advantage they respectfully held in the days of battle around Richmond, at Second Manassas, Fredericksburg, Chancellorsville, Gettysburg, The Wilderness, and at all the many hard-contested battles after the Wilderness. The streams of courage and confidence, do not, as a rule, flow from foot to head—they move downward from head to foot. The bravery of the rank and file of the army he commands is not so inspiring to the general as the manifestation of his own is to them.

Longstreet's game but unsupported and fruitless battle of July 2nd ended at sunset of that day. Whether true or not that he made it unwillingly and directed it half-heartedly, he stayed on the firing line from its inception to its finish, and by his presence encouraged his men to their bravest efforts. Hopeless at last of further assistance from Hill, and none at all coming from Ewell, it only remained for him to hold as much of the ground won as he safely could with the shattered remnants of his command. Quite early in the engagement General Hood was wounded and carried from the field, and the command of his division fell upon General E. M. Law, its senior brigadier. The Texas Brigade was withdrawn from it advanced position, and from the new line formed, pickets were sent forward to watch the movements of the enemy. It was not until 2 A. M. of July 3rd, though, that the First Texas and Third Arkansas, which, during the fighting, had borne well to the left and thus separated themselves from the Fourth and Fifth Texas, reached the new position.

While on the 3rd the gallant Confederates under Pickett and Pettigrew were so heroically battling against no less gal-

HOOD'S TEXAS BRIGADE   195

lant Federals—the one, to break, the other, to hold fast the Union center, the regiments of the Texas Brigade were neither idle nor unexposed to danger. Hood's division was the right flank of the Southern army; Law's brigade guarded the right flank of the division, and next in line to Law's but on its left, all that day stood the Texans and Arkansans, most of the time in line of battle, and all the time ready, at a moment's notice, to move to right or left, or forward, as the exigency might require. For while such a large part of Lee's army engaged, or was held ready to engage, in the tragic struggle far to the left, the time was opportune for a movement from the Round Tops on our right flank, and several tentative ones were made, both by infantry and cavalry. None succeeded, though, and after the loss his army suffered in repulsing the assault upon his center, Meade had little stomach for further battle, big or little. Still, activity on the skirmish lines continued during the whole of that day, and was not entirely lacking on the next.

Nor was General Lee inclined to renew the struggle. In his official report, he says: " The severe loss sustained by the army, and the reduction of its ammunition, rendered another attempt to dislodge the enemy unadvisable, and it was therefore determined to withdraw." Yet he did not withdraw in such haste as to endanger the safety either of the army or its long wagon trains. All day of the 4th he held his army in line waiting for such attack as Meade with his remaining 72,000 men might dare make on the 38,000 Confederates left. But Meade made none; lofty and difficulty of ascent as were Cemetery Ridge and the Round Tops, and skilfully and courageously as they were defended, he had lost 23,000 to Lee's 20,000, and on each day of battle had barely held his ground; if while fighting "on his own dung-hill" strictly in defense, he had so nearly suffered defeat, it would be, he must have thought, suicidal to take the offensive.

In a letter written April 15, 1868, which may be read in full in Volume VII of Southern Historical Papers, beginning on page 445, General Lee wrote:

As to the battle of Gettysburg, I must again refer you to the official accounts. It was commenced in the absence of correct intelligence. It was continued in the effort to overcome the difficulties by which we were surrounded, and it would have been gained could one determined and united blow have been delivered by our whole line. As it was, victory trembed in the balance for three days, and the battle resulted in the infliction of as great an amount of injury as was received and in frustrating the Federal campaign for the season.

On the 4th of July, 1864, save during the hours devoted to caring for the wounded and burying the dead, the two armies rested. Only occasional shots on the picket lines broke a stillness grateful and comforting to Confederates and Federals alike. In the afternoon it commenced raining, at first gently, but as night approached, very heavily—the down-pour continuing all night, and making the march the Texas Brigade began at daylight of the 5th, toward the Potomac at Williamsport, exceedingly difficult and wearisome. But there was no grumbling, no depression of spirits, notwithstanding the fact that with the assurance of their own defeat came the unwelcome news of Pemberton's surrender of Vicksburg and its defending army. For that surrender, the Army of Northern Virginia was in no way to blame, and with troubles of their own at hand, they had neither time nor inclination to bewail it as the great misfortune it really was.

For their repulse on the 2nd,—the first they had ever encountered—the members of the Texas Brigade found comfort in the reflection that it was due, not to the superior bravery of their antagonists, or to any lack of effort on their part, but to the insurmountable physical obstacle with which nature had strewn their line of advance. As said by one of them and endorsed by all within hearing: "Even if we didn't have wings to fly up on top of those steep bluffs and put the Yankees there to making tracks for tall timber, we crippled and slaughtered without mercy or let-up those we met in the lowlands. We whipped them to a frazzle, and good Lord, didn't we put speed in the legs of such of them as tried to get away! Fact is, boys, we won a big and glorious victory before we got to those high, precipitous cliffs and bluffs. There, we butted up against God Almighty's everlasting and immovable handiworks, and we just had to stop."

The march from Gettysburg was unmarked, as far as the

Texas Brigade was concerned, by any incident worthy of note. General Meade was too glad of Lee's withdrawal from Gettysburg to make any determined effort to hold him north of the Potomac, or, when finding that river impassable, Lee halted, to attack him at once. Instead, he waited till the 14th, and then advanced to discover that the Confederate army was across the Potomac and beyond his reach.

From the Potomac, Hood's division moved by way of Culpeper Court House to Fredericksburg on the Rappahannock, halting and staying at first one point and then another on the route, for periods of from two to ten days—its longest stop being at Culpeper. That its marching was slow is evident from the fact that it was not until August 3rd that it reached and camped on the south side of the Rapidan, near Raccoon ford. Thence, it proceeded to Fredericksburg, where, for three weeks, it rested undisturbed by any call to active duty. Along the Rapidan and the upper waters of the Rappahannock, but too far away for Hood's men to hear even the echoes of the guns fired, there was much marching and countermarching, and many skirmishes, but knowing that the corps of Hill and Ewell, and Stuart's cavalry, were the only troops engaged, they stood indifferent. "Let 'em fight, let 'em fight," said a Texan; "it's high time they were doin' it, durn 'em. If the cavalry had kept its place on our right, and if Hill and Ewell's men had come half-way up to the scratch over yonder at Gettysburg, we'd be feasting to-day on brotherly love at Philadelphia, or on terrapin and canvas-back ducks at Baltimore instead of being down here in old Virginia nibbling carefully at our rations lest they run short. Let 'em fight—it's not our funeral."

While neither the fall of Vicksburg nor the reverse with which the Army of Northern Virginia met at Gettysburg weakened its confidence in the final success of the Confederacy, the former event had the effect of curtailing rations. Up to that time the hunger with which it had suffered was due to the failures of commissary trains to keep in touch with the troops they supplied—now it was due to the inability of the Commissary Department to supply the rations needed; up to that date the soldiers stayed hungry only until the wagons came up—now they stayed so all the time, the ration issued having been reduced so largely in quantity. Texas could no longer be depended on for herds of beeves, and economy became the rule enforced by the Commissary-General.

September 3rd Hood's division moved down the river to Bowling Green, a little town on the south side of the Rappahannock, twenty miles below Fredericksburg. Here it remained a few days, when it and McLaws' division was ordered south to reinforce the army commanded by General Bragg, then somewhere in the vicinity of Chattanooga, Tenn. The situation in September, 1863, was not comforting to the South, and many viewed it with grave apprehension. The fall of Vicksburg and the unrestrained possession and control it gave the Federals of the Mississippi River, divided the Confederacy into two distinct theaters of war, neither of which could aid the other in men, material or food supplies. It was now proposed by the military authorities of the North to cut in twain that part of the South east of the Mississippi, and a large and well-appointed Union army, under command of General Rosecrans, was now moving toward the northern borders of Georgia —its aim a march through that State to the sea—its objective point, Savannah, Ga. From west of the Mississippi, the Trans-Mississippi Department, so-called, no aid to the Confederate armies east of that stream could be expected; Tennessee and a large part of Mississippi were in the possession of the Union forces; the Confederate States lying along the Atlantic and Gulf of Mexico were largely exhausted of supplies, and altogether, the situation was one for serious concern.

To drive the advancing Federal armies out of Tennessee, Mississippi, and perhaps, Kentucky, was the need of the hour, and to aid in the accomplishment of that purpose, two divisions of Longstreet's corps were detached from the Army of Northern Virginia and ordered to the reinforcement of Bragg's army. More was hoped for from the movement than in reason should have been expected. General Braxton Bragg did not prove capable of profiting by the aid given himself and his army. The successes gained were not followed up as they should have been.

At what date the Texas Brigade took train at Richmond cannot be stated. It started, and made the journey down to Georgia, in unseated flat and box cars—slept on the floors and tops of these as best it could—and subsisted on hard-tack and uncooked bacon. Save at Wilmington, N. C., where it stayed a day and night and made its only change of train, it had no relief between Richmond and Atlanta from the constant joltings of springless freight cars running over roadbeds made rough by constant usage, and seldom repaired. It arrived at Atlanta on the morning of September 17, and on the 18th boarded a train that carried it to Ringgold, Ga., to the near vicinity of which General Bragg had suffered his army driven. Thence, about mid-day, it marched westward, toward the Chickamauga River and the enemy. Late in the afternoon a body of Federal cavalry appeared in its front, but was soon put to flight by Forrest's Confederate cavalry. The brigade, however, was called into line of battle. While thus formed, General Hood, last seen by it at Gettysburg where he was crippled in the arm, rode from the front, mounted on the sturdy roan horse, "Jeff Davis," that he usually rode in battle. It was with difficulty that a shout of welcome was repressed lest it give notice to the enemy that Confederate infantry was at hand. But every hat was lifted in acknowledgment of Hood's presence as he passed through the line to take his place in its rear.

A few minutes later the Terry Rangers—Eighth Texas cavalry—passed along in the rear of the brigade. It was the first Texas command we had met since the beginning of the war, and as many of them were personally known to us, salutations were exchanged by the lifting of hats and the waving of handkerchiefs.

Next to the Fourth and Fifth Texas—the First Texas, it must be remembered, straggled to Virginia—the Rangers were the first Texas command to volunteer for service east of the Mississippi River. Its ranks filled by the flower of the Lone Star State, it was not long in gaining a reputation for daring that, while seemingly reckless, was too resolute to bring disaster. Its victories many, its defeats few, we Texans of the Virginia army watched its career with an interest not felt in any other troops from our State. In sober truth, it was the only body of Texas cavalry which, emulating the bravery and heroism of Bonham, Travis, Crockett and their compatriots in the Alamo, had won distinction, and for that reason the members of the First, Fourth and Fifth Texas recognized and hailed its members as kindred spirits.

The Federal cavalry dispersed, the Texas Brigade again moved forward, and about midnight crossed the Chickamauga on Reid's bridge, and filing to the left a short distance beyond the stream, bivouacked for the night. The march from Ringgold had been long and fatiguing, and nobody had the heart to blame the boys of the Third Arkansas infantry for surreptitiously impressing into their service the fifty odd horses of the Third Arkansas cavalry, of Harrison's cavalry brigade, whose riders had carelessly tied them in fence corners by the road-side. The victims of the joke, however, found compensation for it when they accepted the invitation extended in the following lines, written on a scrap of paper that was tacked to a tree:

"Tired of long walking and needing a rest,
 Your steeds we have gratefully seized and impressed,
 Feeling it but fair you should do a little walking,
 And put yourself where you can do a lot of talking
 With the Third Arkansas infantry, your old friends and neighbors,
 Who have come from Virginia to share in your labors,
 And, the Lord being willing, the Yankees to smite
 And set them to running with all of their might.
 We'll camp, beyond doubt, after a while,
 Though you may have to foot it, mile after mile;
 But come till you find us—it will give you exercise,
 As well as a heart for gallant enterprise
 When, the Yanks on the run, we follow them close,
 And of bullets and steel, give them a dose."

Because of his loss of a leg at Chickamauga, General Hood made no official report of the part taken by his division in that bloody engagement. If General Robertson or the regimental commanders of the Texas Brigade made reports they have been lost, and at any rate, are not accessible. The only account Hood gave of the battle appears in his book, "Advance and Retreat." This is in the nature of a reminiscence, and as such, comes well within the province of a narrative in which military technicalities are eschewed as far as they may be without risk of inaccuracies. He writes:

JOHN D. MURRAY
Company F, Fourth Texas Regiment

FACING 200

I arrived at Ringgold, Georgia, on the afternoon of September 18th, 1863, and there received an order from General Bragg to proceed on the road to Reid's bridge, and assume command of the column then advancing on the Federals. I had my horse to leap from the train, mounted with one arm in a sling, and, about 3 P. M., joined our forces, then under the direction of General Bushrod Johnson and in line of battle. A small body of Federal cavalry was posted upon an eminence a short distance beyond. On my arrival upon the field I met for the first time after the charge at Gettysburg a portion of my old troops, who received me with a touching welcome. After a few words of greeting exchanged with General Johnson, I assumed command in accordance with the instructions I had received, ordered the line to be broken by filing into the road, sent a few picked men to the front in support of Forrest's cavalry, and began to drive the enemy at a rapid pace.

In a short time we arrived at Reid's bridge across the Chickamauga, and discovered the Federals drawn up in battle array beyond the bridge, which they had partially destroyed. I ordered forward some pieces of artillery, opened fire, and, at the same time, threw out flankers to effect a crossing above and below and join in the attack. Our opponents quickly retreated. We repaired the bridge, and continued to advance till darkness closed in on us, when we bivouacked in line, near a beautiful residence which had been fired by the enemy, and was then almost burned to the ground. We had driven the Federals back a distance of six or seven miles. Meantime, the main body of army crossed the Chickamauga at different points, and concentrated that night in the vicinity of my command.

General Bragg having formed the plan of attack next morning, I was given, in addition to my own division, the direction of Kershaw's and Johnson's divisions, with orders to continue the advance. We soon encountered the enemy in strong force, and a heavy engagement ensued. All that day we fought, slowly but steadily gaining ground. Fierce and desperate grew the conflict, as the foe stubbornly yielded before our repeated assaults; we drove him, step by step, a distance of fully one mile, when nightfall brought about a cessation of hostilities, and the men slept upon their arms.

In the evening, according to my custom in Virginia under General Lee, I rode back to army headquarters to report to the commander-in-chief the result of the day upon my part of the line. I there met for the first time several of the principal officers of the Army of Tennessee, and, to my surprise, not one spoke in a sanguine tone regarding the result of the battle in which we were then engaged. I found the gallant Breckenridge, whom I had known from early youth, seated by the root of a tree, with a heavy slouch hat upon his head. When in the course of a brief conversation, I stated that we would rout the enemy the following day, he sprang to his feet, exclaiming, "My dear Hood, I am delighted to hear you say so. You give me renewed hope; God grant it may be so!"

After receiving orders from General Bragg to advance the next morning as soon as the troops on my right moved to the attack, I returned to the position occupied by my forces, and camped the remainder of the night with General Buckner, as I had nothing with me save that which I had brought from the train upon my horse. Nor did my men have a single wagon, or even ambulance in which to convey the wounded. They were destitute of almost everything, I might say, except pride, spirit, and forty rounds of ammunition to the man.

During that night, after a hard day's fight by his old and trusty troops, General Longstreet joined the army. He reported to General Bragg after I had left army headquarters, and, the next morning, when I had arranged my columns for the attack and was awaiting the signal on the right to advance, he rode up, and joined me. He inquired concerning the formation of my lines, the spirit of our troops, and the effect produced upon the enemy by our assault. I informed him that the feeling of officers and men was never better, that we had driven the enemy fully one mile the day before, and that we would rout him bfore sunset. This distinguished general instantly responded with the confidence that had so often contributed to his extraordinary success, that we would *of course* whip and drive him from the field. I could but exclaim that I was rejoiced to hear him so express himself, as he was the first general I had met since my arrival who talked of victory.

He was assigned to the direction of the left wing, and placed me in command of five divisions: Kershaw's, A. P. Stewart's, Bushrod Johnson's, and Hindman's, together with my own. The latter formed the center of my line, with Hindman upon my left, Johnson and Stewart on the right, and Kershaw in reserve. About 9 A. M. the firing on the right commenced; we immediately advanced and engaged the enemy, when followed a terrible roar of musketry from right to left. Onward we moved, nerved with a determination to become masters of that hotly contested field. We wrestled with the resolute foe till about 2.30 P. M., when, from a skirt of timber to our left, a body of Federals rushed down upon the immediate flank and rear of the Texas Brigade, which was forced to suddenly change front.

Some confusion necessarily arose. I was at the time on my horse, upon a slight ridge about three hundred yards distant, and galloped down the slope, in the midst of the men, who speedily corrected their alignment. At this moment, Kershaw's splendid division, led by its gallant commander, came forward, as Hindman advanced to the attack a little further to the left. Kershaw's line formed, as it were, an angle with that of the Federal line, then in full view in an open space near the wood. I rode rapidly to his command, ordered a change of front forward on his right, which was promptly executed under a galling fire. With a shout along my entire front, the Confederates rushed forward, penetrated into the wood, over and beyond the enemy's breastworks, and thus achieved another glorious victory for our arms. About this time I was pierced with a minie-ball in the upper third of the right leg; I turned from my horse upon the side of the crushed limb, and fell—strange to say, since I was commanding five divisions—into the arms of some of the troops of my old brigade, which I had directed so long a period, and upon so many fields of battle.

Long and constant service with this noble brigade must prove sufficient apology for a brief reference, at this juncture, to its extraordinary military record from the hour of its first encounter with the enemy at Eltham's Landing, on York River, in 1862, to the surrender at Appomattox Court House. In almost every battle in Virginia it bore a conspicuous part. It acted as the advance guard of Jackson when he moved upon McClellan, around Richmond; and almost, without an exceptional instance, it was amongst the foremost of Longstreet's corps in an attack or pursuit of the enemy. It was also, as a rule, with the rear guard of this corps, whenever falling back before the adversary. If a ditch was to be leaped, or fortified position to be carried, General Lee knew no better troops upon which to rely. In truth, its signal achievements in the war of secession have never been surpassed in the history of nations.

The members of this heroic band were possessed of a streak of superstition, as in fact I believe all men to be; and it may here prove of interest to cite an instant thereof. I had a favorite roan horse, named by them, "Jeff Davis"; whenever he was in condition I rode him in battle, and, remarkable as it may seem, he generally received the bullets and bore me unscathed. In this battle he was severely wounded on Saturday; the following day, I was forced to resort to a valuable mare in my possession, and late in the afternoon was shot from the saddle. At Gettysburg I had been unable to mount him on the field, in consequence of lameness; in this engagement I had also been shot from the saddle. Thus the belief among the men became nigh general that, when mounted on old Jeff, the bullets could not find me. This spirited and fearless animal performed his duty throughout the war, after which he received tender care from General Jefferson and family, of Seguin, Texas, until death, when he was buried with appropriate honors.

General Hood parted from his old brigade and division on that second day of battle at Chickamauga. Never again did he command the division, or come in touch with the brigade. For "distinguished conduct and ability in the battle of the 29th," he was recommended for promotion by General Longstreet, and on the 1st of February, 1864, was commissioned as a lieutenant-general, and assigned to the command of a corps in the Army of the Tennessee, then under the leadership of General Joseph E. Johnston.

A mutual confidence and trust, a mutual admiration and love existed between John B. Hood and the Texas Brigade. Each felt it was indebted, and each was grateful to the other. If to Hood's training, teaching and example, was largely due the victories won by the brigade, it was none the less its courage, endurance and unconquerable spirit that uplifted and gave him distinction and promotion. Each trusted the other —Hood, that the brigade would accomplish all he asked of it—the Texas Brigade, that he would make no demand on it beyond its power.

It was this feeling between them that prompted the brigade to adopt and cling to the distinctive title of " Hood's " Texas Brigade—it was this feeling that was uppermost in the mind of Hood, when at Chickamauga, believing himself, perhaps, mortally wounded, he fell from his horse into the waiting arms of members of his old brigade, and as he fell, gave his last order on that field, " Go ahead, and keep ahead of everything," in the words of the command they had so often heard him shout to them in Virginia, Maryland and Pennsylvania. The insistence of the survivors of the command to which that order was addressed on being known as members of Hood's Texas Brigade, is not intended as a disparagement of the

CAPTAIN J. T. HUNTER
Company H, Fourth Texas Regiment

military ability of their subsequent brigade commanders, Generals Jerome B. Robertson and John Gregg. Each of these was brave and capable and his memory is yet cherished in the hearts of the soldiers he commanded; but neither had the personal magnetism of Hood, nor the swinging dash and reckless yet cool disregard of danger, which, from the outset, won the love and admiration of a brigade largely composed of boys just flowering into manhood. And, although both Robertson and Gregg had lived many years in Texas, neither made as just an estimate as Hood, of Texas character, nor felt and acted in such accord with it.

The larger part of the fighting done at Chickamauga was in the somber shadows of thick growths of large pine timber. The soil sterile, it was only now and then that a clearing gave the combatants access to uninterrupted sunlight. Under the trees there was much undergrowth of various kinds. It was difficult for an officer on horseback to get an extended view in any direction, and to footmen it was simply impossible. Short as was the line occupied by the Texas Brigade, neither flank of it could be seen from the other. Therefore, when it is told that the First, Fourth and Fifth Texas and the Third Arkansas went into action side by side, were met by a murderous fire of artillery and musketry, and, by resolute and steady advance and more than one seemingly desperate charge, drove the men from the Western States who so largely composed Rosecrans' army, a distance of fully one mile, about all is said that can be, in description of the fight made by the Texas Brigade on the 19th of September.

As a rule, the Western men of Rosecrans' army were as plucky as the Southerners in the "stand-up-and-fire" or the "lie-down-and-shoot" fights that were so much in vogue in both Rosecrans' and Bragg's armies. As said by Bill Calhoun, "at them ar games, they was powerful hard to handle."

Unaccustomed, though, to have their antagonists rush against their lines in the wild charges so common in Virginia, the Western men were about as easily forced out of the way of the Texas Brigade as had been the foes of that command in the State mentioned. It was a Spanish officer who, as he tendered his sword to his captor at San Juan, Cuba, said in indignant tone: "You Americans do not fight like gentlemen—you rush right up to us and make a personal affair of a battle that should be strictly impersonal." Just so may have thought the Western men we encountered at Chickamauga. Whether they did or not, it is but justice to say that when driven from a position by a charge, they hung together well, and soon recovering from their consternation, formed in battle array at the next good position, ready for the next charge, and that while such charges were being made and until we were quite near them, they fired with an accuracy that inflicted great loss on their assailants.

Referring to official reports and histories for positions of the opposing forces and general description of the battles of the 19th and 20th, place will now be given to an account written by a participant from the view-point accessible to soldiers who moved in line with, or, as officers, close in rear of their comrades.

"Notwithstanding its long and weary tramp of the day before, the Texas Brigade was early astir on the morning of September 19. While munching hard-tack and nibbling at the rancid bacon issued to us at Atlanta, the one absorbing question of the hour was 'What next?' Not a soul of us dreamed that we were then within two miles of fully 45,000 Yankees, and that before the day ended we would be wresting with them in deadly battle. The firing we had heard the day before came, we supposed, from opposing bodies of cavalry, and as the cavalry we were accustomed to in Virginia had never been in sight when we got within ten miles of any considerable body of armed Federal infantry, we took it for granted that 'hoofing it' would be the program of the day. It was, therefore, with astonishment we listened, when Captain Howdy Martin came down from 'Aunt Pollie's' headquarters and announced, not only the near proximity of the Federal army, but the probability that before noon we would be engaged.

"We had barely regained the composure old Howdy's announcement robbed us of, when there broke upon our ears a terrifying roar, the like of which we had never heard in our lives. It came from the direction of Chattanooga, from some place quite a distance from us, and it appeared to be stationary. The earth beneath us seemed to tremble with its concussions, the trees above us to rock back and forth.

"'It's a tornado,' ventured one fellow; 'I was right in the middle of one, up about Dallas, Texas, four years ago, and it roared just like this does. It's time we were hunting for holes, I reckon,' and he began looking around in search of one.

"'It's a stampede of beeves,' volunteered a Texas cow-boy, as he measured with his eyes the girth and height of the tall pine trees beneath which we stood; 'and by the Lord Harry, boys, there must be a million of 'em or they wouldn't make such a racket. If there was a tree in sight that I thought I could climb, you wouldn't catch me standing here—I'd be up on its topmost limb.'

"'You are all mistaken, gentlemen,' interposed the wise man, a school teacher, who, like the jester, Wamba, in the story of Ivanhoe, believed in the doctrine held by Oldhelm of Malmsbury, 'Better a fool at a feast, than a wise man at a fray.' 'It is an earthquake—an upheaval of the crust of the earth, that is tumbling Lookout, and half a dozen other mountains into the Tennessee River. Do you not feel the trembling of the ground under us, and see the swaying of the tree-tops?'

"For two seconds the earthquake theory held our minds fast-bound by its appalling terrors; then the irreverent dare-devil of the regiment came to the rescue. Addressing the wise man, he said: 'It's your cowardly legs, Mr. School Master, that are doing all the trembling and making you imagine the tree-tops are swaying. That isn't an earthquake, a stampede, or a tornedo—it's music. All the bands in the Yankee army are playing, "Hell Broke Loose in Georgia." I've danced all night, many a time, to the tune, but d—d if I ever heard it played quite so loud.'

"The laugh that all joined in, dissipated the solemnity that was fast stealing upon our minds, and just then a comrade who a little while ago had visited friends in Bragg's army, remarked: 'You are all mistaken, boys, and you will find out you are, sooner than you care for. That is the noise of a battle between large forces of Yankees and Confederates.'

"'You are joking, Patterson—you are surely joking,' said an officer; 'that noise is stationary. It neither approaches nor recedes, as it would were troops engaged in battle, and advancing and retreating, as one or the other side gained or lost.'

"' I thought just that way, Captain, the first time I heard such a noise,' rejoined Patterson. ' But I soon learned better. These Yankees and Confederates here in Tennessee and Georgia don't fight like we do in Virginia—they just get within fairly close range of each other, and then coming to a halt, indulge in a stand-up-and-fight, or a lie-down-and-shoot game; there is no charging and counter-charging. When one side gets all the punishment it can stand, it quits, and the victory is awarded to the other side.'

"As usual, Bill Calhoun claimed the last word. 'Well, boys,' he said, ' if we have to stand up or lie down in a straight line, and let the Yankees shoot at us as long as they want to, this old Texas Brigade is going to run like h—ll.'

"An hour passed. Then the brigade was called to attention, and moving forward a mile or more, it halted a half a mile in rear of the troops then holding our front. There we remained fully three hours, at first giving undivided attention to the desultory firing in progress, and then relaxing from strain, falling into an exchange of gossip and pleasantries—the latter, aimed as a rule, at Confederates who expected to win battles without charges. Habe Brahan and myself, I recollect, had a long conversation over long-past college happenings, with Captain Jemmison of the First Texas, who had been one of our class-mates.

"Toward the close of the long wait, Jack Sutherland and I indulged in a friendly smoke and chat. We were both puffing at our pipes when the command, ' Attention!' was given. Jack at once removed his pipe from his lips, and surmising his purpose I said, ' Go on with your smoking, man—it'll be an hour before we get under fire.' ' No, I'll not smoke any more, just now,' he replied, and knocking the ashes and embers from the pipe, he stuck it in his pocket. I held on to mine; it was my last pipeful of the Zarvona tobacco I had brought with me from Virginia, and I felt bound to realize the full benefit of it. But I did not.

"Within three minutes a fierce battle began at the front, and the brigade moved into line of battle—the movement hastened by the divers and sundry bullets, round shot and shells that came flying in our direction. Jack and I stood side by side, and I was still smoking. General Hood rode back from the front, and as he passed through our line on his way to its rear, was greeted by a shout of welcome. He had not gone twenty yards to the rear, though, when a solid shot or shell struck the ground about thirty feet in front of Jack and myself, and ricochetting, passed over, but so close to our heads that I felt the wind of it. It scared me, and, I am confident, my face turned white as a sheet. I pulled my hat down over my pallid countenance, and, fear loving company as well as misery does, stole a glance at Jack's face, and to my relief, it was as white as I believed my own to be. It is hardly necessary to add that I ceased to smoke, and so lost the benefit of half a pipeful of precious Zarvona.

"In another minute the order was given to forward. We had not gone far when we met the troops we were going to reinforce. Of what command they were, I have never learned. They came toward us in squads, and, though not running, were not idling by the wayside. 'You fellers'll catch h—ll in thar,' one of them shouted as he came near us; 'them fellers out thar you ar goin' up agin, ain't none of the blue-bellied, white-livered Yanks an' sassidge-eatin' forrin hirelin's you have in Virginny that'll run at the snap of a cap—they are Western fellers, an' they'll mighty quick give you a bellyful o' fightin'.'

"A hundred yards further the Federals caught sight of us, and their bullets as well as the shot and shell from their well-served artillery came fast and furiously at us, many of our bravest and best falling, dead or wounded, before they pulled a trigger. For almost a minute we failed to locate their line. Then we discovered they were lying down, and shooting from behind trees, fallen logs and other cover, and we commenced firing as we advanced rapidly toward them. Their main body gave way before our impetuous rush, but with a reluctance that was not encouraging, and formed another line a hundred yards in rear of the first. Such of them, though, as had shelter, stood their ground behind it and fought gamely until disabled, or surrounded and forced to surrender. The need to capture such squads compelled our folks to make the battle somewhat personal and individual, and while as a command the brigade moved steadily on, its units fought on their own hook.

"In timber as thick as that in which the battle raged that afternoon, it was impossible for one in the ranks to see what was happening to right or left. To do his share of the work on hand, he could only look straight before him, and tackle the foe immediately facing him. Doing that with all my might and will, incidents occurred within twenty yards of me, to the right or left, that were wholly unwitnessed by me. The truth is, that along about then, the only incidents in which I was particularly interested, were those in which I was myself figuring. All too soon for my comfort, one of these happened, and called a peremptory halt on the assistance I was then giving the Confederacy. Placed hors-de-combat, I hastened from the firing line, and hence have no personal knowledge of what transpired that day, or the next. But I heard a great deal, and part of that hearsay will now be related.

"At home, Jack Sutherland was known as an ardent and indefatigable, if not mighty, Nimrod. His acquaintance with the habits and haunts of deer, turkeys and smaller game, his unerring aim, and his trusty rifle, kept his father's table well supplied with fresh meat. The same qualities that made him a successful hunter in the wilds of Texas, stood him in good stead when, as a soldier in battle, or as a scout or skirmisher, his marksmanship was employed against human beings. During the second day's battle at Chickamauga, Jack pressed far to the front in search of the human game then being hunted. Catching sight of a rock from behind which a lone Mississippian, obviously an estray from his own command, was firing at the enemy, he made for it. 'Glad to see you, comrade—glad to have you with me,' said the Mississippian as Jack found a place beside him; 'I've been having a little picnic here all by myself, and have got lonesome. Help me send some of those Yankees over yonder to kingdom come, will you?' 'Of course I will,' said Jack, as he took aim at one of the blue-coated gentry; 'that's just what I came for.'

"Loading and firing as rapidly as they could, the two had laid more than one enemy low, when, close on their right, a hundred or so Georgians appeared, and each from behind his own tree or rock, commenced firing. They were all that was left of Benning's Georgia Brigade of Hood's division, but the fight was not yet knocked out of them. They were busy loading and firing, when 'Old Rock,'—that was the pet name for General Benning—rode up behind them and shouted, 'G—d d—n you, men, get from behind those trees and rocks, and give 'em hell!' The words were hardly uttered before a shell came along, killed 'Old Rock's' horse, and tumbling the lionhearted rider sprawling on the ground, gave him an instant change of view. Springing to his feet unhurt, he shouted, 'G—d d—n you, men, stay behind those trees and give 'em hell!'

"Five minutes passed. Then, as Jack stood on his feet to take aim, a low-flying fragment of a bursted shell cut in two the straps of both his canteen and haversack, and plowed a furrow across his right shoulder. The blood spurted from the wound, and realizing the need of surgical aid, Jack decided to quit the picnic ground, and make his way back to the field hospital. As he turned to go, the Mississippian cried, 'Leave me your cartridge box, Texas—mine is empty, and I want to stay here as long as there is light enough to get a bead on a Yankee.' 'Cut it off me, then,' said Jack, and that done, he left the gallant Mississippian to continue the fight alone.

"In Company D, of the Fourth Texas, was a German, Julius Glazer. On the afternoon of the 19th—Jack Sutherland says it was the 20th, but he is mistaken—twenty odd of the bravest of the many brave men in the army commanded by General Rosecrans, gathered together in and behind a dilapidated log house built for a blacksmith's shop, and resolved from that point of vantage to contest the advance of the Texas Brigade as long as possible. The house stood at the far edge of the wood through which the brigade was making its way, and on account of intervening timber and undergrowth, could be seen from only a few points along our line. The fire from it was rapid and damaging, but for quite a while our folks failed to discover whence it came. Glazer was the first to locate the spot, and springing forward with a shout, he made for the house, followed, as soon as they saw his purpose, by ten to fifteen First, Fourth and Fifth Texans and Third Arkansans. Their attention directed to Texans on their left who just then came within their view, the Federals at the house had no warning of Glazer's approach until, when within twenty feet of it, he called on them to surrender.

"To this demand the Federals replied by firing half a dozen times at Glazer, and inflicting upon him a couple of flesh-wounds. He acknowledged the courtesy shown him by a more effective shot from his own gun, wounding one of the Federals mortally. But before he could lower his gun, and with the bayonet it carried, guard against attack, two men ran from behind the house and plunged their bayonets into his body. In all reason, Glazer should have fallen to the ground, and laid there content. But he did not; he simply sprang back, and reached for a cartridge. Unwilling to risk a loaded gun in his hands, the two men again rushed at him with levelled bayonets, and in the desperate fight that followed, he placed one of these hors-de-combat. His remaining antagonist was instantly reinforced by another couple of Federals, and Glazer fought the three, and held them at bay, until the comrades who had followed his lead came up and shot down two of the assailants, and the other escaped into the house.

"'Surrender,' was the cry of the Confederates—'Take us if you can,' the answer of the still defiant Federals. And with a pluck useless to themselves, and to the assaulting party, dangerous, the Federals held the house until half of them dead or wounded, the remainder acknowledged themselves prisoners. Then and then only, did Julius Glazer remember his hurts and quit fighting.

"To the question why they did not shoot Glazer instead of attacking him with the bayonet, the lieutenant in command of the squad of Federals replied: 'Because he was a mere boy, and after he fired his one shot we thought it would be cowardly to shoot him. But if the fighting he did against two of our best men at first, and then against three, and that too, after he was four times wounded, is a sample of what you Texans are in the habit of doing, I am going to throw up my commission and return to peaceful pursuits.'"

CHAPTER XII

CHATTANOOGA AND KNOXVILLE

THE Confederates victorious, the Union army in swift demoralized flight, now was the time, it would seem, for instant vigorous pursuit, or for well-planned flank movement—the one promising its measure of advantage—the other, insuring the expulsion of the Federal forces from Tennessee and Kentucky and access to large fields of supply for the now half-starving Southern armies east of the Mississippi. But General Bragg neither pursed nor flanked; instead, he held his troops inactive until, recovering breath and wits, the Federals fortified and intrenched themselves at Chattanooga, and then moved his army within artillery range of their lines and proceeded to invest the city on the east, the only side of it from which his opponent could have no hope of drawing supplies—a course that rendered fruitless a victory gained at such cost of blood and life. It was what General Rosecrans, the Federal commander, most preferred that Bragg should do; Chattanooga was impregnable by direct assault, and with his lines of communication with Nashville unbroken, Rosecrans had well-founded hope of maintaining his army and holding his position until reinforcements arrived.

The Texas Brigade devoted the 21st of September to rest and recuperation. A thousand miles of rough travel, the long and rapid march of the 18th, and the two days of strain and hard fighting its men had undergone, had well-nigh exhausted their energies. That day, Jenkins' South Carolina brigade joined Hood's division, to which it had been previously assigned, at the request of General Longstreet. Ranking General Law by seniority, General Jenkins at once relieved that officer of the command of the division. This was not pleasing to the Texas regiments. They had been too long associated with Law's brigade, and too often under Law's command, not to know and place a high estimate on his courage and ability, and to regard him as the logical successor of General Hood. But the right of protest was not theirs, and they fought as hard and desperately under Jenkins as they would have fought under Law.

On the morning of the 22nd, Hood's division marched in a direction that if pursued would have taken it to the Tennessee River some distance above Chattanooga. That night it bivouacked in the woods, and resuming the march next morning, had not gone a mile when it filed squarely off to the left on a road leading toward Lookout Mountain, in the shadows of which, that afternoon, it found its position in the line of investment. There, about a mile and a half east of the northern foot of Lookout Mountain, its camp just in rear of the first line of breastworks it ever built, the Texas Brigade lay idle and inactive, save for the picket duty its men did along Chattanooga Creek, until the afternoon of October 28th— time hanging as heavily on its hands as the rations on which it subsisted did to its stomachs. It was not accustomed to an unvarying diet of corn meal and lean beef, the only rations issued, and to the muddy and tepid water that alone was accessible to its camp, and bowel complaints prevailed to an alarming extent. Even the privilege of scouting, so liberally extended in the Virginia army, was denied them.

However, the 28th of October brought removal from the line and relief from an idleness that bred discontent. Two Federal corps from the Army of the Potomac, under command of "Fighting Joe" Hooker, having crossed the Tennessee River at Bridgeport, thirty miles below Chattanooga, were moving to the relief of Rosecrans' partly hemmed-in army, and were to camp that night in the vicinity of Wauhatchie, a hamlet just east of Raccoon Mountain, and about two miles west of Lookout Mountain. It was the opportunity for which General Jenkins had been praying. Hood was sure to be promoted to higher rank—his old division must have its own major-general, and why should it not be Major-General Jenkins? And to help along such a consummation, Jenkins proposed to lead Hood's division around Lookout Point, and with it, make a moonlight attack on Hooker's command. Longstreet was more than willing that Jenkins should win the coveted rank

—Law and he had never been in agreeable accord—and to make sure of success, promised to order McLaws' division to support Hood's. He failed to give the order, though, to McLaws, and so Jenkins went unaided.

The plan of assault was well conceived, but its execution and success were frustrated by many blunders, the unwillingness of the veteran troops of the division to engage in a night attack, and the halt of Jenkins' own brigade at the very crisis of the affair to plunder the wagon-trains it had captured. Of the Texas Brigade, only the Fourth Texas was ordered to the firing line. To it was assigned the duty of protecting General Law's right flank. But although it took position to do that effectively, its services were not called into requisition—such of the Alabamians as went to the front that night not staying long enough to even smell danger. What happened to the Fourth Texas is graphically told by one of its members. Before offering that, however, it is well to say that the affair of which it is a partial description is known in history as the battle of Wauhatchie, although always called by the Texas Brigade the battle of Raccoon Mountain. The Fourth Texan says:

"I have often boasted that the Fourth Texas never showed its back to an enemy, but I am more modest since that little affair of October 28, known as the battle of Raccoon Mountain. There, the regiment not only showed its back, but stampeded like a herd of frightened cattle, it being one of those cases when 'discretion is the better part of valor'; and, instead of being ashamed of the performance, we are merry over it. Raccoon and Lookout Mountains, you must know, are separated by Lookout Creek. Between the creek and Raccoon are half a dozen high, parallel ridges, whose tops are open and level enough for a road-way, and whose thickly timbered sides slope at angles of forty-five degrees, into deep, lonely hollows.

"Hooker's corps, of the Federal army, coming up from Bridgeport to reinforce Rosecrans, camped on the night of the 28th, in the vicinity of Raccoon. Imagining that here was an opportunity to win distinction, General Jenkins proposed to Longstreet to march Hood's division to the west side of Lookout Mountain, and by a night attack, capture 'Fighting Joe' Hooker and his corps. Longstreet, of course, offered no objections; success would place as brilliant a feather in his cap as in that of Jenkins, while the blame of defeat would necessarily rest upon the projector of the affair. As for us poor devils in the ranks, we had no business to be there, if we hesitated to risk our lives in the interest of commanding officers.

"The plan of operations appears to have been for Benning's, Anderson's, and Jenkins's brigades to cross Lookout Creek two miles above its mouth, and, forming in line parallel with the Tennessee River, force the Yankees to surrender, or drive them into deep water; while the Texas and Law's brigades should occupy positions west of the creek, at right angles with the river, and prevent them from moving toward Lookout Mountain, and alarming Bragg's army. What became of the First Texas and Third Arkansas, I cannot say, every movement being made at night, but the Fifth Texas guarded the bridge, across which the Fourth marched and thence proceeded in the direction of Raccoon Mountain, climbing up and sliding down the steep sides of intervening ridges, until brought to a halt on the moon-lit top of the highest, and formed in line on the right of an Alabama regiment.

"Here, in blissful ignorance of General Jenkins' plans, and unwarned by the glimmer of a fire or sound of a snore that the main body of the enemy lay asleep in the wide and deep depression between them and Raccoon, the spirits of the gallant Texans rose at once to the elevation of their bodies, and dropping carelessly on the ground, they proceeded to take their ease. But not long were they permitted thus to dally with stern and relentless fate. A gunshot, away off to the left, suddenly broke upon the stillness of the night, and was followed by others in rapid succession, until there was borne to our ears the roar of desperate battle, while the almost simultaneous beating of the long roll in the hitherto silent depths below us, the loud shouts of officers, and all the indescribable noises and hubbub of a suddenly awakened and alarmed host of men, admonished us that we stood upon the outermost edge of a human volcano, which might soon burst forth in all its fury, and overwhelm us.

"The *dolce far niente* to which, lulled by fancied security and the beautiful night, we had surrendered ourselves, vanished as quickly as did the dreams of the Yankees. The emergency came unexpectedly, but none the less surely. Scouts dispatched to the right, returned with the appalling intelligence that between the regiment and the river, half a mile away, not a Confederate was on guard; skirmishers sent to the front, reported that the enemy was approaching rapidly and in strong force. To add to the dismay created by such alarming intelligence, the thrilling whisper came from the left, that the Alabamians had gone 'hunting for tall timber' in their rear. Thus deserted in a solitude soon to be invaded by a ruthless and devouring horde, the cheerless gloom of an exceeding great loneliness fell upon us like a pall—grew intense, when, not twenty feet away, we heard the laborious struggling and puffing of the Yankees as, on hostile thoughts intent, they climbed and pulled up the almost precipitous ascent—and became positively unbearable, when a dozen or more bullets from the left whistled down the line, and the mild beams of the full moon, glinting from what seemed to our agitated minds a hundred thousand bright gun-barrels, revealed the near and dangerous presence of the hated foe.

"Then and there—deeming it braver to live than to die, and moved by thoughts of home and its loved ones—the officers and privates of the gallant and hitherto invincible Fourth Texas stood not upon the order of their going, but went with a celerity and unanimity truly remarkable; in short, they disappeared bodily, stampeded *nolens volens*, and plunged recklessly into the umbrageous and shadowy depths behind them, their flight hastened by the loud huzzaing of the triumphant Yankees, and the echoing volleys they poured into the tree-tops, high above the heads of their retreating antagonists.

"Once fairly on the run down the steep slope, voluntary halting became as impossible as it would have been indiscreet. Dark as it was among the somber shadows into which the fleeing men plunged, the larger trees could generally be avoided, but when encountered, as too frequently for comfort they were, they wrought disaster to both body and clothing; but small ones bent before the wild, pell-mell rush, as from the weight and power of avalanche or hurricane. The speed at which I traveled, let alone the haunting apprehension of being gobbled up by a pursuing blue-coat, was not specially favorable to close observation of comrades, but, nevertheless, I witnessed three almost contemporaneous accidents. One poor unfortunate struck a tree so squarely and with such tremendous force, as not only to flatten his body against it and draw a sonorous groan from his lips, but to send his gun clattering against another tree. As a memento of the collision, he yet carries a face ragged enough to harmonize admirably with his tattered garments. Another fellow exclaimed, as, stepping on a round stone, his feet slipped from under him and he dropped to the ground with a resounding thud, 'Help, boys—help,' and then, with legs wide outspread, he went sliding down the hill, until, in a wholly involuntary attempt to pass upon both sides of a tree, he was brought to a sudden halt, or, as it might be called, a sit-still.

"But adventure the third was the most comical of all. The human actor in it was a Dutchman by the name of Brigger; a fellow nearly as broad as he is long, who always carries a huge knapsack on his shoulders. Aided by this load, he struck a fair-sized sapling with such resistless momentum, that the little tree bent before him, and, straddling it and exclaiming in prayerful, not irreverent, accents, 'Jesus Christ and God Almighty,' with a long-drawn and lingering emphasis on the first word, he described a parabola in the air, and then dropping to the ground on all-fours, continued his downward career in that decidedly unmilitary fashion. His was the novelty and roughness of the ride, but alas, mine was all the loss; for, as the sapling tumbled him off and essayed to straighten itself, an impudent branch of it caught my hat, and flung it at the man in the moon. Whether it ever reached its destination, I am unable to say—the time, the inclination and the ability to stop and see if it did were each sternly prohibited by the exigency of the occasion and the accelerating influence of gravitation. Anyhow, I am now wearing a cap, manufactured by myself, out of the nethermost extremity of a woolen overshirt, and having for a frontispiece a generous slice of a stirrup leather. Colonel Bane well deserves the loss he has sustained; he is not only careless about his saddle, but, as well, of his head, on which he still bears a reminder of the battle of Raccoon Mountain, in the shape of a very sore and red bump.

"But to return to my story. Although I lost my hat, I neither lost physical balance, nor collided with a tree sufficiently sturdy to arrest a fearfully swift descent, as did many of my comrades. Indeed, the scars imprinted upon the regimental physiognomy by large and small monarchs of the forest, are yet numerous, and in some instances, were at first so disguising that the wearers were recognizable, for a day or two, only by their melodious voices. 'Honors' were so 'easy' in that respect, between the members of the regiment, officers as well as privates, that when they at last emerged from the darkness of the woods, and taking places in line, began to look at each other and recount experiences, their shouts of laughter must have reached old Joe Hooker.

"One poor fellow, though, was too sore of body and downcast in spirit, and had been too much trampled upon, to join in the mirth that prevailed. He was a litter-bearer, his name was Dennis, and he was six long feet in height, and Falstaffian in abdominal development. His position in the rear gave him the start in the stampede, and his avoirdupois enabled him to brush aside, or bear down, every obstacle encountered in his downward plunge. But his judgment was disastrously at fault. Forgetting the ditch-like drain that marked the line where descent of one hill ended and ascent of the other began, he tumbled, broadcast, into it. The fall knocked all the breath out of him, and he could only wriggle over on his broad back, and make a pillow for his head of one bank of the drain, and a resting-place for his number twelve feet, of the other. Lying there, his big body looked, in the moon-light, like a rather short butt cut off of the trunk of a large tree.

"The litter-bearer had barely got himself in the comfortable position described, when Bill Calhoun came plunging down the hill with a velocity that left a good-sized vacuum in his wake. Observant by nature, and made the more so by the fear that if he came to grief in his passage of the drain, the Yankees would capture him, Bill no sooner saw Dennis' recumbent body than, taking it for the log it appeared to be, and sure that it spanned the drain, he made a tremendous leap, and landed his foremost and heaviest foot right in the middle of Dennis' expansive corporosity, and on that particular part of it for which the owner had the most tender regard. The sudden compression produced by Bill's suddenly imposed weight, produced as sudden artificial respiration, and giving vent to a howl of agony, Dennis cried, 'For the Lord Almighty's sake, man, don't make a bridge of me!' Bill was startled, but did not lose his presence of mind, and shouting back, 'Lie still, old fellow—lie still! The whole regiment has to cross yet, and you'll never have another such chance to serve your beloved country,' continued his flight at a speed but little abated by the rising ground before him."

Hood's division did not again occupy any part of the line of investment—military operations were in contemplation in which it was to take part. On the day after the Wauhatchie, or Raccoon Mountain affair, the Texas Brigade hid itself from the prying eyes of the enemy in the shady recesses of the timber that grew along the west side of Lookout Mountain, and there the Fourth Texas spent the hours of daylight in ascertaining and repairing the damages to persons and clothing received during the stampede of the night before. The other brigades of Hood's division occupied the front along Lookout Creek—their object, to check any attack which the two Federal corps under General Hooker might be induced to make.

On the afternoon of the 30th, some alarm occurring, the Texas Brigade climbed up the side of Lookout and took position in line under the frowning cliffs by which the level land on its top is encircled. Why it went so high was a question much discussed by the boys. A Fifth Texas man said to one of the Fourth Texas: "It's Aunt Pollie that's done it. He has heard of the speed you fellows made night before last in that stampede down-hill, and he has got an idea from it that he wants to test. If the Yankees line up anywhere below us, he is going to order the brigade to charge them. He calculates, I reckon, that the force of gravity and the momentum we acquire will combine with our bravery to make the down-set—it'll be no onset, you know—absolutely irresistible, and that we'll knock the Yankees, guns and all, into Lookout Creek, and there let the last one of 'em drown."

That night we bivouacked in line on ground so steep and so loosely covered with small shingle and rock that only by bracing our feet against trees could we avoid rolling down-hill. Indeed, many who were careless in lying down, or whose

W. H. BURGES
Company D, Fourth Texas Regiment

slumbers were restless because of the roughness of their couches, did roll until brought to a halt by some obstacle firmly fixed in the ground; and as such obstacles often proved to be the bodies of comrades, the air was occasionally sulphurous. The next day we marched around Lookout Point, and went into camp east of Lookout Mountain; for about this time General Bragg decided that it was time for him to do something.

General Grant had arrived at Chattanooga, and superseded Rosecrans in the command of the Federal army. Hooker had reinforced it with two army corps from Virginia, and Sherman, with a large force, from Memphis, was due to arrive about the 15th of November. Yet, although to his own army had not and could not come any additions, General Bragg reduced its strength by ordering Longstreet, with Hood's and McLaws' divisions and a large force of cavalry, up to Knoxville, to capture or drive out of that portion of Tennessee the Federal forces there, under command of General Burnside. Such a campaign if begun immediately after the battle of Chickamauga would have been not only wise and feasible, but also, a commendable effort to harvest a part of the fruits of victorious battle; now, prohibited by every consideration for the safety of the army Bragg was still allowed to command, it was suicidal.

While protesting that to send his two divisions of infantry and the larger part of the Confederate cavalry on such a mission at such a critical stage of affairs was unwise and foolish, Longstreet, nevertheless, obeyed the order, and at once set about making preparations for the movement. It offered him a practically independent command, and a fine field for military operations, which, if successful, would likely insure him the rank of a full general. Believing, as he said, that if haste was made, Knoxville could be captured and Hood's and McLaws' divisions returned to his army in time to resist any attack on it by the Federals then at and coming to Chattanooga, General Bragg promised ample and speedy transportation and all that was needed in the matter of food supplies. But the promise was not performed, and the troops detached for the expedition did not reach Sweetwater until November 12. There more delay occurred. Wagon-trains were lacking, subsistence stores had not been forwarded, and as a result, Longstreet was compelled to abandon his plan of approaching Knoxville from the east, by way of Maryville, and to cross the Tennessee at Loudon and march directly on Knoxville by way of Campbell's Station.

Passage of the river was effected on the 14th, and daylight had barely dawned on the 15th when Hood's division formed into line of march and hastened in pursuit of the enemy, then known to be in full retreat toward Knoxville. Between him and McLaws' division there was a foot-race—McLaws' effort being to reach Campbell's Station first. But fear lent wings to the Federals, and they won, and gave the Confederates a hot fight at the Station—holding their ground until late in the afternoon, then continuing their retreat, and in the early forenoon of the 16th taking refuge behind their defensive works at Knoxville. Thither followed the Confederates, and by night the town was surrounded by their infantry, cavalry, and artillery.

To the Texas Brigade was assigned a position east of the Holston and below the town—its mission, to assist Wheeler's cavalry in preventing the escape of the enemy in that direction. From that date until the siege was abandoned, it remained under fire, and, perhaps, under a more constant and vigorous one than any other command. Burnside's army was composed almost entirely of men from the Western States, and in them the Texans and Arkansans found foemen as daring, as courageous and as accurate of aim as themselves. It was a kind of hide-and-seek game both sides played; to be seen was to be shot at, and many a poor fellow fell dead or wounded at the moment he felt himself most safe.

But with the time and force at his command, Longstreet had undertaken the impossible. His infantry numbered scarce 12,000, and his cavalry could do no effective work against the fortifications surrounding Knoxville. Burnside, his opponent, had fully 20,000 infantry, and held an interior line that was both naturally and artificially strong. The Confederate commander, however, was determined to make one desperate struggle to gain entrance into the town. Receiving on the 28th a reinforcement of two brigades, Bushrod Johnson's and Gracie's, he ordered a night assault upon Fort Sanders, the key to the

Federal position. It failed to succeed, the troops engaged in it being repulsed with great slaughter.

Half an hour after the fighting ceased, General Longstreet received positive information that the battle of Missionary Ridge had been fought and won by the Federals, then under command of General Grant, and that Bragg's army was in retreat. With this information came an order directing him to rejoin Bragg. As a march to the south and to Bragg's army would not only be over a mountainous and extremely rugged country, but also expose him to pursuit by Burnside and a Federal force then approaching Knoxville from Cumberland Gap, he decided to move north, up the Holston River, into a field offering admirable opportunities for the maneuvering of a small army and soldierly enterprise; moreover, it would take him beyond the reach of Bragg's authority.

To mask the withdrawal of the Texas and Law's brigades from the east side of the Holston, they and the cavalry on their right, on the morning of December 3, made a vigorous demonstration against the Federals in their front. These stood their ground well until about noon; then they abandoned their first line of intrenchments, and took cover in another nearer the river. Night coming on, the two brigades quietly marched to the ferry over the Holston, crossed the river, and, moving around the city, went northward toward Strawberry Plains, as the advance guard of their little army. Silence prevailed and the utmost caution was observed among the Texans and Arkansans until they were well beyond sight and hearing of the Union soldiers they had so long helped to hold in practical captivity. Then, giving expression to their feelings, they made the woods ring and resound with loud and unchecked rejoicings that they were on their way to rejoin " Marse Robert's " army. Some enthusiastic broke into song, and as the opening words of the old melody, " Carry me back to ole Virginny," floated in musical cadence from his lips, a shout went up that made the welkin ring, and there was not a man " with music in his soul " but joined hopefully in the chorus:

" Oh, carry me back to ole Virginny, to ole Virginny's shore."

Crossing the Holston River at Strawberry Plains about

noon, the Texas Brigade bivouacked that night on the open level ground east of the stream. Resuming the march next morning at sunrise, and still the advance guard of Longstreet's command, it moved rapidly on to Rogersville, arriving there on the 8th. On the 9th it went to Bean's Station to support Wheeler's cavalry, then in contention with a pursuing column of cavalry dispatched by Burnside from Knoxville. But, although under artillery fire for a while, it took no active part in the engagement. Remaining at Bean's Station until the 19th, the brigade that day marched down the Holston toward Morristown, and, arriving there on the afternoon of the 22d, went into winter-quarters on the top of a wooded hill, a mile north of the little town. Lacking any assurance of a long stay in them, the men wasted little strength in the erection of cabins. A liberal issue of tents, an abundance of wood and a plentiful and near supply of excellent water, together with a fairly generous distribution of rations, enabled them to make themselves as comfortable as their great need of shoes and clothing permitted. Altogether, their lot as soldiers was not so hard as to warrant special complaint.

Relaxation and more or less of exciting adventure, experienced and related, was furnished by the many details made for scouting west of the Holston River and east of the French Broad. The enemy was held in check on the south by the cavalry which, while the infantry rested in winter-quarters, was almost constantly on the go—fighting, as could be told by the sound of artillery, every day, and aften far into the night. Early in January of 1864, railroad communication was secured with Richmond, Va., and the shoes and clothing, and the mails that came over it to the Texas Brigade, added largely to its comfort and content.

While his army was encamped around Bean's Station, General Longstreet received a telegram from President Davis giving him discretionary authority over all Confederate troops, of whatever service, then in East Tennessee. Invested, temporarily at least, with autocratic power, Longstreet took leisure to do a little pruning among his subordinate commanders. General McLaws was the first officer to be relieved of command, and following him went General Robertson and General Law. With McLaws' removal we have no concern.

Law was relieved of command, beyond doubt, in order to give General Jenkins a better chance of securing the commission of a major-general and the command of Hood's division—it having become known by this time that Hood would be promoted to a lieutenant-generalcy.

Against General Robertson charges were preferred by General Jenkins by express direction of General Longstreet. These did not complain that Robertson lacked ability as a brigade commander, or had been guilty of any unsoldierly conduct on the field. The gist of his offense was that when Jenkins ordered a movement of the Texas Brigade that would entail upon it a long and hurried march over a rough and mountainous country and great hardship, he (Robertson) had informed his regimental commanders that he was opposed to the movement, would require written orders for it, and would obey it under protest; that his men were in no condition for active campaigning, and that he had no confidence in the campaign as conducted.

That these charges did not affect the standing of "Aunt Pollie" with the Texas Brigade, is proven by the fact that not a member of it ever blamed him for what he did; on the contrary, the brigade heartily approved of his course, and its survivors are yet grateful to him for the firm stand he took and for the interest and fatherly solicitude he always manifested in the well-being of his men. The truth is, at that time the Texas Brigade was in worse plight than any brigade in the division. It could get no supplies from Texas or Arkansas, as could and did the other brigades from their home States. However, the charges against its commander went up in smoke. President Davis and the Secretary of War held them frivolous and utterly insufficient to justify, even if proved true, the removal of an able and well-liked brigade commander. Still, rather than remain in a corps with whose commander he was persona non grata, and in a division of which, as then appeared probable, Jenkins would be appointed major-general, Robertson sought and obtained a transfer to Texas, on recruiting service for the army of the Confederacy.

The stay of the Texas Brigade at Morristown was of brief duration. On the 15th of January, 1864, the enemy confronted our cavalry in such strong force that it called lustily for reinforcement. Heeding the call, Longstreet ordered his infantry divisions down to the neighborhood of Strawberry Plains. Before they reached that point, though, the enemy retired, and the Texas Brigade halted at Mossy Creek. It remained there until February 10, and while there the men composing it were invited to re-enlist, for and during the war, last as long as it might. As it was enlist or be conscripted, not a man declined.

From Mossy Creek the Texas Brigade moved down to Strawberry Plains, and, crossing to the east side of the Holston River, took position to support Confederate cavalry then feeling its way toward Knoxville, against which stronghold of the enemy General Longstreet was making a demonstration in hope of bringing troops to its relief, and thus reducing the pressure on the army so lately commanded by Bragg, but now by General Joseph E. Johnston. That object accomplished, and President Davis about that time having ordered all cavalry belonging to Johnston's command to be returned to him, Longstreet wisely withdrew his army from its advanced position and marched it back to Bull's Gap. There Hood's division found awaiting it a commanding major-general in the person of General Charles W. Field, a graduate of West Point, who, as the brigadier-general of a Confederate brigade in Lee's army, had gained considerable distinction. To the Texas Brigade also came a new commander, General John Gregg.

In their respective spheres, both Field and Gregg proved themselves competent and efficient officers. That the former did not win from the division the admiration and confidence it felt for and in General Hood, and that the latter failed to secure such a hold on the affection of the Texas Brigade as Robertson had gained, was due, perhaps, more to lack of opportunity than to any want of merit in either. Of each of them it may be said that in character he was almost diametrically the opposite of his predecessor. Field was of phlegmatic temperament, and seemed indifferent whether the division liked him or not. Gregg's service on the bench in Texas had developed in him an austerity of manner and a positiveness of utterance altogether unlike the free, easy, and somewhat fussy ways of General Robertson that had won for him the sobriquet of "Aunt Pollie." Moreover, Gregg held himself aloof from his inferiors in rank, and so did not afford his men any opportunity to acquaint themselves with the good qualities he undoubtedly had in abundance. In truth, the standard of excellence in a commander for whom they would " do or die," which had been adopted by the members of the Texas Brigade, was John B. Hood. It was impossible that any officer could be to them what Percy Gregg, the English historian, says Hood was; that is, " a splendid soldier peculiarly suited to the command of his reckless, daring and indomitable Texans, with whom he was a special favorite. Commander and men alike exaggerated the proverbial quality of Englishmen—they never knew when they were beaten, or, when they must be."

On the 24th of March, 1864, President Davis wired General Longstreet to make all needful preparations for the march of his command to that of General Johnston, to join in a spring campaign planned by Bragg, who, proven incompetent to conduct the operations of a single army, was yet considered capable of directing the movements of all the armies of the Confederacy from an office in Richmond. April 7, though, Bragg changed his mind, and Longstreet was ordered to rejoin General Lee's army, then holding the line of the Rapidan in Virginia, with all the troops he had carried from Virginia to Bragg's army. Thus it came about, that about the 15th of April the Texas Brigade broke camp at Bull's Gap, and marching to Bristol, took trains to Lynchburg, Va. Remaining there a few days—for there was neither need nor order for haste—it boarded a train for Charlottesville, whence, on the 23d, it marched slowly to the eastward, finally halting and camping near Gordonsville, about twenty-five miles from the battlefield of the Wilderness.

CHAPTER XIII

THE WILDERNESS—SPOTTSYLVANIA—COLD HARBOR—PETERSBURG

On the 1st of May, 1864, the hopes of the Southern Confederacy rested upon the two armies of Lee and Johnston—that of Lee holding the line of the Rapidan in Virginia—that of Johnston, at Dalton, Ga. General Meade was in command of the army opposing Lee's, General Sherman of that confronting Johnston's, and each of their armies was largely superior in numbers and equipment to that of his antagonist. All Confederate ports were blockaded, and along the Atlantic and Gulf coasts the Federals held various important positions. Tennessee, Kentucky, a large part of Mississippi, and parts of Alabama, Florida and Virginia were in practically unopposed possession of the Federal troops. In the Trans-Mississippi department, Arkansas was overrun by them, as well as a large part of Louisiana. In Texas alone, save at Point Isabel, they had no holding.

In March, 1864, Lieutenant-General U. S. Grant was invested with command of the armies of the Union. Looking over the situation, it was apparent to him that the armies of Lee and Johnston could receive little reinforcement except from each other. Therefore he planned a campaign against each that would be so vigorously prosecuted as to keep it busy, and prevent it from aiding the other—these campaigns to begin on the same day. Once begun, there was to be no halt by either. Sherman was to move against Johnston's army, to break it up, to get into the interior of the South, and to inflict all the damage he could against its war resources—his objective points, first, Atlanta, and next, Savannah. Meade's army was to be under Grant's own immediate supervision—his order to Meade being: "Lee's army will be your objective point; wherever he goes, there will you go." The characteristic of the campaign, as stated by Grant in this order, was " to hammer continuously against the armed forces of the enemy and his resources, until, by mere attrition, if nothing else, there shall be nothing left him but submission." His desire was, he told a friend, " to fight Lee between the Rapidan and Richmond, if he will stand." As developed in the field, though, it was to place the Union army between Lee's and Richmond, and to do the " hammering," not by direct and continuous strokes at the Wilderness and other places where Lee did stand, but intermittently, while the Federal army, under his orders, by crab-like sidling, moved southward.

On the 4th day of May, 1864, Meade's army, numbering fully 125,000 men of all arms, and said by one of its officers to be " the best-clothed and the best-fed army that ever took the field," crossed the Rapidan and made its way into what was then, and except to the boldest hunters, still is, a terra incognita, as impenetrable in many places as the jungles of Africa—the Wilderness. What ghastly scenes, what thrilling and horrifying incidents, what terrifying sounds throng to the memories of the survivors of the armies, Confederate and Union, which, for nearly two months, grappled there in deadly struggle! The bloody carnage—the moans and screams of the wounded as they lay helpless on the ground, or limped painfully to the rear—the piles of the dead and the dying—the acrid smell of burning gunpowder—the sickening stench of putrefying corpses—the roaring cannon and the shrieking shells, round shot, grape and canister—the crackling musketry, and the spat or dull thud of hissing, whistling, vengeful bullets—the dark, damp, dense, miasma-breeding forests into which sunlight never penetrated, and the tangled undergrowth of swamplands and morasses, are remembrances that are yet vivid, and at which old soldiers yet shudder.

Strictly, the name, Wilderness, applies to a section of country, ten or twelve miles square, bounded north and east by the Rapidan and Rappahannock Rivers, and lying between Fredericksburg and Orange Court House. Seams of iron ore and traces of gold were discovered there at an early day, and for several generations, more or less mining was done. The forests then growing were cut down to supply fuel for iron furnaces—the first built in North America—and to clear the land for the cultivation of tobacco. The mines finally abandoned, the soil robbed of its fertility, the region was left to nature, and was soon covered with pines, oaks, hickory and other varieties of timber, beneath which grew vines, brambles and all sorts of undergrowth in astonishing profusion. The general surface, while elevated, is undulating, and between the ridges course sluggish streams and lay swamps, bogs and morasses.

But although the Wilderness proper lies as above described, in 1864 it may be said to have extended to within a few miles of Richmond, distant from the battle ground of May 6 about seventy miles on a bee-line, but on the route taken by the armies, nearly, if not quite, a hundred. Across this extension of it run the waters of the Mattapony, North Anna, Little River, South Anna, Chickahominy and other streams of less size and note—their many uncultivated valleys, covered with timber and undergrowth, and often marshy and always miasmatic.

General Lee was neither taken by surprise, nor unprepared for Meade's passage of the Rapidan and advance into the Wilderness. Ewell's and Hill's corps were in their places, and on May 5, in an engagement beginning at daylight and lasting until after nightfall, gave bloody check to the Federal army. On the same day, Hood's old division, hereafter to be designated as Field's, was on the march to find position in the line held by the Confederates. That night it bivouacked within eight miles of the line occupied by Hill's corps, and at 3 A. M. on the morning of the 6th, the Texas Brigade leading the column—moved at a rapid gait to the front. Between daylight and sunrise, when within two miles of the firing line, the noises of volleys of musketry and occasional reports of cannon gave notice that the struggle of the day had commenced, and at the sound General Gregg gave the command, "Double quick!"

"Breaking instantly into a double quick movement," writes a member of the Fourth Texas, "we pressed on toward the Plank Road. Half a mile from it, an order came to Gregg to report, with the Texas Brigade, as soon as possible to General Lee. Reaching the Plank Road, we found it a scene of utter, and apparently, irremediable confusion, such as we had never witnessed before in Lee's army. It was crowded with standing and moving wagons, horses and mules, and threading their way through this tangled mass, each with his face to the rear, were hundreds of the men of Wilcox's and Heth's divisions, which were being driven from their lines.

"Filing to the right as it came into the road, the Texas Brigade continued at a double-quick down it, toward the sound of the firing, for nearly a mile. Then called to a halt, it formed line of battle facing the north side of the road, loaded its guns, and by a right wheel brought itself into position fronting the enemy, on an open hill, the highest probably in the section, and immediately in rear of a battery said to have been Poague's. Not more than three hundred yards in our front was a line of Yankee skirmishers, who, but for intervening pine thickets and large timber, might have done us great damage.

"At this juncture, General Lee rode up near our line. Mounted on the handsome dapple gray horse he bestrode at Fredericksburg in 1862, and which he always rode on the battle-field, he was a picture of noble grace that I can never hope to see again. Having given General Gregg an order to advance at once and check the on-coming enemy, he added: 'The Texas Brigade always has driven the enemy, and I want them to do it now. And tell them, General, that they will fight to-day under my eye—I will watch their conduct. I want every man of them to know I am here with them!' Gregg rode out in front of us, and told us what General Lee had said, and then gave the command, 'Forward!' The word had barely passed his lips when General Lee himself came in front of us, as if intending to lead us. The men shouted to him to come back, that they would not budge an inch unless he did so, and to emphasize the demand, twenty or more of them sprang forward and made an effort to lead or push his horse to the rear. I was too far from him to join in this attempt, or, like any other man in the brigade I would have done so. Exactly what occurred, not even those nearest Lee can tell, but just as they got 'Traveler' headed to the rear, General Longstreet rode up and said something, whereupon General Lee rode silently back through our ranks.

"Then General Gregg again shouted the command to forward, and forward the old brigade went. The enemy's skirmishers discovered our approach before we had gone a hundred yards, and opened a fire on us that killed or wounded many of our best and bravest before they had fired a shot. Three hundred yards further, the leaden hail poured upon us by the skirmishers began to thin our ranks greatly, and five hundred yards from our starting point, we were confronted by a line of battle. This could not withstand our assault, and so fled in confusion. Across the Plank Road was another line, and against it we moved rapidly. The storm of battle was now terrific. Our brigade was alone, no support on our right, none on the left, and an enfilading and terrible fire from the left. The Plank Road ran diagonally across our line of advance, and down the road came the fire of a dozen cannon. But across it we went, and drove the enemy back behind their breastworks, to within a hundred yards of which we advanced. Then it was discovered that a column of the enemy was coming at a double-quick down the Plank Road, with the evident intention of cutting us off, and General Gregg gave the order to withdraw. But the object of our attack was accomplished, General Lee's faith in the Texas Brigade justified. The ground from which two Confederate divisions had been driven, had been recaptured, but at a terrible sacrifice, for one-half of our men were killed and wounded. Of the 207 men of the Fourth Texas that went into the action, 30 were killed or mortally wounded, and 100 wounded more or less seriously. I do not know the extent of the losses in either of the other regiments, but they were likely as great in the Fifth Texas as in the Fourth, both of which regiments crossed the Plank Road. The First Texas and Third Arkansas, however, although advancing and keeping in line with the Fourth and Fifth Texas, did not get to the Plank Road, but fought to the left of it.

"The Fourth and Fifth Texas, the only regiments in danger of being cut off, fell back hurriedly, but not in confusion, and the brigade was soon in line, a couple of hundred yards in front of the battery near which General Lee came to us. As we were forming, another brigade passed over us on its way to hold the enemy in the position to which we had driven him. Ten minutes later we moved to the brow of a hill on the left, and formed in line at right angle to the general line. Then wheeling to the right, we moved down the hill, across a morass and to the summit of another elevation, where we encountered a heavy line of Yankee skirmishers, and in the fight with them lost quite a number of our men, killed and wounded. The skirmishers dispersed, other troops took our place, and we were given a long rest. That evening, though, the brigade drove back a line of skirmishers, and thus held the attention of the enemy until Anderson's and Law's brigades made a flank movement and captured a part of the enemy's first line of breastworks.

"I was not with the brigade in that last affair of the day. Taken sick at noon, I made my way back to the field-hospital, and was there when at 9 P. M. our division marched toward Spottsylvania Court House. Too unwell on the 7th to be fit for duty, I was in the act of leaving the hospital on the 8th to rejoin my command, when Dr. Jones forbade my going, detailed me as a nurse and ordered me to remain there until our wounded were carried back to Richmond. That was not done until the last of April, and before it was, I visited the battle-field twice, once on the 12th, and again on the 24th. At the time of the first visit, its aspect was terrible and sickening. The stench from the putrifying corpses and carcasses of the thousands of men and horses that lay in every conceivable shape and position on the ground, pervaded the air and made impossible any long stay in the gloomy shades of the veritable wilderness in which the battle was waged. All the Confederate dead that could be found had been buried, but the Yankees had not buried a tenth of their dead. Vast quantities of clothing, ammunition and arms lay strewn over acres of ground, the enemy, seemingly, having abandoned the field in too great haste to remove them. I counted five lines of breastworks that had been erected for the defense of the Union army—one, immediately in front of our only line of intrenchments, and the others in rear of that one, at distances of from fifty to a hundred yards apart. In front of the first line the timber had been cleared off for a distance of fifty yards or more. At places, I saw acres of ground, the trees on which were riddled with bullets, and on several portions of the field where small timber and undergrowth only grew, the trees were actually cut in two, and the undergrowth topped at about the height of a man's head. The bodies of our Texas boys, brave fellows all, who had fallen, had been gathered together and buried under a large tree by the side of the Plank Road. Although one large opening in the earth received them, at the head of each was placed a board with his name rudely carved on it, while nailed to a tree nearer the road was another board on which were carved the simple but eloquent words, 'Texas Dead.'

"At the date of my second visit, the road and all the pathways leading into it were alive with worms, and above them swarmed myriads of flies. The flesh had rotted from the corpses and only bones marked the spots where brave spirits had taken leave of their tenements of clay. Most of the clothing left on the field had been appropriated by the citizens living near by, and the arms and ammunition had been hauled away in wagons sent out by the Confederate Secretary of War."

To the daring and successful charge of the Texas Brigade that day, is unquestionably due the check given the enemy at a moment when, Wilcox's and Heth's divisions driven from their positions, the Confederate army was in imminent peril of being cut in two by an unexpectedly early dash forward against its center of Hancock's always hard-fighting corps. That the loss of the open and commanding hill from which it advanced and repulsed the on-coming Federals, would have wrought disaster to his army, and that General Lee so believed, is evident from his presence there, the anxiety he manifested, his message to the Texas Brigade, and his effort to lead it. So, while acknowledging the aid given it by the other commands of Field's division, and by those of McLaws' which fought on the right of Field's, the survivors of the Texas Brigade claim now, as always since that day of struggle and bloodshed, that it saved the Confederate army, and that to it alone belongs that distinction.

Of the day's battle in general, it may be said that from sunrise till 11 A. M., it was fought by Longstreet's corps alone, neither Hill's nor Ewell's corps taking more than desultory parts in it. General John B. Gordon is authority for the statement that had General Jubal Early, at sunrise of the 6th, been less obstinate in his expressed belief that Sedgewick's

corps was close in rear and support of the Federal right flank
—which it was not—or had General Ewell been less under the
domination of General Early, a flank movement by Gordon's
command was not only possible but invited and tempted,
which, assisted by Longstreet's bold and successful assault a
little after sunrise, would either have destroyed the Union
army, or forced it into hurried and disorderly retreat. General Gordon further says that when about 5 P. M. General Lee
rode to his left and was informed by himself of the situation
there, he immediately ordered the flank movement made, and
that but for the lateness of the hour, it would even then have
proven a mortal blow to the enemy.

About ten o'clock in the forenoon Hill's troops, now rested,
were again sent to the front. Longstreet sent Mahone, with
four brigades, to turn Hancock's left, which they did. Then,
moving forward, they rolled up that flank, as Hancock himself said, "like a wet blanket." By eleven o'clock Hancock's
front and both his flanks were driven back, and by noon the
left of the Federal army was defeated and disorganized.
Seeking to press the advantages gained, Longstreet formed
Kershaw's division in line of battle across the Plank Road, and
led it, in person, in pursuit of the now fleeing enemy. He had
gone but a short distance, though, when, mistaken by Mahone's men, then halted in line and facing the Plank Road, for
a Federal officer accompanied by his staff, he was fired upon
and wounded, and the onset of Kershaw's men was checked.
General Lee rode at once to the front, and restoring order,
sent the division forward again, with a part of Field's division on its left. These troops followed the Federals to the
Brock Road, which crosses the Plank Road at right angles,
and there were confronted by a wall of fire, made by the
burning of the front line of the enemy's breastworks, and
also by a more dangerous line of artillery and infantry which
poured shot and shell into their ranks from the second and fully
manned line of works.

Nevertheless, the Confederates drove the enemy from that
second line, and planted their flags on the breastworks, but,
owing to the continued terrible artillery fire, soon fell back a
quarter of a mile to a line they held the balance of that
and all the next day. The outcome of the day's battle was

an advance of the Confederate lines, and the placing of the Union army on the defensive.

Peace and comparatively absolute quiet reigned on the 7th. That night Grant moved his army southward, to Spottsylvania Court House, but when on the morning of the 8th his advance, under Warren, arrived there, it found Longstreet's corps, now commanded by R. H. Anderson, in its front. Thenceforward, until Grant shifted to the south side of the James River, there was little cessation of battle between the two armies; if not all along the lines, it was on this or that flank, or in the center, that Grant " hammered."

To follow the movements of the Texas Brigade and relate them in detail, would be wearisome and unprofitable. It was one of the component parts of a live machine that, although guided and directed by General Lee, seemed to move automatically. In light and in darkness, it shared with comrade commands a relentless, ceaseless and ever-present danger. In the trenches its men looked their perils in the face without blenching, and grew inured to them; in camp or on the march, they swooped down on us unexpectedly—now coming in the guise of bullets from far-off concealed sharpshooters, and again from overhead, when shells from the enemy's long-range cannon burst in the air. Death or wounds came at all hours of the night and day. Absolute safety was nowhere to be found within the zone of five miles in width through the center of which ran the opposing lines of breastworks. Lee's whole force barely sufficient to man the line confronting the enemy's, his soldiers could not be allowed, when relieved from service at the front, to seek resting places beyond the zone, lest, in case of sudden attack, they fail to reach threatened parts of the line in time to avert disaster.

Wherever a halt was made on the firing line, breastworks were immediately erected—the Federals, notwithstanding their overwhelming preponderance in numbers, being as insistent as the Confederates on having such protection. The Confederates soon grew to be experts in the manipulation of the pick and the spade, and when, as frequently happened, such tools were not at hand, and the enemy threatened a speedy attack, resort was had to bayonets—tin-cups and frying-pans and such few axes and hatchets as were carried by individual soldiers. With these and such logs and rails as could be found near, fairly safe breastworks were thrown up in an hour's time.

The rations issued to the Confederates, slender as they were at its beginning, grew less and less as the campaign progressed. Flour became a luxury, corn-bread the staff of life. Hunger—incessant, never-satisfied hunger—prevailed, and the soldiers grew thin and gaunt. Still, on the pound of cornmeal to the man, and the less than half a pound of bacon, or as much of beef which was occasionally issued, Lee's soldiery managed to live and retain the strength and the courage for almost continuous battle with a well-fed foe.

The Texas Brigade moved, as did the other commands in the Southern army, always to the right, and only as Grant's army sidled to its left—Lee's constant effort being, and he seldom failed to accomplish it, to confront the Federals at all times and places. Grant's effort seemed to be, not to crush the Confederate army, but to evade it. But move as secretly as Grant might, Lee was either informed of the movement, or divined it in time to meet it; and dangerous as it often was, to weaken a part of the line then held by him, kept his troops well in front of Grant's.

In the early hours of May 8 the Texas Brigade threw up breastworks along the part of the line assigned to it at Spottsylvania. It was not attacked until about sunset of the 10th. For many hours of the 8th, and all day of the 9th, the dull but incessant roar of small arms and the wicked boom of artillery told of repeated assaults on Ewell's lines on its right, and behind breastworks for the first time and anxious to learn what execution it could do from them, it felt slighted. At daylight of the 10th it appeared that its hopes would be gratified. Fruition, however, was denied until late in the day. Then, having failed after repeated trials, beginning at sunrise, to make headway against either Hill's corps, on the left of Longstreet's, or Ewell's, the enemy as a last resort decided to move against Field's division. Their heaviest blow was directed against the Texas Brigade, and, it must be confessed, they took it by surprise.

Giving no notice of their intentions, five of their brigades, under cover of the heavy timber, crawled close up to the breastworks. Then, with loud huzzas they sprang forward in a seemingly reckless charge. Having made up their minds that they would not be attacked at all that day, the Texas regiments were not as ready as they should have been, and for a few seconds it looked as if the enemy would win the breastworks. But when his hope was strongest, a sheet of flame and a yell of defiance burst from the intrenchments, the bullets mowing the assailants down by the hundreds, and in front of the Fourth and Fifth Texas and the Third Arkansas the onset was soon checked.

The First Texas was not as successful as its comrade regiments in repelling the enemy. About the middle of the part of the line occupied by it a gap, probably forty feet wide, had, for some reason, been left unprotected by breastworks, and into this, a double line of the Union soldiers poured, shooting right and left, and to some extent, using their bayonets. But although taken more by surprise than the other regiments, being habitually more careless, and driven from their works, the First Texans immediately rallied, and joining in a hand-to-hand contest with their assailants, soon drove them back over the works; and as by this time the balance of the brigade was idle and turned their fire on the Federals still in front of the First, they were soon compelled to precipitate flight. But for a while, the affair looked ugly to the Confederates, and troops were hurried to the reinforcement of the Texas Brigade. By the time they arrived, though, the part of the line seized was recaptured, and the Union troops in its front were on the run.

The "Ragged —— First" was a peculiar regiment in many respects. Its personnel were as brave and daring as any, but they were never strong on dress, drill and discipline, as laid down in Hardee's tactics. Their long stay in the cornfield at Sharpsburg, and their repulse there of all the Federal commands that had the nerve to assail them, shows how well they could stand fire, and how vigorously and effectively they could deliver it. While in East Tennessee they took a notion that they could march with greater ease if relieved of the weight of bayonets, for which they had never had need and never expected to have, and they threw them away. When at Spottsylvania quite a number of them felt the points of bayonets in the hands of the enemy, they "saw the point" that such weapons were good things to have, and quiet was no sooner restored than they went in search of them and were soon well-equipped with them—securing many from the abandoned guns of the Federals, and borrowing, "unbeknownst" to the owners, others from an Alabama brigade of another division.

In the matter of dress, as above indicated, the First Texans were neither dudes nor dandies. Their fondness for and frequent indulgence in games of cards, naturally had a disastrous effect upon the seats of their trousers. One day when the army was marching from Sharpsburg toward the Rapidan, General Lee and a distinguished English guest sat on their horses by the roadside—Lee naming the commands by States as they passed, and the Englishman observant and critical, his look, that of admiration. As the First Texas filed by, though, the look changed to one of derision, and noting it, General Lee said: "Never mind their raggedness, Colonel—the enemy never sees the backs of my Texans."

On the 11th, Grant let his army rest. It needed it little less, if any, than Lee's did. On the morning of that day, Grant wired to Washington:

"We have now ended the sixth day of very heavy fighting, the result to this time in our favor. But our losses have been heavy, as well as those of the enemy. We have lost to this time, eleven general officers, killed, wounded and missing, and probably 20,000 men. . . . I propose to fight it out on this line if it takes all summer. The arrival of reinforcements will be very encouraging to the men, and I hope they will be sent as fast as possible and in as great numbers. . . . I am satisfied the enemy are very shaky, and are only kept up to the mark by the greatest exertions on the part of their officers, and by keeping them intrenched in every position they take."

The statement, "I am satisfied the enemy are very shaky," was the outcome of desire they should be, and not of Grant's six days' experience in trying to drive the Confederates. In truth, the Army of Northern Virginia was never more enthusiastic and sanguine of success than it was on that day. Grant's insistence that speedy and large reinforcements of his army would be "very encouraging to the men," is a confession, that discouraged by their failures and appalled by the butchery to which they had already been subjected, and appeared doomed, his own men were shaky. His assertion that only by the greatest efforts on the part of their officers were the Confederates kept up to the mark, is not only absolutely untrue, but is another case where "the wish was father to the thought." And finally, his complaint, for it is nothing else, that the Confederates would fight only from behind their breastworks, is puerile in view of the great difference in numbers of the two armies, and the fact that wherever a Federal command took position, it hastened to protect itself by intrenchments.

On the 12th, although to its right and left the storm of battle raged continuously all day long, the Texas Brigade was not attacked. Demonstrations, however, were frequent in its front, and the men were kept busy watching lest one of these be converted into a real attack, and firing at every Federal and body of Federals that came in sight and within range of their rifles. Both for this purpose, and to repel an assault, they had guns and ammunition in superabundance, gathered from the large supplies left on the 10th by the flying Union soldiers. It was at the great salient occupied by Edward Johnson's division that the real battle of the 12th was waged. The brave, determined assault by the Federals, the courageous obstinacy of the Confederates as they contested the issue whether Lee's center should be broken and his army divided, made the engagement far the bloodiest of the campaign, and christened the salient as the "bloody angle." It was Grant's grandest and most hopeful effort to break Lee's center, and for long hours victory hung in the balance. Success crowned the initial assault made on the apex of the angle by twenty-two Federal brigades. Their approach hidden by the thick woods and a dense fog, these crept up to within a hundred yards of the breastworks, and then charging, captured Johnson's division, and only by the almost superhuman exertions of the Confederates was their advance to the base of the angle stayed, and finally, after the most desperate fighting on both sides, repulsed.

It is wonderful how rapidly information as to what was

occurring, or had occurred, passed from lip to lip up and down the Confederate lines. Hancock's assault at the "bloody angle" was known to the Texas Brigade within three minutes after it began, and so of every other important happening. Jokes, jests and accounts of the ludicrous had as swift transmission, and received a most grateful welcome, for they took the minds of the soldier off the tragic. At nightfall of the 12th hardly had the firing ceased when came the comforting words: "All right on the left," "All right on the right," and "We've had a desperate time of it in the center, but we're not whipped to hurt." While such reports came and were received exultingly, behind them, in cases where the fighting had been severe, we could hear the groans of the wounded and dying, and in the light of our own experiences, see the fast stiffening bodies of the slain. It was war, and it might be the turn next of any one of us to fall wounded or dead, and if wounded, to writhe in pain and agony, or, using musket as a crutch, limp slowly and painfully to the rear. Yet, not a man of Lee's army lost heart, and ceased to be brave, defiant and hopeful.

On the 13th quiet prevailed. On the afternoon of the 14th it was discovered that the enemy had again sidled to the southward, and that night the Texas Brigade was again on the march, this time to the North Anna River. The tramp, however, was interrupted at several points where it halted to confront the threatening enemy, and to build the short line of breastworks that was to be its shield should an assault come. On the 21st it reached the North Anna, marching thence on the 27th, and on June 1st taking position and throwing up breastworks on the identical ridge north of the Chickahominy, from which, in June, 1862, it had helped drive Fitz-John Porter's command, of McClellan's army, to the south side of that stream. Then it faced and moved southeast—now, it faced northwest—the positions of the contending armies being exactly the reverse of what they were in 1862.

The Federal breastworks were too close to those occupied by the Texas Brigade to permit a picket line, and June 2nd was spent in an almost continuous exchange of rifle shots from the main lines. The morning of June 3rd dawned clear and hot, not a breath of air stirring. A day of comparative quiet in prospect, the men were no sooner awake than they commenced reading the morning papers, just out from Richmond, then but seven miles distant, breakfasting as they read on clammy corn-bread and raw bacon—the latter too precious then to be wasted by cooking. Such as had neither paper to read nor rations to eat, strolled up and down the trench, casting occasional watchful glances across the breastworks. Not a man dreamed that an attack would be made by the Union army; our position was too strong.

But the improbable, the wholly unlooked for, happened nevertheless. Grant made preparations for an assault on the 2nd, and Lee, alert to every threat, took steps to defend against it. Half a mile to the left of the Texas Brigade, Kershaw's division guarded a salient, the weak place on the Confederate line, and in front of this Grant massed the half of his immense army, and made his last desperate effort to break through Lee's line and gain a direct "on to Richmond." In the trenches between Kershaw's right and the Texas Brigade stood Anderson's and Law's brigades. These and Kershaw's troops bore the brunt of the assault. Against the Texas Brigade there was scarcely the threat of attack, but, as in their advance the Federals exposed their left flank to its fire, they got it as fast as experienced soldiers could load, aim and pull triggers.

The charge of the Federals was gallant enough to deserve success. They came forward in four lines, about fifty yards apart, and thus presented the fairest of targets for Texas and Arkansas markmanship. But they essayed the impossible; men could not live in the fire poured on them from front and flanks, and although in the first rush a few came within seventy yards of our lines, they halted, about-faced, and fled as fast as legs could carry them. The slaughter was terrible; in the fifteen minutes their struggle lasted, 10,000 Union soldiers were killed and wounded. This assault on the Confederate center was supported by one made at the same hour, a mile or more to the right of the Texas Brigade, by Hancock's corps, which, though fruitless, cost it the loss of 3000 men. The Confederate loss during the day was less than 1300.

At nine o'clock of the same morning Grant ordered the assault renewed. But not a man in the Union ranks moved forward, for not a man of them but knew it was suicidal to undertake the task ordered. Swinton, the Northern historian, is candid enough to say: "The order was issued through these officers to their subordinate commanders, and from them descended through the wonted channels, but no man stirred and the immobile lines pronounced a verdict, silent, yet emphatic, against further slaughter."

Until nightfall of June 7th the Texas Brigade remained at Cold Harbor without change of position, the stench of the unburied, rotting corpses of the Federals slain on the 3rd constantly in its nostrils—Grant having delayed asking leave to bury his dead until the 5th, lest the request be construed as an admission of defeat, and when given permission, having failed to bury the half of them. Relieved then by other troops, it was given a day's rest in a camp in the woods, whence it went over to Totopotomy Creek to hold a position from which Ewell's troops were retiring, against Federal cavalry with which it had a rumpus from which the cavalry emerged considerably the worse for wear. Thence, on the 13th, along with the other commands of Field's division, it went to the south side of James River, crossing that stream on a pontoon bridge above Drury's Bluff, and on the morning of the 16th, taking position in an old line of earthworks at Bermuda Hundreds. Grant, hopeless of forcing his way into Richmond by the route originally chosen by him, was transferring his army to the south side—his aim to capture Petersburg and move against Richmond from that point—and Lee was hurrying his to the support of Beauregard, then commanding an insignificant force at Petersburg.

On the crest of the hill at the foot of which the Texas Brigade lay, stretched a short line of intrenchments from which, a day or two before, the Federals had driven Beauregard's troops. They were now occupied by the enemy in heavy force. For a while an effort to recapture them was in contemplation. At noon all thought of such an attack was abandoned, and the men of the Texas Brigade settled themselves down for a good rest. At 5 p. m., though, Pickett's division was ordered forward to make a reconnoissance in force and discover the strengh and position of the enemy in its immediate front. The gallant Virginians soon converted the reconnoissance into a real attack, and unwilling to meet this, the Federals broke in confusion and fled. The ground open and the Texas Brigade not half a mile from the right of Pickett's men, it witnessed every movement made, and when the Federals broke, a Texas private—who it was, has never been known—shouted: "Now's our time, boys!" The effect of the call seemed magical, for the words had scarce passed the speaker's lips when every member of the brigade sprang to his feet, gun in hand, and leaping over the breastworks, joined in a wild, reckless charge up the slope of the hill on the enemy.

No order was given by any officer; none was needed. Each man wanted to do, just then, while the enemy were in confusion, what he felt sure he would be ordered to do, perhaps an hour later, when the Federals had recovered from their panic, and probably, received reinforcements. There was no alignment, no attempt at any, and such a yell as resounded was never, before or since, heard between Richmond and Petersburg. Company, regimental and brigade officers, followed the lead of their men, and the other brigades of the division joined with a yell in the movement. The outcome was that the Union soldiers in front of the Texas Brigade took to their heels, and it gained the breastworks unopposed—to find them half torn down, and to discover that just over the crest beyond them the enemy had built a strong line of intrenchments, along which were two heavy-gunned and well-manned forts that had the exact range, and poured a brisk but ineffective fire on the dismantled works behind whose low walls the Confederates crouched. The cannonading ceasing when darkness came, the brigade worked all night to reconstruct the captured works. But it was not allowed to enjoy the fruits of its bold, unordered charge and its subsequent labor, for shortly after sunrise it moved to the right, and an hour later was on the cars, speeding toward Petersburg, which but the day before had barely escaped seizure by the Federals.

The siege of Petersburg—it was really the siege of Richmond—commenced on the 18th day of June, 1864. Then it was that the Federal armies of the Potomac and the James. and the Confederate Army of Northern Virginia, under their respective commanders, confronted each other south of James River in the positions they were respectively to occupy until the opening days of April, 1865. Grant wrote to General Meade on the 18th, saying: "Now we will rest the men and use the spade for their protection, until a vein can be struck." That kind of resting suggests the story of the plantation and slave-owner, who, one hot summer's day in the fifties, said to his darkeys when they came from the cotton-field at noon: "Now, boys, while you are resting, you may as well hoe out that five-acre garden patch." It was not a new kind of rest, though, to the soldiers in the Army of the Potomac who had constructed a line of intrenchments which stretched from the Rapidan to James River.

Until the 19th the Texas Brigade moved from place to place in the strip of country, a mile and a half wide, that lay between Petersburg and the semi-circle of intrenchments on the east and south that held the enemy at bay—halting an hour or two here, a day there, or a night at another point. The position then assigned it lay east of the city, far down on the eastern and untimbered side of a long ridge—its left flank south and within five hundred yards of the "crater," the yet visible evidence of the great mine exploded July 30, 1864— its right resting on a rather wide branch which, in its passage eastward through the breastworks, left a gap in them. The Federal line of intrenchments was in the thinly timbered hollow at the foot of the ridge, and in front of the brigade, and for a mile to its left was scarcely two hundred yards from that of the Confederates.

Here for thirty long, weary days the Texas Brigade stayed on guard, under a hot, almost blistering sun, and with only the shade made by blankets and tent-cloths, stretched across such rails and planks as could be brought long distances on the shoulders of its men through an incessant storm of bullets, to protect them from its heat and glare. There was little breeze, scant rain, and much dust. The opposing lines too close together to permit either side to send pickets to the front, the watching of each other and the guarding against surprise was done in and from the main lines, and lest the vigilance exercised there prove insufficient, each side maintained a rifle fire, which, although in the daytime somewhat scattering and perfunctory, was at night an unceasing volley. Through this storm of bullets had to come on the shoulders of commissary sergeants and such men as were detailed to assist them, the rations on which soul and body were barely kept together. The corn-bread, a pound a day to the man, was cooked by details far in the rear; the bacon, a scant fourth of a pound per diem to the man, or the same quantity of tough, lean beef, was brought, uncooked, on the same shoulders, as were also, but only at long intervals, the small supplies of beans, peas, rice and sugar then procurable. Coffee —not more than thirty beans to the man—was a rarity.

The water that satisfied thirst, and in which such provisions as the men dared waste by cooking, were boiled, had to be brought in canteens from a spring on the far side of the branch which made a gap in the breastworks, and to cross that branch, by night or by day, was to risk life and limb—the Federals guarding the gap as they did no other point on the line, and keeping it hot and sizzling with death-dealing bullets. After one man was mortally wounded, and two or three others, seriously, the risk was minimized, and at the same time equitably distributed, by sending, in regular turn, two men of a company, with all its canteens, after water. One of these, carrying all the canteens, would spring across the gap, and if he arrived safe, toss them as they were filled, back across it to his comrade.

To stay in the trenches alive, was to suffer with heat, smother with dust, keep heads below the top of the breastworks, and half-starved, long the more for a "square meal" because there was little else to occupy one's mind. Thoroughly inured to danger as were the Texans and Arkansans, they accepted its presence as inevitable, and now that it stayed by them so constantly, it grew monotonous and ceased to be worthy of more attention than could be given it mechanically and subconsciously. Their experiences of hardship and peril were neither singular nor uncommon. Not a brigade of Lee's army that did duty in the trenches east of Petersburg as long on a single stretch as did the Texas Brigade, but suffered and endured as much during those excessively warm, sultry months of June and July, 1864. Nevertheless, the same Texans and Arkansans welcomed, with unfeigned gratitude, the arrival, on the morning of the 20th of July, of the brigade that relieved them. Up to about that date it had been impossible without great exposure of life, to move troops held in reserve into the trenches—now, it was made easy and safe by long traverses leading from the trenches to points beyond the range of the enemy's rifles.

Gathering up their belongings and shouldering their guns, the members of the Texas Brigade bade what proved to be a final farewell to the scene of thirty days and nights of discomfort, ever-present danger and continuous noise, and their steps quickened by the fear that the tons of powder it was known the Federals were placing under ground somewhere along that part of the Confederate line, would be exploded before they could get beyond reach of its terrors, filed into the long traverse and marched to a point a mile southeast of the city. There, under the shade of trees, near a little stream of clear, running water, and sufficiently far from the firing line to dull the roar of guns, big and little, the brigade rested, held in reserve, nine days that were all the more pleasant because absolutely uneventful. At 3 A. M. of the 28th, however, it marched, without beating of drum or blowing of bugle, to the extreme left of the Confederate line, where, taking refuge in a hollow that ran up into wooded hills, it awaited further orders. An effort to capture one of the enemy's forts was in contemplation, and the brigade had been selected to lead the assault. Some Confederate officer blundered, and surmising Lee's intention, Grant not only reinforced that part of his line, but turned loose his artillery, and for more than two hours the brigade lay under a storm of shells and round-shot which, notwithstanding its ineffectiveness, was far from agreeable.

The project abandoned by Lee, and the artillery fire having ceased, the brigade marched back into Petersburg, and thence, crossing the Appomattox, proceeded to Dunlap's Station, the then terminus of the Richmond and Petersburg Railroad. There it boarded a train and rode to Rice's turnout, whence, leaving the train, it marched across James River, and came to a halt, an hour before sunset, some distance in rear of breastworks, on the heights overlooking that portion of the valley of the James known as Deep Bottom, which were then occupied by Kershaw's division. On the 27th, it seems, Grant had sent a large force to the north side, and to meet it and compel its return, Lee had sent over Field's and Kershaw's divisions. But there was only a little skirmishing done, and a reconnoissance made after sunset developed the fact that the Federals had withdrawn to the protection of their gunboats on the river. That night, Kershaw's division returned to Petersburg, leaving Field's division to guard against another advance of the enemy. Next morning, between daylight and sunrise, such members of the Texas Brigade as were then awake, heard the roar of the explosion of the long-talked-of mine at Petersburg. Confident as they were that the mining had been done under that part of the breastworks so long occupied by the brigade, it is small wonder that they and all their comrades heartily congratulated themselves on their timely removal from the vicinity. Bill Calhoun voiced the sentiment of all when he said: " Well, boys, hit's a d—d sight more comfortabler ter be stannin' here on good ole Virginny *terror firmer* than ter be danglin', heels up an' heads down, over that cussed mine, not knowin' whether you'd strike soft or hard groun' when you lit."

CHAPTER XIV

CHARLES CITY ROAD, DARBYTOWN ROAD, CHAFFIN'S FARM, WILLIAMSBURG ROAD

THENCEFORWARD, until the curtain rose on the last act of the tragedy that culminated at Appomattox Court House, the Texas Brigade remained on the north side of James River. A few days after the affair of July 30 General Grant withdrew from that side the bulk of the troops sent there, and Anderson's, Law's and Jenkins' brigades returned to Petersburg—only the Texas and Benning's brigades of infantry, and Gary's, of cavalry, being left on the north side to protect the Confederacy's capital from attack and capture. General John Gregg was assigned to the command of these.

Peace and quiet reigned until August 13, and in shaded camp and with nothing to disturb its rest, the Texas command felt that its lines were cast in pleasant places. Vegetables were to be had in abundance from the Portuguese, negro and "poor white" truck-farmers of the section, and having been recently paid off, the men fared as sumptuously as their wretchedly small allowance of bread and meat permitted. On the 13th, though, their rest was broken by two Federal army corps, which,, advancing from Deep Bottom, at daylight of the 14th, assailed the Confederate left with a strong line of skirmishers. Their force fully twice that of the Confederates, the latter, in order to cover their front, formed in single line, the men standing six feet apart. As was characteristic of the Federal generals of that day, those in command lost the advantage of their superior numbers by excess of caution and slowness of advance. Not until convinced they had double the strength of the Confederates did they order an attack in force on Gary's cavalry, then holding the Confederate left.

The cavalry was driven from its position, but at that juncture Law's and Anderson's brigades arrived and by a desperate charge regained the line lost. Then came darkness, and with it a rain that lasted until morning, and the conflict ceased. About 10 P. M. the brigades of Wright and Sanders reinforced the Confederates. An hour later the Texas Brigade was ordered to the left to assist the cavalry to check the steady movement of the enemy in that direction, and until nearly sunset of the 16th it played a game of "hide and seek," —the hiders being the two brigades of Union cavalry, which crossing White Oak swamp on the Charles City Road, were moving around the Confederate left toward Richmond—the seekers, the Texas Brigade.

The sky was cloudless, the sun had a full head of steam on; not a breath of air was astir in the dense woodlands through which the infantry brigade marched and countermarched, and water was not to be had except at the slow-flowing wells of the few denizens of the section. Still, the hiding and seeking went merrily and diligently on until, about the middle of the afternoon, the Federal troopers learned that Texas and Arkansas infantry were doing the latter, and decided to quit the game. Leaving a regiment to act as rear-guard, their main body beat a hasty and safe retreat. The rear-guard was not so fortunate. Cornered by the Texas Brigade, about sunset, on Fraser's farm, and cut off from the corduroy on which only was the passage of White Oak swamp feasible, a couple of hundred of them were killed, wounded and captured, and half as many more rode their steeds into the swamp, hoping by some miracle to escape its bogs. The remainder, more daring and sensible, faced the bullets long enough to gain the corduroy road, and go clattering down it, followed by a rifle fire that emptied many saddles before their occupants were out of range. Of those who plunged into the swamp, a few escaped capture, but none a submersion, head and ears, in the foul-smelling ooze into which they and their steeds sank. Quite a number of the men and ten or fifteen horses were pulled out of the mire by the Confederates, but many valuable animals had to be left to die of starvation.

While the Texas Brigade was thus engaged, severe fighting was done on that part of the line it had left the night before. Grant had reinforced his north side contingent until the enemy outnumbered the Confederates three to one, and to hold their lines at all, the latter were driven to fight in single rank. All day long seven brigades of infantry and three of cavalry —all the troops Lee could spare from the south side, numbering at the outside, about 10,000—contested the field against 35,000 Federals; and although at one time they were driven out of their intrenchments, at another, in the late afternoon, they retook these works by a gallant charge in which they inflicted on the enemy a loss of 2500. The total loss of the Union troops during the day was about 6000, and of these, the larger part were negroes. The Texas Brigade lost none killed, and very few wounded—its heaviest loss being occasioned by sunstroke. One of the negroes captured, who was interviewed by a Texan, said: "Yassir, Marster, I use ter lib down dar on de Eas'ern Shoah, an' de Yankees day come erlong an' tole me ter jine de ahmy an' fight fur de brack man's freedom. Dar wahnt no way outer jinin', but fo' God, Marster, dis chile wouldn't nebbah un chawged you white folkses breas' wuks lack we did, eff der Yankkees hadn't er tole us day'd shoot us eff we didn't. Hit war deff eeder way, fur all de Yankees war er talkin' de same way, an' er stannin' right dar behin' us, wid dar guns in dar han's."

Returning to its old position on New Market Heights on the night of the 16th, the Texas Brigade spent the 17th in desultory, long-distance sharpshooting. The enemy appeared content with the defeat of the day before, and so made no movement forward, or to right or left. On the 18th the forenoon passed without incident; in the afternoon there was a cavalry engagement on the Confederate left, and some artillery firing and much sharpshooting at New Market Heights; and that night, despairing of reaching Richmond from the north, General Grant recalled the bulk of his troops to the south side, leaving only two or three negro brigades to guard his pontoon bridge at Deep Bottom. The Confederate commander also ordered all his brigades, save the Texas, Benning's, Bushrod Johnson's and Gary's, back to Petersburg.

On the 21st the Texas Brigade was assigned position at the Phillips house—its duty, to watch the movements of the negro brigades in Deep Bottom, and give notice of any attempt to reinforce them. It remained there five weeks. But they were not idle weeks, for the maintenance of a line of pickets that would cover the whole front of the negro brigades required the daily detail of one-third of its men. But for all that, life at the Phillips house was not unenjoyable. Many vegetables and fruits were in season, and high-priced as they were, they were bought as long as the last two months' pay lasted. Moreover, not only were the Richmond papers brought daily to camp, but the New York *Herald* and other Northern journals were easily to be had from negro pickets, in exchange for the tobacco with which Commodore Dunn, our sutler, kept the brigade so well supplied.

Along toward the last days of September General Grant believed the time ripe for renewed activity on the north side; wherefore, he started 40,000 men in that direction, under General Ord, with instructions to proceed without delay into Richmond. On the 27th these crossed the James River at Deep Bottom, got well into position on the 28th, and at daylight of the 29th, with negro troops in the van and covering their entire front, moved forward against the 3000 Confederates, all told, then between them and their goal. Of this 3000, Johnson's brigade was on the river above Drury's Bluff—Benning's, at New Market Heights—Gary's, guarding the Charles City Road—and the Texas, at the Phillips house, between Benning's and Johnson's, two miles to the right of the one and three to the left of the other. Half way between the Texas and Johnson's commands, was Fort Harrison, then occupied by a small force of Confederate artillery. On the inner line of intrenchments around the city, a mile and a half in rear of the Texas Brigade, and a like distance in rear of Fort Harrison, was Fort Gilmer, which was defended by a few heavy siege guns, under the management of a few trained artillerists and the City Battalion, composed of old men and boys, and such clerks in governmental departments as were able to bear arms. The line to be defended against the 40,000 Federal soldiers extended from Drury's Bluff down the river about eight miles.

With daylight came a dense, obscuring fog, and through it was heard a roar that sounded like the bellowing of ten thousand wild bulls; it was the shout of the negroes as they valorously charged the picket line in their front. A minute later it was learned that the first attack would be up a narrow

creek valley across which ran the Confederate line, and thither
the Texas Brigade hastened. In this little valley the fog was
so thick as to render large objects, a hundred feet distant, in-
distinguishable. Forming in single line, six feet apart, the
Texans and Arkansans awaited the onset of the enemy. They
could distinctly hear the Federal officers, as in loud tones they
gave such commands as were needed to keep their men moving
in line, but until the line approached within a hundred feet,
could see nothing; even then, only a wavering dark line was
visible. As it became so, and as was usual in those days, without waiting for orders, the Confederates sprang to the top of
the low breastworks, and commenced firing—" shooting at
shadows," one of them said.

About the same instant a Federal officer shouted in stentorian voice, " Charge, men—Charge!" But only by the
negroes immediately in front of the First Texas was the order
obeyed by a rush forward that carried a regiment of the poor
wretches up to, and in one or more places, across the breastworks, and right in among the First Texans. The latter, since
Spottsylvania Court House well-provided with bayonets, were
experts in the use of them, defensively and offensively, and in
less than three minutes one-half of the assailants were shot
down or bayoneted, and the other half, prisoners. In front
of the other regiments the darkey charge lasted but a second
or two, and covered not more than five paces. It was, in fact,
simply a spasmodic response to the order. Then the black
line halted, and for a moment stood motionless, obviously de-
liberating whether the more danger was to be apprehended
from the Southern men in front, or the Northern men in rear.
Apparently, they decided on a compromise, for the half of
those that survived the terrible fire poured into their ranks,
threw down their guns, and wheeling, fled to the rear, and the
other half dropped flat on the ground, and lay there until
they were led away as captives.

In effect, it was a massacre. Not a dozen shots in all were
fired by the blacks, not a man in the Texas Brigade received
a wound, and save in the First Texas, not a man was for a
second in danger. The firing lasted not exceeding five minutes, but in that short space of time, if the New York *Herald*
be good authority, a Confederate brigade numbering scant 800

men, killed 194 negroes and 23 of their white officers. Estimating the killed as one-fifth of the total loss, it will appear that about 1000 of the colored defenders of the Union were shot out of service in that five minutes. Of the many negroes who dropped to the ground unhurt, quite a number preferred to serve their individual captors as slaves, to confinement in Southern prisons, and did so serve them until the close of the war.

The firing had hardly ceased when word came that Gary's cavalry and Benning's brigade had been driven from their positions, and were in rapid retreat to the inner line of intrenchments on which stood Fort Gilmer, and that if the Texas Brigade did not "get a move on," and a fast one at that, it would be cut off from Richmond and its comrade commands on the north side. Immediately following that information, came a courier from General Gregg with the more alarming intelligence that Fort Harrison had been captured by the enemy, and with an order that the Texas Brigade report as quickly as possible to Gregg at that point. The capture of the fort, as every man knew, placed the brigade in a critical position, and within a minute it was double-quicking up the outer line of intrenchments it had so long guarded—the broad, level ditch affording not only the shortest route, but as well, the best footing for rapid travel. It had not gone a mile, though, before it was a long, straggling line of panting, perspiring and almost exhausted men.

But no halt was made until Fort Harrison came in view, and General Gregg met it. Having waited a quarter of an hour, perhaps, for the men to close up, he led them around in rear of the fort, intending to order a charge upon it. Before they gained a desirable position, however, Gregg learned that the Federals on the left were rapidly nearing the inner line of intrenchments, and knowing that with these in their possession Richmond was, at their mercy, he ordered the men to make the best speed possible to that inner line. It was a race with them and the enemy which would get there first, but they won, lining up in the undefended works to the right of Fort Gilmer, in the nick of time to prevent their seizure by the Federals. It was the "last ditch" between the Union forces and Richmond, and had they won it then, or at any time within

HOOD'S TEXAS BRIGADE   255

the next eight hours, as by one determined attack on its few defenders—a mere corporal's guard as compared with their 40,000—they might unquestionably have done, Appomattox would have been anticipated by fully six months.

But they made no determined attack; such advances as were made were by unsupported brigades, but to meet even these, and repel them, the Confederates were compelled to hurry from one to another widely separated point, and there fight in single rank and far apart. The Texas Brigade alone defended a line of breastworks a mile and a half long, and to do that each of its men had to be practically ubiquitous. How long they could have held out was not fairly tested, for at 3 P. M. reinforcements from the south side came to their aid and at sight of them the 40,000 Federals abandoned a contest in which, up to that hour, they had held all the winning cards, and fell back to the shelter and concealment of the forests.

The defense of Richmond against odds of more than thirteen to one by the four little brigades that fought so gallantly and obstinately until three o'clock that day, deserves a tribute of praise that has never been awarded them. Excepting as they obeyed the general directions of their officers, the fight was made by the privates alone, each man his own general— the officers, figureheads. The loss of the Federals was about 2300—that of the Confederates, about 100. But for the pluck, the uncommanded pluck of the heavy artillerists and of privates of the Texas and Benning's brigades, Fort Gilmer, the one place where the attack of the Federals seemed most determined, must have fallen, and had it, Richmond would have been in the grasp of the Union army. It was here that Caw'pul Dick, a burly black corporal, met his death. The incident is related in the letter of a Texan, as follows:

"A brigade of negroes, supported—or, rather, urged forward—by white troops, made an assault on Fort Gilmer, but the artillerists there were game, and, by the help of half a hundred Georgia and Texas infantry, easily repelled the attack. Death in their rear as surely as in their front,—the prisoners taken declared that they would have been fired upon by their supports had they refused to advance—the poor darkeys came on, for a while, with a steadiness which betokened disaster to the Confederates. But suddenly the line began to waver and twist, and then there was a positive halt by all, except perhaps a hundred, who rushed forward and, miraculously escaping death, tumbled head-long and pell-mell into the wide and deep ditch surrounding the fort.

"'Surrender, you black scoundrels!' shouted the commander of the fort.

"'S'rendah yo'seff, sah!' came the reply in a stentorian voice. 'Jess wait'll we'uns git in dah, eff yer wanter.' Then they began lifting each other up to the top of the parapet, but no sooner did a head appear above it than its owner was killed by a shot from the rifles of the infantry.

"'Less liff Caw'pul Dick up,' one of them suggested; 'he'll git in dah, suah;' and the corporal was accordingly hoisted, only to fall back lifeless, with a bullet through his head.

"'Dah now!' loudly exclaimed another of his companions; 'Caw'pul Dick done dead! What I done bin tole yer?'

"Yet, notwithstanding the loss of Corporal Dick, it was not until the inmates of the fort threw lighted shells over into the ditch that the darkeys came to terms and crawled, one after another, through an opening at the end of the ditch, into the fort."

Their capture on the 29th of September, of Fort Harrison, was a distinct gain to the Federals. Holding it, General Lee had been able to confine the enemy on the north side to the valley of the James, below Drury's Bluff; losing it, he was compelled to withdraw his forces from the heights north of the James, and place them within a line of intrenchments encircling Richmond, and, at various points, not over three miles from the city. This gave the Federals outlet into the country north of Richmond. Lee, however, did not withdraw without an effort to recapture Fort Harrison, and with it, regain possession of the ground lost on the 29th, for on the 30th he ordered an assault made on the fort by a portion of the troops sent over from the south side. But, though well-managed and made with great vigor and determination, the attack failed of success, and emboldened by the defeat administered their opponents, the Federal commanders led their troops out of the river valley on to the heights from which, for the first time, they caught sight of the high church steeples of the doomed capital of the Southern Confederacy—Kautz's cavalry, supported by several brigades of infantry, taking position on, and building formidable intrenchments and fortifications across the Darbytown Road, at a point six miles from Richmond.

The Texas Brigade took no part in the operations of the 30th, and remained unemployed, save in the performance of arduous picket duty, until October 7th. On that day, at 3 A. M., it was called into line, and with the other brigades of Field's, and several brigades of Hoke's division, marched in the direction of the intrenchments across the Darbytown Road —General Lee having planned a reconnoissance in force, to determine the position and strength of the enemy north of James River. That he deemed this of great importance, is evident from the fact that he directed the movement in person.

Kautz's cavalry was easily handled; attacked at early dawn, from front and flank, by a strong line of skirmishers, it abandoned its artillery, and lost little time in placing itself well in rear of its infantry supports. These occupied a line of well-constructed intrenchments, extending along the crest of a long ridge, in front of which much timber had been felled and fashioned into an abatis exceedingly difficult of passage. Half a mile from and in front of the center of the breastworks stood an uncompleted fort in which were several of the cannon captured—its defenders making but a brief stand against the Confederate skirmish line. Passing to the left of this fort and a little beyond it, the Texas Brigade fell into line of battle, and waited for the other troops to march into position on its right and left—General Lee having planned to use the larger part of the forces he had at hand in a simultaneous advance and assault.

Captain W. T. Hill, of the Fifth Texas, writing of the battle, relates the following incident: "The Texas Brigade formed in line about twenty yards from a dim road, on which, immediately in front of my company, General Lee, unattended, sat on his horse, obviously awaiting reports from members of his staff engaged in forming the troops in line. After quite a little while, one of his aides approached him and saluted, and Lee asked if all the commands were ready for the advance. 'None but the Texas Brigade, General,' said the aide. 'The Texas Brigade is always ready,' commented

General Lee. His tone was not loud, but in the still, frosty air of the early morning, every member of my company could distinctly hear his words."

Another member of the brigade, a private, says:

"It was a case of 'noblesse oblige' with the Texas Brigade—'a ground hog case,' as one of the boys put it. 'Marse Robert' was on the field and had his eye on it, and inspired by the consciousness of that fact, every man in it went forward with the resolve to do his level best. But luck and the odds were overwhelmingly with the Yankees that day. Their position was strong, and every tree of the many lying on the ground over which we charged, pointed its sharpened branches at our eyes, faces, bodies and clothing. No sooner was a fellow out of the detaining clutch of one, than another presented itself, and taking hold of flesh or clothing, held him captive a while. There was no staying in line, and could be none—it was each one for himself, in the effort to get through, over or around the abatis. Yet, the brigade moved gallantly on, by jerks and spurts, until an enfilading fire commenced sweeping down on it from the right, and a look in that direction informed it that Hoke's division had come to a halt. Glancing then to the left, and noting that small headway was being made by the Confederates there, the main body of the brigade halted in a depression, about 300 yards short of the breastworks, in which, to some extent, protection against the enemy's rapid and withering fire was afforded.

"But although the brigade halted short of the breastworks, individual members of it went close to them, and while the fight lasted, the space between brigade and intrenchments was dotted with such stragglers to the front—some of them, indeed, going so far that retreat would have been unwise, and they surrendered. The loss of the brigade in killed, wounded and prisoners was greater than in any engagement since the Wilderness, but there is no record from which exact figures can be obtained. Its most notable loss was that of General John Gregg, who was killed while closely following his command and directing its movements. A brave and capable officer, he had won its respect and confidence, if not its love, and his untimely death was sincerely regretted. His remains were followed by the Texas Brigade to Richmond, and buried

J. B. POLLEY
Private, Company F, Fourth Texas Regiment

in Hollywood Cemetery. He was the last officer holding the rank of brigadier-general that commanded the Texas Brigade, and the battle in which he fell proved the last, worthy of the name, in which the brigade engaged."

Unsuccessful as was the attack of the 7th on the enemy's intrenchments, it sufficed to reveal to General Lee the strength and position of the Federals on the north side, and he did not order a renewal of the assault. Along toward the middle of the day Field's division filed to the left and, taking advantage of protecting hills and hollows, withdrew from in front of the breastworks. The Texas Brigade marched to and took position at the place, four miles from Richmond, where it was destined to remain until the following spring, practically undisturbed by the Federals—General Butler's forces wisely, if not valorously, keeping at long-distance range from its rifles, even when, on the 27th of October, they essayed to force their way into Richmond. On that day, for the purpose, it was said, of strengthening " Lincoln's prospects in the near-at-hand presidential election " of 1864, by a couple of victories, General Grant sent a column of 32,000 infantry and 3000 cavalry to turn Lee's right at Hatcher's Run, fourteen miles southwest of Petersburg, and also ordered General Butler to make a demonstration against Richmond. Neither movement was crowned with success—Hancock, at Hatcher's Run, being not only defeated, but losing heavily in men and cannon, and Butler, on the north side, moving with a caution that defeated his object.

Of the battle of October 27th, Captain W. T. Hill, who was then commanding the Fifth Texas, writes as follows:

" All of Field's division were then on the north side—the Texas Brigade holding the left of the infantry line, and Gary's cavalry being on the left of the Texas Brigade. About the middle of the afternoon, the advance guard of the Federals attacked and drove back to the breastworks a portion of Gary's cavalry, then holding position somewhat in advance of their comrades. The Texas Brigade was instantly doublequicked to Gary's relief, and to cover the front of the advancing Federals, our men stood in single line, about eight feet apart. Benning's and Anderson's Georgia brigades followed the movement to the left, and also fell into single line. Just as the three commands got fairly into line and position, a Federal battery and two regiments of infantry emerged from the woods in our front—the artillery taking position on the north side of the Williamsburg road, and the infantry on the south side. From their movements, it was evident that they were somewhat surprised at finding infantry, instead of cavalry alone, in their front.

"Finally, the Federal infantry moved forward against us. But they came only about two hundred yards when, met by our bullets, they lay down. Their battery did effective work, though, at one time blowing up one of our caissons and compelling our men near it to jump over to the outside of the breastworks. Two men of each company of the brigade were at once ordered to concentrate their fire on the battery, and, if possible, to kill all its horses. Their fire was so accurate and destructive that fearing they would lose the battery for want of teams to pull the guns, the Federals hitched up and galloped away with it, leaving their infantry still recumbent on the ground. They lay there for an hour. Then W. A. Traylor, of Company D, Fifth Texas, sprang over the breastworks and, entirely alone, made for them. I called to him and ordered him to come back and rejoin his company. Halting and facing me, he said: 'But, Captain, these slow-going generals of ours are going to sit still until night comes, and let those Yankees out yonder get away.' And facing to the front again, he continued his solitary advance. But he had not gone thirty yards when, waiting for no orders, the men sprang over the breastworks, and forming in line with him, proceeded to the capture of the Federals. Traylor's line of advance led him to a little gulley quite near our breastworks in which lay, concealed from our view, a brave Federal who had done us much harm by his constant and generally accurate fire. When Traylor was within forty yards of the gulley, this man fired at him, but missing his mark, paid for his gallantry with his life—Traylor firing and killing him. By this unordered advance, several hundred Federals were captured, the greater part of the two regiments having crawled back to the woods. It is but fair to say, that with the Texas Brigade in its unordered advance, went both the Georgia brigades."

It was on the Williamsburg road that the Texas Brigade

was stationed. But at no time during the day did the Federals assault the intrenchments it held, their effort on that part of the line being, seemingly, to frighten the Confederates into precipitate flight, by a show of immensely superior numbers, at a distance never less than a quarter of a mile. Butler had under his command 30,000 men—Longstreet had only 6000. Grant's army then numbered 110,000—Lee's, 40,000; Grant's was well-fed, and well-clothed, and shod—Lee's was starving, ragged, and barefooted—and, if of spirit and resolution, if of courage and honest conviction, Grant's army had possessed a tithe of that which animated Lee's, it could have marched into Richmond any day it pleased. But it lacked even that tithe, and knowing it, General Grant allowed it to remain idle and inactive after October 27th, until the last days of March, 1865. It was, perhaps, wise that he should; many in numbers and well-equipped as the Union army was, its morale was at a low ebb, and had been since his butchery of his men at Cold Harbor, after which they fought but half-heartedly. That truth is confessed in Walker's life of General Hancock, in Greeley's work, "The American Conflict," and in many contemporaneous writings.

At that time—November 1, 1864—and thereafter until April, 1865, Lee's 40,000 Confederates defended and held a line of intrenchments forty miles in length, and stretching from Hatcher's Run, south of Petersburg, to the Chickahominy. To man its entire length they must have stood in single rank, five feet apart. Of guns and ammunition only, of courage and determination alone, had they abundant supplies. Even fuel for the fires needed to warm their shivering bodies was doled out to them with sparing hand, for there was no forage for the skeleton teams that hauled it. The quarter of a pound of bacon and the pound of meal that, under the rules of the War Department, were the daily assignment to each man were barely enough to maintain their strength, but even this allowance failed when the railroads broke down and left immense quantities of such provisions piled up beside their tracks in Georgia and the Carolinas, and for lack of them the daily ration was reduced to less than one-half.

Just across the way, beyond the two opposing lines of pickets and at many places in plain view of the hard-run

Confederates, lay the abundantly-tented winter-quarters of the well-fed and comfortably-clad Federals. Among the Confederates, and ever present to the end, at Appomattox, famine stalked, grim, gaunt, unrelenting, and cold penetrated the thin clothing of the men and chilled them to the marrow—among the Federals, plenty reigned, no man went hungry and none cold. Yet, great as were the material differences between the two armies, it is neither venture nor boast to say that thenceforward until Appomattox the Union army remained convinced and could not be shaken in the belief that any one of Lee's men was equal to any three of its own in fighting ability. Nor can it be doubted by the dispassionate and unprejudiced student of the history of those days that both General Grant and the most able of his subordinate commanders had not only a profound respect for the generalship of Lee, but, as well, a wholesome and abiding fear of it.

Grant confessed as much when, at the outset of his campaign, he declined to maneuver, and declared his intention of exhausting Lee's army by attrition. Its movements, well-directed, there was never a day after May 4, 1864, that the Union army, fighting with spirit, confidence, and obstinacy, could not have brushed the Confederate army out of its way and marched into Richmond. Pluck and daring, resolute and unyielding as it may be, can accomplish little when confronted by equal pluck and daring on the part of such vastly superior numbers as Grant had under his command. Weight tells in any contest.

Winter at hand, and the Federals appearing inclined to a cessation of active hostilities, the men of the Texas Brigade set about the construction of shelters from the cold. These were neither imposing nor very comfortable structures. Little timber had been left standing inside the intrenchments, and that north of them was so jealously guarded by the enemy that it could not be counted on as available. The only lumber accessible was that in deserted buildings, and this, for lack of teams, had to be carried on the shoulders of the soldiers lucky enough to be in time to secure shares in such material. Nails were things of the past—hatchets, saws, and hammers were few—and axes, seldom more than one to the company, were the only tools procurable. But with these, hovels were built which, when roofed with tents, blankets and like makeshifts, and provided with fireplaces and chimneys made of mud and sticks, proved desirable dwelling places for men so long inured to hardship. In them the soldiers cooked, ate and slept, played cards, checkers, cribbage and chess, laughed, talked, jested and joked, and, strange to say, were not altogether unhappy.

Not all of their time, by long odds, though, was spent in the hovels and in idleness. Picketing had to be done against the Federals in their front. This being but a duty and precaution, offered little of adventure and excitement, and these, eagerly sought for, not only were details made of organized and instructed parties of scouts under command of trusted officers, but permissions to scout were given liberally to individuals and parties desiring to operate on their own hook. The organized parties, as a rule, gave little annoyance to the enemy, but the independent scouts went right in close to his camps and kept his men in constant alarm; in fact, during that winter, not a Federal within five miles of the Texas Brigade dared, after nightfall, stray beyond the guarded limits of his regiment's camp, or in broad daylight go far from it alone, lest he be pounced upon by Texan or Arkansan, relieved of his valuables and led into captivity.

The only movement made by the Texas Brigade as a command during the winter of 1864-5 was on the 20th of December, 1864. Its objects and incidents are related by Private J. H. Cosgrove, of Company C, Fourth Texas, as follows:

"The cold, chilly winds of December had stolen all military ambition from the older officers of 'Lee's Army'; the weather, combined with the seeming hopelessness of our cause, had produced that lassitude which, to the practiced eye, is a token of coming dissolution.

"Not so, however, with that indefatigable, red-headed Colonel, who, the winter before, had alarmed the enemy at Plymouth, N. C., and under Hoke's command had gained no small repute as a leader in bold and dashing enterprises. His name was Anderson. Small of stature, quick spoken, leaving more to be understood than expressed, and quite nervous in his movements, he suggested the reconnoissance of the 20th of December, 1864; the last aggressive movement made by the

Texas Brigade, except such as covered the retreat to the Appomattox.

"It was a bitter cold day; a day preceded by times of heavy snow and a freeze which so hardened the crust that it bore up the men, though the artillery sunk through and into the rotten soil, and the cavalry cut it up dreadfully. To add to this, the day was gloomy. Murky clouds hung low and depressed the men's spirits.

"In this weather, Colonel Anderson suggested a dash on the enemy's lines on the 'North Side,' not so much to achieve important direct results as to annoy the Yankees, keep them in the open, and disturb as much as possible their repose. And then important direct results might develop, which could be taken advantage of.

"These did develop, but Anderson with all his dash was not equal in that regard to the Texas Brigade skirmish line. I remember that I was acting Clerk to Haywood Brayhan, Lieutenant Co. F, and since Jack Sutherland's disabling, acting Adjutant, and that as the Brigade moved out to the 'sally port' on the Charles City road, I slipped and fell several times, as I ran along the line of march, delivering the mail to the regiment. At the 'sally port' was a Washington artillery battery which had moved out before us. Some mile or so beyond we took a 'woods' road which led to and intersected the pike to the 'Pottery' and to 'Deep Bottom.'

"As we had scouted all through this country, our Brigade was placed in front, and with Ed Crockett, Dansby, Kay, Bennet Wood and others, I went on the skirmish line, which was made up of Texans and South Carolinians. There were about sixty or eighty of us under command of Major Martin; and sixty or eighty men those late days in the war in Virginia made what was then called a Regiment, in size and front covering. And then the sixty or eighty men were a survival, not of the fit, but of those who were at first the fittest. They were trained, and as Joe Polley would remark, 'tried and true.'

"Just beyond the New Market Pike we struck the enemy's pickets, and with a rush and a yell, ran in on the reserves at the heels of the videttes. Just then it began to snow lightly, and the sight at that moment was indescribably grand.

"At the Yankee reserves' bivouac, fires made from rails

burning their entire length, cast a crimson glow; the snow was lazily drifting in huge flakes; the red flash of the small arms against a white background; the flying enemy—dark from their blue uniforms—and the pursuing Confederates, have left with me a lasting impression. At the moment, I called Crockett's, Wood's and Dansby's attention to the picture, and began to dilate on its sublimity, when some smart-alex of a staff officer, as unpoetic as a mummy, remarked: 'We'll defer your fancies, young man, to a season less serious.' General Fields, riding near, retorted, 'You're right, my Texas friend. It is beautiful. Something like Moscow.' To which I replied, 'General, I hope not in results.' And forward we pushed.

"The 'bitterness' of the cold that day came with a thaw which 'slushed' the snow, and from then on it was to keep feet from frost bite. Mine became so cold at times that, finding an open, unfrozen spring stream, I would bathe them in its icy water to find relief from the cruel pain. All my dry socks went, as did those of all the boys.

"Always moving to the left and obliquely forward, we came, towards the noon of that short winter day, to the broken holly-grown lands, through which deep worn gulleys debouch into the James River's second-bottom land, a plateau following that stream to the coastlands below. I had been all day with Major Martin, Ed Crockett and Dansby, practically, as the last two were nearly always my camp and scouting companions. But in this broken and thickety country I became separated from them. Coming up a deep ravine-side to the crest of a hill covered by scrub pine and holly, with no openings except the stock trail I followed, I came suddenly upon a Yankee skirmisher. We were face to face and not ten feet apart. He was in a stooping position, looking at me from over a large and, as I afterwards found, rotten log. My gun was at an easy trail, and I fired quickly from the hip.

"I hit that log, and the rotten dust flew like a cloud. I knew my best chance was to charge him, and as there was no return fire I was sure I had my man. A step or two and I was at the log, but that Yankee had rolled down the hill and was clean gone. I never touched him; but he was at least worse scared than I was, and that was enough.

"I could hear firing at the hill's foot, and going down its

steep sides I found a South Carolina crowd trying to go through an open apple orchard which the enemy defended from the other side. I clambered over the fence, but a sharp fire drove me to an apple tree, where I heard Dansby's voice: 'Jim, you fool,' he cried, 'what in h —— are you doing in there?' My reply, I remember, was, 'Nothing just now, but you fellows can get me out alive if you'll go around and flank this patch.'

"And go around they did, to my great pleasure, for I thought, for some time, that I was a goner. The Yankees were about 200 yards away, and that apple tree felt so small to me when they would clip all around it. As far as my movements were concerned, I hugged the earth and let them do the shooting. After that, I got with Dansby, and we kept together, all along, till the finish.

"You remember the Dutchman who was so brave and so bad? Well, that day he was with us. He had lately returned from Saulsbury, N. C., where he had served a term for 'mugging' a comrade and robbing him of his money. After his pardon and return Colonel Winker had him marching along the breastworks, two hours on and four hours off, with a placard tacked to his back containing this legend in large letters: 'Stole his comrade's rations'—an offense deadly serious when 6 ounces of flour or meal, and 4 ounces of meat daily, was all we got—except cow peas. But he would fight, and fight as bravely as the best of us. On that cold day, his legs became so swollen he could not drag himself along. The heavy ball and chain he had worn in North Carolina had done him up.

"Doctor Terrell advised him to go to the rear, but he said: 'Doc, I can't do that. My honor as a soldier won't permit it.' Terrell turned to me, with the peculiar smile that wrinkled his nose, and said: 'Well, I'm damned! Cosgrove, how is that for a psychologic phenomenon?' I gave it up.

"Dansby and myself scouted around the enemy's right, and found them not so numerous. We got well behind their line, and into an old saw pit. From this, we began to fire on a horseman out in the open, and soon had him dodging to beat the band. But he was too far away to hit except by accident, and after several shots at him, no accident happened.

"Behind him was a breastwork with troops in it, and a forted battery. This seemed their main line, and built to protect their James River pontoon and their lines along Deep Bottom. We found Major Martin and told him of it. He said he didn't know where the brigade was. Dansby and I were in the same fix, but we told the Major we knew where we were, and he was perfectly satisfied.

"Crockett came up just then and suggested to the Major to charge the Yankees out of the woods, as their fire was annoying and hurting somebody, now and then. 'I gad, boys, we'll do it,' said Martin, and yelled out, 'Charge 'em,' which Crockett emphasized by 'dad blame 'em,' and Dansby and myself more sulphuriously.

"At 'em we went, shooting and yelling like H—alifax. They broke and fled, and we followed across the snow-covered field, close on their heels. Major Martin cried out, 'Go into the breastworks with 'em,' and go we did!

"Do any of you remember Dansby's smile; a grin rather, that covered his face. When we got breath he turned to Martin, and with that grin, remarked, 'Major, don't this beat you?' The Major, dear old soul, laughed and said, 'Well, nighly.' Here we were in possession of the enemy's breastworks, and 'slap-dab' in their rear, as Martin remarked, with about 40 men, and to put it as Dansby did, 'forty miles from nowhere.' Martin's query, 'I gosh, where you reckon the brigade is?' I can hear to this day. A wandering cavalry man was sent to find them.

"In a little while 'our friends, the enemy,' came back with a big force and a battery, and after a sharp fight drove Major Martin and his 40 Texans back to the woods where we had 'flushed' them just before we took their line.

"Here we hung on. They shelled and shot at us, but the Major kept us at it. We found big trees, built fires behind them to keep us warm, and when night fell, the South Carolina brigade found us. General Fields was along and took a look at the enemy, but under a sharp fire, and concluded it was now too late.

"Wasn't that a sad word to us all, many and many the time? Well, the old Major had done all he could, and as he remarked, 'I gad, I couldn't whip the whole Yankee army with forty Texans, but I did carry their works and whip a whole lot of 'em, by gad.'

"Going back to our huts, miles away, through that dark and slush and cold, was one of my most trying experiences, but when I had warmed up, had supper and a smoke, and was cozy in my bunk, I heard the horsemen coming along the Charles City Pike, and remarked to my comrades: 'Well, at least I wouldn't be a cavalryman.'"

CHAPTER XV

APPOMATTOX

FROM and after November, 1864, the Southern Confederacy lay in the throes of fast-approaching death. Its credit, even at home, was gone—its prestige abroad was lost—its resources were exhausted. Following the uplifting excitement of the practically continuous battle which, since early spring, had wasted the strength of the Confederate armies on the firing lines in Virginia, Georgia and Tennessee, and especially after the disastrous ending of Hood's Nashville campaign, a reaction came. The hopes that had sustained and encouraged people and armies grew faint, and to thinking men whose pride could humble itself to an abandonment of its dream of Southern independence and separate nationality, the one and only thing that seemed desirable, or even possible, was an honorable peace.

Of the Confederate soldiers then in the field but a scant fourth were at the front, or, at that late period, could be brought there. Of the remainder, more than half of them stood inactive in the Trans-Mississippi department of the Confederacy—held there as much by their own reluctance to share the danger of active service elsewhere as by the presumed military necessity of securing that section against invasion and devastation. The residue operated in scattered detachments in Florida, Alabama, Mississippi, and eastern Louisiana, and along the Atlantic coast, fighting, it is true, bravely and unflinchingly, but, save the gain of occasional temporary advantage, unavailingly. In brief, except in those sections of the South where Lee's and Hood's armies confronted the enemy, and in Texas, the war, ceasing to be national, had degenerated into the guerilla stage, in which this or that quasi-independent band of partisans sought not so much to aid the cause they espoused as to gratify personal animosities and wreak revenge on personal enemies.

On December 1, 1864, Lee's army held Richmond and Petersburg against the hosts under command of Grant; and Hood's, then marching on Nashville, had just lost its opportunity at Spring Hill to deal the enemy a crushing blow, but at Franklin, though at immense sacrifice, had driven him out of his works and into hurried retreat. General Dick Taylor, in command of a small force of infantry and cavalry, was operating in the vicinity of Mobile, but doing neither harm to the enemy nor good to the Confederate cause. Kirby Smith and Magruder played at soldiering in the Trans-Mississippi department, effecting naught save to keep Federal troops out of Texas. Of the Federal armies, that under Grant confronted Lee's in Virginia—that under Thomas was at Nashville, awaiting the coming of Hood's—that under Sherman was well on its way to Savannah, Ga.—the route over which he had passed marked by a swath of destruction, thirty miles wide, in which not a house or a hovel was left standing—and the others were stationed, in large and small bodies, at points where they might hold the Mississippi River open to navigation, protect lines of communication between supply depots and armies, oppress and despoil the non-combatant citizenship, and by occasional threatening activities furnish excuse for thousands of Confederate soldiers to absent themselves from their commands in the main Confederate armies, in order, they said, to protect their families and homes.

The patrol of the Mississippi River by Federal gunboats had long since prohibited dependence on Texas for beef, cut that State, Arkansas, Missouri and a large part of Louisiana out of the Confederacy, and left them " a law unto themselves." Sherman's march to the sea, and destruction, as he went, of all railroads, together with the Federal occupation of east Tennessee, threatened to cut the remainder of the Confederacy in two. The rolling stock and roadbeds of such lines of railway as led into Richmond were worn beyond even temporary repair, and although at Lynchburg and Danville in Virginia, and at different places in North and South Carolina, large quantities of meat, meal and flour were in storage, they could not be transported rapidly enough to Richmond to supply the needs of Lee's army. It was not defeat that threatened the army—it was famine.

Along about the middle of December came the news that

Hood's army had been disastrously defeated at Nashville, and was retreating, demoralized and in confusion. Much as the movement of that army had been condemned by the military experts in the rank and file of the Army of Northern Virginia, there had always been the possibility that it might succeed, and its signal failure was a shock to the most sanguine. Thenceforward, whatever the desire, hope, and aim of Mr. Davis and his admiring followers, "Lee's miserables," as the soldiers around Richmond and Petersburg called themselves, had at heart only the purpose of securing honorable terms of surrender and peace; a peace that would permit them to return to their homes and begin life anew, not as repentant criminals, but as men who had fought for the right as they saw it, and, having failed, were willing, if no disavowal of their principles were required, to lay down their arms and return to the Union. As it looked to them, and as in fact it was, Lee's was the only effective organized Confederate army left in the field, and on it only could reliance be placed to win —not the independence of the South, or the continuance of slavery—vanished dreams both—but such terms of surrender for the soldiers of the Confederacy as were due to a brave foe from a magnanimous antagonist.

For this purpose, unacknowledged to others and scarcely to themselves, the soldiers in Lee's army held their lines, forty miles in length, with a grip that neither cold nor hunger, nor shot nor shell, could loosen. There was no complaining against the grievous condition of affairs that existed, there was no shirking. Shivering with cold and weak for want of food, they stood always ready for duty, and when on duty, whether on field of fierce battle, or of skirmish, on guard, or on picket, did their devoir as firmly, faithfully, and unshrinkingly as when their hopes were highest and brightest. Yet, lest it weaken the resolution of their comrades, they gave no expression to the thought in their minds that only honorable surrender was possible. Apparently, they still fought for independence—still believed it was to be won. There was no cessation of the jest and the laugh, of pranks and practical jokes; fun and frolic was the order of the day, and sadness of face or speech was discountenanced and seldom witnessed or heard.

The feeling that prevailed among them is well illustrated

by a story told by General Gordon, in his "Reminiscences of the Civil War." A prayer meeting was in progress, but fervent and uplifting as were the petitions to God, there was a touch of humor in the proceedings that was irresistibly amusing. Brother Jones, in behalf of himself and his comrades, was praying fervently for more courage. Not content with asking for it once, he repeated the supplication with even greater fervency. Then he was interrupted by a middle-aged private whose resolute bearing, scarred face and maimed hand gave evidence that he had often heard the bullets whistle; to him it seemed a waste of time to be asking for a virtue already possessed, and springing to his feet, he cried: "Hold on there, Brother Jones! Hold on! There's no sense in asking God for more courage, for He knows we have got plenty of it. Ask Him for more grub—that's what we need most of all." That the old fellow had touched the sore spot, was evident from the amens that escaped on all sides.

In February, 1865, came the Hampton Roads conference between commissioners appointed by Mr. Davis, on the part of the Confederacy, and Mr. Lincoln and Mr. Seward, representing the Union. That it should fail to settle the questions at issue, was a foregone conclusion in the minds of thinking men. Mr. Lincoln had no right to consent to a dissolution of the Union as it existed at the beginning of the war—Mr. Davis, none that would justify him in consenting to a peace based upon the return of the seceding States to the Union. Following the conference, or, to be exact, on the 5th day of February, 1865, Mr. Davis appointed General Robert E. Lee commander-in-chief of all the Confederate armies. Had he done this in February of 1864 much good might have been accomplished. Now it was too late; the Confederacy was gasping for breath, its armies were scattered, disorganized, and, practically, commanderless, and there was no time to gather together and weld the fragments into fighting machines. But Lee accepted the trust and did his best, by instantly calling General Joseph E. Johnston to the command of all the troops in Georgia and the Carolinas, and thereby rebuking Mr. Davis for his failure to retain that officer in command at Atlanta, and for not appointing him as successor to General Hood, immediately after the Nashville disaster.

In the meantime Sherman had accomplished his march to the sea, captured the cities of Savannah and Charleston, and was moving up the coast into North Carolina—his object, to come within such range of Grant's army as would enable that and his own to co-operate against the forces under Lee and such as might follow Johnston. Gripped by famine and tortured by cold as Lee knew his army to be, he yet felt it his duty, in deference to the obstinate insistence of Mr. Davis, to hold it in line as long as possible at Richmond and Petersburg. Untrammeled by the Confederate executive and commander-in-chief, in 1864, he would undoubtedly have abandoned those cities to their fate, and, falling back, as he then might easily and safely have done at any time prior to September, to the mountainous regions of Virginia, in their fastnesses have tried conclusions with his opponent. That it would have been good generalship and the wisest course to pursue, is too far beyond question for argument. Now, but alas, too late, he contemplated that move and began planning for it.

On the 27th of March there was hard fighting in the vicinity of Dinwiddie Court House, in which the Federals gained the advantage. Grant had at this time, in his immediate command, 124,700 men, 13,000 of whom were well-mounted cavalry. To oppose these, Lee had about 45,000, less than 5000 of whom were cavalry, under Fitz Lee, mounted on mere skeletons of poorly fed horses. On the 30th, at Five Forks, Pickett, with a force of 10,000 infantry and cavalry, drove Sheridan from Five Forks back to Dinwiddie Court House; but on the 1st of April, having retired to Five Forks, his command was attacked, front and flanks, and routed. On the morning of the 2d the Federals broke through Lee's attenuated line at a point four miles southwest of Petersburg, then made a general attack, and, unable to stay or withstand it, Lee's army began its first compulsory retreat, as a body, before an eagerly pursuing Federal army. Its retreat, though, was neither precipitate nor disorderly—it was organized and well-conducted, the evacuation of Petersburg not beginning until after nightfall. By that time every Confederate command in position along the forty-mile line of intrenchments had received explicit directions what route to pursue in order to join the main column. Among these was the Texas Brigade, which was still occupying its winter-quarters on the Williamsburg road, northeast of Richmond. The story of its retreat, its surrender at Appomattox, and its return to Texas, is told by Captain W. T. Hill, as follows:

"The Texas Brigade held position north of the James River from the 29th of July, 1864, until April 2d, 1865. During the fall of 1864, it found active and almost continuous employment in watching the enemy and fighting him when occasion permitted or demanded, and because it so often supported General Gary's mounted command, soon won the sobriquet of 'Gary's foot cavalry.' About the middle of October, affairs quieted on the Northside, and settling down the brigade built huts and hovels and went into so-called winter-quarters. With no duty to perform save that of picketing our front, time hung heavily on our hands, and to make it lighter, the men sought recreation and profit in scouting— the government offering $1500 for every horse captured from the enemy. This munificent offer tempted many that would otherwise have remained idle, to active enterprise, and competition for the privilege of going on a scout became so eager that when scouting parties were called for from the different regiments, four times as many persons volunteered as were called for, and, quite often, there was difficulty in settling the question of who got there first.

"On Saturday night, April 2d, 1865, the brigade received orders to be in readiness to march at daylight next morning. Starting at the appointed hour, it marched into Richmond, there boarded cars, and about noon reached the north side of the Appomattox, opposite Petersburg. The regiments composing it were commanded as follows: the Third Arkansas, by Colonel R. C. Taylor; the First Texas, by Colonel F. S. Bass; the Fourth Texas, by Lieutenant-Colonel C. M. Winkler, and the Fifth Texas, by myself, Captain W. T. Hill. Colonel R. M. Powell, of the Fifth Texas, commanded the brigade. Our orders were to take position at the fords and crossings of the Appomattox, and prevent the passage of the enemy to its north bank. That our army on the south side of the stream had abandoned its intrenchments, and was now in full retreat, was evident, for we could see long lines of Federals marching

Captain W. T. Hill
Company D, Fifth Texas Regiment

westward from Petersburg. They made no effort to cross the Appomattox, though, and we had little to do. About 11 o'clock that night the brigade commenced its march westward, bringing up the rear of Lee's army. Fires lighted up the heavens in every direction, the Confederates seeming determined to destroy everything that would be of service to the enemy. Near where the Fifth Texas was stationed on the Appomattox, a house stored with bacon was burned, and as we were without food and hungry, we felt it a hardship not to be allowed to fill our haversacks with bacon before it was destroyed.

"Our march that night and next day was uninterrupted by attack from the enemy. We moved along the railroad leading from Petersburg to Lynchburg, and, like the balance of our army, expected to find a supply of rations at Amelia Court House, where General Lee had ordered provisions to be sent, and where he had been officially informed they had been sent. But it was a mistake, and a fatal one at that; not a pound of the supplies ordered had arrived, but from the store of provisions kept on hand there, the Texas Brigade managed to secure a little meal, which the men made into gruel and ate without salt, none of that having been issued.

"In the hope of the arrival of supplies at Amelia Court House, General Lee held his army there one entire day. This loss of time allowed Sheridan, with his cavalry, to cut him off from Danville, his objective point. Baffled in the attempt, by this route, to join forces with General Johnston, he moved toward Lynchburg. During the day, the Federal cavalry made several assaults on our wagon-trains, and did much damage, but were finally driven off by our infantry. The Federal infantry overtook the Texas Brigade, then the rear-guard of the rear-guard of our army, on the evening of the 5th, after we left Rice's station, and the brigade skirmish line had a hot fight with them—so hot that it had to be heavily reinforced before it drove the enemy back. The battle ended at nightfall, by which time all of our army had crossed the Appomattox excepting our brigade.

"Having crossed the Appomattox, the brigade went into bivouac on the first hills near the stream. The next morning, the 6th, it marched up the river to a high railroad bridge, its purpose to hold the enemy in check till the bridge could be effectually destroyed. It remained in position near the bridge until noon; then a courier came to Colonel Powell, commanding the brigade, with the information that the command was about to be cut off from the main army, and an order for instant and hurried retreat. No time was lost in obeying the order, and marching west along a blind road running parallel with the railroad, we succeeded in eluding the enemy and making our way safely to the wagon-bridge spanning the river. Over that we passed, and moving to the north of Farmville, ascended the high hills in Cumberland County, and on one of them halted. On our way from the High Bridge to the wagon-bridge, we had been compelled to march through the front yard of Colonel Hilary Richardson's residence. There, meeting a citizen of the country, I dispatched a message to Dr. Wood, of Farmville, requesting him to buy all the bread in the town and hold it for my regiment, the Fifth Texas. But, alas, there was not a loaf of bread in the town, and the Fifth had to remain hungry, for when, late in the afternoon, a little meat and corn-meal was issued to it along with the other regiments, its march was resumed before any cooking could be done.

"When we had marched a couple of miles further, one of the Georgia brigades of our division (Field's) was attacked by a brigade of Federal cavalry under General Gregg. The attack was most gallantly repulsed—the Federals losing heavily in killed and wounded, and their commander, Gregg, being captured. While the fight was in progress, the Texas Brigade held position on a hill, overlooking the country for miles around. For the time we could spare to observation, the larger part of both armies was in view: Lee's men, moving rapidly but in the most admirable order, to the west, seeking to avoid attack, not because of fear of it, but lest the delay it caused interfere with the plans of General Lee; Grant's, moving steadily in pursuit, his purpose, seemingly, to get around Lee's right flank. But we had little leisure for watching other movements than those immediately in our front and directed at ourselves. Perched on a high and perfectly open hill as our brigade was, the enemy hidden in the dark at the foot of the hill, and his sharpshooters behind trees, they could see all we did and we could see nothing they did. To escape bullets they could not return in kind, our men, while digging little holes in the ground and building fires of twigs in them, over which to cook their corn-meal gruel, crawled around like so many lizards.

"We held position on the hillside until about 10 P. M. that day, then resuming the march westward, went into bivouac on the night of the 8th, at a point two miles east of Appomattox. During this march, evidences of rapid retreat and fast pursuit began to appear. Cannons, wagons and ambulances in large numbers had been abandoned by the troops ahead of us, for lack of teams strong enough to pull them. Horses already dead, and many others fast dying from exhaustion and for lack of feed, lay in the mud, in and by the side of the road.

"On the morning of the 9th, the Texas Brigade made its last march as a Confederate command. This took it to within a mile of Appomattox, where, after facing, in turn, east, west and north in the effort to meet the threatened but never-coming attacks, we formed in a semi-circle across a road, and began building a breastwork of such material as was at hand—the Fifth Texas, I remember, appropriating a rail fence for the purpose.

"Up to this point, General Gordon, with his corps, led the advance. On the 7th, he had driven before him such of the enemy as sought to stay the retreat. But on the evening of the 8th, he failed to drive them, and on the morning of the 9th, again failed. Lee's line of retreat was blocked, the shattered remnants of his once matchless army were surrounded on all sides. Premonition of the inevitable swept through the air, and a death-like stillness prevailed. Work ceased, hunger stayed its gnawing, and expectant of evil tidings, but yet unprepared for the worst, faces grew grave and serious, and men when they talked at all spoke in whispers. Then, in the afternoon, some of our teamsters came from the front and reported that General Lee had surrendered the army. It could not be, and sure the report was false, the men grew indignant, and for a while the teamsters stood in jeopardy. But their statements were soon confirmed by intelligence of the same purport from other sources, and the men of the brigade, submitting to the inevitable, began to wonder what terms General Lee had obtained for his army, and when and how they would return to their homes. There was no hasty disbandment of company, regiment or brigade. The morale of the men had never weakened, and if Lee had but asked it, there was not a man but would have continued to fight as gamely as ever he had.

"During the afternoon and following night, we learned what terms General Lee had obtained. On the next day, the 10th, his farewell address to the army was read on the color line, the men listening to it in silence, but with tears in their eyes. All felt that he had done his best, all that could be done, and that he had surrendered the army only when every avenue of escape was closed and to struggle longer was to invite destruction. Of what followed, little need be said. Some of the scenes that occurred are indescribable, and many are too pathetic to have place here. And while all were sad at the thought of the end that had come, and of speedy partings with the comrades who had shared their dangers and toils, something of humor crept into their conduct and language. Many members of the Fifth Texas declared that even if they had surrendered to General Grant, he should not have a gun from them that would be serviceable, and to make their threat good, they commenced bending the barrels of their guns, and otherwise injuring them. My attention called to this work of destruction, I told the men engaged in it that no parole would be granted by General Grant to any Confederate soldier who did not deliver his arms in good condition. Convinced that I was right, those engaged in the work of destruction said: ' If that is the case, we'll straighten them back again.' But they made signal failures in their efforts ' to straighten them back again.' Nevertheless, all got their paroles, for there was no inspection of the arms delivered. All that our men did, as they halted in front of a line of armed Federals, was to lean their guns up against huge stacks of those already there. Our color-bearers did the same with the flags they surrendered.

"Official records show that the First Texas surrendered at Appomattox, 133 men—the Fourth Texas, 145—the Fifth Texas, 149—and the Third Arkansas, 130; making, in the aggregate, 557 officers and privates, as the number of the Texas Brigade who surrendered. The three Texas regiments surrendered 427 officers and privates. Estimating their entire enlistment, from the beginning to the close of the war, to have been, in round numbers, of officers and privates, 4000, it will be seen that 3573 are not accounted for. Of these, some were dishonorably absent, many hundreds were dead, and many more hundreds were sick or disabled.

"All the formalities of the surrender over, the question of how we should get back to our homes came to the front. To the Third Arkansas, as brave and noble a regiment as was ever mustered into the Confederate service, this was not as difficult as to the Texans, for it could return to Arkansas by way of Chattanooga and Memphis, which it did. The Texans, though, had further to go, and what route was best to take was a problem that required much discussion. Although many of them stayed in Virginia, and others chose to go to Yorktown and avail themselves of transportation by water, offered them by the Federal government, the majority decided to stay together and, as a command, march to Danville, and there taking passage on a railroad train, go by way of Atlanta, Montgomery and Mobile to New Orleans, where they could find conveyance by water to Galveston, Texas.

"On the 12th of April, after bidding farewell to the Third Arkansas, such of the Texans as had chosen to travel as a command fell into line, and under command of their officers, marched in the direction of Danville. But they stayed together only a day or two. Food was difficult to obtain for as large a party as we were. Many of the men were both weak and footsore, and finding it easier to secure needed provisions by scattering out, they soon began to straggle. Wrong roads were taken, long stops were made, and it was several days after the main body reached Danville, before everybody caught up with it.

"Railroad transportation not to be secured at Danville—Sherman's troops having wrecked all railroads leading to the South—we footed it to Greensboro, N. C. There we were joined by the Texans of Johnston's recently surrendered army, and with them proceeded to Montgomery—footing it most of the way, in couples and squads, all effort to retain organization having by this time ceased. At Montgomery, the Federal provost officer assigned us quarters in a large two-story building, located near the artesian well. Major W. H. Martin, the 'Old

Howdy' of the Fourth Texas, shared with me the responsibility of assuming command of the Texans that came in, whatever their regiment or brigade, and we had our hands full—the major in securing rations as needed, and I in attending to official matters.

"It was seven days before we secured transportation to Mobile, and then we had to work for it. A steamboat arrived, loaded with supplies for the Federal troops in and near the city, and the provost told us that if we would unload it, he would send us to Mobile on it. Informed of the offer, the Texans went to work with such energy as, in six hours, to unload and place in piles on the wharf, a mass of freight that it would have taken the negroes employed for the purpose and working in relays of fifty men, full twenty-four hours to unload. When the job was done, one of our boys, noticing the large quantities of bacon, hard tack, sugar, coffee, pickles, canned goods, wagons, picks, spades and other military necessities, exclaimed: 'Boys, we never could have whipped the Yankees. Look at all them good things to eat, and handy things to work with, and compare them with the little we had!'

"The boat unloaded, we were ordered to report that afternoon at the office of the provost, to have our paroles countersigned. The order was obeyed, and next morning we boarded the steamboat we had worked for, and were soon steaming down the river. But at Selma our boat was halted, we were invited to disembark, and a regiment of negroes, destined for service at Mobile, was ordered on it. We protested, of course, and bitterly, against what some of our men denounced as 'a regular Yankee trick,' but our protest was unheeded, and we had to wait at Selma until the next day. Then another steamboat came along, and taking us on board, carried us to Mobile, where we were assigned to comfortable quarters, furnished with rations, and had our paroles again inspected.

"Six days later, we boarded a steamboat for New Orleans, and landing there, were assigned quarters in a large cotton shed. To offset their kindness in not requiring us to have our paroles again countersigned, the military authorities detailed a company of negro soldiers to guard us. The next morning, every Texan wearing brass buttons, whether of Confederate or foreign make, was accosted by one or the other of these blacks with the order, 'Stop, dah, suh, tell I cuts dem buttins off yer clo's!' But the Texans were quick to 'catch on,' and by cutting off their brass buttons themselves, denied the negroes the great satisfaction of doing so.

"During the nine days we were compelled to stay in New Orleans, awaiting transportation to Galveston, the better classes of the citizens treated us with kindness and courtesy; from people in the lower classes only came incivility. Guarded though we were, we went and came at our pleasure. The Irish ladies of the city could not do too much for us. They visited us at our quarters, and not only insisted on having our cooking done for us, but on our coming to their homes and taking our meals there. In addition, they furnished every one of us with a suit of good clothes.

"On the last night of our stay in New Orleans, Colonel Henry, a grand old 'rebel,' gave the rank and file of the Texans an elegant supper at his house, and Dr. Greenleaf entertained the officers in like manner. Next morning, we went aboard the steamship *Hudson*, at 10 A. M. An hour later a fire broke out in the neighborhood of Colonel Henry's residence. The Texans rushed to the rescue, and not only removed from the old Colonel's house everything of value, without damage to a single article, but placed a watchful guard over it, and when the fire was subdued, carried everything back into the building, uninjured. Then they returned to the steamship, which at 4 P. M. got under weigh.

"All went well until, just before day the next morning, the boat reached the mouth of the Mississippi River, and stuck her nose so deep into the mud that she could neither go forward nor back out. Here we lay an exceedingly long forty-eight hours, under a broiling sun, suffering both with impatience and the discomforts of the bad ventilation and the foul-smelling odors of the bilge-water in the hold of the vessel, where for lack of room on the upper deck more than half of our crowd were compelled to stay. On the second day, two tugs lashed to the *Hudson* but failed to drag her from the mud. At ten o'clock of the third day, much to our relief, a freight steamship came down the river, and taking us on board, steamed for Galveston—arriving there and coming to anchor near the blockading fleet, just after daylight next morning.

She was kept at anchor until noon; then only did General E. J. Davis, commanding Federal troops in the city, give his kind consent to our approaching and landing on the wharf, and that we lost no time in getting ashore, you may well believe.

"Notified in advance of our coming, the good people of Galveston and Houston had arranged for us to take a Buffalo Bayou boat at Galveston, and journeying to Houston in comparative comfort, there partake of a sumptuous banquet. But General Davis had taken no shots at 'rebels' when the bullets were flying, and it was time, he thought, to begin fighting. Having already shown his loyalty to the Union by keeping us out at anchor until noon, he gave another evidence of it by prohibiting the employment in our service of the Buffalo Bayou boat; rebels, he said, were entitled to no courtesies. The only chance of getting us to Houston, the railroad, the Galveston people patched up an old engine until it could be depended on for the fifty-mile run, and hitching to it a lot of seatless flat cars, which the Irish women of the city, God bless them, had swept clean, placed the train at our service. Boarding it about sunset, by midnight we were in Houston partaking of the banquet tendered us by its hospitable people. The next day, rejoicing that we had been spared to again set our feet on Texas soil, and feeling that we had done our duty, our whole duty, and nothing but our duty, we separated, each of us going home."

CHAPTER XVI

ADDENDA

It is from well-meaning but careless friends that we must often pray to be delivered. No man had a greater admiration for the Texas Brigade, or ever stood higher in the esteem of its members, living and dead, than did the late John H. Reagan, and yet, in his memoirs, published after his death, he has unintentionally made a number of mistakes with reference to that command. Coming from one less noted for the truth and accuracy of all his statements, they might be safely left uncorrected; coming from Judge John H. Reagan, Postmaster General of the Southern Confederacy, it is imperative that attention should be called to them in this History of the Texas Brigade. In his " Memoirs," beginning on page 143, appears the following:

In the course of the seven days' fighting around Richmond, there occurred, at the battle of Gaines' Mill, a struggle which has few parallels for heroic courage and valor in all the annals of war. Because of the part taken in it by Texans, I shall relate some of the circumstances.

A part of the Federal force occupied a very strong position on a hill on the east side of Gaines' Mill Creek, with three lines of infantry; one was stationed about a third of the distance from the foot of the hill, the second about half way up, and the third between that one and the top of the hill, which was probably 300 or 400 feet high. Their lines were protected by fallen trees, with a swamp and abatis one or two hundred yards wide in their front. The crown of the hill was occupied by the field batteries of the enemy. In order to attack this position the Confederate soldiers had to advance through a gradually descending open field. Two assaults had been repulsed, when, in the general movement of the forces, Hood's Brigade was brought to its front. General Lee inquired of him whether he thought he could take it. Hood's answer was in the affirmative.

It so happened that the First Regiment of Texas Infantry,

commanded by Colonel John Marshall, was launched against the Federal stronghold. Colonel Marshall was soon killed; the lieutenant-colonel was very seriously and the major mortally wounded before the advance reached the creek, and many others of the regiment were killed or wounded before they got through the abatis. This regiment, with no officer above the grade of captain, drove the three lines of infantry from their defenses, and captured the artillery which crowned the hill, and which had been pouring a deadly fire into the charging columns. A few hundred yards further on the Texans saw two field batteries across a depression of the field. Before they had gone far, however, they were assailed by a brigade of Federal cavalry under General McCook. This was put to flight, and then the Texans again rushed forward and captured the batteries.

The Fifth Texas Regiment, commanded by Colonel Jerome B. Robertson, had also broken through the Federal lines and come in view of what was left of the First Regiment. Robertson's statement made afterward to me was that when he saw General McCook's cavalry moving rapidly to the attack of the First Texas Regiment, and saw the small remainder of that regiment, it made his heart ache, as it seemed out of the question for them successfully to resist such a force. But he said the men quickly aligned and stolidly awaited the attack, and that when the brigade got within range he never saw saddles emptied so fast.

The cavalry recoiled, defeated, and as soon as this was accomplished, and the field batteries taken, the Texans started for a Federal siege battery, nearly a mile further on. General T. J. Chambers, who had followed them, as a looker-on, hastened after them and got them to stop, saying that the enemy was then in their rear, and that if they went forward they would certainly be captured. Colonel Robertson's regiment then joined the remainder of Marshall's, and on their return they found that the gap they had made in passing through the Federal line had been occupied by a New Jersey regiment, which on demand surrendered. The beautiful silk banner of this regiment was sent as a trophy to Austin, Texas, and was after the war returned to New Jersey by the military governor, Hamilton.

The First Texas Regiment went into the battle with more than eight hundred men; but came out of it, after this brilliant exploit, with a roll-call of a little over two hundred. After that on different occasions General Lee urged me to aid him in getting a division of Texans for his command, remarking that with such a force he would engage to break any line of battle on earth in an open field.

That Judge Reagan was in fact writing of the Fourth
Texas instead of the First Texas, is evident from his mention
of Colonel John Marshall, who commanded the Fourth, and
not the First Texas. But Judge Reagan makes a number of
other mistakes. It was east of Powhite Creek, and not east
of Gaines' Mill Creek, that the Federals were stationed—it
was but a regiment of cavalry, and not a brigade, that
charged the Fourth Texas—that charge was made, not before
the Fourth Texas captured the batteries, but immediately
afterwards—it was the Fifth Texas, alone, that captured the
New Jersey regiment—and if any Texans "started for a
Federal siege battery nearly a mile further on" it was the
First or Fifth Texas, and not the Fourth.

On page 194 of the same "Memoirs," Judge Reagan gives
Field's division credit for a battle occurring on August 29,
1864, which did not in fact take place until September 29, and
then, the Texas and Benning's brigades were the only brigades
of Field's division that took part in it, until late in the afternoon, when the enemy had been whipped back. Again, on
page 187 of the same "Memoirs," he gives an account of a
voluntary charge made by the Texas Brigade between Richmond and Petersburg that is not at all in accord with the actual facts, which are given in Chapter XIV of his history.

In the Richmond *Dispatch*, of some date in February, 1865,
appears the following account of the presentation of gold
stars to members of the Texas Brigade selected by their
comrades as most worthy of them. It is to be regretted that
the modesty of the fair donor forbade the mention of her name
by General Lee, and has continued to withhold it. It was a
tribute of Beauty to Valor, that should never be forgotten,
and for which no commendation is too great. The *Dispatch*
said:

> We learn that a very interesting scene occurred some days ago
> in the camp of the Texas Brigade (Senator Wigfall's old command), the occasion being the presentation of some golden stars,
> designed for the brave men of the brigade by a lady of Texas,
> and forwarded through the hands of General Lee.
> After brigade inspection the men were addressed by Senator
> Wigfall in a stirring speech. He said that he would be more
> than man if he did not, and less than man if he could not, feel

deeply and solemnly the changes that had taken place, and the absence of the familiar faces of his former companions in arms. It was not to be considered when or where soldiers die; but how they die. Better a thousand times fill the grave of a brave man than be the slaves of insolent knaves and unprincipled tyrants.

The Senator reminded his old command that the roads were drying up; that a few days would bring the familiar sound of the battle, the roaring of artillery and the rattling of the rifles. There was more bloody work to be done, and they were to prepare for the fray.

Senator Wigfall also took occasion to dispose of the tiresome though oft-repeated story, "rich man's war, poor man's fight." The final reverse to our arms, he said, should it ever come, must certainly fall upon the poor man, the man in moderate circumstances, leaving him no chance to escape. He would inevitably be crushed, whilst the man of wealth and talents and the distinguished officer would buy or demand protection in any part of the world. There would be no refuge for the poor man. The vengeance of the enemy would be poured upon his head and those of his posterity unless he carved out his liberties with his sword and bayonet.

At the conclusion of Senator Wigfall's speech the following letter was read from General Lee:

"Headquarters Army Northern Virginia, Jan. 21, 1865.—Commanding Officer of Hood's Texas Brigade: Sir—I have received from 'a young lady of Texas' some golden stars which she desires may be presented to the brave men of your brigade. Where all are so meritorious and have done so much for the honor of their State, I know it will be difficult to select the most worthy, but from your intimate knowledge of their deeds and conduct in action, you can with more certainty than any other bestow them in accordance with the wishes of the donor. I therefore commit them to you. They are nine in number and said to be made of gold too precious for common use.

"As a gift of a lady from their State, who has watched with pride their gallantry on every field and offered daily prayers to the throne of the Almighty for their happiness and safety, I feel assured they will be highly appreciated and long preserved. I have the honor to be your obedient servant,

"R. E. LEE, General."

The stars were presented to the following named men: William Durram, Company D, First Texas; James Knight, Company H, First Texas; Corporal James Burke, Company B, Fourth Texas; Sergeant James Patterson, Company D, Fourth Texas; Corporal W. C. May, Company H, Fourth Texas; Sergeant C. Wilborn,

Company F, Fifth Texas; Sergeant J. Hemphill, Company H, Fifth Texas; Private J. D. Staples, Company E, Third Arkansas; Private J. W. Cook, Company H, Third Arkansas.

Modesty denies to the individual the privilege of repeating and boasting of the compliments paid him by distinguished men. The same rule is not applicable to a military command, and Hood's Texas Brigade is glad that it is not. Proud of its achievements, its survivors delight to recall and repeat the praises bestowed on its gallantry, its pluck and its endurance, by the great military leaders and men in high civil position who witnessed its conduct on the field of battle.

In a letter written to Hood's Texas Brigade Association a few years before his death, Judge John H. Reagan said:

"I would rather have been able to say that I had been a worthy member of Hood's Texas Brigade than to have enjoyed all the honors which have been conferred upon me. I doubt if there has ever been a brigade, or other military organization in the history of the world, that equalled it in the heroic valor and self-sacrificing conduct of its members, and in the brilliancy of its services."

The following excerpts from a letter written August 6, 1907, to General W. R. Hamby, of Austin, Texas, by General Stephen D. Lee, are too flattering to be omitted:

"If any brigade in the Union or Confederate army should have its history written describing their skirmishes and battles, Hood's Texas Brigade is the one, and if no survivor of that brigade can do this, some brilliant Texan should take the record as found in the Government publications, read it carefully both sides, Union and Confederate, and then converse with the survivors and write a full and complete history of that immortal brigade.

"There were very many splendid brigades in the army on the Confederate side, and while I would not say that Hood's Brigade surpassed them all, still, if I were to select a brigade to do honor to the average fighting Confederate brigade, I would select this brigade. . . .

"It was my fortune to hear the volleys of Hood's Brigade, one of the first volleys in the war, between Richmond and West Point on the York River, when McClellan tried to turn the flank of Johnson's army by getting in his rear with a corps from the West Point landing. That volley of five thousand or more muskets, answered by five or ten thousand in reply, is still ringing in my ears, and I heard no other volleys to equal it till I heard it again at Second Manassas in front of Longstreet's corps in their magnificent charge on that field. I saw them pierce the Federal line at Gaines' Mill; I saw their magnificent charge at Second Manassas, and I witnessed the glory the brigade won at Sharpsburg. They were under my eyes all the time. I saw them go in on the evening of the 16th; I saw them come out to get their rations when they were relieved; I saw them go in again a little before day, on the 17th. I saw them sweep the enemy from their front; I saw them almost annihilated, and even then, I saw them contribute the greater part to the repulse, first of Hooker's corps, then of Mansfield's corps of the Union Army. I saw them hold off Sumner's corps until reinforcements came. I saw them delivering volley after volley lying on the ground not 150 yards from the muzzle of my guns to the east of the Dunker Church. I saw them rise, and pursue the enemy; I saw them broken, shattered and falling back before overwhelming numbers; the few who were left giving the rebel yell with more spirit than the hurrahs of the Union troops."

At the date of the battle of Gettysburg, Dr. Sam R. Burroughs, now a leading physician and surgeon residing at Buffalo, Texas, was one of the wildest and woolliest of the many "wild and woolly" young fellows in the First Texas. Writing of his observations and experiences during the fighting on July 2, 1863, Dr. Sam says:

"Mrs. Wigfall, you know, gave the First Texas a beautiful Lone Star flag made from her wedding dress. When Saint Andrew's cross was adopted as the battle flag of the Confederacy, the unfolding of State flags in action was prohibited. Nevertheless the First Texas carried along with it the flag given it by Mrs. Wigfall. Its bearer was a young fellow under twenty whose name has escaped my memory, but he never unfolded it in battle after the order mentioned was given, until the battle of Gettysburg.

"There, while the Texas Brigade was forming in line of battle, a Federal battery got its range and began to play upon

Dr. Sam R. Burroughs
Company G, First Texas Regiment

it. One of the round shots fired wounded several men of the First Texas and then, passing on, swept the head off of William Floyd of Company F of the Fourth Texas.

"Just as this occurred I saw the bearer of the Lone Star flag begin to pull off the oilcloth case that protected it. Having completed the task he stuffed the case into his haversack and then commenced unrolling the flag.

"'What are you doing that for?' I asked, 'don't you know it's against orders to show but the one flag, and that our battle flag?'

"'Yes, I know what the orders are as well as anybody,' he replied; 'but orders be d—d in a case like this; I am going to straddle the gun that fired that shot and wave this Lone Star flag over it or die a trying.'

"At that moment Hood came in front of the brigade and a dozen voices shouted: 'Have that fence pulled down, General, and we'll take that infernal battery!'

"Hood ordered a detail to level the fence and in less than ten minutes the battery was captured, and that little daredevil bearer of the Lone Star sat astride of the gun which had fired the shot mentioned, waving his flag and yelling loud enough to be heard above the roar of cannon.

"In another twenty minutes the First Texas was engaged in the fierce, and sometimes hand to hand, struggle that occurred in the Devil's Den. During the progress of the fight there, about a dozen of us forged far to the front and finally secured a commanding position high up on the side of Little Round Top.

"Here we commenced shooting at everything Federal that came into view. It was not a one-sided performance, though, for some of the Federals on the field had as much grit as the Confederates, and while we drove them as long as we moved forward, they came to a halt when we did and began firing at us. But we did not mind them as much as we did the determination and good aim of some far-off Yankee whose location for a long time we could not fix. The gun he used made a report like a small cannon, and the balls from it wounded two or three men.

"Long and close watching revealed the fact that he was concealed in the branches of a tall oak tree, fully half a mile distant, and standing in the open. The puffs of smoke from his rifle appeared to proceed from a limb on the south side of the trunk, and, thinking to put an end to his game, our little squad waited until he fired, and then poured a volley into the south side of the tree-top. The return shot came immediately, and demonstrated plainly that we had done no damage. A second time we took aim and pulled trigger, only to be replied to by another puff of smoke out of the tree-top and the whistle of a bullet dangerously close to our ears. Then an Alabamian, 200 yards or more off to our right, gave us the hint we needed. He called out:

"'Say, Texans, you'ns ar', lettin' that ar plaguey sharpshooter fool yer. He don't stay on the limb whar he shoots from. The moment he pulls trigger he jumps for the body of the tree. Eff yer'll all center on that yer'll shorely git him.'

"And 'shorely git him' we did. One of our boys shoved his hat well above the big rock sheltering his body. The sharpshooter fired at it, and just a second later we sent a volley of bullets into the tree-top, this time, however, aiming so as to scalp the trunk of the tree in which our enemy was lodged, and had the satisfaction of seeing the fellow's body come tumbling to the ground.

"'You got him that time, Johnny,' sang out a Yankee that was nearer by.

"'We shorely did,' answered one of our party. 'We saw him drop, and we heerd 'im strike the ground, damn him.'

"These little amenities exchanged with the enemy, we looked to our rear and saw, far down the hill below us, that our main force was making a change of position that would leave us entirely unsupported and subject to capture. That was the signal to us for an immediate retreat, and I don't mind acknowledging that it was precipitate. It couldn't have been otherwise, for not only was our flight downhill, but it was hastened by the bullets of the enemy. I know that I went with the velocity of a shell just out of the cannon's mouth—so fast, indeed, that I could distinctly hear the thunder of the air as it rushed together behind me to fill the vacuum my body left."

The only Texas commands that served in the Army of

Northern Virginia were the First, Fourth and Fifth Texas regiments, and the only Arkansas command so serving was the Third Arkansas. Isolated as these four organizations were, it was but natural that they should be allowed, in a manner, to "weed their own rows" and keep their own records; arduous as their service was, it was equally natural, perhaps, that while "weeding their own rows" on the firing line in a fashion that won them the respect of both friends and foes, they should fail to keep the official records straight and in place.

That they did so fail, is evident from the statement of the Librarian of Congress that "the known statistics of these regiments are so remarkable, that if missing figures can be obtained they will establish a record equalled by few, if any, organizations in the Civil War, or indeed, in modern warfare." It is a rule to judge of the achievements of a military command by its losses in action, as officially stated. Unfortunately, Hood's Texas Brigade was too busy during the war inflicting losses upon the enemy, burying its own dead and caring for its own wounded, to have leisure for insisting that official statements of its losses should not only be made, but also carefully preserved. As a result, such reports of the losses of the brigade as were made were either not forwarded to the Confederate War Department, or, in the upheaval of Confederate war records that followed the retreat of General Lee from Petersburg, were lost, misplaced or destroyed. The same is true with respect to a great many of the official reports of the regimental commanders in the brigade.

General W. R. Hamby, the president of the Association of the Survivors of Hood's Texas Brigade, has given the question of the losses of that command a painstaking and careful study; and although unable to apportion it among the regiments, estimates its total loss, up to and including the battle of Chickamauga, as 598 killed and 3734 wounded, or in the aggregate, 4332. The muster rolls of the three Texas regiments are not on file among the Records of the Rebellion at Washington, and as the number enlisted in each is not to be obtained from official records, it is impossible to determine accurately what proportion of the aggregate loss of a brigade of which the Eighteenth Georgia, Hampton's Legion and the Third Arkansas were parts—the first, until after the battle of Sharpsburg; the second, until January, 1864; the third, from December, 1862, until Appomattox—should be credited to them.

In a pamphlet published by General Jerome B. Robertson shortly after the close of the war, appears a list of names of killed and wounded of the First, Fourth and Fifth Texas at different battles; but, while this list is doubtless accurate as far as it goes, it does not go far enough—no attempt being made to give the losses in those regiments in 1864 and 1865, and the losses of some of the regiments in battles of previous years not being given at all; therefore, it is not published.

BIOGRAPHY

CAPTAIN FRANK B. CHILTON, President of Hood's Texas Brigade Monument Committee, was born in Perry County, Ala., in 1845, and at the age of five came with his parents to Harris County, Texas. Among the first to enlist in Company H, of the Fourth Texas infantry, Hood's Texas Brigade, he participated in all the battles fought by his command until September, 1862, when, on account of his youth, he was peremptorily discharged by the Confederate Secretary of War. Returning to Texas he immediately enlisted in Company B of Baylor's regiment, Majors' Brigade, Green's Division of Cavalry. In 1864 he was elected to a lieutenantcy in his company. After the Louisiana campaign of that year, in which he was disabled from active service by wounds, he was made Commandant of the Post and Provost Marshal of Navasota, Texas. Later, his disability continuing, he was promoted to a captaincy, and assigned to the Reserve Corps, under command of General J. B. Robertson.

Since the restoration of peace between the States, Captain Chilton has been prominent in both the business and politics of the State, and has held several important positions of trust. To him, more than to any other one man, should be accorded credit for suggesting and making possible the erection of a monument to the dead of Hood's Texas Brigade. His efforts have been crowned with success, and the monument will be un-

CAPTAIN FRANK BOWDEN CHILTON
Company H, Fourth Texas Regiment

HOOD'S TEXAS BRIGADE 293

veiled at Austin on May 7, 1910, the forty-eighth anniversary of the battle of Eltham's Landing.

GENERAL WILLIAM R. HAMBY, President of "Hood's Texas Brigade Association" and Treasurer of "Hood's Texas Brigade Monument Committee," resides at Austin, Texas, and holds a prominent place in the financial world. Born in Tennessee, he came to Texas with his widowed mother, in early youth. Among the first to enlist in Company B of the Fourth Texas Infantry, Hood's Texas Brigade, he participated in every battle in which that regiment was engaged until November, 1862, when, on account of disabilities caused by wounds received at Second Manassas and Sharpsburg, he was discharged, being at that date only seventeen years old.

Having returned to Texas in March, 1863, "Bill Hamby," as he was known to his comrades, under orders from General Adam R. Johnson, commanding the Second Brigade of Morgan's cavalry and then in Texas on recruiting service, set out for Kentucky at the head of ten other young men, and after frequent skirmishes with the enemy en route, arrived there and was attached to Helm's Scouts, of the Tenth Kentucky Cavalry, made a first lieutenant and assigned to scout duty at brigade headquarters. In a subsequent reorganization, the latter part of the war, his company became Company H' of the Thirteenth Kentucky Cavalry. He was wounded and captured in July, 1863, and after being exchanged, returned to active duty and was in command of his company—its captain, Neill Helm, having been killed—when paroled April 26, 1865.

After the war closed he was a student, during 1866 and 1867, at Cumberland University, Lebanon, Tenn. After leaving the university he remained in Tennessee until 1882, being, while there, lawyer, journalist, and somewhat in politics, and during the administration of Governor James D. Porter, serving as Adjutant-General of the State, and while so serving, originating and carrying to successful issue the first competitive military drill held in the South after the close of the war between the States. It was as Adjutant-General of Tennessee that he captured the title of general.

Since his return to Texas in 1882, General Hamby has

been a member of the Texas legislature and filled other offices of honor and trust. As a legislator he was the author and secured the passage of the first law of the State in aid of the Confederate Home, established at Austin by the John B. Hood Camp of United Confederate Veterans. To him is due a large share of the credit for building the monument to the dead of Hood's Texas Brigade, that is to be unveiled at Austin, in the Capitol grounds, on May 7, 1910, the anniversary of the battle of Eltham's Landing, the first battle of that brigade, and which it fought unaided by any other command.

CAPTAIN W. T. HILL, one of the members of Hood's Texas Brigade Monument Committee, residing near Maynard, Texas, was born near Selma, Ala., August 16, 1837, and in early youth came with his parents to Walker County, Texas. He graduated from Austin College, at Huntsville, Texas, in the class of 1858, and entered service in the Confederate army as first lieutenant of Company D in the Fifth Texas Regiment of Hood's Texas Brigade, and when his captain, R. M. Powell, became a field officer of the regiment, he, Hill, became the captain of the company.

At the surrender of Lee's army at Appomattox, and indeed, for some time prior to that event, Captain Hill was, as senior captain, present for duty, in command of the Fifth Texas. He was seriously wounded both at Gettysburg and the Wilderness, and was recommended to the War Department at Richmond for promotion to the rank and command of colonel.

Captain Hill was not a "headquarters" officer, but was always at his post and with his company, whether at rest or in action. He was one of those devoted leaders, the typical soldiers of the South, who trod steadily the rough path of duty, from the beginning to the end. Of him, a member of the Fifth Texas once said: "When on duty, whether in camp, on the march, or in battle, Captain Hill was a pretty strict disciplinarian; when off duty, he held every one of his men to be as good as himself, but not a bit better; and none of them was better or braver, for no matter what danger threatened, Hill never flinched from it."

But Captain Hill was not simply physically brave—he was morally brave enough to be an humble follower of the lowly

GEORGE W. LITTLEFIELD
Eighth Texas Cavalry or "Terry Rangers"

Nazarene, Jesus, and to exert his influence in every way possible to make the men of his company Christians. That his religion was not a pretense is evident from the fact that he has been ever since the war, and is now, active in church and Sunday-school work. While as a soldier in the field of war he struck hard for the Southland in which he was born, as a soldier of the Cross he is faithful and untiring.

As a member of the Monument Committee, Captain Hill has been a zealous worker, and has secured many subscriptions. He has also taken great interest in the preparation of the history of the Texas Brigade, and has made valuable contributions to it.

MAJOR GEORGE W. LITTLEFIELD, one of the members of "Hood's Texas Brigade Monument Committee," was born in Panola County, Miss., and came with his parents to Gonzales County, Texas, in 1850. He received his education in the country school, and in July, 1861, enlisted as a private in the Eighth Texas Cavalry, better known as the "Terry Rangers." He was promoted to the rank of second lieutenant in January, 1862, and on May 1st following became a first lieutenant. On May 19, 1862, he was elected captain of his company. On the 26th of December, 1863, he received a wound from a bursting shell and fell to the ground. While lying there unable to rise, and while the battle still raged, General Thomas Harrison, commanding the brigade in which the Rangers served, rode up and looking down at him, said: "Littlefield, I promote you to the rank of major, for gallantry on the field."

But although Major Littlefield returned to his command in the following July, he was too seriously disabled by his wound to do service, and in November, 1864, he resigned his commission and returned to his home in Gonzales County, Texas. Here, although compelled to use crutches until 1867, he engaged in farming. In 1871 he entered the cattle business, and is, to-day, probably the owner of more cattle than any man in the State of Texas. He resides at Austin, Texas, and is prominent in financial circles. He has aided greatly in securing funds for the building of the monument to the dead of Hood's Texas Brigade, and is himself a generous contributor to the undertaking.

ROLL OF OFFICERS AND MEN BELONGING TO HOOD'S TEXAS BRIGADE, WHO SURRENDERED AT APPOMATTOX COURT HOUSE, APRIL 9, 1865.

FIRST TEXAS

F. S. Bass, Colonel commanding regiment; Jno. H. Leete, Adjutant; G. A. Merritt, Assistant Surgeon; D. K. Rice, Captain Co. C; Wm. A. Bedell, Captain Co. L; Jno. N. Wilson, Captain Co. K; J. J. Quarles, Captain Co. G; A. W. Buckner, First Lieutenant Co. C; A. A. Aldrich, First Lieutenant Co. I; H. H. Robinson, First Lieutenant Co. A; T. A. Ardrey, First Lieutenant Co. K; D. M. Mollynatt, First Lieutenant Co. G; A. C. Oliver, First Lieutenant Co. D; M. C. Noble, Second Lieutenant Co. F; Wm. M. Berryman, Second Lieutenant Co. I; Sam P. Torbett, Second Lieutenant Co. H; W. A. Forte, Hospital Steward.

Company A.

2d Sergt., A. Alford; Private, G. Mathews.

Company C.

4th Sergt., J. N. Freeman; Privates, O. G. Armstrong, J. W. Armstrong, H. F. M. Freeman, J. P. Neil.

Company D.

2d Sergt., D. F. Storey; 3d Sergt., E. C. Powell; 1st Corp., J. T. Dixon; Privates, A. J. Adams, W. L. Durham, G. F. Moss, E. W. Oliver, J. W. Smith, S. L. Davenport, P. H. Glaze, W. O. Moore, F. T. Oliver, J. L. Allen.

Company E.

4th Sergt., W. H. Coleman; Privates, J. A. Clarke, S. F. Perry, G. F. Heard, F. M. Mays, R. G. Sands, T. H. Langley, J. T. Longino, J. W. Trowbridge, S. T. Watson.

Company F.

Privates, J. M. Snowden, A. S. Crarey.

Company G.

1st Sergt., G. W. Chambers; 2d Sergt., W. P. Bowen; 4th Sergt., J. Parker; 1st Corp., J. R. Keeling; Privates, L. A. Adams, J. W. Davis, F.

HOOD'S TEXAS BRIGADE

M. Hopkins, T. F. Muin, E. M. Mathews, J. Lewellen, T. G. Seay, W. B. Henry, J. A. Knox, Jas. Ward, S. F. Black, D. B. Chambers, H. Darnell, G. W. Kennedy, J. W. Mathews, B. Y. Milan, J. M. Petty, W. J. Watts, W. B. Kimbrough, M. A. Knox, R. F. Wren, A. P. Cooke.

Company H.

1st Sergt., H. G. Hickman; 4th Sergt., Geo. Hollinsworth; 5th Sergt., C. C. Baker; 1st Corp., J. E. Evans; 2d. Corp., W. H. Moore; Privates, P. A. Blanton, T. R. Edwards, N. Hollinsworth, J. A. Knight, J. M. Herrington, J. Laflin, J. P. Surratt, Jas. Bolton, A. J. Fry, J. Honessburger, Joe A. Knight, T. B. Davidson, L. G. McKinsie, A. N. Fennell.

Company I.

2d Sergt., R. F. Emmons; 5th Sergt., D. B. Bush; Commissary Sergt., A. Aldrich; 1st Corp., J. M. Drawhorn; Privates, J. Harris, F. M. Morris, T. W. H. McCall, D. M. McLean, Chas. Scully.

Company K.

2d Sergt., O. T. Hanks; 3d Sergt., H. S. Bennett; 3d Corp., J. Brandon; 4th Corp., W. F. Brooks; Privates, O. T. Hail, A. J. Preselle, H. C. Powell, A. J. Wilson, B. D. Dunham, W. H. Watson, Joe O. Brown, S. N. Peterson, J. O. Noble, Geo. W. Menefree.

Company L.

3d Sergt., J. C. Pratt; 4th Sergt., W. A. Shelton; Privates, Samuel Clarke, J. Dillon, M. Garrity, John McCarty, R. R. Stoddard, W. B. Von Hutton, M. L. Wagner, R. A. Curtis, L. F. Delardenier, T. L. McCarty, G. A. Merke, H. Soultze, A. W. Wood, Wm. Hoskins, Jas Welch.

Company M.

1st Sergt., T. W. Peary; 2d Sergt., W. A. Roach, 3d Sergt., F. M. Slater; 4th Sergt., G. B. Lundy; 5th Sergt., D. H. Hamilton; Drummer, S. S. Watson; Privates, B. J. Caps, W. F. Eufinger, S. Stubblefield, W. T. White, S. Demirry, T. E. Hathorn, W. Tullous, J. A. White, Jo Wilson.

FOURTH TEXAS

C. M. Winkler, Lieutenant-Colonel, commanding regiment; W. H. Martin, Major; J. C. Jones, Surgeon; J. T. McLaurin, Captain Co. B; R. H. Frank, Captain Co. D; J. T. Hunter, Captain Co. H; E. T. Kindred, Captain Co. F; Haywood Branan, First Lieutenant Co. F; N. J. Mills, First Lieutenant Co. I; J. B. Boyd, First Lieutenant Co. C; J. S. Spivey, First Lieutenant Co. H; J. J. Atkinson, First Lieutenant Co. G; Wm. F. Ford, Second Lieutenant Co. B; G. E. Lynon, First Lieutenant Co. A; J. W.

HOOD'S TEXAS BRIGADE

Duran, Second Lieutenant Co. I; Robert H. Leonard, Hospital Steward; J. R. P. Jett, T. D. Herst, J. H. Collins, D. H. Foster, D. J. Goode, Chas. Warner, P. R. Stamps and Frank Veal, Musicians.

Company A.

2d Sergt., P. H. Walker; 3d Sergt., W. D. Mooney; 4th Sergt., P. J. Deel; Privates, T. W. Fletcher, J. H. Gunn, J. S. Jones, W. H. Pittman, P. Thompson, J. M. Fields, W. A. Hall, A. J. Martin, T. S. Simmons, W. B. Walker.

Company B.

5th Sergt., W. J. Flanniken; 1st Corp., J. E. Jones; 2d Corp., W. J. Tannehill; 4th Corp., A. R. Masterson; Privates, L. B. Cox, A. A. Durfee, N. W. Mayfield, A. R. Rice, J. K. P. Dunson, J. B. Henderson, A. T. Luckett, S. P. Teague, D. A. Todd.

Company C.

2d Sergt., J. M. Adams; Privates, W. Geary, B. F. Merriman, S. W. Montgomery, W. Hearne.

Company D.

1st Sergt., Jas. Patterson; 2d Sergt., A. E. Wilson; 3d Sergt., R. A. Burges; 4th Sergt., S. A. Jones; 5th Sergt., Z. J. Harmon; 1st Corp., J. M. White; Privates, W. H. Burges, A. A. Dimmitt, J. B. Gregory, G. W. Little, F. C. White, J. S. Daniel, W. Dunn, J. F. Holmes, John Rodgers, B. Schmidt, G. A. Hodges.

Company E.

1st Sergt., P. M. Ripley; 2d Sergt., W. W. Dunklin; 1st Corp., E. C. Sharp; Privates, S. J. Billingsley, W. E. Duncan, W. M. King, F. C. Mullins, Jas. Robertson, H. B. Rogers, R. W. Umberson, G. N. Chenault, Samuel Fossett, W. H. Burton, W. A. Pamplin, N. N. Ripley, G. M. Taylor, P. D. Williams.

Company F.

1st Sergt., J. D. Murray; Privates, C. A. McAlister, H. G. Abbott, S. H. Hardoin, Jas. Alford, W. H. Dunn, L. T. Pogue.

Company G.

1st Sergt., L. H. Barry; 2d Sergt., W. M. Baines; 3d Sergt., W. A. Stacey; 5th Sergt., W. J. Grissett; 3d Corp., J. F. Martin; 4th Corp., B. F. Kelley; Privates, Jas. Aiken, D. R. Blackshear, E. C. Davis, C. G. Mooring, S. A. Midkiff, H. F. Plaster, G. S. Qualls, H. E. Shafer, T. G. Wallingford, J. J. Blackshear, J. J. Cooke, G. W. Jones, W. A. Martin, J. T. Muse, J. M. Pinckney, J. S. Reynolds, A. J. Stewart, H. F. Williams.

HOOD'S TEXAS BRIGADE

Company H.

4th Sergt., W. T. C. May; 1st Corp., R. H. Stewart; 4th Corp., J. H. Hall; Privates, T. C. Dillard, R. M. May, Thos. A. Wynne, H. Keiser, A. J. McCowan, W. A. Watson.

Company I.

4th Sergt., R. G. Halloway; Privates, W. B. Allen, J. W. Crabtree, H. L. Harrison, J. W. Holderman, L. W. Rice, W. W. Templeton, M. Barry, A. M. Crossland, J. J. Harrison, J. H. Orendorff, J. R. Shaw, J. H. Treadwell, J. C. Welch.

Company K.

1st Sergt., J. H. Kimbrough; 3d Sergt., M. H. Hodge; 5th Sergt., T. C. Banks; Privates, Jos. Baker, J. M. Campbell, M. Chapman, J. F. Ellege, L. J. Guthrie, J. J. Pickering, A. Boles, L. D. Champion, W. T. Brown, J. F. Gibbons, H. A. Larroo, J. Rice.

FIFTH TEXAS.

Colonel, R. M. Powell; Surgeon, John J. Roberts; Adjutant, Wm. P. McGowen; Ensign, Wm. H. Clark; Sergeant-Major, John M. Smither; Ordnance Sergeant, A. T. Cross; Hospital Steward, W. H. Chadwick.

Company A.

2d Sergt., Chas. F. Settle; 3d Sergt., Joseph H. Shepherd; Privates, Lewis Coleman, George W. Douglas, James Downey, Wm. A. George, John T. Hurtt, James E. Landes, James Stanger.

Company B.

1st Lieut., Ben Baker; Musician, Albert H. Carter; Privates, Emmil Besch, W. H. Carlton, David M. Curry, Wesley Cherry, Thos. T. DeGraffenried, John W. Johnson, Joseph C. Kindred, J. S. Obenshain.

Company C.

Captain, J. E. Anderson; 2d. Sergt., John A. Green; Privates, J. P. Copeland, H. T. Driscoll, E. W. James, T. R. Pistole, J. E. Swindler, P. H. West, H. P. Traweek.

Company D.

Captain, Wm. T. Hill; 1st Sergt., Jno. C. Hill; 2d Corp., Richard Hardy; Privates, Thos. J. Birdwell, Bernard Carrington, Joel Minshew, Martin L. Gilbert, Anthony F. Golding, Abner M. Hinson, Thos. J. Lewis, Robert Staunton, Wm. A. Traylor, Alfred W. Underwood, Wm. P. Wilson, Wm. P. Powell, M. D.

HOOD'S TEXAS BRIGADE

Company E.

2nd Lieut., Bowling Eldridge; 3rd Sergt., Wm. C. LeGrand; 4th Sergt., Sidney V. Patrick; 5th Sergt., George B. Williams; Musician, James Hardeman; Musician, John F. Fields; Privates, M. A. J. Evans, Rufus K. Felder, W. H. Gray, Wm. H. Innes, Wm. R. Lott, Wm. H. McAlister, David O. Patrick, Simon B. Smith, Frank M. Smith, Joseph W. Wallace.

Company F.

Captain, Watson S. Williams; 1st Sergt., Henry V. Angell; 2d Sergt., Cadmus Wilborn; Privates, Basil C. Brashear, Julius Beckman, Saml. E. Perley, Joseph C. Ross, John V. Sloan, Henry C. Shea, Ransom Swiney, Thomas W. Taylor, Frank G. Whittington.

Company G.

1st Lieut., Edward Williams; 1st Sergt., Lucilius W. Caldwell; 3rd Sergt., Wm. W. Smith; 4th Sergt., James Pool; 3d Corporal, James P. Smith; Privates, Geo. A. Bernard, Wm. T. Dyer, Hugh C. Jackson, Elias B. McAninch, Danl. McDonald, David H. Mayes, Wm. A. Nabours, Constantine P. Nance, John B. Small, Andrew J. Tomlinson.

Company H.

2nd Lieut., D. W. McDonell; 1st Sergt., Jacob Hemphill; 2nd Sergt., G. M. Sims; 3d Sergt., Wm. Grayless; 4th Sergt., S. W. Small; Musician, Wm. Cooper; Privates, A. D. Brinkley, A. H. Butler, James Curry, J. A. Chesser, Willis B. Darby, Milton P. Foster, P. K. Goree, Thos. S. Haynie, George H. Johnson, Thompson Kelly, Harvey Rose, J. Shields, J. A. Shaw, James M. Small, S. E. Walters, Robt. T. Wilson, John Reader, Wm. Woods.

Company I.

Captain, Ben I. Franklin; 1st Lieut., Dimas R. Ponce; 1st Sergt., George W. Clampitt; 2d Sergt., Wm. O. Morgan; 3d Sergt., Saml. D. Williams; 4th Sergt., John S. Hafner; Privates, Ben J. Baldwin, Fritz Bettis, Willis G. Blue, James R. Clutt, D. H. Carter, J. W. Deane, James A. Eatman, B. S. Fitzgerald, Robert Fleming, Curran Holmes, A. W. Holt, John D. Howle, Jonathan A. Love, Wm. R. McRee.

Company K.

2d Lieut., J. M. Alexander; 1st Sergt., T. F. Meece; 4th Sergt., A. B. Green; 4th Corp., J. F. Ford; Musician, J. W. Smith; Musician, W. S. Sandall; Privates, R. A. Ashley, J. M. Bowen, J. D. Galvert, A. W. Dunn, A. J. Fairchilds, W. G. Hendly, Henry C. Hirams, Mark A. Hubert, E. Kirkland, W. M. McDonald, B. F. Meekins, D. A. Rowe, U. P. Stephenson, S. D. Waldrop, W. B. Young.

HOOD'S TEXAS BRIGADE

Company D.

Privates, M. A. Lampkin, J. W. Ewing.

Company C.

Private, J. T. Allison.

THIRD ARKANSAS.

Robert S. Taylor, Lieutenant-Colonel, commanding regiment; J. R. Brown, Surgeon; H. T. Kleinschmidt, Assistant Surgeon; G. E. Butler, Chaplain; Josh. Hightower, Captain Co. C; A. C. Jones, Captain Co. G; Frank Thach, Captain Co. H; J. W. Norris, Captain Co. K; Wm. H. Harrison, Captain Co. E; T. A. Anderson, Captain Co. F; J. D. Pickens, First Lieutenant Co. E; R. M. Stribling, First Lieutenant Co. F; J. I. Miles, Second Lieutenant Co. H; Thomas P. Brewen, Second Lieutenant Co. K; J. L. Meel, Second Lieutenant Co. G.

Company A.

2d Sergt., H. A. Ralph; Privates, J. C. Bull, J. D. Geddie, W. C. Hannan, Jas. Day, W. E. Gregory, H. N. Morris, W. A. Moore, J. S. Banks, S. S. Johnson, J. A. Kelly, G. W. Smith, Wash Parks, C. A. Harrold, J. D. Kelley, G. Y. Mock, S. F. Stevens, G. L. Wright.

Company B.

1st Sergt., R. E. McMurray; 5th Sergt., H. B. Lindsey; Privates, J. P. Hughes, Jas. Reid, N. J. Fuller, J. F. Ketchins, S. D. Cobb, Dan'l. Senn.

Company C.

1st Sergt., W. E. Conley; 1st Corp., Chas. W. Jeter; Privates, Robert S. Rust, B. F. Glossup, Jas. T. Burden, Jas. B. Robertson, Jno. A. Ferguson, W. L. Law, S. P. Otts, W. T. Tuggle, T. J. Wilson.

Company D.

1st Sergt., J. A. Harrell; Privates, W. T. Anderson, J. H. Tyner, T. T. Crow, J. H. White, J. S. Bush.

Company E.

1st Sergt., J. S. Grooms; 3d Sergt., Jesse W. Hill; 4th Sergt., J. V. King; 5th Sergt., W. H. Dumas; 4th Corp., L. C. Duke; Privates, J. W. Hill, W. V. Jester, H. F. King, Jno. N. McIlvine, Jno. D. Staples, O. W. Jester, J. R. Jester, Jones Amason, P. H. Reynolds, B. F. Stevens, K. Smith.

HOOD'S TEXAS BRIGADE

Company F.

1st Sergt., W. S. Adair; 2d Sergt., Austin Phelps; Privates, C. R. Buster, T. J. White, S. H. Emmerson, A. J. Grigsby, Wm. Stanley.

Company G.

4th Sergt., L. C. Warwick; 5th Sergt., H. A. Massey; Corp., J. B. Wilson; Privates, W. J. Alderson, J. F. Brooks, M. L. Crumpler, H. J. P. Ferguson, Hill Jones, J. F. Lauderdale, J. A. Moore, E. M. Mitchell, P. A. Beeman, Frank Courtney, A. P. Cummings, G. W. Fuller, W. J. Keeling, D. H. Lewis, R. M. McDowell, V. Q. Warwick.

Company H.

4th Sergt., T. W. Hagood; Privates, Joe. May, J. W. Cook, G. B. McDonald, Jeff Thornsbury.

Company I.

1st Sergt., J. S. Williams; 3d Sergt., W. G. Lockhart; 3d Corp., B. B. Newbern; Privates, Moses Garner, W. H. G. Morgan, E. D. Goza, Robert Ratteree, John C. Jones, J. W. Rhodes, J. M. Robertson, J. S. Shirley, W. T. Brewer.

Company K.

1st Sergt., H. C. Denson; 2d Sergt., J. L. F. Hill; 3d Sergt., M. L. McCurdie; Privates, A. P. Bennett, W. D. Everett, Thomas Morris, D. T. White, J. C. Gilliam, J. H. Fountain, J. C. Phillips, J. H. Campbell, J. H. Goldsby, R. P. Noble, J. H. Albrecht, A. W. Holcomb, Geo. Jackson, R. M. Roberts; Musicians, E. L. Bigham, R. J. Baily, R. J. Lowry, J. D. Randle, G. A. Bailey, J. B. Jackson, G. F. Melton, F. M. Ward, B. F. Ward; Hospital Steward, H. C. White.

MUSTER ROLLS OF FIRST TEXAS

COMPANY A

Harvey H. Black, captain; promoted to lieutenant-colonel of the regiment and killed at Eltham's Landing
Geo. T. Todd, elected captain on reorganization, May, 1862, still living
Wes. Laney, first lieutenant. Became captain January, 1864
Harry H. Robinson, second lieutenant
John H. Leete, V. S.

Jas. Henderson, lieutenant and adjutant of the regiment
Dr. Ewing, surgeon of the regiment
Allen, "Bent"
Allen, J. L.
Alford, Julius C.
Alford, Will; killed in battle
Armstrong, George
Attee, John; killed at Eltham's Landing
Baker, Green

HOOD'S TEXAS BRIGADE

Barron, Charles
Blalock, J.
Blackburn, Frank; killed in battle
Brookshire, Tom; killed in battle
Bird, John; killed in battle
Bebo, C.; killed in battle
Brewer, T. E. (Dick)
Browning, Henry
Bronaugh, David
Chase, R.
Crawford, J. C. (Ball); killed at Gaines' Farm
Carlton, Prof.
Campbell, " Gulie "; killed in battle
Derrick, E. P.; killed at Gettysburg
Derrick, John; killed at Gettysburg
Daugherty, Hugh; killed at Gettysburg
Dudgrove, H.
Durrum, Will
Epperson, H. J.; captured and died in Virginia
Edison, John
Elliott, Bill; killed in battle
Edwards, James; killed in battle
Frazier, O. C.
Gaines, John
Gray, John
Goforth, John
Graham, Chas, J.
Hensey, Hugh
Heisinant, Henry; killed in battle
Heisinant, Boynton
Hawkins, J. Cal.
Higgins, Pat; killed
Hill, J. C.; killed at Sharpsburg
Hudson, Geo. W.

Jacoby, M.; lost leg at Gaines' Farm
Jones, C. D.; killed at Sharpsburg
Jones, Tom; killed at Sharpsburg
Joiner, James; killed at Sharpsburg
Kinty, Joe; killed in battle
Kennedy, John H.
Lane, Ben
Lindsay, Joshua; jaw broken at Chickamauga
McDougald, Will; killed at Gettysburg
Malone, Jas.
McLendon, W.; killed in battle
McMahon, Tom; killed in battle
Mathis, George
Murphy, P.; killed in battle
Postlethwaite, Chas.
Rogers, George; killed in battle
Rogers, Walter
Sikes, B.; killed in battle
Sitzer, M.; killed in battle
Slaughter, H.; killed in battle
Slaughter, ——
Shropshire, ——
Story, Frank
Tawlock, F.; killed in battle
Thompson, G.; killed in battle
Todd, Louis B.
Veal, John
Whitaker, Willis; lost arm
Wimberly, John; killed on Potomac in 1861
Wimberly, W. L.; discharged
Wright, S.
Wright, J. C.
Williams, Chas.; killed in battle
Walton, Doug.

COMPANY B

Anderson, M. B.; wounded, discharged
Banfield, G. W.; wounded, discharged
Bass, Richard
Bass, Robert
Balling, Booker; wounded, discharged
Bradford, Champ.; lieutenant
Bradford, James; discharged

Burns, Larry; discharged
Butler, John
Butler, Chas. W.; killed at Gettysburg
Barter, Fred
Burke, Thos.
Canterberry, Jordan; wounded and transferred
Carr, Frank

Choate, Rufus; killed at Chickamauga
Cox, W. H.; discharged
Collins, Frank; wounded and discharged
De Walt, K. B. Lieut.; resigned
Derrick, George; died at Manassas
Derrick, John
Donnelly, Pat; killed at Chickamauga
Dortch, Joseph; killed at Malvern Hill
Dunnam, Sid; joined Trans-Mississippi army and killed at Mansfield
Dunnam, C. R.; paroled
Dunnam, M. A.; wounded at Manassas
Ellis, Richard; killed at Chickamauga
Evans, James; transferred to Va. regiment, killed
Fontain, H. B.; joined the Trans-Mississippi army and made captain of artillery
Garner, James; killed at Gettysburg
Garner, Wm.; wounded at Malvern Hill, discharged
Gibson, Wm.
Ham, George; killed at Gettysburg
Harding, R. J., Lieut., Capt., and Lieut.-Col.; wounded at Gettysburg and Cold Harbor
Ike, Indian
Johnson, George H.; wounded at Sharpsburg and captured at Chickamauga
Jones, Enoch
Kirksey, Newton; wounded
Kendrich, John
Kennady, Jefferson
Lewis, Green; wounded, discharged
Lowe, Henry B.; Lieut.
Lowe, Daniel; wounded at Gettysburg, discharged
McClannahan, James; killed at Malvern Hill
McDonald, Wm.
McGee, S. H.; wounded at Sharpsburg, discharged
McNally, Jno.; killed at Malvern Hill
McNulty, Henry
Meece, Calvin; transferred to Company K, 5th Texas Regiment
Meekins, P. P.
Meekins, Roderick; killed at Gettysburg
Morris, Benjamin; transferred to artillery
Moore, D. D., Capt.; resigned
Nettles, Thos.; wounded at Yorktown, discharged
O'Gorman, John
Probert, John; killed at Gaines' Mill
Quigley, John
Sandel, Wilborn
Sanderson, Adolph; killed at Chickamauga
Scott, Thomas
Scott, Wm.
Shotwell, John I., Lieut., Capt., killed by bushwhackers, N. C., while a prisoner
Shotwell, T. B.
Shotwell, Wm.
Stevens, James P.; killed at Chickamauga
Smith, U. P.; joined Trans-Mississippi army
Trinkman, A.; engineer corps
Victory, Jack; killed at Gettysburg
Walker, William, Lieut.; killed at Cold Harbor
Westbrook, Nathaniel; killed at Cold Harbor
Ward, Sam. V.; discharged
William, Zack; killed at Gaines' Mill
Woodward, Sam J.; wounded at Wilderness, discharged.
Woodward, Mc.
West, Dr. Jacob
Zeluff, ——
Carraway, L. W.
Love, Robt.; wounded at Malvern Hill, discharged

HOOD'S TEXAS BRIGADE

Walker, George; killed near Richmond, Va.
Rev. Blackwell Dunnam
Sy Hines; transferred to Engineers Corps
——, Bean; transferred to Engineers Corps
Every member of Company B believed dead except P. P. Meekins and R. J. Harding, and probably M. B. Anderson

COMPANY D

Clopton, A. G., Capt.
Hewitt, W. M.; 1st Lieut.
Henderson, W. W., 2d Lieut.
Curtright, C. R., 3d Lieut.
Shropshire, W., Orderly Sergeant; wounded at Sharpsburg, dead.
Morris, Simon, 2d Sergeant; killed at Gettysburg, Pa.
Shaw, Jno., 3d Sergt.; discharged for disability, 1861.
Thomas, Jack, 1st Corp.; mortally wounded at Chicamauga
McDowell, J. H., 2d Corp.; wounded at West Point
Blalock, Rube, 3d Corp.; died of bayonet wound at Spottsylvania
Henderson, J. B., 4th Corp.

PRIVATES

Allen, D.
Adams, T. J.
Adams, A. J.
Bean, Andy
Blackwell, Jas.; one of Hood's trusted scouts
Bryan, Thos.
Bryan, Felix; retired for wound in '63
Bartlett, Dan; lost arm at Sharpsburg
Barker, Dug.
Barnard, Joe; discharged
Brown, Ed.; killed at Sharpsburg
Cook, J. P.; wounded at Chickamauga
Colly, Albert
Colly, Wm.
Connally, Scott
Connally, Raddy; killed at Sharpsburg
Covey, Chas.; killed at West Point (or Eltham's Landing)
Covey, Thos.
Childs, H. C.
Carlow, Jas. A.
Dobbs, Wm.; killed at Gettysburg
Droomgoole, Jack; captured
Dudley, Jas.
Davenport, S. L.
Dennis, Pone; mortally wounded at Gaines' Farm
Dennis, Tom.
Dickson, T. J.; wounded at Sharpsburg
Durrum, Jake; killed at Sharpsburg
Durrum, Wm. L.; wounded at Chickamauga, received gold medal for bravery
Dunklin, Jas.; wounded three times
Dean, Jas.; transferred
Day, Wm.; captured
Easley, Jas. S.; wounded at Chickamauga
Ellington, Wm.
Floyd, Richard
Floyd, R. A. H.; wounded at Gettysburg
Frazier, Ed.
Grogard, Thos.
Griffin, Big.
Glaze, P. H.; wounded at Chickamauga
Glage, J. R.
Graham, Chas.
Gibson, Robt.; killed at Gettysburg
Hewitt, Joe.
Henderson, B. F.
Houston, A. A.
Hines, Ben.
Hartzo, Labe

Hopkins, Columbus; killed at The Wilderness
Hughes, Frank
Hass, Henry; mortally wounded at Gettysburg
Jackson, W. C.; killed at Sharpsburg
Jackson, W. R.; killed at Sharpsburg
Lockett, Wm.
Lindsey, Dave
McCoy, H. C.; wounded at Sharpsburg
Moody, Sam.
Moss, W. O.; mortally wounded at Chickamauga, was given a gold medal for bravery
Moss, G. F.; was transferred from 8th Ga. Regt. to Company D, 1861
Moss, A. M.; was transferred from 8th Ga. Reg. to Company D, 1861
Mathews, Sol.
Mixon, Chap.; killed near Richmond
Moore, Jno.; mortally wounded near Richmond
Murray, W. W.
Milligan, Larkin
McAlpine, Thos.
McAlpine, Jas.; deserted
Miles, J. Foster; killed at Gettysburg
Miles, Aquilla; wounded at Chickamauga
McClellan, Wm.; killed at Gettysburg
Mitchell, Frank
Noward, Jas.; transferred.
Oliver, W. S.; wounded at Gettysburg.
Oliver, A. C.; wounded at White Oak Swamp
Oliver, W. H.; mortally wounded at Chickamauga
Oliver, F. F.; wounded near Richmond
Oliver, Jno. A.
Oliver, H. P.
Oliver, W. A. T.; wounded at Sharpsburg
O'Rear, J. P.; lost leg near Richmond, '64
Powell, E. C.; wounded several times, through the chest at Chickamauga
Porter, J. W.
Perryman, Maje
Pickett, L. L.
Petty, Thos.
Robinson, Wm.
Robinson, Jno. C.; wounded in the mouth at Chickamauga
Reynolds, S. F.
Richardson, A.
Snellgrove, J. P.; wounded at Chickamauga
Simms, Dave; wounded at Gaines' Farm
Story, R. F.; lost portion of his hand at The Wilderness
Smith, Joe; wounded twice
Snow, Geo.
Snow, Wm.; killed at Sharpsburg
Snow, Robt.
Sasser, Wm.
Shaw, Jno.
Smith, J. W.
Sartin, Wm.; killed at Sharpsburg
Slade, Thos.
Trice, Jas.; transferred
Therrell, Abe; killed near Gaines' Mill
Thomas, Jack, Lieut.; when mortally wounded at Chickamauga
Thomas, Lucian; killed at Gettysburg
Taylor, Bill
Wear, Henry; transferred
Williams, W. W.
Wood, Jack; wounded at Sharpsburg
Wise, ——
Wood, Bailey
White, Joe.
Watson, Jno.
Sledge, Nat. M.
Chesser, ——

July, 1861, Capt. Clopton was promoted to Major. The company was commanded by Lieut. Hewitt until the reorganization, 1862. Lieut. C. R. Curtright drilled the company.

HOOD'S TEXAS BRIGADE

COMPANY E

The following members of the "Marshall Guards" were mustered into the Confederate service on June 6th, 1861—the company afterwards becoming Company E, of the First Texas:

F. S. Bass, Captain
E. H. Baxter, 1st Lieut.
A. D. Burns, 2d Lieut.
J. K. Taylor, 3d Lieut.
Adam Hope
J. R. Pogue
J. M. Pears
W. E. Turner
T. P. Ochiltree
J. R. Bullock
C. H. Fields
S. H. Burnham
W. Finney
B. R. Brasil
W. L. Langley
A. B. Peal
J. A. Lindsey
W. H. Coleman
J. H. Coleman
C. H. Morrison
W. T. Clark
W. D. Prescott
J. R. Boone
Henry Stone
M. A. Chivers
J. W. Smith
James W. Pope
Thomas Steele
G. W. Willingham
R. Lloyd
E. A. Earnest
R. S. I. Burns
J. H. Hendrick
W. B. Preston
R. Stephens
J. F. Rudd
S. T. Watson
M. McKinney
T. M. Sloan
W. Campbell
Chas. Woodson
L. N. Levy
R. S. Clark

E. M. Ewing
D. L. Wilson
John Smith
S. A. King
T. H. Langley
R. Childers
Geo. McQueen
G. W. Stauts
W. C. Scott
A. F. Wiggs
Joe Marks
W. P. Rawls
J. M. Taylor
Thomas McKay
Ben. S. Pope
William Boodworth
S. W. Webb
Pratt Hughes
G. A. Peete
J. O. Bradfield
Marcus Gillett
J. A. Clark
J. W. Gillian
James Norwood
G. F. Heard
Howell Austin
John Burke
B. W. Webb
J. W. Webb
R. F. Joyce
S. F. Perry
Clinton Perry
E. O. Perry
H. E. Perry
J. D. Campbell
J. W. Trowbridge
James Spradling
C. H. Ward
T. J. Longino
Riley G. Sands
M. B. Turrentine
W. F. Woodward
James Hayes

HOOD'S TEXAS BRIGADE

Robert Marshall
Lee Trimble
J. C. K. Mullay
J. A. Lawson
David Dunn
Rev'd Collins
Jos. Robertson

R. V. Phillips
W. J. Purnell
J. S. Vandergraff
W. D. Haynes
A. A. Allen
Franklin Mayes
D. M. Walker

COMPANY F

Work, P. A., Capt. and later Lieut.-Col.
Willson, S. A., 1st Lieut. and later Capt.
Landers, Robt., 2d Lieut.
Rock, I. D., 3d Lieut.
Bullock, James
Benedict, ——
Brady, ——
Buvley, ——
Bradshaw, Ben
Barclay, Thomas
Bush, ——; was killed in battle
Bush, Dr.
Blacksher, William
Bostic, ——
Crier, Manuel; killed in battle
Crier, Morris
Crier, William; killed in battle
Chance, Dock
Chance, Zeke
Chance, Dan
Cravey, Jack
Durham, Thomas
Durham, Richard
Dean, ——
Eskridge, Thomas; killed in battle
Evans, James
Engleking, ——; killed in battle
Gilder, U. M.
Goodman, William
Graham, Jack; killed in battle
Grimes, William
Hooker, Robt.
Hooks, Gill
Holloman, Burrell; killed in battle
Harvill, Henry; wounded
Hinds, James; died of wounds
Hinds, James, Jr.

Hamilton, Tillman; killed in battle
Hamilton, Ed.
Holmes, William
Hanks, Amos; wounded in battle
Jones, Henry C.; died of wounds received in battle
Jones, Samuel; wounded in battle
Kindrell, James
Long, Green
Minter, John
May, Dr.
McMellon, Dunkin; killed in battle
McDurmot, Hugh
Moore, Henry
Nicks, W. P.
Noble, Milton, and later Lieut.
Poole, William; wounded in battle
Poole, Josh; wounded in battle
Phillipps, James
Phillips, John
Prewitt, Argalus
Perryman, James
Pate, ——
Rigsby, A. J.; late Captain of Company
Rountree, Andrew
Runnels, Perry; killed in battle
Smith, Milton
Shide, ——; killed in battle
Snowden, Jasper
Smith, Sergt.; killed in battle
Steadman, Bug.
Steadman, Eli; died in army of wound received in battle
Steadman, John
Scott, William; killed in battle
Smith, Zack
Sims, Cubb
Smith, Abe

Snow, Dr.; killed
Sharp, Charley
Tompkins, D. C.
Tompkins, Jasper
Tolbert, Dr.
Travis, John
Van Vleck, Julius; was killed in battle
Welch, Thomas; killed in battle
West, ——; died in army from a wound received in battle
Wiggins, William
Ward, Joseph
Wackter, J. J.
Wammack, Green
West, Isaac
Wooton, Albert; died in army of wound received by accident

COMPANY G

Copied from original muster roll at surrender at Appomattox, by Willis J. Watts of Company G, 1st Texas, April 10, 1865, day after surrender.

Woodward, J. R., Capt.; promoted to Major, died of wound
Jemmison, E. S., 1st Lieut.; promoted to Captain, wounded at Gaines' Mill
Dale, Matt, 2d Lieut.; elected Major, killed at Sharpsburg
Campbell, Ben. A., 3d Lieut.; killed at Gettysburg
Rose, T. J., O. Sergt.; promoted to Lieut., wounded at Sharpsburg
Harris, Matt, 2d Sergt.
Kimbrough, Wm., 3d Sergt.
Holley, J., 4th Sergt.
Box, Lina, 5th Sergt.
Wright, C. F., 1st Corp.; lost arm at Wilderness
Hopper, Wm, 2d Corp.
Montgomery, Mat., 3d Corp.
Cantley, Zeb., 4th Corp.; killed at Sharpsburg

PRIVATES

Aspley, M. J.; killed at Sharpsburg
Allen, Phil T.
Admas, Levi
Barnes, N. R.
Bradley, Hy.; wounded at Chickamauga
Brighman, Wm.; killed at Ft. Harrison
Bowen, Estes
Bowen, Pat., Sergt.
Burgess, J.
Bottoms, Smith; killed at Sharpsburg
Black, Sim; disabled at 2d Manassas
Blackshear, Seb.; disabled at Sharpsburg
Buttler, Richard; killed at Sharpsburg
Butts, Jas.; disabled at Wilderness
Burrough, S. R.
Copeland, J. C.; killed at Wilderness
Cone, Jack; killed at Sharpsburg
Cone, Hy.; disabled at Wilderness
Cook, A. P.
Crombie, Dr. A. C., Assist. Surg.
Croghan, Pat.; deserted
Chambers, D. C.
Chambers, A. J.
Chambers, W. D., O. Sergt.
Colvin, Jim; deserted
Corder, Jim; killed at Wilderness
Downs, G. B.; killed in battle, 1864
Duval, J. D.
Debard, ——
Duval, W. A.; killed at Gettysburg
Darnell H.
Duval, Richard
Derdan, Jim; disabled at Sharpsburg
Davis, J. W.
Dagg, Ed.; killed at Chickamauga
Feles, M. M.; killed at Sharpsburg
Gibson, L. H.
Fondren, Bud.; transferred
Goad, J. O.; lost leg at Farmville, Va., 1865, last fight
Garner, W.
Groomes, Lewis; wounded at Chickamauga

Goodwin, Chas.
Hickey, T. C.
Heperley, J. C.
Hoffman, Hy.; deserted
Hoover, W. P.; killed at Sharpsburg
Hopkins, Frank
Hallum, B. A.; killed at Sharpsburg
Hazellwood, W. T.; killed at Chickamauga
Hambey, Marsh
Henry, W. B.
Holloway, Jim; disabled at Gettysburg
Hicky, W.
Hill, R. C.
Honeycutt, Hy.; disabled at Gettysburg
Jordan, Bruce
Johnson, Jas.
Johnson, John
Knox, M. A.; disabled at Sharpsburg
Knox, Joe
Kenneday, Geo.
Kenneday, Jos.
Keeling, Jno.
Kyle, Geo.; killed at Chickamauga
Lindsy, Jno.
Lewellyn, J. E.
Lewellyn, Alf.
Lottie, N. S.
Lynch, H.; deserted
Leath, Dan.
Mynatte, Park; died of wound at Chickamauga, Ga., was 2d Lieut. of Company
Mynatte, D. M.; elected Lieut.
Mathews, A. M.; disabled at Gaines' Mill
Mathews, J. W.
Mathews, F. M.
McKnight, Robt.; disabled at Gaines' Mill
Mahle, Henry
Main, T. C.; wounded
McKinzie, Robt.; deserted
McKinzie, Tom.
Morris, Chas.
McFarland, C. R.; killed at Sharpsburg
Milan, John; lost leg at Gettysburg
Milan, B. Y.
Morgan, J.
McCannahan, Rube; absent without leave
Morite, J.
Mallard, Mark; deserted
Newson, Elias; disabled at Wilderness
Newson, John
O'Brien, Martin; killed at Eltham's Landing
Owens, H.; deserted
Parker, John
Parker, Ira; died from wound at Chickamauga
Parkes, B. F.
Parkes, Joe
Posey, Ed.; killed at Sharpsburg
Posey, Jack; killed at Sharpsburg
Petty, Robt.
Petty, Jno. N.
Pitts, Jesse
Pugh, J.
Quarles, J. J.; elected captain
Rudd, J. S.
Rockwall, ——; deserted
Reaves, Chas.
Ratcliff, A. T.; wounded at Gettysburg
Read, Jeff.; now dead
Read, N. D.
Rountree, Sam.; killed at Gaines' Mill
Stinson, J. C.; was killed at Gaines Mill
Stinson, Cal.
Spurrier, Nathan
Seay, Tom; living
Sorrell, J. C.; absent without leave
Spring, L.
Scott, J. G.
Stephens, J.
Shamburger, Tom
Stalcup, Jasper; disabled at Wilderness
Scarbrough, Geo.
Scarbrough, M.
Sawyer, B.; deserted

HOOD'S TEXAS BRIGADE

Thompson, A.; disabled at Wilderness
Ward, R. K.
Ward, Jim; disabled at Second Manassas
Watts, F. J.; lost arm at Sharpsburg
Watts, B. F.
Watts, W. J. N.; was wounded five times
Watts, A. J.; wounded three places
at Chickamauga, disabled at Wilderness
Woodhouse, W. D.
Woodhouse, J. T.
Woodhouse, Chas. W.; killed at Gaines' Mill
Wren, W. C.
Wren, Dick
Wren, Richard
Williamson, Jos.

COMPANY H

Captain, A. T. Rainey
Captain, W. H. Gaston
Lieut., Bedford Parks
Lieut., W. R. Miller
Lieut., Jno. Stevenson
Lieut., R. H. Gaston
Lieut., J. L. Spencer
Lieut., R. J. Rhome
Lieut., S. P. Torbett
Lieut., J. T. Smith
A. M. Finnell
J. R. Jones
J. E. Hickman
O. Q. A. Capps
H. G. Hickman
E. G. Eell
W. A. Ford
W. Arnwine
A. A. Anderson
A. A. Adkinson
J. B. Bussey
P. A. Blanton
J. Baldwin
Tom Butler
M. A. Berry
J. Briggs
Jno. Baker
Wm. Barton
A. C. Baxley
C. S. Bolton
W. S. Beard
R. R. Birdwell
Geo. Beauchamp
Tom Brilley
J. R. Beers
C. C. Baker

J. A. Bolton
C. Cecil
J. J. Clarke
J. A. Counts
Geo. Colton
G. W. Culpepper
A. F. Cox
J. R. Crutchfield
I. Cotney
Dock Cantrell
Wm. Derrough
J. M. Doherty
L. L. Evans
J. Evans
Felix Embry
A. F. Erwin
G. R. Edwards
W. Foster
Jno. J. Foster
A. J. Fry
N. H. Freeman
H. B. Fontaine
M. V. Fry
W. H. Gray
B. Goble
G. W. Grisham
J. A. Graham
J. A. Griffis
J. F. Gibson
S. Garrett
J. J. Herrington
J. M. Herrington
J. B. Hanks
J. C. Hollingsworth
G. Hollingsworth
N. Hollingsworth

W. Hollingsworth
J. H. Howell
Alf. Horton
I. Honingsburger
W. N. Haynes
Fred Horton
Jno. Henry
W. Hammer
D. M. Horton
S. S. Hones
D. L. Hill
M. Jacobs
Lee King
Jno. Jones
J. Loftin
G. W. Lumpkin
L. G. McKenzie
James Marshall
W. J. Mansell
W. G. Middleton
J. V. Moon
Fayette Martin
N. A. Mendedhall
Caleb McBryde
J. H. Moore
J. P. Mullinax
J. A. Norris
J. B. Nichols
F. R. Oldham
A. C. Perry
—— Patrick
J. Reid
J. E. Rudd
M. Reynolds
Geo. Small
D. C. Stewart

HOOD'S TEXAS BRIGADE

F. Smith
J. P. Surratt
R. Simpson
S. L. Scott
J. M. Steincipher
Joe. Smith
J. E. Sides
C. Strotherl

W. M. Simpson
Jim Tubbs
J. G. Titten
M. Taylor
A. F. Taylor
J. M. Tillman
Morgan Tillman

W. Williams
J. T. Woodall
W. M. Woodford
A. J. Knight
W. H. Knight
J. A. Knight
Jno. A. Knight

COMPANY K
1st TEXAS

Benton, B. F., Capt.; killed at Gaines' Mill
Price, F. B., 1st Lieut.
Massey, J. C., 2d Lieut.
Bates, B., 3d Lieut.
Ardrey, T. A.
Benton, Jesse
Brown, J. O.
Brandon, John
Bennett, H. C.
Brooks, Wm.
Bryant, Wm.; deserted
Bryant, Sebe
Bullock, Thad W.
Burneman, Sam.; killed at Chattanooga
Brandon, Joe
Buckley, J. M.
Coleman, Mason
Cureton, Wm.; killed
Crownsen, Jesse
Connor, R. T.
Cooper, ——
Chambers, Wm.; killed at Gaines' Mill
Coe, Wm.; killed
Cureton, John
Davis, G. W.; killed at Wilderness
Dunham, B. B.
Davidson, W. R.
Davidson, Tom B.
Day, Steve
Evans, Jim
Evans, ——
Elison, A.
Drawhon, Monroe

Finley, Wm.; killed
Fall, J. C.
Fall, H. V.
Forsythe, Lafayette
Ford, H. H.
Ford, John D.
Gray, Wm.
Gray, ——
Houston, Mal.
Housman, Jim.
Hail, Jesse; killed at Sharpsburg
Hail, Joe J.
Hail, Oscar
Hooper, Sam.
Howard, Wash.; deserted
Haughton, John
Hunt, T. C.
Hanks, O. T.
Harris, Tom.
Haughton, P.
Irvine, Tom.
Jacobs, Matt.
Lanier, Tom.
Lain, Joe; killed at Malvern Hill.
Lanier, Clem.
Miller, Ned; killed
McNally, Pat.; deserted
McLendon, Alf.
Menefee, Geo. W.
Menefee, Tatum
Mason, Lafayette; killed
Massey, J. V.; shot at Suffolk
Murphey, Tom.

Moseley, Henry E.
Mattox, Cicero
Mayo, Lewis; killed at Gaines' Mill
McAlister, ——
Matthews, Sim.
McMahan, Charlie
Norfolk, Jim.
Noble, Ike
Noble, R. T.
Norvell, Tom.
Patton, Henry
Patton, Sam.; killed
Patton, James
Pool, Amos
Peterson, S. M.
Peterson, John
Proceller, A. J.
Price, Elijah
Powell, Henry A.
Pierce, Joe.
Parker, Joe.
Parker, John
Quinn, Wm.; killed
Ridley, Jim.
Ronbro, David
Ruddell, Ike
Sowell, J. J.
Sanders, John
Strother, W. F.; deserted
Stallings, Jas. A.
Sharp, Anderson; deserted
Sharp, Marion; killed at Gettysburg
Sherrod, R.
Thomas, Oscar

HOOD'S TEXAS BRIGADE

Tucker, F. H.
Tucker, R.
Wilson, J. N.
Wilson, A. J.
Wilson, W. J.
Waterhouse, Jim.; killed
Watson, Wm. H.
White, Wm. T.
White, Wm.
Walker, ——
Warford, Sam.
Wade, ——

COMPANY L

COMMISSIONED OFFICERS

Capt., A. C. McKeen; wounded Eltham's Landing
1st Lieut., W. A. Bedell; wounded Sharpsburg and Wilderness
2nd Lieut., J. C. Thompson; killed at Sharpsburg
3rd Lieut., J. M. Baldwin; wounded Second Manassas

NON-COMMISSIONED OFFICERS

1st Sergt., A. W. Smith
2d Sergt., Robt. R. Armstrong; wounded at Chickamauga, killed at Wilderness
3d Sergt., W. F. Richardson
4th Sergt., W. B. Robinson; wounded at Chickamauga
1st Corp., A. P. Forsythe
2d Corp., W. P. Randall; killed at Second Manassas
3d Corp., R. S. Robinson; wounded at Malvern Hill
4th Corp., Geo. A. Branard; wounded at Knoxville

PRIVATES

Alsbrook, Joseph; wounded at Sharpsburg, killed at Chaffin's Farm
Bowman, Joel; killed at Sharpsburg
Buckley, E. C.
Bolling, C. L.
Blessing, S. T.; wounded at Sharpsburg and Darbytown
Brandt, A.; wounded at Chickamauga
Baker, G. B.
Brown, W. J.; wounded at Seven Points, killed at Gettysburg
Brown, Joseph; killed at Eltham's Landing
Barber, W. J.; killed at Dundridge, Tenn.
Barnett, Thos.
Burke, Daniel
Cady, D. C.
Cole, Fred; killed at Wilderness
Clark, Samuel; wounded at Wilderness
Crawford, E. C.
Coffee, John; wounded at Eltham's Landing
Cummings, James; wounded at Gettysburg
Collins, M. E.
Collins, James
Carnes, Wm. E.; wounded at Chaffin's Farm
Carpenter, S.; was killed at Sharpsburg
Curtis, R. A.; wounded at Knoxville and Petersburg
Dillon, John
Delesdernier, F. L.
Elmendorff, D.; wounded at Chickamauga
Farquar, A. M.; wounded at Gettysburg
Fralich, John; wounded at Chickamauga and Spottsylvania
Frank, Jacob; killed at Sharpsburg
Garity, M.
Gearing, F. A. G.; wounded at Wilderness
Gillis, J. P.; wounded at New Market Heights
Hawkins, G. B.; wounded at Gaines' Mill
Hoskins, Wm.; wounded at Sharpsburg
Hagan, Charles
Hanson, John; wounded at Sharpsburg

Jones, A. W.; wounded at Sharpsburg
Jackson, W. F.
Jackoliff, Robert; killed at Sharpsburg
Kelso, Aaron; killed at Darbytown
Kingsley, Chas. H.; wounded at Sharpsburg and Chickamauga
Lake, T. W. C.
Leach, Wm.; wounded at Chickamauga
Lazarus, S. S.; wounded at Chickamauga
Lewis, Jack; killed at Chickamauga
Merke, G. A.
Melhausen, T. A.; killed at Gettysburg
Murphy, J. W.; wounded at Chickamauga
McCarty, T. L.
McCarty, John; wounded at Wilderness
Mahoney, J. P.
McCorqudale, E. A.; wounded at Gettysburg
Nagle, James; wounded at Chickamauga
Nagle, Joseph; wounded at Gaines' Mill
Nicholson, John.
Nelson, John.
Poupot, John; killed at Gaines' Mill
Prater, Virgil
Pickett, John
Porter, W. H.; killed at Gettysburg
Pratt, J. C.; wounded at Chickamauga
Rourcke, Jas. O.; wounded at Sharpsburg
Rourcke, Noah
Robinson, W. M.
Rogers, Geo.
Shepherd, W. G.; wounded at Chickamauga
Schadt, Wm.; wounded at Chickamauga and Wilderness
Schadt, Chas.; killed at Eltham's Landing
Scott, A. J.
Scott, G. W.
Stoddard, B. R.
Smith, S. B.; wounded at Gaines' Mill
Sable, Jack
Stansberry, N.
Sims, S. D.; wounded at Eltham's Landing
Shelton, W. A.; wounded at Seven Pines
Smith, J. M.; wounded at Sharpsburg
Southwick, J. W.; killed at Gettysburg
Schultz, Henry; wounded at Wilderness
Schmidt, Frank; wounded at Wilderness
Starke, James
Taylor, W.; wounded at Gettysburg
Thompson, L. A.; wounded at New Market Heights
Townsend, L.
Von Hutton, W. B.
Vidor, Chas.
Vandegraff, S.
Worsham, Saml.
Worsham, James.
Waters, John; killed at Gettysburg
Wakelee, A.; wounded at Darbytown
Welsh, James; wounded at Sharpsburg and Wilderness
Wood, A. W.; wounded at Chickamauga and Knoxville
Williams, Chas.
Wagner, M. L.
Young, Wm.
Zimmerman, Wm.; killed at Sharpsburg

COMPANY M

NOW LIVING

Captain, W. J. Towns
D. H. Hamilton
Sebastian Domino
George Lock
James Jones

HOOD'S TEXAS BRIGADE

Wm. Blackshear
Sam Stuberfield
Wm. Roach
Jas. White
George Lundy

DIED SINCE THE WAR

Sam Watson
Dick Bennett
Cecil Wagner
M. A. Dunham
John Wilson
Jos. McMinn
Robert Capps
Wm. Forsythe
Elijah Ivery
J. Watter
Marion Burke
George Bowers
Wm. Goodson
Crockett Dunlap
Reason Hutto
John Steward
Ephraim Dial
John Ballamy
John Polk
I. D. Lovett
Willis B. Tullos
Harvey Pinson
Wm. Sylvester
Wm. Moore
John Blacksnear
Captain Ballinger
J. H. Hawthorne

Jas. Hawthorne
Isaac Wright
Richard Strawther
Buck Strawther
Zeb McClain
Thos. Peavy

DIED DURING WAR OF SICKNESS OR WOUNDS

Harvey Newman, Presley Brownlee, John Harrell, John Hutto, John Hood, Arch Davis, Joseph Barley, Jas. Hughes, Warner Jones, Sam Chamberger, John Henderson, Thos. Henderson, Henry Sweat, Robert McIntyre, Robt. Perry, George Wagner, Wm. Rogers, Newton Lundy, Dr. Wallace, Wm. Vick, Jas. Hines, E. McMinn, J. Lancaster, Wm. Martin, Jas. Stanler, Wm. Johnson, Jas. Skinner.

KILLED IN BATTLE

At Second Manassas, Willis Reading; at Sharpsburg, Lieut. Sanford, Shade Boach, Jeff Bowman, Jas. Story, Chas. Stewart and Joshua Boon; at Wilderness, James Martin, Green Morgan, Wade Turner and Oliver McBryde; at Chickamauga, Lieut. Sissell, Jack Adams, George Oglesby, John Stephens, Joseph Ratcliffe; at Siege of Petersburg, W. C. Evans, J. M. Motes and J. B. Eaves.

MUSTER ROLLS OF FOURTH TEXAS
COMPANY A

Dr. J. C. Jones, Surgeon
J. C. G. Key, Capt. of Co. A.; wounded
S. H. Darden, 1st Lieut.
J. H. McCain, 2d Lieut.
Bomer, R., 3d Lieut.; killed at Wilderness
H. Merchant, 1st Sergt.
G. E. Lynch, 2d Sergt.; wounded
L. John Adam; wounded at Seven Days' Battle

M. H. Alice; wounded
W. W. Brown; killed June 17, 1864
A. P. Brown; killed at Gaines' Mill
R. G. Barton; wounded at Gaines' Mill
S. Baker
R. Bostic
W. Cavett; lost a leg at Gettysburg
J. Cox
J. Clark
C. Kerthadly

HOOD'S TEXAS BRIGADE

C. McCathern
P. McCalister
J. Colwell
J. W. Deel; wounded at Gaines' Mill
P. Deel
S. A. Drenan; killed at Chickamauga
J. Dering
M. C. Dagle; deserted
W. Dwight
J. Dickerson; killed at Wilderness
J. Drenan
W. Eldridge; wounded at Gaines' Mill
J. Futch
A. Futch
Ed. M. Francis, Color Sergt.; killed at Chickamauga
W. Francis
F. Fletcher
J. Fields
F. Finley
J. Grose
J. Grundy
—— Goldsticker; killed at Gettysburg
H. Gunn
J. Haggerty, Jr.
John Hopkins; wounded at Second Manassas
—— Hite
A. Hilard; wounded at Gaines' Mill
W. Harrison
W. Hall
R. Hammon; killed at Sharpsburg
V. Garth; killed at Gettysburg
A. Jones
R. Jones
W. Johnson
J. Jones
L. Dement
H. Kerr
J. H. Key; wounded at Gaines' Mill
H. Key
R. Lockridge; wounded at Gaines' Mill
T. Lyle; wounded at Gaines' Mill
C. Lankster; killed at Petersburg
W. D. Mooney; wounded
T. H. Munford; wounded

S. Mooney
C. H. Munce; wounded
A. Martin
J. Melhorn
A. R. Melhorn; killed at Gaines' Mill
D. McDaniel; killed at Chickamauga
J. Murphy; wounded at Gaines' Mill
Chas. Moned; wounded at Gaines' Mill
J. McCarty; wounded at Gaines' Mill
Sergt. Geo. E. Lynch; wounded at Second Manassas
D. Martindale; killed at Sharpsburg
F. Natians; killed at Gettysburg
R. Natians; deserted
H. Owens
W. Pitman
H. Pangle
R. Stamps
J. Stringfield; wounded
D. Strong; wounded
—— Scanlon; killed at Wilderness
J. Simson
P. Chadoin
L. Chadoin
H. Stegall
J. A. Surrett; wounded at Gaines' Mill
W. H. Stanfield; wounded at Gaines' Mill
T. Simons
R. W. Thomas, Sergt.; wounded at Second Manassas
T. J. Thomas, Sergt.; killed at Second Manassas
P. Thomson
T. Vann; wounded at Second Manassas
Q. Van; wounded at Second Manassas
W. Walker
E. R. Walker; wounded at Second Manassas
—— Wallace
J. A. Woods; wounded at Gaines' Mill
—— Watkins
B. Terrell
T. B. Stanfield; wounded at Second Manassas

HOOD'S TEXAS BRIGADE

COMPANY B

"TOM GREEN RIFLES"

B. F. Carter, Captain; promoted to Lieut.-Colonel July 10, 1862, mortally wounded at Gettysburg July 2, 1863

Wm. C. Walsh, First Lieutenant; promoted to Captain July 10, 1862, was permanently disabled at Gaines' Mill and since the war has served eight years as Commissioner of General Land Office

James T. McLaurin, Second Lieutenant; promoted to Captain

Robert J. Lambert, Third Lieutenant; mortally wounded at Gaines' Mill

Frank L. Price, First Sergeant; promoted to Adjutancy of regiment

Oliver Flusser, Second Sergeant; killed at Sharpsburg Sept. 17, 1862

M. C. McAnelly, Third Sergeant; killed at Second Manassas

T. W. Masterson, Fourth Sergeant; promoted to Lieutenant

John T. Price, Fifth Sergeant; promoted to Lieutenant

Niles Fawcett, First Corporal; killed at Second Manassas

M. T. Norris, Second Corporal; killed at Gettysburg

Stephen H. Burnham, Third Corporal; killed at Second Manassas

Robt. H. Clements; wounded 1862, Fourth Corporal, died at Confederate Home in 1899

PRIVATES

Adams, A. M.
Adams, Lee
Black, Lem; killed in Virginia, 1863
Blakey, Hart G.; killed at Sharpsburg
Bonner, Bud.
Bonner, Cal.
Bonner, Wash.
Burdett, Thomas P.
Burdett, Mike
Burdett, Wm. E.
Burnham, Frank
Burk, J.; permanently disabled at the Wilderness
Buchner, C. A.
Callaghan, John; killed at Sharpsburg
Calhoun, Wm. C.; wounded at Seven Pines
Campbell, A. C.
Carpenter, W. G.; wounded in 1864
Cater, Thos. E.
Caton, W. H.; disabled by wounds in 1863
Chandler, W. M.
Colvin, Garland; wounded at Gaines' Mill and Gettysburg
Cooper, Sam.; wounded in 1863
Cooke, "Pet"; severely wounded at Gettysburg
Cox, Louis B.; wounded in 1864
Crozier, Granville H.; wounded at Gaines' Mill and Second Manassas
Donahue, John
Davige, Robert A.
Dearing, Jas. H.; one of Longstreet's sharpshooters, killed in 1864
Dohme, C. A.
Dunkin, G. W.; died in 1862 of wounds received at Second Manassas
Dunson, J. K. P.; wounded in 1862
Durfee, A. A.; wounded in 1864
Falls, J.; killed in Virginia in 1862
Flanikin, Wm. J.; wounded in 1864
Ford, Wm. F.; promoted Lieutenant, wounded in 1863
Foster, Wm. K.
Freeman, Pony
Freeman, C. L.; wounded at Gaines' Mill
Fawcett, B. K.; disabled at Sharpsburg
Giles, Val C.; wounded at Gaines' Mill
Gregg, Alex.

Girand, F. W.
Glasscock, Thos. A.
Gould, Uriah
George, M. A.; lost an arm at the Wilderness
Grumbles, Perry; promoted Sergeant, killed at Gettysburg
Griffith, John
Hamilton, H.; wounded at Gaines' Mill
Hamby, Wm. R.; wounded at Second Manassas, disabled at Sharpsburg
Hamilton, S. W.
Haralson, Chas. L.
Hawthorne, A. J.
Horton, W. H.
Haynes, J. J.
Henderson, J. B.; wounded once in 1863
Hill, L. D.
Hoffler, G. W.; killed at Sharpsburg
Holden, D. W.
Hopson, Briggs W.; wounded at Gaines' Mill
Howard, Ball; killed at Sharpsburg
Howard, Jeff.
Hughes, J. J.
Horn, P.
Herbert, Wm.; wounded in 1863
Jones, A. C.
Jones, Etanial; killed in 1863
Jones, Joe E.; wounded in 1863
Jones, J. K. P.; killed at Chickamauga
Keller, Wm. A.; lost an arm at Gaines' Mill
Keller, J. H.
Lessing, Wm. H.; permanently disabled at Sharpsburg
Lightfoot, W. H.
Luckett, Alfred T.; wounded at Sharpsburg
Maier, H.; killed at Sharpsburg
Marcham, R.
Mayfield, Newton W.; wounded in 1864
Mayfield, Eph.
Minor, Arthur
McGee, Jno. F.; wounded at Second Manassas and Sharpsburg
McMath, M. W.
McMullin, Barney
McPhaul, C. M.
Masterson, A. B.; wounded at Gettysburg
Millican, Ed. H.
Mosely, Sidney E.; lost right leg in battle in 1864
Moss, Wm. V.
Morris, Charles L.; killed at Knoxville
Neuendorff, Max; wounded and discharged in 1862
Nichols, A. W.; wounded at Seven Pines
Nichols, Geo. W.; wounded at Second Manassas, killed at Chickamauga
Piper, Wm. L.; wounded at Second Manassas and Sharpsburg, discharged
Plagge, C.
Puckett, Lim.
Railey, J. D.; wounded in 1862
Rice, A. R.
Roberts, A. S.; wounded at Second Manassas
Robertson, Geo. L.; wounded at Gaines' Mill, disabled at Sharpsburg
Robertson, Robert R.; wounded in 1863
Rose, Geo. W.
Rushton, Chas. H.; wounded at Gaines' Mill and Second Manassas
Rust, Robt. S.; seriously wounded and disabled at Sharpsburg
Ripetoe, James
Stone, S. T.; disabled at Chicamauga
Strohmer, Frank; wounded once
Summers, Jno. S.; killed at Gaines' Mill
Schuler, John; seriously wounded at Gaines' Mill
Stein, Isaac; lost an arm at Second Manassas
Sheppard, J. L.
Tannehill, Wm. J.; wounded at Gaines' Mill
Teague, S. P.; wounded in 1862

HOOD'S TEXAS BRIGADE 319

Tatum, J. M.; killed in Virginia in 1863
Thomas, Jas. H.; killed at Second Manassas
Thomas, Mark; wounded at Gaines' Mill and Second Manassas
Todd, D. A.; wounded in 1862
Wheeler, Jno. G.; lost arm at Darbytown
White, J. A.; wounded and died
Wilson, Sam. C.; wounded at Gaines' Mill
Wright, Jas. A.; wounded in 1862
Woodward, Logan
Whitesides, H. A.; disabled at the Wilderness
Wright, Peyton A.
Price, John; a negro who followed his master, Lieut. John T. Price, into the service. He was faithful to the end, and after the war voted always with the Democrats of the State. He is now dead

COMPANY C

Townsend, W. P., Captain; promoted to Major, lost foot at Manassas
Barziza, D. U., 1st Lieut.; wounded at Gettysburg
Turner, B. F., 2d Lieut.
Wood, P. S., 3d Lieut.; mortally wounded at Gaines' Mill
Grizzle, J. P., 1st Sergt.; elected Lieut., killed at Darbytown
Davis, H. W., 2d Sergt.; wounded at Gettysburg
Roberts, J. C., 3d Sergt.; lost arm at Gaines' Mill
Galloway, J. I., 4th Sergt.; lost leg at Second Manassas
Simmons, J. H., 5th Sergt.; killed at Chickamauga
Streetman, A. P., 1st Corp.; killed at Gaines' Mill
Livingston, M. L., 2d Corp., Lieut., and Captain; wounded at Chickamauga and Gettysburg
Hill, J. W. M. P., 3d Corp.; lost arm at Gaines' Mill
Adams, J. O., 4th Corp.; killed at Malvern Hill

PRIVATES

Adams, J. M.; wounded at Wilderness
Acruse, P.; disabled at Wilderness
Alexander, W. J.; wounded at Sharpsburg
Alexander, ——; killed at Sharpsburg
Allday, Peter
Barziza, P. J.; wounded at Sharpsburg
Brown, P. A.; killed at Gaines' Mill
Barton, Lem; lost right arm at Sharpsburg
Barton, John; lost right arm at Sharpsburg
Barton, Frank; wounded at Gaines' Mill and Chickamauga
Bailey, W. L.; wounded at Gaines' Mill
Burns, Joe
Butler, ——
Beavers, T. B.; wounded at Gaines' Mill and killed at Wilderness
Beavers, M.; wounded at Gettysburg
Blackburn, Green; killed at Wilderness
Boyd, J. B.; elected Lieut., wounded at Wilderness and before Richmond
Cosgrove, J. H.; wounded at Wilderness
Corley, Wilks; killed at Petersburg
Chambers, G. J.; killed at Sharpsburg
Coe, E. N.
Drennan, J. H.; wounded at Gaines' Mill and Cold Harbor
Drake, J. H.
Davis, Louis
Davidson, Riley, killed at Sharpsburg
Easter, M. L.; killed at the Wilderness
Eddington, H. F.; killed at Darbytown

HOOD'S TEXAS BRIGADE

Elder, Geo.
Field, F. L.; killed at Gettysburg
Foster, H.; lost right arm at Gaines' Mill
Foster, R.; wounded at Malvern Hill
Frost, H.; mortally wounded at the Wilderness
Griffin, J. H.; killed at Chickamauga
Garrett, J. M.
Goodman, J.; wounded at Gaines' Mill and Wilderness
Gillmore, Harry
Gear, W. E.
Gary, W.
Hearne, William
Herndon, Jacob; killed at Gettysburg
S. J. Mitchell; wounded at Chickamauga
Herndon, Ed.
Herndon, A.; killed at Petersburg
Hunter, W. R.; killed at Gaines' Mill
Henderson, J. S.; killed in battle
Hamman, W. H.
Hixson, G. M.; killed at Darbytown
Hyson, ——; killed at Petersburg
Haynes, Richard
Harris, Bazley
Jones, D. C.
Jones, W. A.
Jones, J. J.; killed at Chickamauga
January, Jno.
Kirk, W. S.; killed at Second Manassas
Kensey, D.; killed at Chickamauga
Keith, L. D.; wounded at Richmond
Livingston, Jesse; wounded at Second Manassas and Gettysburg
Lofton, Silas
Love, Ogle
Montgomery, Whit.; wounded at Spottsylvania Court House
Marshall, W. W.; lost arm at Gaines' Mill
Marshall, Ben
Marshall, W. H.
Merriman, B. F.; wounded at Gaines' Mill and Wilderness
McClinton, Jas.; killed in battle

Moore, R. E.; wounded at Petersburg
Moore, M. C.; killed at Petersburg
Marsh, Joe.
Norwood, Alexander; killed at the Wilderness
Noble, Jas.
Norton, W.; killed at Chickamauga
Olive, J.; killed at Sharpsburg
Rutherford, Robt.
Reese, W.; killed at Chickamauga
Robertson, J. R.; killed at Gaines' Mill
Robertson, Frank
Robertson, B.
Rymes, B. W.
Reed, Ashley
Ray, Y. B.
Smith, J. A.; mortally wounded at Chickamauga
Smiley, W. J.; killed at Gaines, Mill
Smiley, J. R.; killed at Gaines' Mill
Smiley, J.; wounded at Wilderness
Sneed, J. W.; wounded at Gaines' Mill
Steele, W. C.
Tindall, O. H.; lost foot at Wilderness
Talbot, Y. O.
Tolbot, Augustus
Vaughn, P. H.
Vandusen, H.; wounded at Gettysburg
Wood, Bennett, wounded at Gaines' Mill, Second Manassas and Wilderness
Wood, E. O.; wounded at Second Manassas, killed at Chickamauga
Wood, J.
Webster, E,; wounded before Richmond in 1864
Wilson, J. M.; killed Second Manassas
Wilkins, E.
Whiddon, W. G.; killed at Second Manassas
Wells, Lou
Roberts, J. C.
McVoiman, B. F.

HOOD'S TEXAS BRIGADE 321

COMPANY D

Bane, Jno. P.; Capt., promoted to Col.; wounded at Gaines' Mill
Martin, Chas.; 1st Lieut.
Holloman, T. H.; 2nd Lieut.; killed at Gaines' Mill
Duggan, Ed.; 3rd Lieut.
Davis, Robt.; 1st Sergt.
Jeffries, Dudley; 2nd Sergt.; and 1st Lieut., wounded at Second Manassas
Jefferson, John R.; 3rd Sergt.; wounded at Manassas
Patterson, Jas.; 4th Sergt.
Wipprecht, Chas.; 5th Sergt.
Dibrell, Jno.; 1st Corp.
Wilson, Alex. A.; 2nd Corp.; promoted to Adjt.; wounded twice
Hudgins, Meck; 3rd Corp.
Smith, W. Pitt; 4th Corp.
Armstrong, D. H.
Allen, Adolphus
Aikin, Wm.; killed in battle, think Gettysburg
Anderson, Chas.
Baker, Jno. W.; wounded at Wilderness
Baker, Joseph
Butler, Geo.; killed at Gaines' Mill
Butler, Jas.; killed at Gettysburg
Burges, W. H.; wounded at Sharpsburg
Burges, R. J. (Dick); wounded at Manassas
Burges, Robt. A.; wounded at Wilderness
Burges, Gid.
Calvert, Lott; wounded at Gaines' Mill
Cabiness, Thos.
Cody, E. J.; killed at Chickamauga
Cox, Thos.; wounded at Gaines' Mill
Campbell, Jas.; killed at Chickamauga
Courtney, Seymour; deserted
Davis, Wm.; killed at Sharpsburg
Davis, Robt.
Davidson, —; killed at Gaines' Mill
Daniel, Jack
Duare, Alex.; killed at Gaines' Mill
Dimmitt, Jas.; wounded at Sharpsburg
Dimmitt, Nap.; wounded at Gaines' Mill
Dimmitt, Alamo
Dunn, M. S.; wounded at Gaines' Mill
Dibrell, Chas.
Ewing, Thos.; wounded at Gaines' Mill
Ewing, Finis
Erskine, A. N.; killed at Sharpsburg
Erskine, A. M.; wounded at Gaines' Mill and Sharpsburg
Ehringhans, W. F. H.
Franks, R. H. (Hat); promoted to Lieut. and Captain, wounded at Sharpsburg
Fennell, Isham; wounded at Gaines' Mill and died
Flores, Manuel
George Moses
Gregory, Jno.
Green, W. S.; wounded at Gaines' Mill, killed at Gettysburg
Gordon, Alonzo; wounded at Gaines' Mill and died
Glazier, Fritz; killed at Gettysburg
Glazier, Julius; wounded at Chickamauga
Harmon, Wm.
Harmon, Zack
Herron, Andrew; killed at Gettysburg
Herron, Jas.
Harris, Wm.; wounded at Cold Harbor and Spottsylvania Court House
Hudgins, Geo.
Hadges, Geo. A.; wounded at Gettysburg and Wilderness
Holmes, J. F. N.
Henry, Arch.; deserted
Jordan, P. E.
Jefferson, Thos.

Jefferson, ——
Johnson, Ig.; promoted to Lieut.; killed at Manassas
Jones, S. A.; wounded at Gaines' Mill and Chickamauga
Jones, R. H.; wounded at Manassas
Knight, Geo.; promoted to Captain, dead
Le Gette, Jesse; served to Second Manassas, discharged
Longstreet, Geo.; wounded at Gettysburg
Lackey, R. J.; wounded at Gaines' Mill and died
Lewis, Chas.
Leonard, Asa; wonded in battle
Lynch, Thos.; (Laplander)
Little, G. W. (Ben); wounded at Gaines' Mill
McClaugherty, W. H.; promoted to Captain, wounded at Wilderness
McNeely, Jul.
Means, Reub.
Merriwether, Thos.; wounded at Fort Gilmore
Maddox, Levi
Millet, Leonidas; killed at Gaines' Mill
Mitchell, ——.
Manning, Merret; killed at Wilderness
Mays, Nelson; killed at Gettysburg
Morison, Robt.
Miller, M. E.; wounded at Gaines' Mill
Park, Dr. Robt.
Park, Thos.; wounded at Gaines' Mill and died
Parent, E. J.
Pierce, Aaron; killed at Gaines' Mill

Rutledge, Osborne; deserted
Russell, Wm.
Rhodes, R. A.; wounded at Manassas
Reich, Cornelius; promoted to 1st Lieut.; killed at Gaines' Mill
Redus, Wm.
Rogers, Jno.
Rogers, Mike
Reeves, J. R. (Rankin)
Shuniate, Wm.; killed at the Wilderness
Smith, Jno.
Smith, Jack, D.
Smith, Paris, wounded at Gaines' Mill and Wilderness
Smith, M. V. (Pony); wounded at Sharpsburg, Chickamauga and Gettysburg
Smith, Thos.
Smith, Ezekiel
Saunders, Frank; wounded at Gettysburg
Smith, Wm.
Sanders, Geo.
Sanders, Stewart
Singleterry, Jno. U.
Wilson, Wm.; wounded at Gaines' Mill
Watson, Thos.
Schmidt, Baltzer
Woods, A. H.; promoted to Lieut.; killed at Chickamauga
Whitehead, Jas.; killed at Manassas
White, Jas. M.; wounded at Gaines' Mill and in some other fight
White, J. M.; No 2
White, Fred
Young, Jno.; wounded at Gaines' Mill
Yeaker, ——; deserted

COMPANY E

Ryan, E. D.; Captain
Brandon, J. M.; 1st Lieut.
Sublett, D. L.; 2d Lieut.
Billingsley, J. C.; 3d Lieut.
Killingsworth, A.; 1st Sergt.
Smith, J. C.; 2d Sergt.
Ripley, P. M.; 3d Sergt.; now living

HOOD'S TEXAS BRIGADE

Dunklin, W. W.; 4th Sergt.
Dean, R. S.; 5th Sergt.
Majors, J. B.; 1st Corp.
Young, B.; 2d Corp.
Walters, A. J.; 3d Corp.
Long, J. H.; 4th Corp.

PRIVATES

Ashmead, G. L.
Aycock, B. L.; now living
Blocker, J. C.
Billingsley, S. J.
Bible, Noah
Bible, Phil. C.
Burton, W. H. P.; now living
Clark, J. E.
Clark, J. B.
Cowden, W. B.
Chenault, G. N.
Chambers, S. H.
Chapman, J. B.
Dunklin, T. L.
Duncan, W. E.
Donally, H. M.
Decherd, A. P.
Decherd, D. M.
Delk, W. G.
Edwards, B. G.
Fitzhugh, D. C.
Freeman, R. L.
Fossett, Sam
Green, Geo.

Good, D. J.
Hunt, J. F.
Holloway, L. D.
Hirst, T. D.
Hughes, Josiah
Harrington, J. A.
Harrison, J. H.
Hicks, W. M.
Hicks, H. K.
Holden, J. W.
Hannah, W.
Hill, Eldon
Irven, W. H.
Johnson, J. W.
Johnson, John
Jones, R. M.
Lehman, Joe
Loyd, W. J.
Leonard, R. H.
Manahan, J. H.
Makeig, T. M.
Miller, T. D.
Mullens, C.
Mullens, T. M.; now living
Mullens, W. T.
Morgan, A. B.
Madden, C. P.
Moor, N. P.
McGee, Green
Norwood, T. L.
Famplin, W. A.
Peters, L. C.
Ross, W. M.
Robinson, J. A.

Robinson, S. A.
Robinson, James
Robinson, W. S.
Reed, J. C.
Rogers, W. D.
Rogers, H. B.
Rogers, J. L.
Roberts, Abner
Ragsdale, J. B.
Rotan, W. T.
Ramsey, (perhaps F.)
Ripley, N. N.
Selman, T. J.
Sandefur, L. G.
Smith, J. S.
Smith, Joe. S.
Sharp, E. C.
Taylor, G. M.
Terry, J. C.
Tilley, Ed.
Umberson, R. W.
West, John C.
Wideman, C. A.
Williams, T. D.
Willis, J. B.
Wollard, Andy; now living
Worsham, E. L.
Worsham, J. N.
Worsham C. G.
Wilson, G. H.
Way, C. B.; now living
Whitehead, C. M.
Young, T. H.

COMPANY F

Ed. H. Cunningham, Captain—After Sharpsburg, went on Hood's staff
John F. Brooks; First Lieutenant—Disabled at Gaines' Mill
L. P. Hughes; Second Lieutenant—Lost arm at Sharpsburg
L. P. Lyons; Third Lieutenant—Killed at Gaines' Mill
Haywood Brahan; Orderly Sergeant—later Lieutenant—wounded at Appomattox
Chas. S. Brown; Second Sergeant—Sergeant-Major. Killed at Wilderness
John D. Murray; Third Sergeant—Often wounded, but stuck
Eli Park; Fourth Sergeant—Lieutenant. Killed at New Market Heights
W. A. Bennett; Fifth Sergeant
R. H. Skinner; First Corporal—Disabled at Sharpsburg

324 HOOD'S TEXAS BRIGADE

Daniel M. McAlister; Second Corporal—Mortally wounded at Gaines' Mill
E. T. Kindred; Third Corporal—Lieutanant and Captain
Charles A. McAlister; Fourth Corporal—wounded at Gaines' Mill

PRIVATES

Adams, J. T.
Abbott, H. G.
Alford, James
Allen, George; lost arm at Second Manassas
Aylmer, G. G.; disabled at Gaines' Mill
Brown, Ossawatomie
Bedell, A. M.
Brantley, J. E.
Breckenridge, ——
Brieger, J. G.
Buchanan, L.
Brooks, Cincinnatus
Camp, T. P.
Cohea, A. T.; wounded and died at the Wilderness
Cook, John
Cunningham, Thos.; died of wounds received at Gaines' Mill
Copeland, Sol.; killed at the Wilderness
Crigler, R. T.; later Lieutenant. Disabled at Wilderness
Campbell, John
Clark, Joseph
Currie, J. B.; lost a leg at Chickamauga
Crockett, E. R.
Dansby, Harrison
Dial, Augustus A.; disabled at Gaines' Mill
Downing, Ed.; killed at Gaines' Mill
Dreyer, H.
Dunn, W. H.
Fishburn, J. A.
Elliot, John
Floyd, William F.; killed at Gettysburg
Gabbert, H. H.
Givens, Wm.; disabled at Chickamauga
Goodloe, Calvin
Goodloe, Wm. P.
Goodwin, Benj.
Graham, J. C.; wounded early in war
Green, W. A.; disabled at Gaines' Mill
Hahn, Ferdinand; wounded, disabled
Harbour, C.
Hardoin, A.; killed at Gaines' Mill
Hardoin, S.
King, W. R.
Harwell, J. H.; disabled at Gaines' Mill
Henderson, C. F.; killed at Gaines' Mill
Henderson, B. G.; killed at Sharpsburg
Hollander, W. M.; disabled at Gaines' Mill
Houston, Russell
Howard, Russell
Johnson, J. N.
Johnson, W. C.; disabled at Chickamauga
Jones, A. R.
Jones, Wm.
Kahr, N.; killed at Gaines' Mill
Kindred, J. B.
Kindred, John; killed at Gaines' Mill
Kindred, Clay; killed at Sharpsburg
Kindred, J. P.
Koolbeck, G.; killed at Gaines' Mill
Love, J. P.; killed at Sharpsburg
Meisner, Ed
Maus, Peter; wounded at Gaines' Mill
McCann, T. J.; wounded at Gaines' Mill
Mayfield, Jas.; killed at Knoxville, Tenn.
Menifee, Q. M.; lost leg at Sharpsburg and discharged.
Menger, Oscar; disabled at Gaines' Mill
Morris, Wm.
Murray, J. C.; killed at Gettysburg

HOOD'S TEXAS BRIGADE 325

Murray, R. W.; lost leg at Wilderness
Pengra, M. M.; disabled at Gettysburg
Penn, Pat.; killed in picket skirmish Sept. 29, 1864
Penn, Abe; disabled at Chickamauga
Pickett, M.; killed at Gaines' Mill
Pogue, L. S.
Polley, J. B.; lost a foot at Darbytown
Quick, Jacob; wounded somewhere
Riggs, John; killed at the Wilderness
Roberts, John
Rumley, J. J.; wounded and retired
Sampson, Ed. J.; killed at Gaines' Mill
Schweitzer, Geo.; wounded and retired
Selp, M. M.
Sargeant, A. H.; wounded, retired
Smith, Henry; wounded at Sharpsburg and retired
Smith, Albert
Sneed, Albert; disabled at Second Manassas
Sullivan, R. A.; killed at Gaines' Mill
Summerville, Jas.; lost arm at the Wilderness
Sutherland, Jack; later Adjutant, disabled at Darbytown
Thornton, H. G.
Webber, S.; killed at Sharpsburg
Wallace, E. F.
Weir, Henry
Wiseman, Jas. O.
Wolff, S.; killed at Second Manassas
Wood, G. W.; wounded in 1863
Maddox, John
Crenshaw, M.
Naurath, Wm.
Dockstadder, Oscar
Veal, Frank
Warner, Chas.

COMPANY G

Adkinson, John J., Lieut.; wounded
Adams, Sam H.
Aikens, James O.; wounded
Allen, W. J.
Arnett, David
Bassett, Robert H.; Lieut. and Adjt. of the regiment; disabled at Chickamauga
Bessett, Noah H.; wounded, died in Texas.
Barry, Wm. E., Lieut.; disabled at the Wilderness
Barry, L. Howard, O. Sergt.; was wounded several times
Barry, John D.; killed at Chickamauga
Barry, Thos. W.
Baines, Thos. W., Sergt.
Baines, Wm. M.
Barnes, John T.
Baker, Jesse W., Lieut.
Barker, James, Scout
Beecher, R. A., O. Sergt.; killed at Gettysburg
Blackshear, Robt. D.; wounded at Sharpsburg and Spottsylvania Court House
Blackshear, Jas. J., Sergt.; wounded
Blackshear, Duncan R.; wounded twice
Blackshear, E. T.
Boozer, H. D.
Bookman, J. M. (Bob), Lieut.; killed at Chickamauga
Butts, Lewis D., Lieut.; killed at Gaines' Mill
Buffington, Tom C., Lieut. and Captain
Brietz, A. C., Ordnance Sergt.; wounded at Wilderness
Bowen, Allen
Chambers, G. C.; killed at Sharpsburg
Churchwell, Thomas; killed at Chickamauga
Carley, Martin F.
Closs, T. O.; killed at Gettysburg
Chatham, Wm. B.; wounded at Wilderness

Cruse, A. J.; killed at Gaines' Mill
Cotton, H. T.
Collins, Daniel; Chief Bugler from commencement to Appomattox, dead
Cook, J. J.
Dance, John T.; wounded at Gaines' Mill
Dawkins, F. A.
Damm, Frank; wounded at Gettysburg
Davis, Ed. C.
Daffan, Lawrence A.
Davis, John A.
Dunham, Jas. H., Lieut.
Duke, Joseph G.; mortally wounded at Chickamauga
Eckolls, Wm. R. A.; lost an arm at Gaines' Mill
Ferrell, Davis S.; killed at Gettysburg
Finley, J. R.
Fields, Drury H.
Floyd, Chas. E.
Floyd, Wm.
Flournoy, Jas. J.; wounded at Gaines' Mill
Gay, G. A.; disabled at Gaines' Mill
Gould, Jas. L., Sergt.; mortally wounded at Gettysburg
Green, John E.; killed at Gettysburg
Griffin, David C.; wounded at Gaines' Mill
Grissett, Wm. J., Com. Sergt.
Giles, Jas. J.
Giles, E. D.
Giles, P. L.
Giles, Dan
Haddon, Mack E.; killed at Second Manassas
Harrison, M. M. (Smoky)
Hasson, Robert; lost leg at Darbytown
Helmer, Edward
Hadon, Jas. J.
Hiett, J. W.
Heyman, George
Hubbell, N. L.
Hughes, W. T.
Hutcheson, J. W., first Captain of Company G; killed at Gaines' Mill

Jackson, Isaac
Jackson, Job; lost leg at Sharpsburg
Jones, W. S.; killed at Gaines' Mill
Jones, N. B.
Jones, Geo. W.
Jones, I. Newton
Kay, Eli
Kennard, A. Drew
Kendall, J. L.
King, Jno. H.
Lawrence, Groce; killed at Wilderness
Livingston, A.
Loggins, Dr. Jas. C.; lives at Ennes, Texas
Loper, Wm.; deserted
Martin, Wm. A.
Martin, Jno. F., Sergt.
May, J. W. T., Color Guard; wounded at Second Manassas
McCowen, John; killed at Chickamauga
McDaniel, Ben H.
McClenny, Wm.; killed at Wilderness
McGregor, Wm. B.
Midkiff, E. P.; killed at Gaines' Mill
Midkiff, J. A.; wounded at Wilderness
Montgomery, Joseph
Moss, George R.
Mooring, Chas. G.; wounded several times
Mooring, J. S. (Bob); wounded at Wilderness, disabled
Muldrew, Jno. T.
Muse, Jas. T.; wounded at Gaines' Mill
Nix, John L.; wounded at Gettysburg
Nelms, Everard P.; wounded at Gaines' Mill
Nettles, Joseph H.
Neal, French
Pearce, Ben. W.; wounded at Sharpsburg
Pearce, Ed. W.; lost hand at Gaines' Mill
Parnell, Jas. C.

HOOD'S TEXAS BRIGADE

Patterson, Wm. R.
Peteet, W. B.
Peteet, J. Monroe; wounded at Gaines' Mill
Pinckney, Jno. M.; wounded several times
Pinckney, Richard H.; youngest soldier in regiment
Plaster, Joseph H.; wounded at Gaines' Mill and Wilderness
Plaster, Frank
Qualls, George S.; Color Corporal
Reynolds, J. S.
Rogerson, John; killed at Gaines' Mill
Roach, John, Lieut.; killed
Roco, A. C.
Rowe, H. T.
Robinson, John
Stacey, John J., Color Corporal; wounded at Gettysburg
Scott, J. B.; killed at Gaines' Mill
Scott, Garrett; killed at Sharpsburg
Schultz, W. A.
Shaffer, Henry E.
Smith, W. H.
Silverbaugh, A.; killed at Chickamauga
Spencer, Chas. W.; mortally wounded at Eltham's Landing
Stewart, A. Jackson; wounded at Gettysburg
Stacey, Willis A.; wounded at Gaines' Mill and Wilderness
Terrell, E. Tom., Asst. Surgeon
Terrell, Wm. H.
Tidwell, Wm. C.
Thomas, J. W. (Gotch)
Trant, John; wounded at Gaines' Mill and killed at Sharpsburg
Turner, Jasper
Tierner, Wesley
Wilson, Walter S.; wounded at Second Manassas
Watson, A. E.
Webb, Frank X.
Whitehurst, J. K.
White Mathew D.
White, Caleb; was killed at Gaines' Mill
Whitesides, A. Hoxcey; captured at Gettysburg and drowned in effort to escape
Whitlock, A. T.
Williams, Henry F.
Williams, Jas. J.; wounded at Gaines' Mill
Wood, Dan A.; wounded several times
Ward, Chas. H.
Womack, M. S.; captured at Gettysburg
Wood, Rufus H., Sergt.
Wallingford, T. G.; litter bearer

COMPANY H

Captain, P. P. Porter; killed at Gaines' Mill
1st. Lieut., James T. Hunter; was wounded often
2d Lieut., Tom M. Owens; killed at Gaines' Mill
3d Lieut., Benton Randolph; disabled at Gaines' Mill
1st Sergt., C. E. Jones; killed at Second Manassas
2d Sergt., S. Y. Smith
3d Sergt., J. S. Rudd
4th Sergt., Nelse A. Myer; killed at Gaines' Mill
5th Sergt., J. W. Lawrence
1st Corp., H. T. Sapp; wounded at Eltham's Landing, 1862
2d Corp., Z. Landrum; disabled at Gettysburg
3d Corp., G. L. P. Reed; Hospital Steward
4th Corp., A. C. Morris
Musician, J. R. P. Jett

PRIVATES

Allen, Ben H.; killed at Gaines' Mill
Bullock, B. F.
Bell, O. W.

Barzo, Henry; killed at Gaines' Mill
Bascom, G. F.
Brent, Thos. A.; killed at Second Manassas
Beck, Jacob
Cartwright, E. W.
Cartwright, Jas.; killed at the Wilderness
Chilton, F. B.
Connelly, Jas.; disabled at Gaines' Mill
Copeland, W. E.; disabled at Gaines' Mill, lost a foot
Conroe, C. M.; killed at Gaines' Mill
Dawson, R. C.; killed at Second Manassas
Damm, Adam
Edmison, J. S.
Fisher, W. S.; lost a foot at Gaines' Mill
Faulkner, A.
Finley, Howard
Farrow, D. D.
Griggs, Green; disabled in 1864 in Virginia
Gilliham, J. H.; killed at Gaines' Mill
Hall, J. H.; died of wound in 1864
Hatch, L. B.
Howard, C. S.
Howard, N. F.
Holt, A. C.
Hahn, A.
Hopkins, J. C.
Harrison, D.; deserted
Holmes, M. C.; lost a leg at Second Manassas
Keyser, G. W.
Kipps, G. W.; killed at the Wilderness
Kerr, W. C.
King, S. P.; killed at Second Manassas
King, F. G.
Long, John
Lemon, J. W.
Landrum, Z.; killed at Gaines' Mill
Landrum, W. J.
Lewis, Jas. L.; killed at Second Manassas
Lewis, Clint; killed at Gaines' Mill
Loper, Wm.
Lackland, J. M.
Martin, W. L.; killed at Gaines' Mill
Mathews, L. A.
McCowan, A. J.; disabled in Tennessee in 1863, wound in knee
McDaniels, Y. L.; disabled in 1864, wound in leg
Meyers, M. F.
May, Thomas
May, D. G.; disabled at Gaines' Mill
May, W. C.
May, R. M.
Milliken, Wm.
McGraw, Wm.
Nevill, D. E.
McGraw, Wm.
Petty, T. T. M.
Peacock, Wm.; killed at Chickamauga
Parker, Wm. A.; color bearer, was wounded at Sharpsburg and died
Peasley, G. A.
Rogers, J. P.
Reynolds, Ben.; killed at Gettysburg
Randolph, D. J.
Ransom, R. W.; killed at Second Manassas
Steward, J. R.
Sanderlin, J. M.
Savage, Ed.
Stewart, J. E.; lost leg in battle, 1862
Stewart, R. H.
Sharp, J. H.; killed at Petersburg
Seay, A. B.; disabled by wound in in 1862
Seargeant, Thos.
Spivey, J. S.
Stratton, Robert
Travis, Henry; killed at the Wilderness
Tucker, D. J.
Tedford, R. J.; disabled by wound in leg at Chickamauga
Thigpen, E. C.
Thigpen, G. C.
Taylor, Alex.

A Genuine Soldier Boy of 1861
16 Year Old
(Taken in Richmond, Va., 1861)

FRANK BOWDEN CHILTON
Company H, Fourth Texas Regiment, Hood's Texas Brigade,
Army of Northern Virginia; later, Captain C. S. A.

HOOD'S TEXAS BRIGADE

Thomas, J.
Taliafero, J.; disabled by wound in arm at Gettysburg
Tyler, R. L.; killed at Gaines' Mill
Waltrip, C. M.
Wallace, J. M.
Watson, Wm. A.
Wilcox, T. W.
Wynne, G. A.; killed at Sharpsburg
Wynne, J. A.
Wilkes, T. O.; killed at Gaines' Mill
Wade, F. H.
Anders, R.
Bryant, W. L. B.; killed at Gaines' Mill
Cartwright, L. C.; lost arm in battle in 1865
Cathey, B. H.
Cude, Wm.
Clepper, L. C.
Dillard, T. C.
Dowdey, B. C.; disabled by wound in leg, 1864
Dale, G. W.
Collier, A. H.
Ellis, Jack; killed at Gettysburg
Farrow, Sam W.
Faulkner, A.; killed at Gettysburg
Gafford, R. D.
Watson, H. C.; killed at Second Manassas
Quigley, R.; killed at Gaines' Mill
Conklin, Jas.; killed at Wilderness

Keeble, Ed.
Smith, John; killed at Chickamauga
Stanfield, John; killed at Chickamauga
Jeffers, M. S.
Wilkes, B. B.
Kirby, J. A.; killed at Chickamauga
Keyser, Henry
Lewis, Wm.
LeVenture, Louis
Town, Jacob L.; was killed at Knoxville
Leach, M.
Meyers, T. J.
Mitchell, T. R.; deserted
Steussey, J.; lost an arm at Gaines' Mill
Steussey, M.; lost a leg at Gaines' Mill
Smith, John L.; disabled in Virginia in 1864
Sergeant, Jas. B.; disabled at Gaines' Mill
Sanders, C. B.
Rankin, Robt.
Talley, J. C.
Talley, Reuben
Taylor, C. T.; disabled in battle in 1863
Wynne, T. A.
Wynne, S. W.; killed at Second Manassas
Fox, Richard; killed at Sharpsburg

COMPANY I

C. M. Winkler, Captain
J. R. Loughridge, First Lieutenant; disabled
J. R. Oglebia, Second Lieutenant; resigned and returned
B. J. C. Hill, Third Lieutenant; resigned
Mat. Beasley, First Sergeant
S. M. Riggs, Second Sergeant; killed at battle of Chickamauga
J. D. Caddell, Third Sergeant; killed at Petersburg, 1865

W. G. Jackson, Fourth Sergeant; wounded and disabled Oct., 1864

PRIVATES

Astin, J. H.; disabled and discharged
Allen, W. B.
Armstrong, R. C.
Barry, A.
Barry, M.
Beasley, J. R.
Beasley, Jesse; killed at Second battle of Manassas

HOOD'S TEXAS BRIGADE

Barnet, J. R.
Brewster, A. J.
Bales, W. H.; disabled at Gettysburg
Boynton, G. S.
Black, James R.
Bias, A. J.
Bishop, John
Crab, E. S.; disabled in Second battle of Manassas
Crabtree, J. W.
Crawford, R. W.
Carroll, W. E.; killed at Chickamauga
Childress, B. F.; killed at Chickamauga
Crossland, A. M.; wounded and disabled at Ft. Harrison
Casady, J. M.
Duran, J. W.
Duncan, Ira P.
Dillard, E. P.
Dozier, ——; killed in battle
Fondran, W. A.; killed at Gaines' Mill
Franklin, B. F.
Fagan, Jas. G.
Fuller, W. W.
Fuller, Jas. L.; killed at Wilderness
Foster, J. A.; disabled in 1864
Foster, G. W.; disabled Oct. 7, 1864
Foster, M. L.
Garner, E. M.; killed at battle of Antietam or Sharpsburg
Green, J. T.
Green, John
Gregory, R.
Gregory, John; wounded, disabled
Herbert, J. H.; wounded at Second Manassas, disabled
Holloway, R. G.
Harrison, J. J.
Harrison, H. H.
Hill, Jack; killed in September, 1864
Hill, J. H.; wounded at Sharpsburg
Haldeman, J. W.
Hagle, Joe.
Henderson, G. W.
Harris, J. O.; killed at Gettysburg
Hamilton, J. D.

Hamilton, J. L.
Harper, Frank
Jefferson, W. R.
Jordan, I. C.
Killian, H. L. W.; wounded at Sharpsburg
Kennedy, Thomas; wounded and discharged, 1864
Knight, Tom
Lemons, A. M.; wounded and disabled September, 1864
Lumas, J. M.
Lanham, J. B.; wounded at Sharpsburg and discharged
Lea, ——
Miller, R. S.
Mills, N. J.; elected lieutenant of Co.
Massey, J. H.; wounded and disabled at Chickamauga
Morris, T. R.; killed at Second battle of Manassas
Mitchell, W. H.
McMorris, J. M.
Melton, I. E.
Meador, A. L.
Neal, J. H.
Neal, Jeff.
Platt, W. G.
Pickett, John; wounded at Second Manassas and discharged
Polk, J. M.
Osborn, Paddy
Osborn, Sandy
Orendorff, J. H.
Pursly, Lewis
Pennington, C.
Rice, L. W.
Rice, R. N.
Rushing, M. D. L.
Sessions, J. T.
Sessions, E. G.
Smith, Pulasky
Smith, W. T.; killed at Gettysburg
Smith, W. G.
Simmons, J. W.
Stokes, Cornelius; killed June 2, 1864
Steward, J. D.; wounded and disabled at Gaines' Mill

HOOD'S TEXAS BRIGADE 331

Spence, W. T.; killed at Second Manassas
Shaw, J. R.
Terrell, S. B.; killed at Suffolk, February, 1863
Templeton, Wm. W.
Templeton, N. B.
Treadwell, J. H.
Utzman, J. L.
Walker, J. C.; killed at Chickamauga
Walker, H. E.; killed at Wilderness
Wade, R. H.; disabled at Gaines' Mill
Waters, Ezekial
Warren, B.
Weil, Sol.
Welch, Mike
Welch, John
Westbrook, J. H.
Westbrooks, W. H.
Westbrooks, George
Fortson, J. R.

COMPANY K

Captain, Wm. H. Martin
1st Lieut.; M. O. Clanahan
3d Lieut., W. D. Rounsavall

PRIVATES

Anding, John
Allen, J. M.
Allen, J. W.
Antle, Milton
Ball, B. L.
Barham, C. J.
Bowles, Axom
Bradley, J. F. T.
Baker, Joseph
Boyd, James
Banks, T. C.
Brown, W. B.
Carguilo, W. A.
Cox, B. M.
Champion, L. D.
Campbell, A.
Campbell, J. E.
Campbell, J. M.
Clanahan, W. R.
Chapman, M.
Chapman, J.

Carter, Hugh
Derden, W. L.
Elledge, H. D.
Elledge, J. F.
Edwards, W. L.
Forrester, Thomas
Forester, Joel
Green, J. J.
Green, D. N.
Guthrie, L. J.
Gibbon, J. F.
Guiger, John D.
Godwin, Wesley
Hodge, M. H.
Hobgood, T. J.
Hight, F. M.
Heard, J. D.
Hamby, John
Hilliard, E. C.
Holland, F. M.
Isaacs, William
Kimbrough, J. H.
Loop, G. R.
Larue, A. J.
Lemox, A. C.
McCall, J. C.
McNealy, T. G.
Martin, R. B.
Martin, Alfred

Martin, Henry
Norvell, Robert
Owen, S. T.
Owen, J. D.
Owen, S. Trice
Paul, R. B.
Pattillo, B. A.
Pickering, James
Price, Russell
Price, W. B.
Phillips, H.
Pairr, W. R.
Richardson, W. E.
Rice, John
Rounsavall, James A.
Rounsavall I. M.
Rogers, J. H.
Rogers, S. S.
Roushing, G. H.
Ross, C. C.
Redmon, R.
Swindle, J. M.
Smith, F. J.
Tubbs, Robert
Wilton, W. T.
Weisensee, C. P.
Whittaker, W. F.
Williams, E. J.
Wigginton, William

MUSTER ROLLS OF FIFTH TEXAS
" BAYOU CITY GUARDS "

COMPANY A

W. B. Botts; was Captain, promoted to Lieut. Col., and resigned
W. H. Sellers, 1st Lieut.; went with Gen. Hood West. Died in Texas

HOOD'S TEXAS BRIGADE

J. R. Hale, 2d Lieut.
D. C. Farmer, 3d Lieut.; Captain
J. E. Clute, Orderly Sergt.; killed at Gaines' Mill
W. D. Cleveland, 3d Sergt.
E. A. Noble, 4th Sergt.; wounded at Second Manassas
E. R. Moore, Corporal
John Leverton, 2d Corp.; wounded at Gettysburg, Pa.
Justus Davidson, 3d Corp.
J. A. McMurty, 4th Corp.; wounded at Manassas
J. Aurbach; discharged
John B. Bell; wounded at Manassas
C. M. Botts
Jasper Barron
William Barron
A. J. Burke, Jr.
Sam Bailey; wounded at Manassas and Gettysburg, killed at Spottsylvania Court House
M. F. Berry
Geo. W. Bottler
T. E. Bigbee; missing at Boonesboro, Md.
Robert Burns; Regimental Commissary
George Butler
H. C. Bell
W. H. A. Cyrus
R. Capps; deserted
B. R. Currin
W. H. Chadwick
W. F. Clark
W. A. Clark
S. Cohn; killed at Gettysburg
J. A. Cameron
M. J. McCullock
T. H. Clark
C. W. Doggs; killed at Gettysburg
G. H. DeLesdernier; killed at Gaines' Mill
Jas. Downey
B. S. Dyer; wounded at Sharpsburg
Geo. M. Douglass
J. W. DeLesdernier; wounded at Manassas
Isaac Elsasser
A. H. Edey
B. Pugh Fuller; 3d Lieut.
W. F. Farrell
D. N. Fleming
C. B. Gardner; wounded at Second Manassas
J. H. Garrison; wounded at Gettysburg
W. A. George
C. P. Horn; deserted
S. D. Hughs
R. G. Hollard
G. C. Holbrook; deserted
J. T. Hurtt
T. Kesse
J. A. Kennard; deserted
William Kelly; wounded at Second Manassas
J. M. Lee
T. W. Lubbock
J. W. Landigsen
J. E. Landes; wounded at the Wilderness
Horace Livingston
W. McDowell; killed at Gettysburg
F. Loberque
J. V. May
C. H. Merriman
J. S. Norton
O. O. Malley; wounded at Second Manassas and Chickamauga
Thos. O. Donnell
F. M. Poland
R. W. Phelps
Nicholas Pomeroy; wounded at Second Manassas and Gettysburg
John Reily
T. H. Rievly; wounded at Gettysburg
H. R. Rogers
G. H. Robins; wounded at Chickamauga
J. J. Sweeney
Jas. Stanger
B. C. Simpson; wounded at Manassas and Gettysburg
J. H. Shepherds; wounded at Wilderness
Wm. Sims
H. G. Settle; wounded at Petersburg

HOOD'S TEXAS BRIGADE

Chas. Settle
Chas. Seldon; deserted
W. A. Tryon
H. P. Tools
I. Tressam
A. C. M. Taylor
V. Vandergen
A. Wolff; killed at Sharpsburg
S. B. Webber; deserted

D. W. Walker; killed at Manassas
D. Wilderson
C. Whitaker
W. A. Cook
The following named parties, wounded at Manassa, Va., died at Warrenton, Va.: J. A. McMurty, John Massenburg, John DeLesdernier
S. O. Young; enlisted Jan. 1, 1865

COMPANY B

John C. Upton, Captain; became Lieut.-Col., killed at Second Manassas
J. D. Roberdeau, 1st Lieut.; became Captain, wounded at Second Manassas, Sharpsburg and Gettysburg
J. H. Bullington, 2d Lieut.
Ed. Collier, 3d Lieut.; disabled permanently at Petersburg, Va.
W. D. Denny, 1st Sergt.; killed at Eltham's Landing
B. M. Baker, 2d Sergt. and Lieut.; wounded at Second Manassas and Gettysburg
J. C. Kindred, 3d Sergt.
D. H. Henderson, 4th Sergt. and 1st Lieut.; killed at Gettysburg
Ellis Putney, 5th Sergt.
John Buchanan, 1st Corp.
John C. Miller, 2d Corp.; killed at Gettysburg
Wm. Pinchback, 3d Corp.; killed at Second Manassas
J. H. Whitehead, 4th Corp.; wounded at Gettysburg
John B. Wall, 5th Corp.

PRIVATES

Auerbach, E.; killed at the Wilderness
Burton, W. H.; killed at Bermuda Hundred Front
Besch, E.; wounded three different battles
Byers, W. F.
Bently, W. L.
Bruce, J. S.; wounded at Second Manassas

Baker, J. D.
Baker, A. H.; killed at Sharpsburg
Bostick, S. R.
Burford, Phil.
Bridge, A.
Behue, G.
Carter, J. T.; killed at Gettysburg
Carter, A. H.; wounded at Gaines' Mill
Carter, A. V. L.; killed at Second Manassas
Coffee, C.
Cabanis, Max
Carroll, Jim.; wounded at Gaines' Mill
Cherry, W. S.; wounded at Gaines' Mill and Gettysburg
Carleton, W. H.
Currie, D. M.; wounded
Collins, Pat.; wounded at Second Manassas
Cooper, Jasper
Cooper, Newton
Darden, W. J.; wounded at Sharpsburg and disabled
Dickinson, J. C.
DeGraffenreid, T. T.; wounded at Boonesboro
Dolan, John; deserted
Daggett, M.; killed at Second Manassas
Dickey, G. W.
Edgar, John
Enke, August; wounded at Gaines' Mill and disabled
Flanagan, M.; deserted
Graf, John; wounded at Wilderness

Gaines, John R.; killed at Gaines' Mill
Gegenrarth, Geo.; wounded at Chickamauga and disabled
Grace, A. J.
Harris, Dr. T. W.
Harris, F. R.
Harbert, W. J.
Humphrey, R. I.; wounded at Second Manassas, killed at Petersburg
Howard, I. A.; killed at Gettysburg, with colors
Harvey, John B.; wounded at Gettysburg, disabled
Hurley, D.; wounded at Freeman's Ford
Hurley, M.; killed at Gettysburg
Haynes, Blythe
Haynes, Henry; killed at Gettysburg
Hendrick, Hiram
Hart, W. S.; killed at Chickamauga
Higgs, J. F.
Hoffman, Wm.; killed at Sharpsburg
Hahn, Jacob; wounded at Gaines' Mill
Hare, W. S.
Hanks, John
Johnson, J. W.; wounded at Second Manassas and Gettysburg
Johnson, Wm.
Jenkins, John M.
Kolbow, John; killed at Sharpsburg
Kaepke, F.; killed at Malvern Hill
Lahey, John; wounded at the Wilderness
Lynch, C.; wounded at Gaines' Mill, disabled
Lundy, P.; wounded at Second Manassas
Legg, Andrew
Manhart, F.
Murphy, F. M.
Morrissey, John; wounded at Sharpsburg
Monroe, George; killed at Sharpsburg
Mathee, Fritz; killed at Freeman's Ford
McMillan, A. P. M.; deserted
McCormick, John
McCormick, S. L.
McNeilus, D.; killed at Sharpsburg
McLeod, M. W.
Nelms, W. F.; wounded at Second Manassas, killed at Gettysburg
Obenschain, J. S.; wounded at Chickamauga
O'Neill, John; killed at Gettysburg
Perkins, J. R.
Pratt, Henry; wounded at Second Manassas
Penelton, Henry
Priest, John
Ray, J. R.
Reynolds, Jas.
Ratican, John; wounded at Gaines' Mill, disabled
Roberts, T. J.; wounded at Freeman's Ford
Rhodes, Wm.; wounded at Second Manassas
Sheppard, Webb; wounded at Second Manassas, with colors
Sloan, A. G.; killed at Gettysburg
Stroud, B. F.
Scherer, Riley; killed at Eltham's Landing
Senne, Henry; wounded at Eltham's Landing, disabled
Snell, W. T.; wounded at Second Manassas
Smith, John C.; wounded at Second Manassas
Stephenson, William
Shields, Chas.
Sanders, W. L.
Stafford, R. E.
Stoneker, W. J.
Slayton, Wm.
Tanner, C. B.
Tatum, C. S.
Terrell, Hunt; wounded at Gettysburg
Terrell, C. M.
Trainor, John; wounded at Second Manassas and Gettysburg
Taylor, T. O.
Taylor, F. M.; deserted

HOOD'S TEXAS BRIGADE

Umbarger, John; killed at Second Manassas
Welck, T.; deserted
Weston, C.; deserted
Wallace, J. W.; deserted
Wilson, J. C.; killed at Gettysburg
Woodhouse, P.; wounded at Second Manassas and Gettysburg
Carrigan, J.; killed at Second Manassas

COMPANY C

COMMISSIONED OFFICERS
D. M. Whaley, Captain
J. J. McBride, 1st Lieut.
W. G. Wallace, 2d Lieut.
J. E. Anderson, 2d Lieut.

NON-COMMISSIONED OFFICERS
Lee Tubb, 1st Sergt.
Z. L. Logan, 2d Sergt.
T. J. Pridgen, 3d Sergt.
J. C. Cox, 4th Sergt.
E. W. Black, 5th Sergt.
G. A. Pruitt, 1st Corp.
J. T. Adkinson, 2d Corp.
P. B. Perry, 3d Corp.
G. F. Border, 4th Corp.
P. K. McKenzie, Musician
H. L. Olrick, Musician

PRIVATES
Jesse Anderson
J. T. Allison
A. B. Allison
Robert Allen
Z. P. Bell
Edward Bell
T. J. Boykin
B. W. Bristow
E. H. Bristow
G. G. Barbee
J. H. Brewer
F. M. Braden
William Boykin
Wm. Brashear
A. Brashear
H. W. Boyd
J. F. Coston
D. O. H. Coston
J. M. Copeland
J. P. Copeland

J. S. Crosby
James Deatley
A. J. Dunlap
H. B. Dunn
Z. Y. Dezell
E. M. Dezell
J. M. Driscol
H. T. Driscol
W. V. B. Duncan
J. C. Dickson
J. B. Durgan
J. E. Ellis
C. A. Ellis
B. D. Elkins
J. B. Farris
J. A. J. Fryer
Thomas Foley
J. A. Green
J. C. Green
J. W. M. Green
John Garrison
Wiley Graham
J. B. Graham
Strickland Graham
J. G. Gouch
Marion Garey
Benjamin Henry
W. H. Gough
Berry Hicks
R. H. Hays
J. H. Hailey
S. W. Erwin
E. W. James
John Caloway
A. A. Jones
Asbury Lawson
Thomas R. Lee
J. E. Lacey
W. L. Long
Lacey Lusk
Emmitt Mulholland

D. W. Moore
Sterling Moody
G. W. Mills
Ransom McKenzie
James Merideth
A. P. Moss
William Murchinson
James W. Neighbors
John Neighbors
B. D. Nunnery
Joe S. New
Benjamin Perry
B. D. Page
Thomas R. Pistole
David Price
J. H. Pool
E. P. Parker
P. G. Phillips
J. J. Pridgen
B. R. Perry
T. M. Robinson
Joe. L. Ross
Joseph Rose
E. H. Sawyers
B. S. Stewart
W. B. Simmons
G. A. Shillings
James E. Swindler
J. D. Stephens
J. S. Skinner
J. M. Scott
H. P. Traweek
C. C. Traweek
Richard Turner
Sam. Thomas
James Underwood
Henry C. Wynch
P. W. West
James M. Wallace
R. F. Webb
F. M. Williams

HOOD'S TEXAS BRIGADE

James Williams
W. K. Williams
M. T. Welsh

Jefferson Walker
William Watson
C. M. C. Whaley

Eli Yow
J. K. Yeldell

COMPANY D

R. M. Powell, Captain; promoted to Colonel, wounded and captured at Gettysburg, commanding brigade at surrender of Appomattox Court House
W. T. Hill, 1st Lieut.; promoted to Captain, wounded at Gettysburg and Wilderness, commanding regiment at surrender
A. C. Woodall, 2d Lieut.; promoted to 1st Lieut., wounded at battles of Knoxville and Darbytown
Campbell Wood, 3d Lieut.; promoted to 2d Lieut., wounded at Gettysburg

NON-COMMISSIONED OFFICERS AND PRIVATES

Abercrombie, Milo B.
Abernathy, Henry; killed at Gettysburg
Adickes, E. J.
Allen, William H.
Alston, Angus, D.; killed at Gaines' Mill
Alston, Robert
Alston, Willis W.; wounded at Gettysburg and Wilderness
Alverson, Jno. T.; killed at Spottsylvania Court House
Bass, J. M.
Birdwell, T. J.
Bowden, J. G.
Brantley, R. A.; promoted to Sergt., wounded at Second Manassas
Brown, M. C.; killed at Chickamauga
Brown, R. C.; wounded at Malvern Hill
Burden, Jack
Burden, Joseph C.; killed at Second Manassas
Burke, Eph.
Burton, I.; wounded at Wilderness
Caldwell, O. H. P.; wounded at Second Manassas, deserted
Campbell, John
Campbell, D. M.
Campbell, W. B.
Carrington, Bernard; wounded at the Wilderness
Coleman, W. G.; wounded at Gettysburg, lost his foot
Cotton, Robert
Cotton, John A.
Cotton, John W.; wounded at Second Manassas
Cox, L. A.
Cunningham, Nat.
Cunningham, Frank
DeCapree, A.
Dickie, J. A.; wounded at Chickamauga
Dikeman, Wm.
Douglass, N.; wounded at Second Manassas, killed at Gettysburg
Edwards, T. J.
Elmore, Joseph
Eskridge, George; killed at Gettysburg
Estill, Ben. D.; killed at Second Manassas
Estill, Black; killed at Second Manassas
Ewing, J. W.
Eutzler, C. C.
Farthing, W. G. W.; promoted Sergt., lost leg at Gettysburg
Franklin, S. J.
Gilbert, Jas. E.; wounded at Gettysburg, Chickamauga and the Wilderness
Gilbert, Martin L.; wounded and permanently disabled at Chickamauga
Golding, Anthony; wounded at Gaines' Mill and Fort Harrison

HOOD'S TEXAS BRIGADE

Grant, Geo. A.; wounded at Gaines' Mill and Fort Harrison
Griffin, Robert H.; killed at the Wilderness
Gwynn, William A.
Hardy, Richard; wounded at Gettysburg
Harris, J. K. P.; mortally wounded at Second Manassas
Harrison, J. S.; wounded at Seven Pines
Henry, Z. P.; killed at Williamsport, Md.
Harper, William
Hightower, J. A.
Hill, A. T.
Hill, C. T.
Hill, J. C.; promoted to Sergeant, wounded at Gettysburg
Hinson, A. M.
Hewitt, Robt.
Hanks, ——
Hume, F. Charles; wounded at Second Manassas
Irving, Henry
Kearse, Calhoun
Keeble, Edwin A.; wounded at the Wilderness
Keenan, Walter; wounded at Darbytown
Latchman, Ernest; wounded at Second Manassas, killed at Gettysburg
Lamkin, M. A.; wounded at Second Manassas
Lewis, William H.; killed at the Wilderness
Lewis, W. E.; killed at Wilderness
Lewis, T.J.; wounded at Chickamauga
Lucas, ——
Maas, Louis; killed at Second Manassas
Malone, Thomas
Marshall, James
McDade, Jas. A.; killed at Gettysburg
Minshew, Jacob
Minshew, Joel; wounded at Gettysburg
McGilvary, William
Morris, Robert
Mitchell, Charles
Mitchell, Leroy; promoted Corporal, wounded at Gettysburg
Murphy, M.; deserted
Murray, J. A.; promoted Sergeant
Murray, J. H., Jr.
Myers, William, H.; wounded at the Wilderness
Neatherly, J.
Nelms, Jesse C.
Nelms, W. M.; killed at Second Manassas
Page, K. J.; wounded at Seven Pines, Gettysburg
Parker, I. N.; wounded at Gettysburg
Pearce, W. J. C.
Perkins, ——
Powell, W. P.; wounded at Second Manassas
Pirtle, Samuel; killed at Sharpsburg
Randall, I. B.; wounded at Gettysburg
Reynolds, Dr.
Ridgeway, F. M.; killed at Sharpsburg
Robertson, J. R.
Robinson, J. M.; promoted Sergeant, wounded at Second Manassas, lost leg at Chickamauga
Rome, W. B.; wounded at Chickamauga, lost leg at Wilderness
Ross, S. P.; killed at Gettysburg
Rose, Joseph
Sanders, Alonzo
Saunders, William; killed at Knoxville, Tenn.
Scott, Thomas B.; lost leg at Malvern Hill
Scott, Jno. A.
See, A.
Seale, J. R.; wounded at Second Manassas
Shackleford, Ed.
Shanaski, Charles; wounded at Gettysburg
Shaw, Jas. T.; killed at Spottsylvania
Spivey, W. F.; killed at Second Manassas

338   HOOD'S TEXAS BRIGADE

Smith, W. O.; wounded at Second Manassas
Smith, R.
Smither, J. M.; promoted to Corp., Sergt.-Major, wounded at Chickamauga, Bermuda Hundreds
Stanton, Robert; wounded at Second Manassas, missing at the Wilderness
Strayhorn, ——
Traylor, A. H.; wounded at Chickamauga
Traylor, J. H.
Traylor, W. A.
Tomlinson, John; killed at Chickamauga
Tomlinson, James
Turner, William; killed at Gettysburg
Underwood, A.
Walke, W. C.; promoted to Corporal, wounded at the Wilderness
Warren, Walter
Watson, Thos. L.; promoted to Corporal, killed at Chickamauga
Williamson, Peter J. Gray; killed at Gettysburg
Williamson, Jack
Wilson, Luts; deserted
Wilson, W. P.
Wood, Robert
Woodson, Philip; discharged
Woodson, C. T.
Wynne, William D.; killed at Second Manassas
Yoakum, George

COMPANY E

John D. Rogers, Capt.; resigned
Thomas A. Baber, 1st Lieut.; disabled
R. T. Harper, 2d Lieut.; disabled
Thomas Nash, 3d Lieut.; killed
James H. Littlefield; promoted
A. J. Stevens
Walter S. Norwood; promoted
A. J. Hall
W. B. W. George
M. M. Felder
Milam Gay
John T. Sedgely
Hardy Allen; killed
Richard Allen
Thos. J. Armitage
D. F. Adair
Chas. C. Allen
Chas. Brown
John Booth; killed
W. G. Bunger
James C. Buster; killed
James A. Cartwell
John W. Cousins
George Cooper
Moses Cooper; killed
Atrus M. Clay
Sam. T. Cofield
Sam H. Dean; killed
F. A. Eldridge
B. Eldridge
M. A. J. Evans
Geo. Ewing
John T. Fields
Rufus K. Felder
Cornelius E. Farquhar; killed
Felix Farquhar
James T. Farmer
W. H. H. Gray
J. R. Goodwin
James B. Gee
Leonard Gee
John Gee; he was transferred
John L. Garrett
James S. Hutchinson; killed
Julian H. Hutchinson; killed
Leonidas Holliday
John N. Henderson; disabled
Francis M. Hendly
Ruf. G. Harper
James H. Hardiman
Joseph E. Henery; killed
James T. Hurt; killed
Robert W. Hargrove
Andrew Hill
Bernard Kavanaugh
W. C. Legrand
John Lott
J. B. Lott
Lamb S. Lockett; killed
E. E. Maxey
Thomas McCoy
Thomas H. Mullins
Newton N. Mullins; killed
Wm. A. Muir
Wm. T. Muse
John Mayfield; killed
Charles E. Moncrief; killed
Fatin Meadows
Duncan W. McPherson
John May
W. H. McCalister

HOOD'S TEXAS BRIGADE

Frank M. Nash	B. J. F. Smith	W. H. Innis
R. S. Niblett	Joseph Sherman; killed	J. F. Wray
David O. Patrick	James W. Spann; killed	George Counts; killed
S. M. Patrick	Frank M. Smith	C. S. Goodwin; killed
N. E. Petty; killed	A. J. Trainer; killed	Ira Hill; killed
Robert W. Pearson; killed	James F. Toland	Thomas Weathersby; killed
	Robert S. Toland; killed	
J. J. Roberts; promoted	Sam H. Watson; killed	Henry Pollock; killed
John S. Roberts	Robert D. Wilkinson	Dan Batts; killed
John H. Roberts	George B. Williams	Wm. R. Lott
Patrick H. Rogers	John L. Wilcox	Leonard Moore
Richard Ringgold; killed	Jefferson Wright; killed	Joe George
Chas. J. Rice	Joseph W. Wallace	William Stevens; killed
Jule A. Ranald	F. M. Williamson	John Walthall
Wm. Sensebaugh; killed	L. E. Mattox; killed	John L. Dulany
Simon B. Smith	Jesse B. Lott	J. H. Smith; killed

COMPANY F

F. J. Whittington	Isaac Oxford	Sivan Giroux
Wm. McIvey	Sam Godwin	Dr. Cook
Wm. Fletcher	John Tutt	—— Mobra
D. A. Tilton	—— Truax	Chas. Brashear
Henry Griffith	Tom Smith	—— Moody
Wm. Bryant	Cadmus Wilborn	—— Dormick
Andrew Bryant	Davis Rashall	Arthur H. Edy
Beasley Dugat	M. Fitzgerald	J. C. Ross
Henry Whitlock	Jeff. Chaison	—— Kauffman
John Church	Wm. Pemburton	—— Myers
Jim Johnson	Jno. Spencer	King Bryant
Blair Johnson	—— Fortescue	Sol. Curbillo
Albert Dugat	John Smith	Julius Schultz
Edmun Hart	Jack Wilson	Ed. Pruett
Neal Dorain	Ed. McCarty	Pryor Bryant
Pink Buckston	Jim Karlow	L. V. Cobb
D. Toups	Peter Mallery	Dr. Noah
"Sargent" Evans	Pryer Choat	Jem Howell
Tom Coogan	Tom Leonard	R. N. Keith
Mike Whalin	Jack Little	John White
Dallis Bryan	Bill Taylor	S. Stephenson
G. W. Starnes	Dick Berry	—— Starks
Earnest Branch	Mc Stricklin	—— Nobles
Isaac Linscott	Jim Booth	

COMPANY G

J. C. Rogers, Capt.; wounded, promoted to Major·
John Smith, 1st Lieut.; promoted to Captain
Sam Streetman, 2d Lieut.; killed
Lu. Battle, 3d Lieut.; discharged
W. J. Terry, 1st Sergt.; promoted to 3d Lieut., killed
W. A. Nabors, 2d Sergt.
Ben. Green, 3d Sergt.; wounded and died

HOOD'S TEXAS BRIGADE

Ike Jackson, 4th Sergt.; wounded
B. F. Nabours, 1st Corp.
J. L. Stewart, 2d Corp.
J. P. Smith, 3d Corp.
A. H. Brown, 4th Corp.; wounded

PRIVATES

Allison, S. P.; wounded
Bigbee, T. M.; promoted to Sergt., wounded
Bellah, S. H.; wounded
Bounds, J. H.
Bean, E. M.; promoted to Lieut., wounded
Beal, D. R.; wounded
Blackman, W. J.
Blackman, M. W.
Bracken, ——
Bracken, Thos.; lost his arm
Blackburn, W. P.
Bollinger, F. M.; killed
Cross, Antonio
Cooper, W. V. L.; wounded
Cunningham, A. P.; wounded
Carson, D. H.; killed
Clarke, J. C.; killed
Cooley, Benj.; killed
Converse, George
Ditto, Alex.
Evans, James; wounded
Ford, G. M.; killed
Fleming, H. P.
Ford, J. L.
Gafford, J. C.
Griffin, Robt.; killed
Garrett, W.
Hawkins, J. H.; wounded
Holt, H. P.
Hairstone, A. B.
Huffman, J. A.; wounded
Hill, W. V.
Hale, Charles
Hobbs, M.; deserted

Hardcastle, James
Harmon, John
Jones, G. A.; killed
Jones, Wash.; wounded
Jones, A. E.; wounded
Jackson, H. C.
Jolly, John; killed
Jackson, C. J.; wounded
Jones, Dick; wounded and died
King, Ben
Lawrence, J. L.; killed
Lewis, John
Mayes, D. H.; wounded
McAlister, J. H.
McKinney, J. M.
McDonnald, E., Jr.; killed
McDonnald, David; killed
McDonnald, E., Sr.
McDonnald, Daniel; wounded
McKnight, Ed.
Mayes, R. B.; wounded
Morey, Harvy; wounded
Middleton, N. D.
Nance, C. P.; wounded
Ogdon; Milton
Pemberton, W. J.
Peaks, W. W.; killed
Pool, James; wounded
Pool, I. M.
Pendarvis, Wm.
Richie, R. W.; wounded
Rowe, H. H.; killed
Small, J. B.; wounded
Stedham, Lewis
Sharp, S. W.; killed
Sharp, Antony
Smith, W. W.; wounded
Sherrell, J. G.; wounded
Sherrell, James
Sherrell, David; killed
Sherrell, Al. J.; wounded
Stedham, Al. J.; wounded
Stedham, James; killed
Sharp, Robt.; wounded
Shelton, J. D.; wounded

Turnham, R. C.
Tuttle, W. P.
Tarver, W. H.; wounded
Tomlinson, J. B.; killed
Thompson, J. E.
Valient, W. A.
Walker, S. H.; killed
Webb, J. W.
Walker, Tandy; killed
Watson, R. E.
Youngs, W.; killed
Tomlinson, A. J.
Austin, J. T.; wounded
Anderson, Bunk; killed
Adams, Carey; killed
Allen, John; wounded
Bryant, J. W.; deserted
Barnard, Geo.; wounded
Benge, J. J.
Caldwell, L. W.; promoted to Orderly Sergeant, wounded
Chance, David; deserted
Cook, James
Dyer, W. T.
Duke, Thomas
Evans, Dan
Edwards, Jas.; wounded
Frazier, James
Garrett, Mike; wounded
Henderson, Robt.
Hill, W. W.; wounded
Jones, Joseph; killed
Jackson, Andrew; killed
Lankford, Thos.
Lankford, Daniel; deserted
Long, Thomas; wounded
Locklin, Jesse; killed
Miller, L. W.; wounded
McPrewett, Wilson
McAninch, E. B.; wounded
Moore, John; wounded
Moore, Wash.; killed
Monroe, John; killed
Pool, E. W.; wounded
Price, Fred

HOOD'S TEXAS BRIGADE

Ross, Carroll; wounded
Richardson, ——; wounded
Ray, ——; killed
Ray, ——; killed
Sharp, H. H.
Shirley, Madison
Stiles, John
Williams, S.; promoted to Lieut., wounded
Watson, James; wounded
Ward, Chas.; killed

COMPANY H

John S. Cleveland, Captain; wounded at Manassas and Gettysburg
W. S. Maxey, 1st Lieut.
Wm. Robinson, 2d Lieut.; promoted to 1st Lieut., wounded at Second Manassas, killed at Wilderness
Burney Byrd, 3d Lieut.
S. S. Stanley, 1st Sergt., 3d Sergt., and 2d Lieut.; wounded at Manassas
L. H. Woodall, 2d Sergt., 1st Sergt.; wounded at Manassas, killed near Richmond
G. M. Sims, 3d Sergt., 2d Sergt.
E. M. Osborne, 4th Sergt.; wounded at Second Manassas
J. S. Stone, 1st Corp.; wounded at Second Manassas
D. W. McDonald, 2d Corp., 3d Lieut., and 2d Lieut.
Wm. Wood, 3d Corp.; wounded at Sharpsburg and Gettysburg
L. J. Goree, 4th Corp.; wounded at Second Manassas

PRIVATES

Brinkley, A. B.
Brinkley, Chris.
Brinkley, Amos
Butler, A. H.; wounded at Chickamauga
Bell, R. R.; wounded at Second Manassas
Barber, Jonathan; wounded at Second Manassas
Ball, Bill; killed at Darbytown
Curry, James
Cuney, J. C.; wounded at Second Manassas
Chesher, J. A.; wounded at Second Manassas and Wilderness
Cooper, Bill (Musician)
Coleman, ——
Cunnungham, Pete
Carter, George
Carr, James
Davis, Bill
Darby, W. B., 3d Lieut.
Dansby, Uriah
Dowdy, Jim
Dooley, Tom
Dowden, Charlie
Foster, Milton O.
Fitzgerald, T.; wounded at Gaines' Mill and died
Fitzgerald, F. M.; killed at Gettysburg
Freeman, Ben; wounded at Second Manassas
Fridge, J. E.; wounded at Gettysburg
Ferrell, Bill
Foster, Bud; wounded at Sharpsburg
Floyd, William
Grayless, William, 3d Sergt.
Goree, E. K.; wounded at the Wilderness
Goree, P. K.; wounded
Grace, M. B.; wounded at Second Manassas
Grace, John W.; wounded at Second Manassas and Chickamauga
Bains, R.; killed at Second Manassas
Bass, James; wounded at Chickamauga
Carter, George
Graves, J. C.; wounded at Gettysburg
Gibson, Ben
Gainor, Wm.
Gillam, M.
Hemphill, Jacob; wounded at Second Manassas, Sharpsburg, Wilderness and before Richmond
Haynie, Tom
Hall, C. L.; killed at Second Manassas

House, W.; wounded at Second Manassas, killed at Sharpsburg
Hampton, T. L.; wounded at Second Manassas and Wilderness
Harris, Coon
Huffman, Ned
Hogue, Bill
Hubert, Mile
Hough, Trav
Johnson, George H.
Jones, W. G.; killed at Spottsylvania
Jennings, J. A.; killed at Chickamauga
Jennings, Ben
Jett, Levi
Jett, Voll
Kirby, Josiah
Kirgin, E. M.
Keyes, Jim; deserted
Keyes, Jno. H.
Kelley, Thompson
Lee, R. E.; wounded at Manassas and Chickamauga
Lewis, George
Lewis, Jim
Maxey, Finney
Martin, Dan
Martin, Bud
Martin, Charles
McGee, Bill
McGee, Jesse
McDonald, C. F.; killed at Gettysburg
McCormick, Maxey; wounded at Winchester
McCracken, Dave; wounded at Wilderness
McLean, ——
McCann, Wash.
McNulty, Frank
McNeeley, Dr. H.
New, John; wounded at Manassas
Obar, George
Pannell, D.; killed at Second Manassas
Pinson, J. C.; wounded at Wilderness
Pinson, West
Pinson, Newt.; killed at Darbytown
Reeder, John
Rose, Harvey; wounded at Gaines' Mill and Chickamauga
Robinson, James
Robinet, James; wounded at Gettysburg and Wilderness
Ross, Mat.
Raines, E.
Ross, J. B.
Small, S. W., 4th Sergt.
Small, J. M.
Shields, Isaiah; wounded at Second Manassas
Shaw, J. A.
Shaw, E.; wounded at the Wilderness
Simpson, Hiram
Sprott, T. B.; wounded at Second Manassas and Chickamauga
Stephenson, S. V.; killed at Gettysburg
Stephenson, John; wounded
Stevenson, Jarrett
Simmons, T. J.; killed at Chickamauga
Simmons, Wiley
Spires, Steve
Steele, George
Steele, Andrew
Tarkington, Jno. L.; wounded at Gettysburg
Templeton, W. M.; wounded at Fredericksburg, killed at Second Manassas
Wilson, Robert T.; wounded at Chickamauga
Walters, S. E.; wounded at Second Manassas
Vincent, La.
Weathers, J. R.; killed at Gettysburg
Whitmier, Jesse W.
Wicks, William; killed at Kelly's Ford
Wicks, L. B.; wounded at Freeman's Ford
Underwood, W. A.

HOOD'S TEXAS BRIGADE 343

COMPANY I

Captain, Jerome B. Robertson; became Brigadier-General, commanding brigade
1st Lieut., Tacitus T. Clay; became Captain, lost leg at Darbytown
2d Lieut., John W. Kerr; became Adjutant-General of the brigade
3d Lieut., Ben J. Franklin; wounded at Second Manassas
3d Lieut.; Chas. A. Graham; killed at Gettysburg
Ord. Sergt., Jas. P. Drake; killed at Sharpsburg
2d Sergt., H. S. Tarver; wounded at Gettysburg
3d Sergt., J. T. Hairston
4th Sergt., H. O. Robertson; wounded Gettysburg
5th Sergt., Robt. A. Park; wounded at Sharpsburg
1st Corp., Wm. O. Morgan; wounded at Second Manassas and Gettysburg
2d Corp., John W. Flanagan; promoted to lieutenantcy
3d Corp., Geo. W. Clamptt; wounded at Gettysburg and Wilderness
4th Corp., Wm. H. Holmes

PRIVATES

D. B. Allen; wounded at Second Manassas
John Andrews
Joe Atkinson
Geo. W. Baldwin; wounded at Second Manassas, killed at Wilderness
Ben. J. Baldwin; wounded at Gettysburg, Chickamauga and Wilderness
Thos. Banner
Martin Banner
Bat. Baker; killed at Sharpsburg
W. R. Barlow; wounded at Wilderness
Oliver P. Barton; wounded at Wilderness
Thos. Bates; wounded at Second Manassas and killed at Gettysburg
Wm. T. Blackburn; wounded at Chaffin's Farm
J. H. Blue; wounded at Gettysburg
Jerome Blue
C. D. Blue
W. G. Blue; wounded at Second Manassas
Jas.,Brady
Fritz W. Bettis
Alex. G. Beaumont
D. H. Carter
Oscar Chase
Jas. R. Cliett; wounded at Seven Pines
Timothy Conway
John Connor; wounded at Wilderness
Wm. Crabtree; wounded at Second Manassas, killed at Chickamauga
J. T. Cross; wounded at Gaines' Mill
J. W. Dallas; wounded at Second Manassas
John Davis; wounded at Chickamauga, killed at Wilderness
John Dean; wounded at Gettysburg, killed at Wilderness
J. Watt Dean; wounded at Wilderness
James Diggs
John Dick; wounded at Second Manassas
S. S. Driscol; wounded at Second Manassas, killed at Chickamauga
Ed. Dunn; killed at Sharpsburg
T. P. Dudley; wounded at Knoxville, killed at Darbytown
F. C. Edney; wounded at Seven Pines
Jas. A. Eaton
D. E. Flannegan; wounded at Second Manassas
Robert Fleming; wounded at Wilderness
Robert E. Fitzgerald
Ben S. Fitzgerald
Pat Goodlett
Josh. S. Grant; wounded at Wilderness

Chas. H. Graves
June W. Graves; killed at Chickamauga
Jas. N. Guess
Joe Hallum; wounded at Gaines' Mill
Wm. Haley; wounded at Second Manassas, killed at Gettysburg
John H. Hardy
Hammett Hardy
Richard J. Haynes; killed at Gaines' Mill
W. T. Harris; wounded at Gaines' Mill and Second Manassas
John S. Heffner; wounded at Gettysburg
R. A. Higgason
Green Hill
John C. Hill
Wm. B. Hill
Jas. D. Holmes; wounded at Chickamauga
Wm. A. Holmes; wounded at Wilderness
Curran Holmes
Jas. L. Holmes; killed at Gettysburg
A. W. Holt; wounded at Chickamauga
John D. Howell; wounded at Sharpsburg
Robert Howell; wounded at Sharpsburg
John Hoval; wounded at Wilderness
A. B. Hood; wounded at Wilderness
Robert W. Hudson
E. C. Hughes; wounded at Wilderness
Hugh Jackson
Walker Kerr
J. W. Kilby; killed at Chickamauga
Abram Lee
M. O. Lipscomb
Jonathan Love; surrendered at Appomattox
J. A. Mack; deserted
Harmon C. Martin
Jeff. Montgomery
Whit. S. Montgomery
Robert Mitchell
Drew F. Morgan; wounded at Sharpsburg, killed at Chaffin's Farm
S. A. Morris
Parrott W. McNeese
Ed. H. McKnight; wounded at Second Manassas
W. B. McRae; wounded at Freeman's Ford
Thos. J. Newman; wounded at Sharpsburg
G. Ober
Hugh Parker
Dell Perkins
Dimas R. Ponce
J. W. Powell; wounded at Wilderness
Ben Qualls
Dr. D. H. Robertson; wounded at Second Manassas
Frank Robertson
W. B. Roysten; killed at Second Manassas
C. D. Seward; killed at Cold Harbor
Wm. Short; wounded at Gettysburg
John Short; wounded at Second Manassas; killed at Chickamauga
R. H. Spence; wounded at Second Manassas, killed at Knoxville
J. H. Stephens
Will S. Stephens
Thos. Sutherland
W. F. Thomas; wounded at Second Manassas
Jas. R. Thomas
J. W. Tooley; wounded at Chickamauga
H. W. Waters; wounded at Gaines' Mill
Loot Ward
Lewis Wells; wounded at Gaines' Mill
W. S. Weatherby
Clem Wiebusch
Sam'l M. Williams

HOOD'S TEXAS BRIGADE 345

COMPANY K

Turner, I. N. M., Captain; wounded at Seven Pines and Manassas, killed at Suffolk
Hubert, R. W., 1st Lieut.; promoted to Captain, wounded at Manassas and Gettysburg
Thornton, S. B., 2d Lieut.
Jones, J. F., 3d Lieut.
Henry B. W., 1st Sergt., 2d Lieut.; killed at Manassas
McKinnon, N. B., 4th Sergt.; wounded at Manassas
Turner, Joe, 2d Sergt., 2d Lieut.; wounded at Manassas and Chickamauga
Beard, J. F., 3d Sergt., 1st Sergt.; wounded at Freeman's Ford, killed at Chickamauga
* Meece, T. F., 5th Sergt., 1st Sergt.; wounded at Manassas, Gettysburg, and White Oak Bottom
Tracey, Blount, 1st Corp.
Craig, Z. Q., 2d Corp.
Cochran, J. W., 3d Corp.
Oats, Nathan, 4th Corp.; wounded at Manassas, killed at Chickamauga
Allbritton, Lafayette
Adams, J. J.
Alexander, J. M., 2d Lieut.; wounded at Second Manassas and Darbytown road
* Armour, J. H. C.
* Ashley, R. A.; wounded at Sharpsburg, Gettysburg and White Oak Bottom
Bayless, W. U.; killed in 1864
Best, M. W.
* Bowen, J. M.; wounded at Second Manassas
Braswell, W. N.; wounded at Manassas
Burch, Joe
Burroughs, T. J.
Butler, John T.; wounded at Gaines' Farm
Butler, Aaron
Butler, James
Butler, Fred.; wounded at Manassas and Chickamauga
Calvert, Tom
* Calvert, J. D.; wounded at Gettysburg
Cannon, J. J.
Carr, A. B.
Clark, B. C.
Collins, R. B.; wounded at Gaines' Mill
Crouch, Julius
Crouch, Henry
Davis, A. C.
Davis, Frank
Davis, B. F.
DeWalt, N. B.
DeWalt, Waters
Dorsey, C. C.
Dortch, L. B.; wounded at Second Manassas, both eyes shot out at Chickamauga
Dunn, J. W.
Dunn, Simeon; killed at Gettysburg
* Dunn, Alfred; wounded at Second Manassas and Wilderness
Easterling, Henry A.; wounded at Second Manassas
Fairchilds, A. J.; wounded at Chickamauga
Fields, V. B.
Fields, R. R.
Fields, W. H. H.; wounded at Gettysburg
Fraser, W.
* Ford, J. F.; wounded at Gettysburg
Geiger, John
Green, H. R.
* Green, A. B., Corporal, 5th Sergt.;

* NOTE.—Those marked with a * were at the surrender of the army at Appomattox, Va., April 9, 1865.

wounded at Manassas, Wilderness, Darbytown road
Hamm, Geo. W.; transferred to Co. B, 1st Texas, killed at Gettysburg
* Hendly, W. D. C.; wounded at Sharpsburg and Gettysburg
Hendley, J. A.
Henry, T. W.; killed at the Wilderness
Hervey, V. T.
Hester, J. N.
* Hirams, H. C.; wounded at the Wilderness
Hirams, Sam
Hobbs, J.
Holton, David
* Hubert, M. A.; wounded at Gettysburg
Hubbard, B. C.; wounded at Wilderness
Hudson, Ed.
Hurt, B. H. N., 1st Lieut.; wounded at Second Manassas
Hutton, G. A.
Jewel, W. E.
Johnson, J. H.
Jones, J. M.
Julian, E. H.
Julian, John
Kale, John P.; wounded at Second Manassas
Keith, J. C.
Killingsworth, J. M.
* Kirkland, Elzy; wounded at Chickamauga
Knox, Z.
Lewis, G. W.
Lewis, Joe
Lockhart, Wesley
Lockhart, ——
Lockhart, C. H.
Lott, J. T.
Matthews, T. C.; wounded at Manassas
Matthews, W. H.; wounded at Gettysburg

Matthews, J. W.; wounded at Manassas
McClenny, ——
McCoy, J. W.; wounded at Manassas
McCoy, W. J.
McCormick, John
McCrorey, T. W.; wounded at Chickamauga, killed at the Wilderness
* McDonald, W. M.; wounded at Chickamauga
McKee, J. F.; wounded at Manassas, killed in the Wilderness
Meece, C. W.; wounded at Gettysburg
Meece, J. P.; wounded at Gettysburg
* Meekins, B. F.; wounded at Second Manassas
Myers, G. B.
Naulty, T. D.
Nettles, W. D. S.; wounded at Chickamauga
Nettles, J. H.
Oates, Isaiah
Oliver, Joseph
Peebles, J. W.; wounded at Gaines' Mill
Pierrot, Gus; wounded at Gettysburg, killed at Cold Harbor
Ritchie, Austin
Ritter, Louis
Rone, Jerry; wounded at Second Manassas
* Rowe, D. A.; wounded at Hay Market, also Suffolk campaign, Wilderness, Darbytown
Reese, J. F.
Salles, B. A.
* Sandall, W. S.; wounded at Sharpsburg and Gettysburg
Sawyer, J. H.
Schooler, Sam
Simpson, L.
Slatter, L. J.
Smith, J. W.; wounded at Second Manassas

NOTE—Those marked with a * were at the surrender of the army at Appomattox, Va., April 9, 1865.

Smith, J. P.; wounded at Gaines' Farm
South, N. J.
Speights, C. A.
* Stevenson, U. P.
Sterling, M.
Sterling, John
Stevens, Ike
Stevens, John W.
Stewart, Wiley; wounded at Second Manassas
Suttles, Ike
Towns, J. R.
Treadway, Dick
Turner, W. H.
Turner, C. H.
* Waldrep, S. D.; wounded at Gaines' Farm and Wilderness
Walker, J. A.
Walker, W. A.; killed at Sharpsburg
Ward, W. J.; died from wounds received at Second Manassas
Wiley, Nelse; killed at Wilderness
Wilson, H. W.
Wilson, J. B.; died from wounds received at Freeman's Ford
* Young, W. B.; wounded at the Wilderness and Fort Harrison

*NOTE—Those marked with a * were at the surrender of the army at Appomattox, Va., April 9, 1865.